THE THOUSAND-YEAR FLOOD

THE OHIO-MISSISSIPPI DISASTER OF 1937

THE THOUSAND-YEAR FLOOD

〰〰〰

DAVID WELKY

The University of Chicago Press

Chicago and London

DAVID WELKY was born and raised in St. Louis, the consummate midwestern river town. He received a BA in history from Truman State University in Missouri and an MA and PhD, both in history, from Purdue University. He has written widely on American culture and society in the interwar era and is the author of *Everything Was Better in America: Print Culture in the Great Depression* and *The Moguls and the Dictators: Hollywood and the Coming of World War II.* He is currently associate professor of history at the University of Central Arkansas in Conway, Arkansas, where he lives with his wife and two children.

The University of Chicago Press, Chicago 60637
The University of Chicago Press, Ltd., London
© 2011 by The University of Chicago
All rights reserved. Published 2011.
Printed in the United States of America

20 19 18 17 16 15 14 13 12 11   1 2 3 4 5

ISBN-13: 978-0-226-88716-6 (cloth)
ISBN-10: 0-226-88716-2 (cloth)

Library of Congress Cataloging-in-Publication Data

Welky, David.
    The thousand-year flood : the Ohio-Mississippi disaster of 1937 / David Welky.
        p. cm.
    Includes bibliographical references and index.
    ISBN-13: 978-0-226-88716-6 (cloth : alk. paper)
    ISBN-10: 0-226-88716-2 (cloth : alk. paper)
    1. Floods—Mississippi River Valley—History—20th century. 2. Floods—Ohio River Valley—History—20th century. 3. Disaster relief—United States—History—20th century. 4. New Deal, 1933–1939. 5. United States—Politics and government—1933–1945. I. Title.
    HV6101937.M57 W45 2011
    363.34′93097709043—dc22

                                        2011014875

♾ This paper meets the requirements of ANSI/NISO Z39.48-1992 (Permanence of Paper).

To KMW, my own flood baby

Women and children were screamin', sayin', "Mama why must we go?"
Women and children were screamin', sayin', "Lord, where must we go?"
The floodwater have broke the levees and we ain't safe here no more.
LONNIE JOHNSON, "Flood Water Blues" (1937)

CONTENTS

PREFACE

WHENEVER I SAID I WAS writing a book about the 1937 flood, people inevitably asked whether I meant the 1927 flood. I assured them that, no, I really meant 1937—it was even bigger than the earlier crisis. This comment generally produced a grunt of either incomprehension or suspicion and a quick change of topic because my conversation partners had reached the limit of their knowledge on the subject. They were aware of the great Mississippi River flood of 1927, the subject of a marvelous documentary and several excellent books, but they were certain they had never heard of any flood in 1937. Those who knew me well suspected I was making the whole thing up as a joke at their expense.[1]

I have been known to spin a yarn, but to the best of my knowledge I have never fabricated a natural disaster. An enormous flood, the worst river flood in American history, really did paralyze the Ohio valley and much of the lower Mississippi valley in January and February 1937. President Franklin Roosevelt had to shift from celebrating the start of his second term to dispatching tens of thousands of New Deal employees to fight the water. Red Cross executives organized their agency's largest peacetime relief effort to that point in its history. By the time the crest passed, the flood had killed hundreds of people, buried a thousand towns, and left a million people homeless. Some of those communities never came back, at least not in any recognizable form, and all of them were changed.

For all this, the 1937 flood is a catastrophe lost to historians. It merits scant attention in classrooms, textbooks, or even books about the Depression era. My first encounter with the flood was a brief mention, perhaps a sentence, in a survey of the 1930s. It sounded impressive enough that I dropped a mention of it into my PhD dissertation. In retrospect I am baffled that I had never heard of the flood, because much of my personal and professional life has orbited around it. I grew up in St. Louis. With the exception of New Orleans, no city is more closely associated with the Mississippi River basin that encompasses the Ohio. St. Louis's history is to a great extent a story of man's relationship with water. Every time I stood on the river landing I watched a muddy current that was destined to mingle with the Ohio within a day or so. In my life the river was a constant presence, a literal presence. It was something to drive across, a backdrop for television commercials, the setting for occasional visits to the old Goldenrod Showboat. Like my heartbeat, the river was rarely contemplated yet always there.

My adult years kept me circling around the flood. I became a historian of the 1930s, a decade replete with both natural and manmade disasters. During a visit to Pittsburgh I stood atop Mount Washington to watch the Ohio's ongoing birth and rebirth at the junction of the Allegheny and the Monongahela. Watching this triple union, I laughed to realize that every drop of the water enjoyed one shining instant as the leading edge of the Ohio River. Later I moved to Arkansas, site of some of the worst moments in the flood's early days. Trips to see my family took me through Arkansas's old sharecropper region—a district that in 1937 swarmed with flood victims seeking safety—then carried me into the Missouri bootheel, another scene of great suffering. From there the highway passes just west of the setback levees of the Bird's Point spillway, a structure that will play an important part in the following pages. Finally, I made several visits to Memphis, where I navigated streets that once echoed with footsteps from tens of thousands of refugees. All this time I knew nothing of the flood, and I had no idea that life was familiarizing me with places destined to carry great personal significance.

One day I noticed that casual reference to a 1937 flood I had made years earlier. Resolving to learn something of this catastrophe, I soon discovered that apart from a handful of quickie recaps appearing a few months after the crest, no one had written a book about it. And from that realization came this work.[2]

This project took me all over the eastern half of the United States. It gave me an opportunity to revisit familiar archives, investigate cities I had never seen, and explore towns I had never heard of before I delved into my research. I learned in Cairo, Paducah, Shawneetown, and the other places my journey led me that the people of the Ohio valley were eager to discuss the flood—it was not so much a lost disaster as one that has gone into hiding. It's still there if you know where to look for it. It seemed that everyone I met had a story to share once they established that I was interested in 1937, not 1927. They convinced me that the flood never really passed to the sea. Today it rolls down the valley as a torrent of memories, some of them firsthand and others passed from generation to generation like prized heirlooms.

These stories touch on a few consistent themes. Many people express amazement that they or their ancestors had endured a calamity of such inconceivable magnitude. Survivors of the disaster remember it with crystal clarity twenty, fifty, sixty years later. Their descendants exhibit profound respect for the sacrifices their parents or grandparents made during the wet, frigid weeks of early 1937. Such admiration suggests that those people were somehow different from us, that the Americans of 1937 were better equipped to handle a crisis. This implies that a social decline has occurred over the past seventy-five years, that present-day Americans are too weak, ineffectual, or pampered to fight a rising river, run from their homes, or rebuild cities. It reflects a longing for a simpler time when neighbors cared for each other and communities stuck together.

Memories of the 1937 flood are bound up in how we understand the present. We use the disaster to evaluate ourselves, our families, and our society, and the modern world usually comes up short. Recent remarks about the crisis appear within the context of Katrina, the hurricane that devastated New Orleans in 2005. The botched federal rescue campaign and horrifying scenes of suffering inside the Louisiana Superdome are seared into the nation's consciousness. From the safe distance of seventy-five years the response to 1937 appears smooth, competent, and effective in comparison. Again there is a feeling that they were better than us. Back then, the argument goes, Washington knew what it was doing. Back then Americans knew how to take care of themselves. Back then we were a better people.

Ideas raised in these accounts touch on the questions I asked while researching this book. Were they superior to us, or is that assertion another example of Greatest Generation nostalgia? Did they have it right back then, or were personal and government responses beset with shortcomings? How did victims respond to the flood? Were their actions noble or lamentable? What if anything did they do to prevent another such incident? What do the answers say about who Americans were?

One more question haunted me: Why did this happen? That buckets of rain fell in early 1937 seemed insufficient to explain an emergency of this magnitude. Americans had populated the Ohio valley ever since there was an America. Century-old towns flooded to the rooftops. Had it never occurred to anyone that building a city next to a thousand-mile river carried risks? Had no one taken precautions against the inevitable? I carried this question around the valley. I asked it when I drove through the Memphis fairgrounds, former site of an overcrowded refugee camp. I asked it when I stood just south of Cairo at the intersection of the Ohio and Mississippi Rivers. I asked it when I walked the Louisville riverfront. I asked it when I read documents housed at the Franklin Roosevelt Library in Hyde Park, New York, and at the National Archives in College Park, Maryland. Why did this happen?

The answer is long, involved, and fascinating. Understanding why the flood of 1937 happened, and why it happened as it did, requires us to examine choices made long before the Great Depression began. Human folly is as much to blame for the deluge as is impersonal nature. Greed, ignorance, passivity, and overconfidence combined to discourage an amicable accord with the environment and left the Ohio valley vulnerable. My purpose here is to explore the origins of that vulnerability, the response to the flood itself, and the world the flood created.

INTRODUCTION

~~~~~~~~~

"THEY ARE ALL TRYING to blame this on me," Nebraska senator George Norris laughed as he pointed at a knot of shivering reporters watching Franklin Roosevelt prepare to take the oath of office. Norris had championed the Twentieth Amendment to the Constitution, a modification that advanced the inauguration from March 4 to January 20. This wet, chilly gray day in 1937, the first day of FDR's second term, marked the new date's initial application. Inauguration morning brought more of the relentless precipitation that had turned Washington, DC, into a swampy morass. Residents scuttled through near-freezing temperatures and a nasty mix of rain and sleet. Tiny rivers streamed down Pennsylvania Avenue, and small ponds capped with skins of ice dotted the National Mall. Resentful correspondents ribbed the senator for forcing them into this mess. They groaned when a cheerful Norris reminisced about the March 1909 blizzard that had compelled William Howard Taft to recite the oath indoors.[1]

President Franklin Roosevelt, smiling to the crowd from the rostrum, was oblivious to their carping. His aura of stolid resolution mocked both the storm and the thirty pounds of iron braces encasing his paralyzed legs. FDR had spent the past few days polishing his inaugural address in the comfort of the White House and was determined to put on a good show for a nation that was just now lifting its head after years of punishing economic hardship. As he had four years earlier, Roosevelt began inauguration day with a special service at St. John's Episcopal Church. Rain hammered the roof as Reverend Endicott Peabody, his old headmaster from

1

Groton prep school, asked God to grant Roosevelt the wisdom and strength to lead the nation through what was presumably his final term in office. The president's family and close friends filled the pews behind him. They represented an array of faiths, an assortment of Catholics, Jews, and Protestants huddling in God's house to seek shelter from the elements.[2]

After the service FDR's party returned to the White House to prepare for the public ceremonies. Advisers urged the president to read his address indoors rather than braving the elements. Roosevelt pondered their suggestion for a moment before asking whether anyone was waiting outside to hear him speak. Forty thousand or so, they replied. That was a small gathering by inauguration standards, far smaller than four years earlier, but many of those people had huddled for hours under soggy hats, umbrellas, and newspapers to catch a glimpse of the president. Roosevelt flashed his trademark smile and said, "If they can take it, I can." The ceremony would go forward as planned. Manservants helped him into a limousine that was soon speeding down Pennsylvania Avenue toward the Capitol.[3]

Roosevelt, for all his bravado, had no great desire to stand in a storm. Noon found him stewing in the Senate sergeant-at-arms' office, chain-smoking cigarettes as he chatted with Secretary of State Cordell Hull about Japan and talked economics with Secretary of War Harry Woodring. Treasury Secretary Henry Morgenthau lightened the mood when he cracked open a flask of scotch. Morgenthau took a furtive pull before passing it to Interior Secretary Harold Ickes. Fortification against the weather, the old warhorses laughed. Roosevelt stalled until 12:20, twenty minutes after his first term expired, before giving the sign to go. Aides helped the president to his feet as his son James braced to receive his father's weight. The two locked arms, steadied themselves, and shuffled into the downpour.[4]

Temporary shelters erected over the Capitol's main portico offered little protection against the weather. A frigid wind hurled the downpour sideways under the roof, leaving the luminaries beneath it as wet as the thousands gathered below. Roosevelt pressed on against the storm, twice halting his speech to wipe his face but otherwise refusing to acknowledge the rain. Millions in dry living rooms listened to the patrician voice emanating from their radios. Some of them nodded when the president lamented that one-third of Americans remained "ill-housed, ill-clad, ill-nourished" and beamed when he promised to use the nation's "great wealth of natural resources" to elevate living standards. The throng outside the Capitol ignored these applause lines. Heavy rain and ankle-deep mud dampened their enthusiasm, and the substandard amplification system prevented most of them from hearing anything Roosevelt said. The seats behind the president were nearly empty by the time he finished speaking. Apparently few of the dignitaries could "take it."[5]

Roosevelt insisted on returning to the White House in an open touring car so the crowds lining the route could see him. He smiled and waved all the way home. Eleanor tried to do the same as she sat beside him in a saturated fur coat. FDR accepted a brief alcohol rubdown before presiding over a buffet luncheon for six hundred. He then clamped on his sodden hat to go review the ninety-minute inaugural parade. Declining a chair, he stood at attention as dripping cadets, midshipmen, and Marines marched before him. Rain fell on president and plebe alike.[6]

Once the last soldier passed, the Roosevelts went back inside to host a tea for three thousand wet guests. The festive mood inside the White House stood in stark contrast to the atmosphere four years earlier, when fears of a complete financial meltdown had cast a pall over the proceedings. Economic indicators were favorable, the Depression appeared to be waning, and the lopsided election results suggested that a broad majority of voters favored the New Deal. Roosevelt's guests knew that, unlike the financial storms of 1933, the squall beating the White House today would soon blow over.

Roosevelt excused himself from the celebration late that evening to indulge in a rare moment of privacy. His extended family had already retired for the night. Eleanor was enjoying a concert at Constitution Hall with former first lady Edith Wilson. A master of compartmentalization, FDR resolved to savor a few untroubled hours rather than worry about the perils ahead. An autoworkers' strike that had brought General Motors to a standstill, his as yet unannounced scheme to pack the Supreme Court with liberal justices, his plan to slash the federal budget in response to improving financial conditions, his upcoming initiative to reorganize the executive branch—these issues could wait. He probably paid no attention to the weather, as he had done his best to ignore it all day.[7]

Press secretary Stephen Early found Roosevelt in a buoyant mood when he phoned to relay the newspapers' reaction to the inaugural address. "You can't guess what I'm doing," the president teased. "Playing with your stamps," Early replied. "That's right," FDR laughed, "rather a nice contrast to inaugural evening four years ago." They reminisced about that first night in office. Early recalled the panic that gripped FDR's economic team as they debated the national emergency into the wee hours of the morning. Roosevelt and Early agreed that things were better now and that even sunnier days lay ahead. After wishing the president a good night, the secretary sat down at his typewriter to record his thoughts. Two decades of working alongside Roosevelt had not diminished his amazement at the president's uncanny serenity. "He had brought about such changed conditions, that he could sit alone . . . with nothing more to do or worry about than [to] toy with his stamp collection," Early typed. He reminded himself to keep FDR's schedule light over the next few days. He had earned a break. Early, his tasks for the day completed, turned out the lights and collapsed into an exhausted sleep.[8]

Outside his window, the rain pounded the streets of Washington, DC. It filled every low spot, overflowed gutters, and poured into the rivers that carried it toward the sea.

ABOUT EIGHT HUNDRED MILES west of the capital's meticulous grid of streets and a world away from the festivities surrounding the inaugural, northeast Arkansas and southeast Missouri cowered as rain muddied the region's dirt paths and fallow fields. Most who lived in these places epitomized Roosevelt's ill-housed, ill-clad, and ill-nourished class. They saw no marble monuments outside their homes, only vast treeless tracts waiting to receive cotton seeds. Despondent shacks, an occasional plantation manor, hulking cotton gins, and weathered barns with ads for patent medicines painted on their roofs interrupted the monotonous landscape. Other than these markers, the area was so flat and featureless that people could discern the curvature of the earth on the horizon.

Recent troubles had bedeviled a region where all times were hard times. A tremendous Mississippi River flood a decade earlier had killed about one hundred people and destroyed tens of millions of dollars worth of property. The Great Depression struck just as memories of the inundation were fading. Disastrously low cotton prices crippled tenant and landowner alike. Most farm families earned less than two hundred dollars a year. They survived on a meager diet of cornbread, molasses, and fatback. Malaria and pellagra ravaged a society more familiar with folk remedies than with doctors. Uneducated croppers, day laborers, and backwoods squatters ascribed medicinal qualities to turpentine, lard, and hog-hoof tea. They wasted their pennies on love potions, carried lucky bones in their pockets, and wore red flannel next to their skin to ward off rheumatism. Their

4

housing was so shoddy that, according to an old saying, they studied as-
tronomy through the holes in the roof and geology through the gaps in the
floor.[9]

Vicious weather punished the area during the opening weeks of 1937.
Heavy precipitation coincided with a cold snap to unleash the worst ice
storms anyone could remember. Each cloudburst pushed the Mississippi
higher. Smaller rivers running parallel to it—the Black, the Little, the
St. Francis—also rose. Flooding began in mid-January. Water covered
farmland made fertile by millennia of overflows that had deposited vital
nutrients into the soil. In a sense it was frequent inundation that attracted
settlers to this region. Now that same phenomenon was driving them out.
Rich and poor alike sought refuge in nearby towns or braved treacherous roads leading east to Memphis. Others fled west to Crowley's Ridge,
a line of hills arcing 150 miles from southeast Missouri to the river town of
Helena, Arkansas. Evacuation proceeded at a deliberate pace. Floods were
common here, so people with little to lose and nowhere to go stayed put
until water lapped at their doorsteps.[10]

By inauguration eve they knew this was no typical flood. National
Guardsmen, enrollees in the New Deal's Works Progress Administration
(WPA), and local volunteers scoured riverbanks for danger spots in need
of sandbagging. Armed patrols watched for anyone aiming to dynamite
a levee to force water over one bank while relieving pressure on the opposite side. Some detachments received shoot-to-kill orders after a series of
near-miss attempts to breach barriers. "We simply cannot afford to take
chances," one engineer explained.[11]

Area officials and the Army Corps of Engineers believed the massive
levees on the Mississippi would hold. They were less certain about the
shoddier works lining smaller rivers. Thousands of men formed human
chains that packed sandbags atop the walls. These gangs toiled day and
night with brief pauses to grab some food, take a nap, or look heavenward and pose the question on everyone's mind: When will it stop raining? Higher went the stacks, and higher went the rivers. Dozens of minor
levee failures spilled brackish water across thousands of acres of farmland.
A breakthrough in the Missouri bootheel swept two Corps of Engineers in-
spectors and a WPA supervisor into the river. The trio clung to a telephone
line until rescuers arrived. "It was the best telephone conversation I ever
had," one survivor laughed.[12]

Americans elsewhere gave scant attention to the crisis in the Midwest.

Bold headlines about Roosevelt's inauguration relegated the flood to inside pages. Arkansans and Missourians living west of the Mississippi valley, in what was then the eastern edge of the Dust Bowl, worried more about a shortage of rain than a surplus. "My Dear Sir," a farmer from Fryatt, Arkansas, sixty miles west of the flooding, wrote to newly inaugurated governor Carl Bailey, "The people of this country has elected you for govener with the faith that you will help the people in this drough stricken country and have ask me to rite you this is five years of straight drough with us of course."[13]

Miserable flood victims bagged levees, ran for high ground, or sat in refugee camps while Roosevelt waved to a bedraggled but spirited crowd in Washington. Anyone familiar with hydrology and meteorology knew the worst was yet to come. Confined by levees as it roared toward the Gulf of Mexico, the Mississippi had risen so high that the water acted as a wall preventing minor streams from emptying into it. The Mississippi instead backed up into its tributaries as if cascading over a waterfall. Arkansas and Missouri rivers could not drain to the sea until the Father of Waters first disgorged its load.

And more water was coming. The same storms that pummeled midwestern sharecroppers dumped billions of gallons into the Ohio valley. As streams from Illinois to Pennsylvania crept higher, Red Cross and Coast Guard workers swung into action along a thousand-mile front. Washington, however, remained distracted as officials enjoyed the inaugural celebration and weathermen convinced themselves the rain would end soon. There is "no threat of a serious flood," one forecaster told a federal official. His confidence made little sense, for all that water in the Ohio had to pass the waterlogged Missouri bootheel and Arkansas delta before it reached the ocean. Additional rain might transform an inconvenience into a disaster.[14]

Mississippi valley residents saw black mountains of angry storm clouds bearing down from the southwest. They knew the rain was not letting up anytime soon. But neither the tenant farmer running for his life nor the president enjoying his stamp collection anticipated how bad the situation was going to get. Something was coming that would destroy towns, fracture communities, and forever change the Ohio valley. The worst river flood in American history was on its way.

Engineers label floods according to the likelihood of their occurrence. A "hundred-year flood" has a 1 percent chance of striking in any particular year and is far more severe than a "twenty-year flood," which has a 5 percent chance of hitting during that same period. These designations represent odds rather than absolute predictions, since twenty-year floods could come in consecutive years and two hundred years might pass between hundred-year floods. Although important to professionals calculating the risk of damage to a given location, for the layman these designations serve mostly as informal guides for evaluating the magnitude of a disaster. So while there is no way to determine the truth of what river men said in January 1937, their assertions show how they viewed the inundation passing before them. In that eighth year of depression, in those first days of FDR's second term, they said that what began in rural Arkansas and Missouri before spreading eastward across the Ohio valley was something no American, living or dead, had ever witnessed: a thousand-year flood.

A REPORTER FOR THE *Louisville Courier-Journal* printed a conversation he had overheard between a sightseer and an elderly man who was peering at the river. "Some flood, eh?" the tourist remarked.

> "The only flood I ever saw," the gentleman said.
> "Just move here?"
> "No, lived here all my life. Went through five high waters, but this is my first flood."

People groped for words that captured what they were witnessing. Major General John Craig did as well as anyone. "It's the worst thing that ever happened," he concluded after flying the length of the Ohio. Others spoke of the disaster in biblical terms, imagining themselves as modern-day Noahs subjected to God's awful wrath. Victims recognized it as a once in a lifetime event, perhaps a once in many lifetimes event.[15]

The overflow surpassed all estimations of the Ohio's potential strength. At one point the river's entire 981-mile run stood above flood stage, as did tributaries from Pennsylvania to Illinois. Communities gasped as water surged fifteen feet above previous records. Buildings, farms, and cities once considered untouchable disappeared beneath the waves. Water covered 15,000 miles of highway, disrupted railroad traffic across the eastern half of the United States, and ravaged communications networks. It devastated rural areas, decimated urban infrastructures, and gutted industries. Hundreds of people either drowned or died from pneumonia and other illnesses.

These events prompted an unprecedented relief effort. Red Cross officials dispatched the largest staff ever assembled for a disaster operation. Railroad companies shunted freight cars to clear tracks for trains stuffed with emergency supplies. East Coast fishermen heaved dories onto flatbeds headed for the valley. Sympathizers from around the world donated money and essentials.

Washington, DC, also mobilized its resources. Although previous administrations had put charities and local groups in charge of relief and rehabilitation matters, Franklin Roosevelt's New Deal placed federal authorities at the center of national affairs. Americans now looked to their president rather than to a governor or mayor. Administration officials saw the flood as an opportunity to showcase their philosophy of government. The Works Progress Administration and the Civilian Conservation Corps (CCC) paid hundreds of thousands of unemployed people to defend towns from inundation, transport victims to safety, and reconstruct the shattered valley.

As the presence of these public relief bureaus suggests, the thousand-year flood was very much a New Deal catastrophe. It tested the New Deal's assumption that an activist administration stocked with enlightened experts could guarantee all Americans a basic level of security. An ineffective response could undermine popular support not just for a government, but for an entire theory of government. New Dealers already operated under the premise that the government should provide cradle-to-grave protection against economic calamity. Flood damage widened that umbrella to include acts of God. The deluge also solidified support for centralized power over environmental matters and emergency relief. Discussions about preventing future superfloods assumed that Washington, not the states or private interests, bore primary responsibility for shielding citizens from natural disasters.

Washington-based officials worked alongside private entities and local leaders to manage the crisis, organize the recovery, and chart the Ohio basin's future course. These interactions raised questions about whether the New Deal functioned more effectively when it acted from the top down or from the bottom up. Both the central government and the grass roots believed they knew what was best for the valley and they aimed to achieve their goals with minimal interference from the other side. The flood provides a chance to examine how well, and to what extent, New Deal policies operated on the local level. It resulted in a mixed bag of good works, dashed idealism, bureaucratic overreach, and stubborn parochialism. On the whole, New Dealers did a better job of navigating the short-term emergency than of realizing their long-term objectives. In the end, however, anyone who spends much time looking around the Ohio valley or other river basins should understand that much of what they see came from the Depression era. Legislation, physical structures, attitudes about coexisting with natural forces, the very parameters for how one lives alongside the river all reflect the New Deal world.

The disaster shines a penetrating light on New Deal conservation policies. More than any previous president, Franklin Roosevelt came into office hoping to reshape Americans' relationship with nature. Dust storms, soil erosion, deforestation, waterborne pollution, and runaway rivers signaled a society living in dissonance rather than in harmony with the environment.[16] Drawing on ideas dating to the time of his distant cousin Theodore and even further back, FDR aimed to put the country's use of resources on a more rational, efficient, and scientific path. Ambitious New Dealers intended to centralize resource management through a national planning board tasked with maximizing Americans' ability to harness nature's gifts in ways that minimized environmental damage. Opposing them were entrenched interests that clung to older, which is not to say wrongheaded, understandings of government's role in conservation and flood control. Planning advocates seized on the unprecedented overflow to press their agenda, but instead of serving as the climactic moment for a century-long discussion about conservation, resource use, and planning, it became a missed opportunity. A better one never came along. Different environmental priorities carried the legislative day, with enormous consequences for the Ohio valley and the entire nation.

Other conflicts rooted in the politics of the 1930s swirled around the inundation and its aftermath. Floodwaters exposed the limitations of New Deal agricultural and labor policies. FDR's administration generally supported workers desiring to organize and bargain collectively. It also aimed to increase purchasing power and improve living conditions in rural areas, often without much success. A ragtag collection of sharecroppers called the Southern Tenant Farmers' Union (STFU) stood at the nexus of these two issues. One of the groups that emerged from the government's new tolerance of unions, the STFU believed it could use the floodtime chaos to achieve victory in its clash with exploitive planters. Instead it suffered a grievous blow that deprived its impoverished members of their best hope for overcoming elite domination.

The flood also offers a snapshot of America's racial mores under the New Deal. Rising waters awoke memories of the 1927 Mississippi River flood. African Americans had suffered disproportionately during that event, and they did so again a decade later. Black residents of the Ohio and Mississippi valleys dwelled in less desirable, more flood-prone areas and had fewer resources to draw on than whites. Black "flooders" encountered discriminatory treatment at the hands of prejudiced refugee-camp administrators. Authorities in some places rounded up African Americans as forced laborers. Roosevelt had an up-and-down relationship with African Americans, and at times the New Deal acted contrary to their best interests. But by inserting Washington further into local affairs, the flood also opened up possibilities for improving treatment and equalizing rights.[17] The administration did its best to impose a color-blind approach toward flood victims. Although Roosevelt's subordinates could not always enforce nondiscrimination edicts, their efforts at impartiality distinguished them from the Coolidge administration, which was generally apathetic toward the widespread bigotry that occurred in 1927.

Some communities handled the 1937 flood with relative aplomb and rebounded in good form. Others came apart at the seams and never recovered. Understanding why communities weathered the storm with varying success requires us to examine their histories in some detail. In some cases a town's short- and long-term response to the catastrophe reflected historical developments that stretch back to its birth. This is not to say that cities were predestined to succeed or fail, but rather to note that the circumstances of their founding and the decisions earlier generations made established traits and characteristics that became more evident during moments of extreme crisis.

Hard times create opportunities for dramatic change. Ruined villages and shattered lives offered vivid reminders of the need for a new relationship with the environment. Humans cannot control the rains. They can only tailor their lives to avoid angry waterways. Nature causes floods, man causes flood damage. Decisions made long before sharecroppers occupied squalid cabins and long before Franklin Roosevelt delivered his inaugural address redounded against the valley. Hardy pioneers had taken up positions along the river for what at the time were rational reasons. They concerned themselves with how best to exploit the river, whether for trade, defense, or nearby resources, instead of asking how the river might affect them. In doing so they failed to consider the Ohio as an actor in their world. In 1937 that neglect backfired on their successors.[18]

Hoping to avoid future catastrophes, Depression-era Americans debated ways to reconcile their way of life with the dangers of living near a river. Today millions of Americans from Pittsburgh, Pennsylvania, to Cairo, Illinois, and millions more outside the Ohio-Mississippi valley, live in a world created in no small part by the choices made three-quarters of a century ago.

THE RIVER

～～～～～

THE MISSISSIPPI, NOT THE Ohio, seems the quintessential American river. It is the Father of Waters, the Muddy Mississip, Old Man River. It is the Delta Blues, Memphis barbecue, the Gateway Arch. The Ohio is a tributary, a feeder, an eternal second fiddle that will never achieve mythic status. Compared with the rowdy Mississippi, known for devouring towns overnight and for shifting its channel at a whim despite engineers' concerted efforts to hold it in check, the placid Ohio lacks sufficient ambition, or power, or panache, or whatever transforms long rivers—which at 981 miles it clearly is—into iconic rivers. Rather than trickling down from mysterious mountain springs, it enters the world in straightforward fashion at the Allegheny's confluence with the Monongahela. Rather than pouring triumphant into the ocean, the ultimate destination for all the earth's water, it yields before completing the journey, as if handing off a baton to the anchor leg of a relay team. When it meets the Mississippi at Cairo, it concludes its run with a whimper. A demarcation line extends from shore to shore where the Ohio's blue-green current merges with the Mississippi's brackish brown flow. The Mississippi regains its muddy color within a few miles of the union, barreling toward New Orleans with no indication of the stream it has just subsumed.

The rivers' names further diminish the Ohio. Mississippi derives from the Algonquin word *misi-sipi*, or "great water." Ohio comes from the Seneca word *oheeyo*, meaning "beautiful water." It is an apt though modest moniker, for the Ohio was a beautiful stream. Henri Joutel, a member of the Sieur de La Salle's 1681 expedition that claimed the valley for France, noted its "extraordinarily clear" water and gentle current. Subsequent generations of Frenchmen dubbed it La Belle Rivière. Thomas Jefferson, the first great American naturalist, concurred with their assessment. He called the Ohio "the most beautiful river on earth."[1]

Even though the Ohio is not the Mississippi, dismissing it as nothing more than beautiful overlooks its importance. Its drainage basin draws waters from fourteen states and encompasses almost 204,000 square miles, roughly equivalent to the combined territories of Italy, Austria, Hungary, and Belgium. The valley has long been one of the nation's primary breadbaskets. Its fertile soil nurtured vast fields of corn and oats and supported meadows teeming with cattle, pigs, and chickens. The river's gentle, predictable current allowed industrialists to float coal, steel, and gravel to markets around the country, fusing the eastern half of the United States into a single economic unit.

Native tribes such as the Shawnees viewed the Ohio as a unifying force fostering transportation and communication between faraway clans. Eighteenth-century colonial conflicts transformed it into more of a dividing line than a shared space. Both the French and British Crowns coveted the territory's rich resources. Great Britain established a nominal claim in 1744 when the Iroquois League sold George II's agents most of the upper valley for a pittance. The British government chartered the Ohio Company of Virginia to exploit its new possession, charging the directors, who included future revolutionary George Mason and George Washington's half-brothers Augustine and Lawrence, with the task of settling several hundred thousand riverside acres.[2]

King Louis XV of France had no intention of letting this land grab go unchallenged. In 1749 he dispatched Pierre Joseph Céloron de Bienville to establish a French presence in the valley. Céloron was an old military hand who had commanded forts at Detroit and elsewhere in France's New World colonies. In the 1730s he participated in a punitive mission against Chickasaws who were disrupting trade routes near present-day Memphis. By all accounts a man of deadly seriousness, Céloron believed his new mission would extend the glory of France and was determined to infuse his actions with an aura of ceremony and dignity suitable to that noble goal. Clad in his parade best, he marched two hundred infantrymen and a team of guides from Montreal to the Ohio's headwaters at present-day Pittsburgh, where he supervised the construction of sturdy rafts that conveyed the expedition downstream. At every junction with another river, his men disembarked to perform a rite of conquest. As banners waved and soldiers in dress uniforms stood at attention, Céloron buried a small lead plate that declared Louis's ownership of the surrounding property and warned area natives, few of whom could read, to renounce their alliances with the British. A trooper nailed an announcement calling attention to the hidden plate to a tree, a priest said a prayer, the company fired a salute, and the squad reboarded their boats to push farther west.[3]

France reinforced Céloron's symbolic claims with a hardheaded campaign to propagandize local tribes and strengthen its military force. Britain countered with its own cordon of forts and employed a combination of bribery and threats to woo the natives. The French and Indian War resolved the dispute in Britain's favor, as France abandoned its North American settlements under the 1763 Treaty of Paris. Britain's hold on the region proved short-lived. A new American republic wrested the river away in 1783, although the British maintained a shadow presence until the War of 1812 finally pushed them out for good.

With ownership of the territory decided, at least on paper, a slow trickle of pioneers penetrated the valley in the late eighteenth century. Land speculators staked out plots, hunters roamed the woods, and missionaries searched for souls to save. The river became the new republic's first east-west superhighway as it carried people and goods from established areas near the Atlantic coast into the untrammeled territory beyond the Alleghenies. Opportunities seemed limitless for anyone with the guts to journey into a wilderness teeming with dangers ranging from hostile natives to disease-bearing mosquitoes. "The land it is good my boys you need not to fear," declared the 1810 poem "Banks of Ohio." "'Tis a garden of Eden in North America: / Come along my lads and we'll altogether go / And we'll settle on the banks of the pleasant Ohio."[4]

In its demography the valley replicated the diversity seen back east. Sons of patrician tidewater planters, doughty New Englanders, Dutch exiles from New York, Irish transplants, German immigrants, and descendants of French colonizers peppered the region. Pockets of free and enslaved African Americans occupied the bottom rung of the emerging social hierarchy. Settlers represented a mix of the legitimate and the shady. Shakers, Owenites, Rappites, and other utopianists set up near ramshackle communities. Homesteaders and artisans shared space with shysters and squatters. Industrious businessmen coexisted with drunken down-and-outers. Together they carved out a new world that boasted commercial and cultural links with both New England and the South. A string of towns sprang from the forests and bottomlands, most of them founded by profiteers intent on grabbing a piece of the fortune passing by them on rafts, flatboats, and steamboats.

Antebellum city builders gave little thought to the consequences of developing acreage the jealous Ohio claimed as its own. Money-minded developers exacerbated the natural process of flooding when they denuded the land of water-retaining forests, drained swamps, and plowed up grasslands to plant farms, stores, and cabins. Topographical realities added to the potential for severe high waters. Hills crowding the Ohio's shores confine overflows to a narrow channel. With few escape routes, water piles up on itself until it climbs high above normal levels. An Ohio flood is like pouring water into a glass, where it rises high but leaves the surrounding area dry. In contrast, a flood on the Mississippi's broad plains acts like water spilled on the kitchen floor: it spreads far but stays low.

Residents endured seven major overflows before the Civil War, one during the war, and many more in the late nineteenth and early twentieth centuries. These floods did little damage because the preindustrial valley offered few substantial targets. With local economies dependent on the free flow of commodities, removing physical obstacles to trade took precedence over protecting residents from inundation. Summers often saw the Ohio drop low enough to bring commerce to a standstill. A depth of one foot was not unknown. Highwater seasons brought other risks as captains foundered on unmarked shoals and pierced their hulls on driftwood or the submerged trees known as sawyers.[5]

In 1824 Congress appropriated $75,000 to clear snags on the Ohio and Mississippi. Secretary of War John C. Calhoun badgered Speaker of the House Henry Clay into amending the act so as to place the Army Corps of Engineers in charge of the project. Clay's assent initiated a long history of military control over interior waterways. Calhoun claimed the assignment would keep the Corps in fighting trim. He further insisted that his men could do the job more efficiently than private operators, a curious contention because the Corps promptly contracted out the work.[6]

Improving the channel demanded ceaseless labor. The Ohio's current constantly threw up new obstructions. Every rise dragged more driftwood and sawyers into the river. Work ebbed and flowed according to the mood in Washington. Sarcastic boatmen referred to snags as "Polkstalks" in the 1840s because President James Polk vetoed every waterways bill that reached his desk. Millard Fillmore, on the other hand, lobbied for channel funds, a policy his successor Franklin Pierce reversed. Scores of Ohio River steamboats sank as a result of this on-again, off-again approach to internal improvements. Removing obstructions did nothing to insulate vulnerable communities from high water. Congress cited the Constitution's interstate commerce clause as a legal justification for navigation improvements. Responsibility for flood control fell squarely on states and localities.[7]

It took until 1850, almost seventy years after the United States claimed the Ohio valley, for the government to sponsor a far-reaching survey of the crucial waterway. The man who conducted it, the respected engineer Charles Ellet Jr., suggested imaginative ways to improve navigation and combat floods. Future studies disproved some of Ellet's conclusions and exposed gross simplifications in others. Even so, had experts analyzed, modified, and implemented the outline he proposed in *The Mississippi and Ohio Rivers*, it is possible that the 1937 flood might never have happened, or at least would have been far milder. Critics instead dismissed Ellet. It took another eighty years, a revolution in environmental attitudes, and a political sea change to give credence in the halls of power to his vision of a national program that treated land and water as an intertwined ecosystem subject to human manipulation.

Ellet was an energetic jack-of-all-trades who at various points in his life became an expert in bridges, canals, railroads, hydraulics, weaponry, and economics. With his brilliance came a profound impatience that made him quick to attack contrary opinions and bitter that he never found greater fame. Frequent bouts of ill health exacerbated his harsher tendencies. He was above all an individualist, reluctant to work as part of a team or follow a logical career path. Ellet went where his interests took him, bouncing from job to job in search of better things. In many ways he reflected the United States at midcentury—mechanically inclined, committed to self-betterment, obsessed with wealth, and eager to weave the Union's disparate threads into a cohesive economic unit.[8]

Ellet's abrasive personality came from his father, a foul-tempered former hardware salesman who exchanged his business in Philadelphia for a run-down farm after his three-year-old son died. Charles's mother, Mary, was a more admirable character whose poise tempered some of her husband's gruffness. Farm life did not come naturally to Mary, an educated woman from a middle-class Jewish family. Charles Jr., her eldest surviving

Charles Ellet. Photo courtesy istockphoto.com.

child, also despised the countryside. His innate aptitude for math inspired dreams of escaping the farm to become an engineer.[9]

Ellet's goal fit the times. The 1820s saw a boom in canal construction soon matched by a flurry of railroad building. Transportation companies needed bright young men who could perform complex calculations as they tramped through the wilderness. The work required no formal education— Ellet had received some informal tutoring but never attended school. Instead, it demanded a capacity for learning on the fly. No American university other than West Point even offered a degree in civil engineering when the precocious seventeen-year-old signed on in 1827 as an assistant engineer for a Pennsylvania canal builder. His primary qualification was that he was strong enough to schlep equipment through the undergrowth as he marked a path for the diggers following behind.[10]

The budding engineer honed his surveying, mathematical, and map-making skills during a two-year stint with the Chesapeake and Ohio Canal Company, a venture intended to link the Ohio River with the Atlantic Ocean. When legal difficulties bogged down the ambitious project, Ellet left for an extended tour of Europe. With its fantastic structures and intellectual cachet, the Old World was a popular destination for American mechanics hungry for inspiration and prestige. Ellet gaped at magnificent French cities, canals, suspension bridges, railroads, and reservoirs. It was all so unlike the rudimentary towns and primitive infrastructure he knew from home. His fieldwork matured him as an engineer. He came home with an awareness of new trends in the profession and a burning desire to surpass European achievements.[11]

Ellet spent the next decade building canals and railroads while searching for an opportunity to introduce America to his new love, the suspension bridge. Marriage did nothing to blunt his determination to succeed. If anything, his thirst for fame grew as he labored to support his bride. Ellie Ellet was in many ways her husband's opposite. A patient, good-natured woman, she endured innumerable separations over their twenty-five-year union as Charles pursued his career and his dreams. She viewed his frequent leave-takings as part of the burden of marrying an up-and-comer. He spent more time in the wilderness than at home during these busy years and always kept one eye on the glorious destiny he imagined for himself. Imposing order on the American backwoods was not enough to fulfill him. Hurried meals in secluded taverns offered snatches of time to sketch out future projects that might push him into the national spotlight. After absentmindedly shoveling food into his mouth, the young man with a mission would store his dreams, stuff his notes into his saddlebags, and ride off down the line to renew the more prosaic task of surveying.[12]

A propensity for rubbing employers the wrong way kept Ellet on the cusp of unemployment even after his *Essay on the Laws of Trade* (1838), an attempt to establish scientific principles for setting freight rates, gained him a measure of recognition in professional circles. Frequent bouts of dizziness, weakness, and indigestion further soured him. His impressive six-foot-two stature combined with his narrow features and prominent nose to produce an awkwardness many found off-putting, especially in conjunction with his arrogance. In photographs he looks not at the camera but into some undefined middle distance, as if contemplating his next venture rather than interacting with the person standing before him.[13]

Ellet craved the attention that came from a bold engineering statement. He spent months trying to literally sell a bridge to towns along the Ohio before finally winning a contract to build a suspension bridge over the Schuylkill, not far from Philadelphia. Following a successful job there he signed a high-profile contract to span the Niagara near its famous falls.

The engineer's first challenge at Niagara was to extend a wire across the gorge, a puzzle he solved with a showman's flair. Ellet promised a five-dollar bounty to any boy who flew a kite over the falls. Young Homer Walsh cost him five dollars and gave him a significant prize; he used the kite string to drag a series of progressively thicker cords across the gap. Eventually he had in place a wire capable of serving as a foundation for the rest of the bridge. His thirst for publicity shone throughout the building. Ellet's journey across the falls in an iron basket dangling from the bridge cable silenced critics who questioned the strength of his construction. "The trip was a very interesting one to me—perched up as I was two hundred and forty feet above the Rapids, and viewing from the center of the river one of the sublimest prospects which nature had prepared on this globe of ours," he wrote with undisguised glee. A few weeks later he steered a speeding horse-drawn buggy across the temporary wooden catwalk connecting the two shores.[14]

Between foolish displays of bravado, Ellet quarreled with his suppliers and his clients at the New York Railroad Company. Ellet's hatred of his employers grew so intense that he rolled cannons to either side of the chasm and threatened to pulverize anyone approaching "his" property. Then he simply walked away, leaving behind a half-finished bridge. John Roebling, who had bid against him for the original contract and later oversaw initial construction of the Brooklyn Bridge, finished the job several years later. Roebling used Ellet's structure as a scaffolding for his own span before dismantling the earlier work.[15]

An undaunted Ellet threw himself into a project to cross the Ohio at Wheeling, West Virginia. The undertaking brought more headaches. Ellet had carpenters, riggers, and stone masons hard at work when a steamboat consortium filed an injunction on the grounds that the bridge was too low to allow vessels carrying tall smokestacks to pass beneath. Pennsylvania railroad interests who feared the bridge would cut into their business backed the lawsuit. To represent them they hired Edwin Stanton, a tenacious, no-nonsense attorney who later served as Lincoln's secretary of war.

It took years of legal wrangling, and eventually an act of Congress, to clear the way for the bridge's completion.[16]

Its opening solidified Ellet's status as one of America's premier builders. He reveled in the attention. Then, a few months after the bridge opened, disaster struck. Gale-force winds snapped suspension lines and ripped the decking to shreds. A petulant Ellet exonerated himself. "The shock to my reputation may be greater or less," he wrote to Ellie, "but I do not deserve to suffer on account of mismanagement. I did what was right, and I will stand the account." Repairs began almost immediately despite Stanton's injunction to stop them. As he had at Niagara, Ellet lost patience and stepped aside before the bridge reopened. His departure again paved the way for John Roebling to step in and finish another job.[17]

Ellet never pursued another bridge assignment. Approaching middle age and weary of his itinerant life, he sought a challenge big enough to restore his tarnished reputation yet theoretical enough to allow him to work from home or with minimal travel. It is no surprise that he chose the improvement of the Ohio and Mississippi Rivers as his culminating work. He had spent decades bending streams to serve man's needs by either channeling them to benefit trade or erecting bridges that overcame their power to disrupt commerce. Now the waterways would serve his personal needs.

His observations at Wheeling gave him enough material to produce *Navigation of the Ohio and Other Rivers* (1851), a pamphlet outlining a plan to tame the Ohio. In it he proposed constructing three or four reservoirs on headwaters tributaries that would retain water in floodtime, release it during low-flow seasons, deliver hydropower to America's booming industries, and supply drinking water during droughts.[18]

Ellet's plan was simple, elegant, and devoid of factual evidence. Powerful senators including Mississippi's Jefferson Davis and Kentucky's Henry Clay nevertheless championed his request for funds to explore potential reservoir sites. Their bid stalled amid the chaos surrounding passage of the intricate Compromise of 1850. The engineer got a second chance that fall when Congress appropriated $50,000 for a topographical and hydrographical survey of the lower Mississippi. He applied to lead the mission, then withdrew when the War Department asked him to serve on a three-man board. "[I] do not wish to work in partnership," he complained. Fellow civil engineers lobbied on his behalf. Army officers touted their own candidate, talented West Point graduate Captain Andrew Atkinson Humphreys, a brilliant engineer whose ambition and orneriness may even

Andrew Atkinson Humphreys. Library of Congress Prints
and Photographs Division, Brady-Handy Photograph
Collection. LC-DIG-cwpbh-00528.

have exceeded Ellet's. A Solomonesque President Millard Fillmore split the
appropriation to allow each man to submit his own findings.[19]

Humphreys attacked the job with rabid enthusiasm, always pushing his
handpicked team for more data, more facts, more information. He worked
absurd hours, even denying himself the luxury of writing to his wife because it kept him from his labors. The captain prowled the river in an im-
maculate dress uniform, as if trying to intimidate the Father of Waters
into surrendering its secrets. He tasted mud dredged from the bottom like
a primitive hunter eating his prey's heart to capture its soul. And always
he kept one eye on Ellet, a stranger become his worst enemy because they
shared a goal. Humphreys hated anyone who stood between him and his
destiny. He had not yet begun writing when an acquaintance informed
him that Ellet was crafting a final draft. This news pushed the captain over

the edge. Collapsing from exhaustion, he removed himself to Philadelphia for an extended rest. The army shut down the survey and transferred Humphreys's instruments and records to storage in Louisville.[20]

Ellet opted for a more relaxed approach. Like Humphreys, he set up headquarters in Louisiana. Unlike the captain, he brought his family along for company. He conducted few field experiments and ate no mud. Instead he took his wife to hear the singer Jenny Lind and fretted about the high cost of living in New Orleans. Humphreys derided his competitor's approach. "I cannot understand how any man can be willing to assume charge of a work without making it his business to know everything about it from A to Izzard," he told a colleague. Ellet planned to simply modify his earlier conclusions about the Ohio to fit the larger stream. There was no reason for him to hang around New Orleans any longer than necessary. He loathed its brutal heat, rowdy saloons, and carnival spirit. "[I] have pretty near come to the conclusion that instead of controlling these floods I would do service to the work to sweep away the whole concern," he confided to his mother.[21]

The family retreated to their Illinois home in fall 1851. Ellet composed his report as the recuperating Humphreys lay in bed, unable to complete the work he viewed as the culmination of his career. On Halloween the engineer handed Congress a slender document bearing the unimaginative if precise title "Report on the Overflows of the Delta of the Mississippi."

Brief though it was, the piece upended conventional wisdom regarding the sources of a waterway's behavior. Earlier researchers had argued that the bed of the Mississippi was constantly rising owing to sediment deposited in its channel. Flood control therefore required constructing ever-higher levees to compensate for the river's inexorable climb. Ellet instead, and correctly, asserted that the bed remained relatively constant and rising flood levels reflected artificial changes on the river. "The water is supplied by nature," he explained, "but its *height* is increased by man." Americans elevated flood crests when they drained the bayous that held runoff, flattened water-absorbing forests, and confined water within levees rather than allowing it to spread over its natural floodplains.

Convinced that the nation could engineer its way out of the problem, Ellet recommended rectifying past errors by constructing yet another series of manmade works. He suggested that reforestation might help, though he gathered no evidence to prove it. He put more enthusiasm into his proposal to build several spillways to divert excess water from farmland and settled areas. The engineer suggested expanding Louisiana's Atchafalaya Bayou; running a channel from Bonnet Carré, about twenty-five miles upstream from New Orleans, to Lake Pontchartrain; and other endeavors.[22]

As in his earlier publication, Ellet presented reservoirs as the crucial piece of the waterway control puzzle. A series of dams on the Allegheny, Tennessee, Kanawha, and other tributaries would guarantee year-round navigation and end the flood menace throughout the Mississippi watershed. He did not list exact sites—a problem for future surveys—but insisted that reservoirs were good investments because the value of the property they protected would exceed construction costs regardless of their precise location. Reservoirs might also heal the country's festering sectionalism. Americans viewed waterways selfishly, endorsing only improvements that enhanced local navigation or shielded their own land from inundation. Ellet reasoned that his plan united all Americans behind Washington's leadership. It represented a national solution to a national problem.[23]

Seeking the greatest possible exposure for his ideas, Ellet began writing a book that blended the stunning sweep of "Report on the Overflows of the Delta of the Mississippi" with the more focused *Navigation of the Ohio and Other Rivers*. The resulting work, *The Mississippi and Ohio Rivers* (1853), outlined an environmental revolution on the cheap. Ellet promised Americans flood control, year-round navigation, a dependable water supply, and nearly limitless hydropower for about one million dollars—the price of a few dams—plus a small annual outlay to employ the twenty or so men required to operate and maintain the system. He tailored his appeal to the age of Manifest Destiny. God intended for his favorite nation to domesticate the rivers, and the Ohio in particular seemed a divine gem awaiting polishing. It was wide enough to carry the largest steamboats yet so gentle that it required neither locks nor diversionary canals. "All that is left for the ingenuity and enterprise of man to accomplish," he concluded, "is to build a few stone walls across some of the tributary streams, and hold back a small portion of the surplus water in the lakes that are there already formed, and then provide common sluice-gates to emit that water into the channel when it is needed." If only Congress would listen to him. If only the public would demand that its representatives act. If only America would recognize his genius.[24]

Ellet's desire to engineer a safer, more prosperous future placed him squarely within a centuries-old tradition in Western thought. Writing around 1600, English philosopher Francis Bacon, the man who popularized the concept of basing knowledge on observable evidence and empirical testing, articulated a powerful critique of humanity's role in nature. "The world is made for man . . . , not man for the world," he argued. Bacon wanted to manufacture a more fertile, more productive, more useful environment. He believed men of science like himself could manipulate natural processes as if tweaking an inefficient machine. Bacon drew his ideas from the popular Christian assumption that God created the earth for man's benefit. According to this line of thinking, nature was a benevolent entity that expressed God's love for his creatures. As God's agent on earth, it was man's privilege to manage all life on it however he saw fit. Carl Linnaeus, the eighteenth-century Swedish botanist, merged this reading of Scripture with Bacon's secular approach. God constructed the universe as a precisely functioning machine where all parts had a purpose, he argued. Once scientific minds divined the inner workings of that machine, they could improve its workings to increase human comfort.

These arguments implied the desirability of conquering nature, of wrenching it from its heaven-directed course onto a path of man's choosing. This philosophy dovetailed well with Ellet's era of industrialization. Clear-cutting forests, stripping ore-bearing mountains, and relocating rivers in the name of economic progress became an extension of God's hand. Americans reasoned that had God not loved us so, he would not have given us all these wonderful resources and the power to exploit them.[25]

Still recuperating from exhaustion, Captain Humphreys watched with fury as his rival grabbed the honors he craved. At his request an associate organized his voluminous notes into a feeble progress report. It took another two years before Humphreys felt well enough to apply for a new assignment, this time to study European rivers. That mission got him out of the United States for eighteen months without lifting his spirits. His rage mounted whenever a European colleague inquired about Mr. Ellet's remarkable study. Humphreys gained another escape when his friend, Secretary of War Jefferson Davis, sent him to investigate possible routes for transcontinental railroads. But try as he might, he could not break the Mississippi's hold on him. He spent four years lobbying to reopen the survey before winning approval in 1857. Energized by this second chance, he transferred his records to Washington, settled into office space near the War Department, and began writing his vindication.[26]

Humphreys's peers were busy launching attacks against Ellet. W. Milnor

Roberts, a respected civil engineer with wide experience in railroads and canals, penned a scathing critique that appeared in the *Journal of the Franklin Institute* in the midst of a congressional debate on funding reservoir surveys. Ellet's plan "cannot be practically carried out now, or at any future time," Roberts insisted. His calculations indicated that restraining the Ohio demanded far more and far higher dams than Ellet suggested. A network of low dams along the river could create a series of pools suitable for year-round navigation without affecting flood crests. Higher dams might diminish crests, but only by retaining water needed to provide adequate depth for navigation. Commerce was therefore incompatible with protection. In addition, high dams would submerge towns, mills, railroads, and valuable bottomlands beneath their manmade reservoirs. Roberts urged Congress to support trade rather than flood control. He proposed fifty low dams on the Ohio that would guarantee a minimum depth of six feet, thus ensuring clearance for all commercial vessels. His forceful argument and close friendships with associates of President James Buchanan carried the day. Legislators dismissed Ellet's plan and advanced Roberts's.[27]

The Civil War derailed the river improvement program. It also silenced the nation's foremost advocate of reservoirs, reforestation, and spillways. Ellet offered his services to the Union soon after Fort Sumter fell. He spent months butting heads with his old nemesis, Secretary of War Edwin Stanton, before securing a commission to construct a fleet of steam-powered rams. Ellet's armada performed well in its first scrap, an encounter with Confederate ships just north of Memphis, but its creator suffered a leg wound during the battle and died a few weeks later.[28]

Ellet was therefore in no position to defend his theories when Andrew Humphreys and his research partner Henry Abbot released *The Physics and Hydraulics of the Mississippi River* a few months before the fight at Memphis. Their text oozed with authority, bristling with charts, maps, and columns of figures gleaned from Humphreys's painstaking experiments. Their party had tested every assumption and questioned every accepted truth in a single-minded quest to understand the forces governing the volatile waterway. "Thus," Humphreys asserted in a typically self-aggrandizing passage, "every important fact connected with the various physical conditions of the river and the laws uniting them being ascertained, the great problem of protection against inundation was solved."[29]

Humphreys disputed Ellet's findings at every point. He claimed that swamps worsened floods because they discharged water into rising rivers.

Reforestation promoted rather than mitigated flooding because trees helped create rain and because clearing undergrowth enabled the earth to absorb more precipitation. Flood control reservoirs were "admirable" but impracticable. Humphreys justifiably dismissed Ellet's spotty research. "No opinion of the care with which [his] measurements were made or even of the method employed, can be formed from the published report," Humphreys sniffed. The captain's perusal of his rival's diagrams did persuade him that "the exactness of measurement deemed essential in the operations of this Survey was not attempted by Mr. Ellet."[30]

Humphreys rejected spillways even though he agreed that the "general principle" behind them was "unquestionably correct." They were too expensive, imperiled navigation, and would likely cause the river to cut a new main channel. Here the captain fell victim to pique, since his own research indicated that these fears were groundless. He plowed forward regardless, infused with a confidence bred from monomania. With outlets, reservoirs, and reforestation off the table, Humphreys had nothing left except levees, forcing him to undermine his own conclusions. He observed in the report's opening pages that his survey had "rendered untenable that position of the advocates of the exclusive use of levees." Later on, however, he declared that a system of levees running from near the mouth of the Ohio down to New Orleans would provide "*absolute security*" against any flood nature could concoct.[31]

Subsequent events gave Humphreys the power to implement his misguided agenda. The captain rose rapidly through the ranks during the war, becoming a brigadier general within months of the first shots. He saw action at Fredericksburg and Gettysburg and, after earning a promotion to major general, helped pin down General Lee at Appomattox. In 1866 he became the army's chief of engineers. Meanwhile, his report assumed its place as the definitive statement on the Mississippi River and, by extension, American rivers as a whole.[32]

One of his initial acts as chief was to appoint fellow Ellet detractor W. Milnor Roberts to conduct the first army-sponsored study of the Ohio River. Roberts's team spent three years producing 118 gorgeous hand-drawn maps that provided a complete hydrological portrait of the stream. This accomplishment gave Roberts the credibility needed to gain support for his canalization plan. Congress began allocating funds in 1875 for a dozen small dams that ensured a six-foot channel. Later modifications expanded the program into a network of fifty-one dams that created a nine-foot channel. Each barrier consisted of boards attached to a metal framework hinged to a concrete foundation on the river bottom. In times of low water crews snared the top of each wicket with a grapple and pulled it upright to create a temporary dam. They lowered the walls during high water so traffic could move through freely. On October 29, 1929, President Herbert Hoover momentarily escaped the tumbling stock market and the first signs of an economic crackup when he traveled to southern Illinois to dedicate the final dam in the chain. Engineers began modernizing the system in the 1960s and 1970s when they replaced aging structures and enlarged locks, a process that continues in the twenty-first century. It exists today essentially as Roberts envisioned it more than a century earlier.[33]

Roberts's and Humphreys's unimpeachable credentials compelled the Corps of Engineers to embrace a "levees-only" policy that suppressed exploration of alternative methods of preventing overflows. A horrific 1889 dam break near Johnstown, Pennsylvania, that killed 2,200 people further soured the nation on storage reservoirs. Conservative West Point professors lent scientific authority to this distaste. Their courses reduced flood control to a question of levees versus reservoirs, portraying the two as antithetical rather than as complementary tools. Generations of students ingrained this orthodoxy into the rivers community. Engineers ignored contrary theories, such as those of conservationist George Perkins Marsh, who in his 1864 *Man and Nature* agreed with Ellet that erosion control, reforestation, and headwaters dams provided more effective flood control than did levees.[34]

The Ohio valley received little attention during the late nineteenth century. Washington concentrated its efforts on the Mississippi River and on cataloging the natural resources of the mysterious lands west of the hundredth meridian. For most legislators the pressing outdoor issue of the day was devising ways to exploit land and water, not ways to protect people from natural disasters. Resource management meant finding the most profitable methods of doling out public lands to powerful interests. This period saw massive federal giveaways, most notably the tens of millions of acres handed to railroad companies, but also generous terms given to corporations seeking water and mineral rights in various parcels.[35]

Progressive Era reformers used a different language to talk about rivers and about the environment in general. Their ideas drew from the works of Marsh and other writers, including naturalist John Muir and explorer John Wesley Powell, who argued that men of science should develop plans to use scarce resources in rational ways rather than allowing the unregulated rape of the environment to continue. These scientists would report to a centralized planning agency operating under the auspices of the executive branch. Powell contributed another idea that transformed discussions of waterways and flood policy when he insisted that environmental legislation should use the river basin as its organizing unit because the land and water within a basin constituted a unique ecological entity and must therefore be treated as a single whole.

Talk of unified watersheds, resource scarcity, wise use, centralized planning, and scientific minds meshed well with the turn of the century political climate. Progressive reformers sought to bring order out of the chaos of an urbanizing and industrializing America. In terms of the environment, that meant placing trained experts in charge of federal conservation programs. In 1907 John Muir's friend Teddy Roosevelt convened an Inland Waterways Commission tasked with outlining "a comprehensive plan designed for the benefit of the entire country" along these scientific lines. Its 1908 report called for the federal government to construct a series of multipurpose dams capable of providing both hydroelectricity and flood control. As part of this blueprint the panel plotted a system of one hundred reservoirs to protect and electrify the Ohio valley. Commission members also recommended creating a single agency under executive command to administer these projects and devise long-term environmental plans.

Congress rejected a bill to implement this program. Legislators objected to the costs of improving the nation's rivers and refused to relinquish their power to authorize river projects. The Corps of Engineers also lobbied hard against the bill. Its representative on the commission dissented from the 1908 report on the grounds that it distracted the government from its responsibility to improve navigation and that its proposed central planning board was unwieldy and unnecessary, not to mention uninterested in letting the Corps have its way on water issues. The Corps's more scientific objections reflected the thinking of Andrew Atkinson Humphreys and ignored most of environmental scientists' recent findings. Military engineers continued to argue that forests did not affect water flow and that reservoirs could not prevent floods. Levees were the best way to protect riverside communities.

Roosevelt's successor, former secretary of war William Howard Taft, granted the Corps of Engineers a virtual monopoly over river policy. For the moment it seemed unlikely that talk about basinwide development, multipurpose dam projects, and national planning agencies would ever translate into action.[36]

A tremendous flood in 1913 exposed the consequences of inactivity. Spring rains sent the Muskingum, Miami, Scioto, and Wabash Rivers to record levels and killed hundreds of people. Army engineers who thought they had the rivers under control reconsidered their assumptions. Chief engineer William Rossell named a commission to explore "measures for prevention of damage by floods to works constructed for the improvement of navigation," a carefully worded order designed to keep the Corps within established constitutional limits to its authority. Some committee members demanded revolutionary change. Lieutenant Colonel Francis Shunk, commander of the Corps's Pittsburgh district, pleaded for more gauging stations, better maps, and surveys of possible reservoir sites. Sounding more like a Roosevelt Progressive than a dutiful army engineer, he urged higher-ups to broaden their thinking. "The question of flood prevention cannot stand alone," he wrote to the chief engineer, and "cannot be made independently of a general plan of regulation of streams for all purposes—navigation, power, water supply, sewage disposal, etc."[37]

Shunk's superiors showed little interest in his proposals and allocated only enough money to keep the board limping along. "It is evident that nothing in the way of obtaining the desired information can be done with such an allotment," Shunk said of Washington's parsimony. After much debate and little new research, the board ratified a thoroughly conventional agenda based on the conviction that levees should be the centerpiece of any flood protection program. Chief Rossell applauded this conclusion in part because he feared that a new waterways initiative might allow other government bureaus to poach some of the Corps's power. He made it clear, albeit with murky language, that "divided control will be productive of results which will not be the most economical and will be less satisfactory than the people have a right to expect."[38]

Rossell's conformist thinking sparked outrage in some circles. A citizens' group in Dayton, Ohio, hired Arthur Morgan to find a better way to control the Miami River basin. Morgan, who headed a Memphis engineering firm and later chaired the Tennessee Valley Authority, brought an open mind to the job. His examination of topographical maps and rainfall records convinced him, despite everything he thought he knew, that reservoirs provided the simplest means of flood protection. Surveys suggested that the area abounded with possible sites even though the Corps insisted there were no good sites in the Miami valley. Morgan, a longtime reservoir skeptic, enlisted other doubters to check his figures. They agreed that the army was wrong. Over the Corps's objections, a consortium of public and private interests raised $32 million to build the five dams Morgan outlined. The region has never experienced serious flooding since the final reservoir opened in 1922, not even in 1937.[39]

Besides changing some opinions on reservoirs, the 1913 inundation also renewed interest in federally funded flood control. The House of Representatives organized a standing flood control committee in 1916. Congress passed a resolution the next year calling for "a comprehensive plan or plans for the development of the water resources of the United States." No blueprint emerged because President Woodrow Wilson never bothered to appoint any members to the national waterways commission the resolution created. In that same session legislators voted the first ever appropriation for flood control levees, as opposed to levees designed to improve navigation. America's entrance into World War I a few days later stalled momentum for federal protection. Except for the Miami Conservancy District and a few towns with floodwalls of uncertain quality, the Ohio valley remained undefended.[40]

A horrendous Mississippi River inundation in spring 1927 shook Washington from a decade of lethargy. Over 600,000 people fled as water covered 25,000 square miles of farmland. Scores of levee breaks exposed the folly of a slipshod, ad hoc defense. A predictable cry ensued for better flood control, preferably funded by the federal government. President Calvin Coolidge, a strict conservative on budget matters, conceded that political considerations demanded a new waterways law. Chief engineer Major General Edgar Jadwin, an irritable traditionalist who opposed federal financing and wanted above all to ensure that the Corps maintained authority over flood works, assumed the chore of writing one. Jadwin focused the bill on the lower Mississippi. He stressed the need to reinforce levees but rejected reservoirs based on a few perfunctory surveys. The general did break from the Corps's levees-only policy when he endorsed floodways, including some that Charles Ellet had recommended in the 1850s.[41]

Sections of the Missouri bootheel experienced serious flooding owing to inferior barriers that crumbled when the river rose. Jadwin, in what proved the most contentious part of his plan, wanted to convert a 131,000-acre slice of that territory, known as Bird's Point, into a floodway. Under his proposal, engineers would leave the portion of the rebuilt Mississippi River levee that fronted Bird's Point lower and weaker than the adjoining areas. Water would top this section, known as a fuse plug, before it climbed high enough to endanger the rest of the structure. A successful fuse-plug operation would redirect millions of gallons of water from the main stream. Setback levees several miles to the west of the fuse plug steered the artificial river downstream before it reached the small towns outside the floodway. Jadwin justified the destruction of Bird's Point with figures indicating that the floodway would divert enough water to save Cairo, Illinois, the largest town in the vicinity, from inundation.[42]

"The Jadwin Plan proposes a greater hardship than has resulted from any flood," Missouri senator Harry Hawes complained. Bird's Point residents mobilized against a scheme that imperiled their homes to save someone else's. Gatherings of angry landowners denounced the spillway as "unfair and unjust to our section." And they resented the bill's requirement that locals pay a portion of the cost of levee projects. If Jadwin got his way, they would have to fork over money to destroy their own farms. "We are asked not only to cut our throats, but we are to pay for the operation," Hawes bellowed. Missourians countered with proposals to raise Cairo's levees or to elevate that town above the floodplain. Army engineers deemed their alternatives too expensive to merit consideration.[43]

Congress wrote the spillway into the 1928 Flood Control Act despite testimony that it might be less effective than Jadwin predicted. After paying Bird's Point landowners ten to forty dollars an acre for the right to inundate their property whenever the government considered it necessary, the Corps erected a wall of setback levees five miles inland that could one day form the right bank of a manmade branch of the Mississippi. Tests later concluded that the floodway would cut less than three feet off flood heights at Cairo, not the six feet the general claimed. Meanwhile the Ohio flowed on, largely unhindered by levees, floodwalls, or reservoirs.[44]

Commerce Secretary Herbert Hoover was one of the few people to benefit from the 1927 flood. Hoover parlayed his role as the government's coordinator of relief work into a public relations bonanza that advanced his political aspirations. Elected president the following year, the former mining engineer understood that the federal government must expand its role in bringing flood protection, irrigation, and hydropower to the nation. He urged private interests to take the lead but wanted Washington to encourage development by disseminating accurate survey data. He also pressed the notoriously hidebound Corps to explore new approaches to flood control.

The process of prying the army from its barnacle-encrusted moorings had begun several years earlier when Congress enabled a series of river studies known as the 308 Reports, so named because they were authorized under House Document 308. This directive sent Corps officers into the field to seek out potential reservoir locations, determine the feasibility of hydropower plants, and gauge the value of possible navigation improvements. Their work brought them into contact with local levee boards, power company engineers, university professors, and other experts whose perspectives shed new light on old problems.[45]

Flood control and river development fascinated Hoover, who firmly believed in manipulating nature to serve man's purposes. Not only did he encourage the 308 surveys, he also helped launch Boulder Dam and other projects that undercut the army's phobia about reservoirs. Hoover convinced the reluctant Corps to open a Waterways Experiment Station in Vicksburg, Mississippi, that simulated improvements in a controlled environment before workers broke ground on the real thing. Tests performed on scale models of watersheds allowed engineers to determine the impact of spillways on flood heights and proved that reservoirs could in some cases reduce crests to manageable levels. These advances discredited the levees-only policy for all time. But they came too late to lessen the deluge that rolled down the Ohio in 1937.[46]

BOAT TRAFFIC ON LA Belle Rivière soared in the 1930s. The stream, however, remained a low priority for engineers obsessed with mastering the lower Mississippi. A person cruising the Ohio at the nadir of the Great Depression passed many scenes reminiscent of the era before massive flood works. Vast piles of sand and gravel dredged from the riverbed awaited transport to market. Barges loaded with coal, petroleum, iron, and steel muscled past the decrepit homes of "shantyboaters," aquatic nomads who eked out a living by fishing and day labor. An occasional showboat tied up to a dock, its jangling calliope inviting curiosity seekers to partake of its mélange of singing, dancing, and comedic acts. Human settlements interrupted long stretches of silent forest rather than the other way around. Some communities demanded attention—Cincinnati, with its tall towers; Louisville, the gateway to the South; Cairo, the stubborn city perched along two rivers. Others slipped past with less drama, anonymous outposts crowding the Ohio for reasons not immediately apparent. One of these small communities was destined to play a prominent part in the coming disaster.

Salt, not water, drew settlers to what became Shawneetown, Illinois. French trappers discovered saltwater springs in the early 1700s near what is today the Saline River. They erected a small fort and began extracting the precious mineral through the same evaporation process that ancient Greeks, Romans, and Egyptians had used centuries earlier. The Shawnee Indians also coveted the salines, which they called the Great Salt Spring or the Great Half Moon Lick. Their hostility forced out the French in the 1730s but could not dislodge the British colonists who began drifting in at mid-century.[47]

An influx of migrants after the Revolutionary War included the area's first permanent white settler. A blacksmith and gunsmith from Indiana named Michael Sprinkle opened a store in 1800 atop the ruins of Indian campgrounds a few miles downstream from the Ohio's intersection with the Wabash. Rugged pioneers who shared his desire to carve profits from the wilderness set up around his business. They named their settlement Shawnee Town, later collapsing it to a single word.[48]

Sprinkle's village thrived despite periodic scuffles with the tribe that gave the community its name. Bears, buffalo, and other game provided abundant food, and the lucrative springs anchored the growing town to its riverside location. Shawneetown became the trans-Allegheny west's principal source of the salt needed to preserve food before the invention of refrigeration. One to two thousand people, most of them slaves, labored in the salt camps. Salt was so important that Illinois's first constitution outlawed slavery "except within the tract reserved for the salt works near Shawneetown."[49]

The federal government wanted to entice settlers to the vital district. It hired surveyors to lay out a town plat, then started selling tracts in 1814 despite doubts about the location's safety; a flood in 1813 prompted one government engineer to recommend moving the settlement to higher ground. "It is certain that no building can safely be erected on that site," he wrote. Both Washington and the locals ignored his advice. As if on cue, a flood put the town under twenty feet of water the next year. "It appears a most unfortunate site for this town has been made," the commissioner of Shawneetown's land office informed Congress.[50]

Land-hungry Americans disregarded these warnings. By 1820 Shawneetown's population topped 3,000, making it one of the larger communities in what was still considered the Far West. Boatmen knew it as the primary laying-up point and commercial center between Louisville and Cairo. As they meandered downstream they sang, "Some row up, but we row down / All the way to Shawneetown." Wagons lined up to cross the Ohio on Shawneetown's ferry, Illinois's best connection with Kentucky and the South, and a well-traveled road linked the village with St. Louis. Its economy diversified as the river trade grew—distilleries, tanneries, gristmills, and taverns enriched local merchants serving the waterborne trade. The frontier community harbored enough wealth that it boasted a jewelry store, an unusual luxury for that part of the world.[51]

Shawneetown was one of the young republic's financial centers. One often told and much relished tale recalls four businessmen who trekked more than three hundred miles to request a $10,000 loan from local bankers. "Since none of us have heard of your village, Chicago," the financiers told the applicants, "we have decided that you are just too far from Shawneetown to amount to anything." Looming just yards from the river, the bank on Main Street provided the most tangible evidence of prosperity. The building was a four-story brick-and-stone masterpiece of Greek Revival architecture. Five magnificent Doric columns supported a broad portico capped with a triangular pediment similar to the ones gracing the White House and the United States Capitol. Its lavish interior boasted marble counters, ornate fireplaces, and carved wood paneling. The bank served as the community's central landmark. Groups gathered on the steps to chat and descended into the basement to vote. One nine-foot slab of granite wall still bears a depression caused by generations of knife carriers' using it as a whetstone.[52]

Shawneetown, for all its affluence, remained a rough-and-tumble town. Local leaders constructed a jail before addressing such extravagances as schools and churches. Highbrow settlers in imported silks peered down their noses at buckskin-clad transients who frequented sleazy riverside saloons. Drunkenness was common, and brawls were frequent. Boatmen referred to a hard-drinking Sabbath as a Shawneetown Sunday. "Not a single soul made any pretensions to religion," one shocked missionary reported after a visit.[53]

And then there was the water. Water gave the village life, and sometimes death. Fetid odors emanating from nearby marshes and cypress swamps sent women reaching for scented handkerchiefs. Spring rains tumbled down the hills into the natural basin where Michael Sprinkle had set up shop. Disease-carrying mosquitoes bred in the stagnant pools dotting poor riverside neighborhoods. Residents accepted the Ohio's frequent floods as an inevitable fact of life, for without the river there would be no Shawneetown.[54]

Shawneetown passed its prime in the late nineteenth century. New salt works in Michigan and elsewhere had broken its monopoly. A burgeoning railroad network diverted trade and migrants to Cairo, Chicago, and St. Louis. Townfolk clung to a glory-bound past as they rehashed tales about Abraham Lincoln's visit to stump for the Whig Party, John James Audubon's overnight stay, and Ulysses S. Grant's honeymoon sojourn. Shawneetown's literary types told anyone who would listen that Mark Twain and Charles Dudley Warner had based *The Gilded Age*'s (1873) silver-tongued con artist Colonel Beriah Sellers on local farmer Mulberry Sellers. The Marquis de Lafayette's brief stopover during his 1825 tour of America remained a staple of conversation.[55]

A spring 1898 rise on the Ohio elicited little concern in a village accustomed to coexisting with the river. The *Shawneetown News* insisted that the levee offered "safe protection against all future danger from inundation." Overconfident residents saw no reason to seek higher ground or to protect their property.[56]

April 3, Palm Sunday, brought a scene reminiscent of one of the Romantic landscapes so popular at the time. A warm spring sun cast rich reds and oranges on the Ohio. A gentle breeze discouraged flying insects and dispersed the prevailing stench. But the idyll shattered just as the sun sank beneath the horizon. Without warning, the river punched through the wall. An angry wave barreled through the gap, killing twenty-five people and obliterating two-thirds of the town within minutes. Church bells pealed a futile warning as terrified survivors scrambled onto roofs, climbed trees, and clung to debris. Hundreds crammed into the bank and the four-story Second Empire–style Riverside Hotel across the street. With telephone and telegraph wires down, refugees had no way to summon help. Several volunteers undertook a harrowing overnight journey to a nearby town. Unnerved and unsure of the situation at home, they sent Governor John Tanner a desperate cable claiming that four or five hundred had perished.[57]

Relief boats arrived within forty-eight hours of the breach. Tanner arranged for tents and emergency rations and persuaded the McKinley administration to dispatch a federal steamer to remove animal carcasses that imperiled public health. The governor resisted calls to summon the legislature into a special session to approve relief funds. Private citizens should finance rehabilitation efforts, he insisted. Briefly the focus of national attention, the catastrophe exited the national consciousness when McKinley declared war with Spain three weeks later. Food and clothing donations lagged far behind needs, and community leaders begged for additional aid. They focused their efforts on Chicago, the city they had so famously snubbed decades earlier, but raised only one-quarter of their $100,000 goal. Spurned by private donors and ignored by a government committed to individual responsibility, the village rebuilt as best it could with the few resources at hand.[58]

Fifteen years later, the 1913 inundation inspired talk of abandoning Shawneetown. One merchant even offered to donate land for a new town site. Nothing came of the proposal. Rather than solving the flooding problem, the city put its head down, repaired its levee, and started over. Shawneetowners acted out of inertia and blind loyalty to the past. Already puffed with stories of their village's illustrious past, their sense of self-importance had nearly burst when the Mississippi River swallowed the dying settlement of Kaskaskia in 1910. That channel shift left Shawneetown as Illinois's oldest city. It bore that title with pride through the Roaring Twenties and into the shadows of the Great Depression.[59]

CHAPTER TWO

ROOSEVELT AND THE RIVERS

〜〜〜〜〜

OCTOBER 20, 1811, DAWNED crisp and clear over Pittsburgh. The docks along the Monongahela hummed as flatboats arrived from upstream or prepared to set off into the wilderness. For all the bustle, only one slip had a crowd around it, and a most unusual crowd at that. Pittsburgh's nabobs generally avoided the seedy river rats who kept the city going in those days before steel. Today, however, the elite joined the hoi polloi to witness the start of a bold endeavor: Nicholas Roosevelt was going to launch the 148-foot steamboat *New Orleans* on its way to the mouth of the Mississippi. Everyone present, whether powerful or humble, respected the affable engineer's nimble mind, mechanical wizardry, and powerful yet unthreatening self-confidence.

Roosevelt had always loved the water. At age thirteen he built his first "ship," a little paddleboat that cruised a pond near his family's New York home. Since then the intellectual polyglot had achieved national prominence through collaborations with Robert Livingston, one of the drafters of the Declaration of Independence; Benjamin Henry Latrobe, his father-in-law and architect of the United States Capitol; and Robert Fulton, creator of the first viable steamboat, the *Clermont*. Today marked the opening chapter of his life's greatest challenge. He aimed to become the first to pilot a steamboat the two thousand miles from the Ohio headwaters to the Gulf of Mexico. A successful voyage would link northeastern manufacturing centers with southern agrarian concerns to form a cohesive and prosperous commercial empire. An unsuccessful voyage might cost him his life.

In 1809 Roosevelt had navigated a flatboat from Pittsburgh to New

Orleans and back, so he knew the perils awaiting him. Sandbars and snags studded the river bottom. Epidemics raged along the route. Tecumseh's crusade against white expansion had the Ohio's north bank close to war. Ruthless pirates controlled long stretches of water.

Roosevelt's headstrong—some said foolhardy—wife Lydia had accompanied him on his previous trip while pregnant with their daughter Rosetta. Now a precocious toddler, Rosetta was waiting for her parents on board the *New Orleans*. Lydia insisted on joining her husband for a second risky voyage even though she was expecting again. Onlookers clucked in disapproval as she waddled from the shipyard office to the boat.[1]

Nicholas and Lydia waved to onlookers as the *New Orleans* belched a mass of black smoke from its twin stacks and chugged out into the Ohio. The ship maintained a twelve mile an hour clip as it wound through virgin forests rich with the vivid colors of fall. Its deafening engine attracted curiosity seekers from isolated cabins and frontier towns.

As Roosevelt had planned, eight days into its trip the *New Orleans* halted in Louisville so Lydia could give birth. The village owed its existence to its location at the Falls of the Ohio, a series of limestone ledges that rendered the river impassable during the low-flow time from midsummer through early winter. In the 1770s explorer George Rogers Clark had erected a fort at that strategic point as a base of operations against British defenses in the Old Northwest. After the Revolutionary War the surrounding civilian community, originally known as "Falls of the Ohio," renamed itself in honor of America's chief ally, France's Louis XVI. In 1811 Louisville boasted a population of one thousand. Most of its businesses revolved around either the labor-intensive portaging of boats and cargo around the falls or the less-demanding job of satisfying the needs of sailors waiting to renew their journeys. With his mechanical inclinations, Roosevelt no doubt admired these crews at work as he strolled past the warehouses, hotels, and taverns lining the riverfront. He also used the layover to his financial advantage by ferrying people upriver for one dollar a head.[2]

The family resumed its expedition in early December, several weeks after Lydia delivered a healthy boy named Henry Latrobe Roosevelt. They had not been on the water long when a violent tremor shook the boat. Crewmen exchanged glances, looked around at the silent wilderness, then shrugged and returned to their tasks. The unremarkable landscape grew ominous as the *New Orleans* approached Cairo, Illinois, a threadbare settlement at the Ohio's junction with the Mississippi. Waves buffeted the prow and uprooted trees drifted across the ship's course. Shoreside buildings lay in heaps. Evidence of some cataclysm grew once the steamboat glided into the Mississippi's agitated waters. Muddy waves heaved the *New Orleans* from side to side like a toy boat in a bathtub.[3]

Six hours past Cairo, Roosevelt's crew maneuvered through a bend in the river that turned them north before veering west to pass in front of New Madrid, Missouri, a popular stopover for roughneck Ohio and Mississippi river boatmen. The town resembled a war zone. A catastrophic earthquake had leveled houses, swamped the riverfront, and transformed the plains behind New Madrid into a lake. Bewildered animals and people wandered through the wreckage in a daze. Victims begged Roosevelt to take them on board. He told them his vessel was full and held his course without stopping. The ship reached New Orleans four weeks later, its crew still unnerved by the destruction but jubilant to have opened America's inland waterways to steamboats.[4]

Besides becoming one of the first white men to witness a natural disaster in the Ohio-Mississippi valley, Roosevelt also paved the way for basinwide development. His expedition promoted future expeditions that connected the East, Old Northwest, and South into a vast mercantile, transportation, and communications network. Improved access to goods and trading lines encouraged Americans to construct great centers of industry and commerce along the Ohio. In one of those tragic yet delicious twists of history, the remarkable regional growth Nicholas helped create guaranteed that the devastation of 1811 paled compared with what his distant relative Franklin faced in 1937.[5]

FDR APPROACHED THE 1937 Ohio disaster with a solid understanding of streams. Although river reforms never topped his agenda, he and his New Dealers nudged the country toward a waterways philosophy that connected land- and water-based problems in order to pursue flood protection, erosion control, reforestation, improved navigation, greater hydroelectric capacity, and other benefits. Roosevelt revived the arguments of Charles Ellet, John Wesley Powell, and Progressive reformers from his cousin Teddy's administration. He also revisited earlier discussions of centralized planning boards that reported directly to the president. What was different now was that the second President Roosevelt operated within the context of the Great Depression. Economic difficulties undermined confidence in established beliefs, creating possibilities for new ideas—

or ambitious old ones—to take hold. FDR also had a strong motivation for putting people to work on construction projects. Under the New Deal, conservation served as a means for combating unemployment as well as an attempt to rationalize resource use.[6]

New Deal conservationists faced numerous obstructions. In many ways planners had to start from scratch because the Corps of Engineers' 308 Reports had only recently provided the knowledge base needed to craft informed environmental legislation. Entrenched interests in Congress and the army engineers were accustomed to directing waterways matters. Roosevelt's bid to expand executive control over this cozy system touched off turf wars that were often more about power than policy. Cash-starved local governments looked to the federal government for leadership on flood control. Washington, however, needed time to overcome past negligence, expertise to develop viable programs, and motivation to commit vast sums of money to hypothetical rather than immediate problems. None of these factors clicked into place fast enough to save the Ohio valley.

Franklin Roosevelt spent much of his life considering environmental issues. He possessed little of Nicholas's mechanical ability but shared his love of boats and the water. Like Nicholas he understood the commercial and ecological importance of the nation's inland waterways. A childhood spent playing in the lush orchards crowding the hill behind the family mansion; his backyard view of the Hudson River valley; and his lifelong reverence for America's most famous nature lover, Theodore Roosevelt, made FDR environmentally aware from an early age. As a young man he developed into a full-fledged conservationist, which in the Progressive Era meant that he supported sustainable use and scientific management of nature's bounty. He converted the family's Hyde Park estate into a showpiece for environmental planning, organizing a multiyear schedule for planting and harvesting trees that maximized financial rewards while ensuring a long-term supply of lumber. Roosevelt also found inspiration in the early twentieth-century Country Life crusade, a movement interested in cultivation methods that promised stability for a new breed of idealized, close-knit rural communities. Its ideas later manifested themselves in President Roosevelt's Resettlement Administration and his infatuation with greenbelt settlements.[7]

Environmental issues defined Roosevelt's otherwise lackluster career as a New York state senator. His position as chairman of the Senate's Forest, Fish, and Game Committee gave him a bully pulpit for championing reforestation. Later, as governor, he proposed planting trees on one million acres of abandoned farmland. Roosevelt confirmed his belief in centralized planning when he initiated a statewide soil survey. When the Depression hit he instituted a relief program that hired the unemployed to work in New York's woodlands, a precursor to the Civilian Conservation Corps he launched during his first hundred days in the White House.[8]

FDR's love of forests blossomed as he looked to adjust government policies to respect the interconnectedness of nature. Unlike W. Milnor Roberts, designer of the Ohio River's movable dam system, he saw conservation and commerce as complementary rather than contradictory ends. As the Democratic Party's 1920 vice presidential candidate, he urged Congress to replace its reliance on piecemeal "pork barrel" river projects with a single agency that set waterways appropriations and developed long-term goals. FDR kept pushing for a centralized policy through the 1920s while remaining vague on the specifics.[9]

Roosevelt sharpened his rhetoric after the government's anemic response to the 1927 Mississippi flood. He blasted Coolidge's refusal to summon Congress into emergency session and chided the stingy administration for ignoring the devastated region's cries for help. Combining his genuine concern for flood victims with an intuitive feel for what was possible and what was politically desirable, FDR advised Democratic allies to pass a relief package generous enough to seize the moral high ground. Do not waste time bickering over detailed flood control, hydropower, and reclamation proposals until you rehabilitate damaged homes and levees, he warned. With an election on the horizon, the canny politician believed hesitation meant electoral disaster. "President Coolidge will, if left alone, make flood relief a purely Republican family matter," he told sympathetic senators, "and will put any blame for delay . . . on the Democratic Party."[10]

FDR attacked Coolidge's inactivity throughout his 1928 gubernatorial campaign. Candidate Roosevelt also supported a movement to appoint a nonpartisan committee to oversee federal rehabilitation programs. He endorsed the 1928 Flood Control Act but feared with good reason that public interest in the issue would wane before Congress could extend reform beyond the lower Mississippi. Legislation to encourage power development, improve navigation, reduce waterborne pollution, and prevent floods required time, patience, and meticulous engineering surveys. Hasty action might produce a boondoggle bill that funded projects without considering their place in a national, comprehensive plan.[11]

Roosevelt ran for president at a moment when talk of national planning was once again in the air. Private-sector planning flourished in the 1920s as industrialists sought to rationalize output, manage growing corporate bureaucracies, and predict future demand for their products. What was good for General Motors, General Electric, and Standard Oil took time to reach the halls of political power. World War I witnessed a temporary flurry of planning in Washington. As the election of 1932 approached, however, the government had no coordinated economic policy, monetary policy, tax policy, agricultural policy, or environmental policy. There was no general agreement on what planning entailed or how far it should go. Roosevelt's Democratic Party included ideological heirs of Woodrow Wilson, who distrusted permanent bureaucracies, and of Teddy Roosevelt, who saw them as acceptable so long as they operated efficiently. Always eager to hear competing voices, FDR drew members of both factions into his inner circle. But even had there been a rough consensus on the desirability and purpose of planning, Washington lacked the qualified personnel and administrative institutions needed to develop and execute long-term strategies.[12]

Depression era writers recalibrated and updated Progressive theories of centralized planning. George Henry Soule's *A Planned Society* (1933) and Lewis Mumford's *Technics and Civilization* (1934) and *The Culture of Cities* (1938) mark some of the genre's high points. Soule and Mumford, who both had connections with the Roosevelt administration, heralded centralized planning as a means for elevating output and standards of living. Without planning, Mumford explained, society developed chaotically, resulting in an "empire of muddle." Soule agreed, describing the United States as "a body without a central nervous system, without a brain."[13]

Inspired by the Soviet Union's experiments with a planned economy and convinced that a selfish spirit of hyperindividualism had driven their country to economic ruin, they encouraged far-seeking leaders to defy entrenched political interests, conservative courts, and materialistic businessmen who refused to acknowledge the need for collective action. A national planning board staffed with dispassionate experts could foster cooperation between businesses, coordinate studies and data, and set production and wage goals. Regional boards could perform much of the legwork, leaving the central agency to focus on the big picture. Interaction among the local, state, and federal levels was pivotal to the success of this setup. For these strategies to be successful, all relevant parties needed a say in formulating long-term policy.

Of the two, Mumford spoke more directly about environmental planning. Like the Progressives, he saw conservation not as wilderness preservation so much as the study of how to put every acre to the best possible use. Ruthless, unplanned exploitation created dust bowls and other environmental disasters. Mankind must instead accommodate the land, letting its features, not our wishes, dictate its function. Responsible public administrators reporting to a centralized agency could determine what tracts made ideal farmland, rangeland, or mining territory. Even plots best suited as parks or swampland played a role in the man-made ecosystem. Like John Wesley Powell, Mumford thought of the natural world as a set of regions that planners needed to treat as unified wholes.[14]

Candidate Roosevelt integrated these discussions into his thinking. Centralized agricultural planning proved of particular interest. FDR saw conquering the Depression as primarily a question of raising purchasing power in rural areas. A planning agency could stabilize farm life by calculating growers' optimal output levels, promoting soil conservation, and electrifying farms. Delivering power to rural America would generate new demand for consumer goods manufactured in cities and thereby bring recovery to urban America. Roosevelt felt the same way about the benefits of planning in 1936, when he told a gathering of Democrats that "nationwide thinking, nationwide planning and nationwide action are the three great essentials to prevent nationwide crises."[15]

Political scientist Ernest Griffith wrote that "from the viewpoint of national planning, the New Deal has been like Don Quixote who mounted his horse and rode off in all directions at once." Roosevelt's inauguration opened the door to hordes of fresh-faced bureaucrats eager to rationalize American life. The short-lived National Recovery Administration attempted to substitute cooperation for competition in the business world. The Agricultural Adjustment Administration worked to put the farm economy on a long-term basis. Conservationists salivated at the prospect of adopting a holistic, planned approach to nature. By middecade, activists such as Soil Conservation Service chief H. H. Bennett were speaking of "total conservation," the merger of all federal environmental activities into a single Department of Conservation.[16]

As Griffith observed, the problem with this sudden flurry of activity was that there was a sudden flurry of activity. New Dealers wanted to accomplish everything at once. The proliferation of agencies created bureaucratic disputes, poor coordination, and redundancies. Roosevelt, who had a hard time saying no and enjoyed setting advisers with ideological conflicts against each other, did little to straighten tangled lines of authority.

New Deal conservationists nevertheless took remarkable strides during FDR's first term. They collected mountains of data, identified complex problems, and mapped out possible solutions. They planted millions of trees, expanded the use of soil-friendly farming techniques, and tamed many unruly rivers. Like their predecessors from the Progressive Era and before, however, they failed to create a permanent, centralized environmental planning commission that formulated long-term strategies based on the concept that nature operated as a unified whole. Internal divisions combined with external foes, in the form of congressional detractors and their allies in the Corps of Engineers, to defeat New Dealers' attempt to link flood protection with other land- and soil-based priorities.[17]

Roosevelt began his presidency with a hazy sense of what to do with American rivers. He wanted to treat waterways as a single interconnected system in order to simultaneously address several interlocking problems. Not being an engineer or a scientist, he had no real idea of how to reach this vague objective. At times he could not even distinguish between the many agencies involved in water policy. "Who and what is the Mississippi River Commission?" he asked an adviser. "I understand there is a vacancy on it but I cannot find anything about it." FDR took more than two years to fill the position.[18]

Roosevelt's dawdling stemmed in large part from his focus on more immediate economic concerns. The president nevertheless celebrated important triumphs in his effort to house environmental matters within the executive branch rather than with Congress or the Corps of Engineers. Regionalists achieved a huge victory when Roosevelt created the Tennessee Valley Authority (TVA), a single bureaucratic entity that modernized the impoverished valley through channel improvements, erosion control, and hydroelectric dams. John Wesley Powell would have been proud. FDR envisioned TVA as a test case for the nationally coordinated watershed-based rivers policy he wanted. He tipped his intention to make TVA a jumping-off point rather than a landing place when in a January 1934 message to Congress he advocated an agenda of "carefully planned flood control, power development, and land-use." Obliging legislators passed a resolution asking the president for a plan. This request enabled him to explore options without interference from nosy congressman or the Corps, groups he saw as not interested in a comprehensive waterways program.[19]

The resulting Committee on Water Flow was a blue-ribbon panel with little real power. Roosevelt ordered the secretaries of war, labor, agriculture, and the interior, and other members, to evaluate existing water supply, pollution, irrigation, drainage, erosion, power, navigation, and flood control proposals as a first step toward outlining a long-term agenda directed from the White House, not the Capitol. FDR promptly undercut his expansive aspirations when he asked for a report within three weeks, an absurd deadline considering the mountain of material members needed to digest.[20]

Development of the Rivers of the United States ended up taking three months to prepare and was still a rush job. Harried committeemen cobbled together material from earlier surveys rather than conducting original research. Other than asserting the need for more studies, they offered few specific recommendations. This ambiguity reflected divisions within the commission. Secretary of War George Dern protested the undertaking as an end run around the Corps of Engineers. He wanted Congress to approve lump-sum appropriations for waterways spending, then allow the army to assign project priorities based on its own internal calculus.

Three months was ample time to confirm suspicions that the Ohio River was a mess. The Committee on Water Flow lamented wasteful agricultural practices that eroded farmland and stripped hillsides of trees. It decried the torrents of waterborne pollutants that mines, factories, and sewage systems poured into the stream. The commission ranked flood control as less important than these problems but suggested as an afterthought that damming upstream tributaries offered the best way to reduce crest heights. It proposed a $210 million network of thirty-nine reservoirs, all of them above Cincinnati. Complete protection also required floodwalls and other works that the committee rejected as economically unjustifiable.[21]

The Committee on Water Flow's recommendations cluttered desks in Washington without prodding Congress to consider a comprehensive rivers agenda. As if to acknowledge the panel's shortcomings, Roosevelt appointed a second study group, the Mississippi Valley Committee (MVC), even before the first commission concluded its review. FDR hoped rivalries between the overlapping boards might produce innovative solutions. The

MVC instead created confusion. White House staffers already drowning in an alphabet soup of new agencies sometimes called it the Mississippi Valley Commission or conflated it with the Mississippi River Commission, the bureau responsible for building levees and maintaining navigation channels on the lower Mississippi. Even Roosevelt had a hard time keeping the two straight.[22]

MVC officials spent months studying reports and examining sites throughout the Ohio-Mississippi watershed. Interior Secretary Harold Ickes and other members fended off attacks from congressmen who saw the group as a bureaucratic assault on the Corps of Engineers. The board's 1934 report, which made expanding hydropower supplies a higher priority than controlling high waters, seemed to confirm this charge. Its section on flood control called for a dramatic expansion of the Interior Department's mission and a reduction of that of the levee-building Corps. Ickes's concerns permeated the document. "We cannot plan for water unless we also consider the relevant problems of the land," it observed. The MVC called for reducing water runoff through reforestation, restoring grasslands, and retiring marginal lands from cultivation. Its wide-ranging approach to flood control included the use of dams, channel improvements, reservoirs, levees, and floodways. These proposals, which mirrored ideas Charles Ellet had raised decades earlier, left little room for the traditionalist Corps.[23]

FDR remained distracted by urgent financial concerns, wary of the cost of a comprehensive waterways act, and loath to expend the political capital needed to shift congressional loyalties from the Corps of Engineers to an executive-controlled body. He sensed little public enthusiasm for expensive river projects. With these obstacles in mind, FDR prolonged the status quo by shuffling the MVC into a larger entity, the National Resources Board, later renamed the National Resources Committee (NRC). Roosevelt asked the group to set the nation's agenda on "the physical, social, governmental, and economic aspects of . . . the development and use of land, water, and other national resources." The NRC's illustrious membership reflected the weight Roosevelt put on it. Harold Ickes chaired the outfit. The secretaries of war, agriculture, and labor reprised their roles from the defunct Committee on Water Flow. Commerce Secretary Daniel Roper joined the team, as did FDR's uncle, Frederic Delano, a veteran of the city planning movement. Longtime public power advocate Morris Cooke led a subcommittee tasked with evaluating and setting priorities for over two thousand proposed watershed projects.[24]

Roosevelt hailed the NRC's early 1935 report as a stride toward a comprehensive environmental agenda. In reality, other than prioritizing existing proposals, the NRC report did little more than restate the MVC's conclusions. Ickes's board again advocated erosion control, reforestation, and hydropower. Its discussion of flood control again derided the Corps of Engineers' discredited levees-only stance and embraced the idea gaining traction within conservation circles that small dams across headwaters offered more effective flood control than levees, a notion Ellet had raised nearly a century earlier. Like the Committee on Water Flow, the NRC offered little evidence to support its conclusions because it had reviewed existing surveys rather than conducting its own.[25]

Roosevelt's efforts produced widespread resentment and few concrete results. Congressmen from landlocked districts saw no reason to support expensive programs derived from the musings of academics. The rivers and harbors bloc complained that the administration's deliberate pace endangered their constituents. Representatives on both sides favored the old ad hoc system of constructing flood works. Army engineers were men of action. They knew their business, provided tangible results, and, unlike the aloof executive-branch groups, cultivated important legislators. Critics, including some in the Corps, asserted that Roosevelt was more interested in consolidating executive power than in fabricating a workable water policy.[26]

FDR's conflict with Congress escalated when a New England inundation in summer 1935 prompted about one hundred flood control bills. A proposal by House Flood Control Committee chairman Riley Wilson of Louisiana to herd hundreds of projects approved by the Corps of Engineers into a single $400 million package, $75 million more than Congress authorized under the 1928 Flood Control Act, emerged as the frontrunner. Legislators sensing a boondoggle in the making tacked their pet proposals onto the bill. Republicans hoping to inflate the bill's price tag enough to make it politically unpalatable joined in the frenzy. California Democrat John Hoeppel introduced a sarcastic amendment to "build a dam around the United States Treasury to protect the taxpayers." But the conservatives' tactics backfired when the bloated proposal squeaked through the House after swelling to almost $500 million.[27]

Wilson's bill seemed destined to sail through a Senate desperate to recess after a long session. New York senator Royal Copeland whisked it through the Commerce Committee and presented it to the full floor before most of his peers had even read it. A bipartisan group of conservatives chastised colleagues for their willingness to pass the expensive proposal sight unseen and with minimal debate. Their arguments persuaded a slight majority to vote to recommit the bill until the next session.[28]

FDR played a decisive role in stopping the Wilson-Copeland Act. He saw it as contrary to his desire for comprehensive, rational, executive-driven river reform, a diversion on the march toward national planning and total conservation. Roosevelt also found the bill's stipulation that the federal government assume all construction costs financially onerous and unfair to states that would receive minimal benefits. The president implored congressmen to be patient and dispatched budget director Daniel Bell to denounce the pork-laden bill in closed-door meetings with senators.[29]

Harlow Person's *Little Waters*, issued a few months later, revitalized the debate while bolstering Ickes and others who doubted traditional protection methods and wanted to treat rivers as part of a unified ecosystem. Person was one of the anonymous cadre of New Dealers floating around the capital, a member of both the National Resources Committee and its predecessor, the Mississippi Valley Committee. Like his friends Morris Cooke and Soil Conservation Service director H. H. Bennett, he was fascinated with the possibility of using the government to scientifically manage natural resources. His book echoed arguments that Ellet, Ickes, and others had made for years. In contrast to their turgid studies, *Little Waters* excited public interest in flood control. FDR incorporated its signature phrase, "upstream engineering," into his conversations about waterways.

Person painted a dismal picture appropriate to an era of depression and dust storms. Complacent Americans, he claimed, could no longer exchange environmental stability for short-term material gain. Their voracious consumption habits had led to clear-cut timberlands, overgrazed prairies, and exhausted underground aquifers. "The United States is not a 'permanent country,'" Person warned, "and is on the way to joining decadent parts of China and Asia Minor, once opulent and magnificent, but now stripped of their fertile soils and buried in the dust of destructive exploitation of resources."[30]

Person's conclusions on flooding drew particular attention. He insisted that rather than rushing water to the sea through narrow channels of levees that elevated rather than lowered crests, engineers must instead slow its journey by reinvigorating denuded forests, grasslands, and marshes that could absorb precipitation before it reached flood-prone rivers. Small check dams and reservoirs on headwaters would prevent additional water from reaching swollen streams. His plan offered all citizens, not just experts, a role in solving waterways problems, an angle that fit the collective spirit of the New Deal. They could all contribute to the common good through conscientious land and water usage on their own property.

Many economists speculated that the country had reached its maximum prosperity and should therefore make the most of the finite wealth available rather than pining for an economic boom that would never come. Person's talk of exhausted resources and national impermanence conveyed a similar message. It was time to cede territory that belonged to rivers and accept flood control rather than aim for absolute flood prevention. Such pessimism contradicted the country's usual self-confidence, but with the Depression entering its seventh year, optimism felt out of touch with reality.[31]

Public officials seized on headwaters dams as a panacea despite Person's insistence that neither upstream engineering nor any other act of man could stop floods. A major overflow in spring 1936 gave these misguided interpretations the ring of authority. It had been a harsh winter across the Northeast. Snow piled up in huge drifts. Frigid temperatures froze lakes and rivers. Miles of ice floes, some of them twenty-five feet thick, clogged the Ohio. Spring thaws sent melted ice and snow pouring into mountain gullies, creeks, the Allegheny, the Monongahela, the Connecticut, the James, the Potomac, and the Ohio. Frozen, saturated soil whisked additional rainfall into bloated streams.[32]

New England felt the impact first. Pittsburgh came next. The Steel City knew floods well, having survived eighty in the previous eighty-four years. Government meteorologists predicted a thirty-four-foot crest there, nine feet above flood stage but five feet below the record mark.[33] Waters instead hit forty-six feet as simultaneous peaks on the Allegheny and Monongahela pushed the Ohio twenty feet higher in a single day. The Golden Triangle, Pittsburgh's commercial heart, sat twenty feet underwater. The rise sent 30,000 people running from crumbling neighborhoods near the riverside and punished upstream industrial areas.[34]

Pittsburgh sustained half of the 107 flood-related deaths. Scenes of desperation occurred as far downstream as Cincinnati, where several thousand residents fled the low-rent riverfront warehouse district. Deadeye marksmen saved Portsmouth, Ohio, by shooting thousands of muskrats tunneling through temporary barriers. Binghamton, New York, went under while its leaders testified at flood control budget hearings in the capital. Civilian Conservation Corps enlistees from around Washington, DC, sandbagged the Washington Monument and Lincoln Memorial against the churning Potomac. Workers at the Red Cross's national headquarters hustled files out of basement offices in case water backed up through the sewers.[35]

The contentious Wilson-Copeland debate, the release of *Little Waters*, and the $200 million in damages from the springtime inundation captured the nation's attention. Supporters of check dams and retention ponds observed that the recent disaster originated from tiny streams, not major rivers. Secretary Ickes and his allies claimed that the calamity exemplified the need for reforestation. Roosevelt supported reforestation and soil stabilization—and the New Deal was active in those capacities—but he suspected that those remedies alone could not prevent overflows. He also knew the March flood almost guaranteed that Congress would pass a hefty waterways act. FDR wanted to steer the debate toward a comprehensive environmental program that situated flood control within a broader natural resources agenda under the National Resources Committee's supervision. Senate Commerce Committee chairman Royal Copeland defied the president when he asked the chief of the Corps of Engineers, Major General Edward Markham, to devise a plan for the committee's consideration. His request reflected Congress's long-standing ties to the Corps and its disdain for Roosevelt's NRC.[36]

Lawmakers offered Markham little input or direction beyond stipulating a $300 million spending target. Their vagueness frustrated the general. "It seems to me that the Corps of Engineers cannot recommend anything here very intelligently until the committee itself, or the Congress itself, tells us what line to pursue," he complained. "It is difficult for us to recommend what ought to be done . . . because we have no compass."[37] Within a week of Copeland's request, the general cobbled together a proposal that introduced scores of projects missing from the previous year's bill. For the most part it posed flood control as a straightforward engineering problem that amateurs unnecessarily complicated when they tossed hydropower, water supply, and land-based issues into the mix. He showed little interest in reforestation or soil erosion and insisted that the Corps of Engineers must maintain control over waterways.[38]

The Senate's quick action prompted a rapid response from the White House. Agriculture Secretary Henry Wallace, who had a vested interest in expanding programs within his bureaucratic domain, interrupted FDR's yachting vacation with a telegram warning about the Copeland bill. Roosevelt wired his disapproval to congressional leaders. Mitigating floods was "only one phase of the subject . . . inextricably tied in with other projects and cannot be separated from them," he wrote. He promised to veto any bill that did not address "all forms of land misuse" or that denied the NRC an important policymaking role. FDR ordered Wallace, Ickes, and Secretary of War George Dern to stall the legislation until he finished his cruise. This was more than a dispute about two versions of a bill. Two philosophies of environmentalism,[39] tied to two philosophies of government, were colliding. New Dealers proposed a government built to address long-term difficulties in a rational, organized manner. They favored accommodation with the natural world, adapting to its contours without retreating altogether. Congress and the Corps looked to conquer more immediate problems in a way that asserted man's absolute authority over nature.[40]

Ickes and other administration officials eager to make the NRC paramount in water issues seconded Roosevelt's belief that the bill was "thoroughly unsound." Their opposition forced a few amendments without changing the core of the legislation. FDR did rebuff demands from river districts that the federal government meet the entire cost of protecting them from high water. He insisted that locals must share the burden lest flood control return to its pork barrel roots. Communities would focus on worthy endeavors so long as they footed part of the bill. As modified, the act required Washington to cover construction costs, leaving states or localities to purchase land needed for levees and reservoirs and pay operations and maintenance bills. FDR's inability to win amendments making the NRC permanent or vesting it with any real power left the Corps of Engineers in charge of waterways improvements.[41]

The $300 million Flood Control Act of 1936 authorized hundreds of projects but did not appropriate enough money to conduct surveys or start construction on the vast majority of them. Construction would not have begun even had Congress allocated funds, because states needed to buy land before work could commence. The law nevertheless represented a turning point for inland waterways. For the first time, Washington assumed responsibility for national flood control policy. Ohio valley residents would reap the benefits from nine reservoirs slated for construction in the Allegheny-Monongahela basin and five more on the Kanawha and Licking River basins in West Virginia and Kentucky.[42]

Roosevelt hoped to fold the 1936 Flood Control Act into a comprehensive program under NRC auspices. He ordered another report from the committee by the time Congress passed the bill. *Drainage Basin Problems and Programs* landed on the president's desk a few weeks before Christmas. Like other New Deal era studies, the NRC's compendium did a better job of listing problems than of detailing solutions. It again concluded that a paucity of basic data made committing to any specific plan of action premature. Researchers had spotty information on precipitation rates, streamflow, evaporation, and water quality. They required more statistics concerning erosion's impact on flooding and more accurate topographical maps.

Above all, the document insisted on the need for a unified rivers program under NRC leadership. "Far too often," it observed, the country had resorted to "orderless, unintegrated treatment of water problems." NRC members crowed that they—with little cooperation from the Corps of Engineers, which played a minimal role in writing *Drainage Basin Problems*— had taken an important step toward this goal. Members tagged thousands of proposed projects as either viable or pointless. They opened lines of communication with federal agencies, state planning boards, and local organizations. This was national planning as George Soule and Lewis Mumford envisioned it. Washington encouraged input from all levels of society, forging a harmony of interests that invested the various parties in whatever strategies emerged from their deliberations.[43]

Drainage Basin Problems expressed horror at conditions in the Ohio valley. "Some cities are practically drinking their own and their neighbors' sewage," it noted. Cities dumped their waste downstream rather than treating it. Runoff from breweries, mills, tanneries, mines, and sewage plants had transformed La Belle Rivière into a cesspool. Flood control provided another vexing issue. Reservoirs on tributaries might offer some security, but most proposed sites were not economically viable. Delegates suggested a more defeatist agenda. "It might be cheaper," the document stated, "to prevent the construction of new buildings in flood zones, and gradually to eliminate those now threatened as they become desolate."[44]

The report had no more policy impact than the other environmental studies issued during Roosevelt's first term. Even so, New Dealers racked up numerous accomplishments during those four years. FDR's subordinates transformed a debate about where to place massive engineering works into a far-ranging discussion that probed man's impact on the environment. Bureaucrats identified weak spots, set priorities for future study, and started mobilizing all levels of government behind a coordinated flood control program.

Roosevelt was by then fully aware of the publicity value of flood control works and other infrastructure projects. Federally funded dams, irrigation canals, and hillside terraces provided what Neil Maher called "physical advertisements for the New Deal." Communities learned that a Civilian Conservation Corps facility, a Works Progress Administration grant, or a Public Works Administration building drive brought outside revenue and improved the quality of local life. FDR never hesitated to use job programs to sell other proposals or enhance his own popularity. Like a new courthouse or repaved street, a waterways improvement stood as a living reminder of the importance of electing New Deal Democrats. Moreover, the nation as a whole grew more conscious of the benefits of conservation as environmental projects proliferated and as Americans cycled through the CCC, WPA, and PWA. What was once a movement limited to academics and the elite became democratized once the average joe learned ways to stabilize his relationship with the earth and grew to appreciate the merits of rationalized resource consumption. If done well, a comprehensive flood control program would enhance both public awareness of conservation and FDR's political stature.[45]

The president instead perpetuated the venerable American tradition of responding to natural disasters rather than anticipating them. He never made flood control a top priority within his environmental agenda even though he knew that rivers menaced cities built on floodplains. Forests occupied his mind more than rivers, and Interior Secretary Ickes placed soil above water. His insistence on executive domination over waterways stymied progress by straining his relationship with Congress and the Corps of Engineers. Finally, Roosevelt articulated no specific outline for his ill-defined comprehensive approach to rivers. Nor did he persuade Congress to relinquish its demand for immediate, piecemeal action to solve local waterways problems. At this point the public displayed little enthusiasm for a speculative venture in centralized environmental planning, a proposition that sounded possibly socialist and assuredly expensive. It is hard to blame FDR for his inability to cast aside decades of precedent in four short and extraordinarily busy years. He made laudable efforts in fields where his predecessors had made none. Even had Congress approved a massive overhaul of the Ohio valley on the first day of his presidency, and found some way to pay for it, it is unlikely that the resulting system would have been fully operational by January 1937.

NEITHER PLANNERS, CONGRESS, NOR the Corps of Engineers gave much thought to Shawneetown. The historic community on the Ohio was too small and economically irrelevant to merit a place in their grand designs. Shawneetown did, however, benefit from the increased funds for flood control that began appearing under Herbert Hoover. In 1931 Mayor William Brinkley pried $100,000 from Washington to bolster the wall the village had repaired at its own expense after the 1913 disaster. New Deal dollars saw the project through to its completion in 1934. The enhanced levee loomed so high that passing boats could not see the village behind it. Shawneetowners joked that the sun rose at nine in the morning, when its first rays topped the wall. Shorter days seemed a small price to pay for security and the economic boom sure to follow the town's fortification. An edifice built to confine actually freed the community to realize its bright future. From another perspective, it acted as a prison that isolated the village from the outside world. Preserving Shawneetown's river heritage meant physically separating it from the Ohio.[46]

Shawneetown in the 1930s remained a relic of the past. Hitching posts lined its unpaved Main Street. A pump house and watering trough stood across the street from the magnificently incongruous bank. Lumber companies, a flour mill, a barrel-stave mill, and a small sand and gravel plant provided most of the area's scarce employment opportunities. The harddrinking toughs who patronized a floating roadhouse named Moon Mullins proved that Shawneetown's rough-and-tumble side survived into the twentieth century. Bootleggers proliferated during Prohibition and stuck around after repeal. Prostitutes and gamblers paraded in the streets as openly as during the steamboat era.

Yet signs of rebirth abounded. The Public Works Administration constructed a system that delivered fresh drinking water instead of stagnant well water. A new highway brought hopes that increased traffic would enrich local merchants. The school board built a two-story brick high school near the hilltop spot considered for a new town site after the 1913 inundation. Shawneetown's annual Corn Day celebration drew guests from surrounding counties for a week of agricultural displays, dances, and concerts.

A rising generation of local leaders drove this renaissance. Many of the old elite departed after the 1898 flood convinced them the village had no future. Hustling go-getters filled the void atop the social ladder. Many were newcomers—meaning they had lived in Shawneetown less than twenty-five years—who valued the area's rich history both as an inherent treasure and as a marketing tool. These young businessmen chided self-satisfied elders who had "made their pile and are just holding on to it till they die." They worked through such organizations as the Kiwanis Club to refashion the sleepy town into a bustling burg.[47]

The new elite forged a tight-knit clique that played cards together, drank together, went to church together, and attended club meetings together. Although they had no recognized head, Max Galt was as much the leader as anyone. Born in Omaha, Nebraska, in 1896 as the first of James and Carrie Galt's two sons, he was a booster through and through. James's railroad job brought the family to Shawneetown in 1909. In his youth the precocious Max played baseball with future community leaders including Al Lowe, scion of an established business family, and Carroll Goetzman, heir to the Goetzman Brothers Grocery and Bakery. Two years of high school sated Galt's thirst for formal learning; he dropped out at age sixteen to pursue a career in banking. His military service during World War I interrupted his budding career without derailing it. Galt cemented his social status when he married Carroll Goetzman's sister Marie in 1919. Their union gave him access to his in-laws' considerable banking and agricultural interests and brought him into the community's inner circle.[48]

Galt plunged into numerous ventures with admirable aplomb. He ran an insurance company with Carroll Goetzman and parlayed his charm, intellect, and phenomenal memory into the top spot at the First National Bank. Though a benevolent dictator, he treated the bank like his personal fiefdom. Galt often dug into his wallet to make loans to people on the street. He rarely bothered to record these transactions. "They'll come in and let me know when it's due," he would laugh before strolling off, whistling through his teeth like a man without a care. Such nonchalance concealed a steel-trap mind. Writing a loan in a ledger struck him as an unnecessary formality because he knew pretty much everyone in town. Galt belonged to the right organizations and attended dinner parties with the right people. He was as close to an institution as the village had. "When Mr. Galt died," one resident later remarked, "I expected the town to dry up and blow away."[49]

For all Galt's bonhomie, Shawneetown in the 1930s was more a collection of distinct circles than a cohesive society. Its 250 African Americans lived in a world of their own, as in so many towns across the valley. Most worked as unskilled laborers or domestics. They were the first to lose their jobs when the Depression hit. Nearly all of them survived on relief checks. A few saloons served them so long as they stayed in the back room. The town's segregated school system made no provision for educating black students beyond eighth grade. No Colored Allowed signs adorned restaurant windows.[50]

"Shawneetown is one-third white people, one-third white trash, and one-third niggers," one local politician commented. Village elites, as they did with African Americans, denied the "white trash" a say in community affairs. Poor whites would never have admitted how much they had in common with African Americans. Economic misery ranged widely. Most poor families, black or white, rented small, rickety houses. One-third of the children walked to school in bare feet. "We've always had that class here," an upper-class Shawneetowner snorted. "God creates classes. . . . They're born worthless." Class indeed defined everyday life. Prosperous families worshipped at the Methodist, First Baptist, and St. Mary's churches. Poor white families attended the Church of God or the General Baptist Church. Blacks worshipped at a different Baptist church. Wealthy families belonged to the 4-H Club, the Kiwanis Club, the Lions Club, and the Masonic Lodge, organizations that excluded the impoverished majority. Social partitioning extended to the grave. One undertaker served upper-class whites and another handled poor whites and African Americans.[51]

The Depression exacerbated social tensions. Farmers displaced from nearby agricultural districts poured into the village to seek work. Elites and established lower-class residents denigrated these newcomers as "peckerwoods" who stole jobs and relief dollars from more deserving candidates. "They lived in dirt-floor houses, they ate sow-belly and pone, and now they come in here," people complained.[52]

Galt and his friends hoped to transform Illinois's oldest settlement from a hidebound place where "even the stray dogs are too lazy to bark at you" into a vigorous business center. Everyone knew the Ohio was key to the town's future, whether because of river life's alleged character-giving properties or, more concretely, because of its transportation and commercial potential. Residents clung to the Ohio through good times and bad. Their commitment to a patch of sandy soil reflected the loyalty, or perhaps complacency, that British immigrant Morris Birbeck detected after purchasing some acreage in 1817. "Shawneetown," he wrote, "I account as a phenomenon evincing the pertinacious adhesion of the human animal to the spot where it has once fixed itself. As the lava of Mount Etna cannot dislodge this strange being from the cities which have been ravaged by its eruptions, so . . . the Ohio with its annual overflowings is unable to wash away the inhabitants of Shawneetown."

Birbeck's wonder would have struck the Shawneetowner of 1937 as a cause for smugness rather than concern. Inhabitants saw themselves as gritty survivors who had withstood nature's terrible fury. After a generation without a major flood, they believed they were immune from the river's ravages.[53]

Their disregard for the Ohio's power mirrored a confidence seen throughout the valley. Cincinnati and other upstream communities believed 1936 was the worst the river could give. Many downstream cities had gone decades without severe damage. Washington spun its wheels as it delayed finding solutions to problems identified years earlier. So, as FDR drafted his second inaugural address during those wet January days, the Ohio snaked through its valley much as it had four years earlier—or, for that matter, twenty-four years earlier. The thousand-mile river remained an afterthought in a system obsessed with the Mississippi and with bureaucratic prerogatives.

As winter settled over the land, people from Pittsburgh to Cairo watched the Ohio meander past as it had since time immemorial. Cairoites and Shawneetowners dozed behind levees tall enough to create an illusion of invulnerability. Paducahans and Lousivillians inured to the inconvenience of minor rises assumed the Ohio would never exceed historic highs. Prosperous Cincinnatians peered down at the river from hilltop homes while the poor watched from waterfront shacks. And so the Ohio rolled on past scores of cities, towns, and crossroads, past farmland, countryside, and hills, past millions of Americans grown accustomed to its placid current.

Then it started raining.

MOVING OUT, MOVING IN

~~~~~~~~

EAGER CHILDREN ROSE WITH the dawn, rushed to their windows, and drooped when they discovered that 1936 would not be a white Christmas. Sleepy parents rolled out of bed feeling more cheerful about the weather. It had been a warmer than usual December in the Ohio valley. Temperatures rose into the lower forties with minimal morning frost and less snowfall than expected.[1]

Benevolent weather contributed to a general sense of well-being. Economic indicators had stabilized after years of precipitous declines. Americans assumed that FDR's recent victory meant four more years of New Deal activism. An early spring seemed a given when temperatures touched the sixties soon after Christmas. Light rain moistened America's northeastern quadrant in the last week of December without dampening the cheerful mood. Trees and plants drank as the soil grew heavy with water. Trickles of runoff started dripping into creeks and streams. The Ohio and its tributaries crept above the uncharacteristically low depths seen before the holidays but remained far below flood level.

Confidence prevailed as Americans hung new calendars. "There are ample indications that 1937 . . . is to be one of the best years this community has known in a long time," crowed the *Cairo Evening Citizen and Bulletin.* Roosevelt's banishment of Old Man Depression paved the way for an economic revival sure to benefit the industrial heartland. "The outlook hasn't been so good since 1929," the paper concluded. Similar sentiments appeared seventy-five miles upstream in Golconda, Illinois, where the *Herald-Enterprise*'s editor urged readers to seize control over their destinies after years of helpless drifting. "Our lives are not shaped by inexorable fates," he declared. "We make them mostly by our own efforts or errors." The paper's words bore more truth than intended, for inexorable fate, in the form of nature's fury, was about to exploit Ohio valley residents' past efforts and errors.[2]

The first days of crisis inspired contradictory movements. Flooded-out people forsook the Ohio valley and Mississippi delta at the same time as hundreds of thousands of private and public relief workers entered. The calamity spread beyond Arkansas and Missouri within a few days of Roosevelt's inauguration. Unusual weather conditions sent the swollen Ohio and its tributaries crashing into cities throughout the basin and rushing toward the buried Mississippi bottomlands. With the crest still off in the indeterminate future, the downpour began exploiting cracks in the region's social foundations, pressing at weak points that could burst at any moment.

There is no great mystery to what caused the 1937 flood: it rained. A lot. About 165 billion tons—close to 41,250,000,000,000 (quadrillion!) gallons—of ice, snow, sleet, and rain pummeled the Ohio valley in the month following Christmas. Certain areas on the lower Ohio absorbed twenty-five inches of precipitation. Between ten and fifteen inches drenched upstream communities. Decades of apathy, poor planning, and bickering left residents without an adequate flood control program or local protective works. They had no choice but to "take it."

Ecclesiastes 1:7 captures the essence of the flood cycle. "All the rivers run into the sea," it reads, "yet the sea is not full; unto the place from whence the river comes, thither they return again." Hundreds of tributaries flow into the Ohio, which empties into the Mississippi, which exits into the Gulf of Mexico. Water from the Gulf then evaporates, travels north on the prevailing winds, and falls on the ground again, where it enters rivers and underground aquifers to begin the cycle anew. This sequence of rain, drainage, and evaporation has prevailed since time immemorial. Without it life on the earth could not exist.

Every so often nature unleashes a variant of this cycle so extreme that it harms rather than aids humankind. Americans awoke that beautiful Christmas morning unaware that nature had already played a wild card. A powerful high-pressure network was sucking moisture-laden air from the Caribbean into a giant clockwise spiral that blanketed the Mid-Atlantic states. Two titanic weather systems squared off as that front's warm, wet air repelled dry polar air sweeping down from the northwest. Between them lay a climatological Maginot Line that took the form of a low-pressure trough running east by northeast over the Ohio valley.

That channel drew moisture through it like a giant vacuum. A Wagnerian drama played out as warm, humid air collided with its cool, dry counterpart, an atmospheric clash that induced storm clouds to discharge their burden. The storm's proximity to the Ohio and its lower tributaries had a disproportionate impact on river heights because the ground had little chance to absorb precipitation before it encountered a stream. Fortunately, the same arctic front that guided rain along the Ohio kept the air over the Missouri and upper Mississippi rivers dry. Had they too received abnormal rainfall, a concurrence of conditions meteorologists dismiss as improbable, the resulting flood on the Mississippi below Cairo might have attained biblical proportions.

These storms would have been inconsequential had the two high-pressure fronts broken up and moved on. Instead, they dug in. Four huge storm waves navigated the low-pressure gutter between them before the aerial gridlock dissipated. An initial cycle dumped seven inches of rain on the Tennessee River basin between the day after Christmas and the first days of the new year. A second, lasting from January 6 to January 12, delivered some of the most intense sleet that Illinois, Indiana, and Kentucky had seen in decades. A third the next week poured seven to ten inches of rain on the Tennessee, Cumberland, and Wabash valleys. Rivers in Ohio, Illinois, and Indiana broke levels last seen in 1913 even before the fourth wave began.[3]

Many meteorologists predicted that snow and subfreezing temperatures would slow the waters' rush to the rivers. Others expected a high-pressure front out of the Great Plains to dislodge the mountain of tropical air. Neither hope materialized. Temperatures just above freezing in Ohio, Indiana, Illinois, Missouri, Kentucky, and Tennessee added to flood victims' misery without halting the rise. Moreover, the troublesome duo of stalled fronts refused to yield to the dry western air before first shepherding a final series of storms that unleashed the heaviest precipitation yet.[4]

The sequential nature of the storms intensified the overflow. Floods are most dangerous when they contain multiple crests. River channels were already so full from the post-Christmas downpours that they could not carry precipitation from subsequent cloudbursts. Water stacked on top of itself to send levels higher than a single storm of comparable magni-

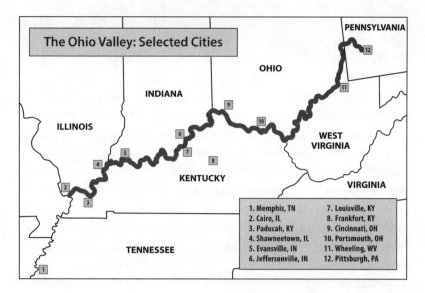

The Ohio Valley: Selected Cities

PENNSYLVANIA

OHIO

INDIANA

ILLINOIS

WEST VIRGINIA

KENTUCKY

VIRGINIA

TENNESSEE

1. Memphis, TN	7. Louisville, KY
2. Cairo, IL	8. Frankfort, KY
3. Paducah, KY	9. Cincinnati, OH
4. Shawneetown, IL	10. Portsmouth, OH
5. Evansville, IN	11. Wheeling, WV
6. Jeffersonville, IN	12. Pittsburgh, PA

tude could have produced. Tributaries lost their battles to empty into the engorged Ohio. With a wall of water blocking their normal exits, rivers had no choice but to back up into surrounding lowlands. The Ohio itself was far beyond its capacity to empty fast enough to save the communities along its banks. And valley residents looked heavenward on inauguration day to see another wall of gray cumulonimbus clouds heading their way—the leading edge of the fourth wave.

It is curious if not particularly significant that the first forecast of disaster came from a crank correspondent to the White House. William Hillinger of Hazel Park, Michigan, wrote several letters to Franklin Roosevelt over the years bearing alleged insights into the future. In October 1936 he reminded the president of his more or less accurate prediction of recent high waters in Texas. "Please permit me to warn you of another flood in some of these states or in the Mississippi or Ohio River Valley which may occur in January 1937," he wrote. "At the present time I am not able to determine the exact locality," Hillinger concluded, adding: "I hope that this is of some help for you."[5]

FDR's subordinates handled Hillinger's missive without disturbing the president. Warnings of impending natural disasters should come from the U.S. Weather Bureau, not some random loony. Unfortunately, bureau analysts struggled to determine what impact the dark clouds massing over the valley might have. "We cannot . . . forecast the amount and location of rain in advance of its fall," Weather Bureau River and Flood Division chief Merrill Bernard told a congressional committee in 1939. "We can decide that we are to have rains of a certain character, but we haven't quite reached that point where we can bring them into a quantifiable forecast."

That inability to predict short-term weather patterns haunted the Ohio valley during the thousand-year flood. Meteorologists with little idea what tomorrow would bring revised their crest forecasts daily or even hourly. They could not with any certainty tell people whether to stay or leave. Their constant hedging frustrated citizens who demanded that their weathermen tell them what the weather had in store for them. Millions suspected that their predictions amounted to little more than guessing. With good reason, they tuned out official announcements and relied on their own instincts. Tempting as it is to charge the messenger with incompetence, it is important to remember that weathermen did not have the satellites that allow their modern counterparts to see days into the future. Government forecasters labored under additional handicaps that dated back to the first days of their agency.[6]

There is no obvious explanation for Americans' peculiar fascination with the weather. Perhaps it lies in their close association with the frontier wilderness and feeling of connection with the natural world. Or maybe it grew from a conviction that they could control their environment if they mastered its rules. Possibly it reflects the new republic's grounding in the Enlightenment's emphasis on scientific processes and systematizing knowledge. For whatever reason, climate conditions enthralled the Founding Fathers. George Washington kept a detailed weather diary until the day he died. Fellow Virginian Thomas Jefferson ducked out of drafting sessions for the Declaration of Independence to purchase a thermometer and barometer that he used to register twice-daily readings for decades to come. Consummate tinkerer Benjamin Franklin collated data from a small army of observers to support his theories on storm behavior.[7]

The United States took its first official interest in the weather in 1870, when Congress directed military personnel to record climate conditions and to notify ships in the Great Lakes, Gulf of Mexico, and Atlantic Ocean of approaching storms. The government vested the War Department's Signal Corps with this mission because, as the bill's sponsor explained, "military discipline would probably secure the greatest promptness, regularity, and accuracy in the required observations." Members of the new weather bureau had no special training or particular interest in meteorology.[8]

Although the Signal Corps looked to shed these unwanted tasks at the earliest possible moment, its responsibilities grew as time passed. An expanding telegraph network enabled, or rather obligated, the corps to extend its observation services across the country. A central office in Washington received updates on temperature, humidity, wind direction, wind velocity, and cloud coverage three times a day from three hundred field stations. A quartet of analysts converted the data into twenty-four-hour forecasts that they transmitted to railroad companies and the Associated Press. Newspapers began printing elementary weather maps, albeit with little information about the mysterious areas west of the Rocky Mountains.[9]

In 1873 the Signal Corps initiated a primitive flood forecasting service, administered by a single employee, that used reports telegraphed from a handful of undermanned river stations to guess at future river levels. In reality the service offered little more than advance word that some kind of high water might be coming. Its inability to make solid crest predictions made it difficult to know whether to run from an upcoming rise. The War Department, with its limited understanding of river behavior, had to focus on a few large, sluggish waterways that acted in conventional ways. It had little insight into smaller, more volatile streams prone to flash flooding.[10]

After years of trying to unload the weather service, in 1890 the War Department finally convinced Congress to transfer the burden to the Department of Agriculture. Military men breathed a sigh of relief. No longer did the Signal Corps have to balance mundane data gathering with suppressing labor riots and fighting Indian wars.

The Weather Bureau modernized once it escaped its military roots. Marconi's new wireless enabled it to receive information from remote regions and deliver storm warnings to ships at sea. Its scientists employed kites and balloons to study upper-air conditions, methods long used in Europe for predicting weather on the ground. Americans lagged far behind the cutting edge of storm forecasting. Europeans better understood how high- and low-pressure fronts produced various climate conditions and were therefore able to predict storms; their New World counterparts could only follow existing ones.[11]

As of 1937 officials received reports from about a thousand precipitation stations, an impressive-sounding network nevertheless incapable of providing sufficient data on potential or actual floods. Bureau chief Willis Gregg called the river service "inadequate" and its flood-research capabilities "woeful." It needed more rainfall stations along tributaries and more facts on snowfall in mountainous headwaters regions. Communication between substations and district headquarters was spotty. Fiscal limitations prevented employees from recording information between ten at night and six in the morning. Recent budget cuts closed dozens of branches.[12]

Flood prediction had changed little since the Weather Bureau's formative years. Officials based their projections on rain in sight, meaning precipitation that had already fallen or was likely to fall within the next twenty-four hours. Calculations beyond the immediate term relied more on guesswork than on science. Ohio valley residents wanting precise information about crest heights found that following predictions was like climbing a staircase with inconsistent risers between treads. Each day brought prophecies of levels ranging from several inches to several feet above yesterday's prediction. This wild inconsistency left residents unsure whether to stay or leave and raised doubts that local forecasters had any idea what they were doing.

The uncertainty in Cincinnati, the largest city on the Ohio, demonstrated that rising waters flummoxed even the most experienced hands. Chief meteorologist W. C. Devereaux had spent twenty of his thirty years in the profession with the Weather Bureau in the Queen City. A fastidious man who kept his mustache in perfect trim and his graying hair precisely slicked, he was regarded by colleagues and community alike as a top-notch monitor of river conditions.

Even though Devereaux knew his section of the Ohio as well as anyone, his ability to predict its behavior extended only to the next day or two. He announced on January 17 that the river might run full. Devereaux anticipated a mild inundation when the river broke its fifty-two-foot flood stage the next day. He soon jumped his crest prediction to sixty feet, inches shy of the peak during last year's flood and eight feet higher than he had announced twenty-four hours earlier. Devereaux held to his revised forecast for the next few days. The *Cincinnati Enquirer* assured readers of his credibility. He had proved "almost uncannily correct" in similar moments, the paper observed. The weatherman raised his prediction again when the Ohio topped sixty feet on the twenty-first. At this point the usually confident observer threw up his hands: "It is impossible to say how high the river will go because we do not know how much more rain to expect," he sighed.[13]

Devereaux's dilemma exposed his organization's core weakness. After

half a century as an independent agency, the Weather Bureau still had almost no idea what the weather would be the next day. He revised his crest
forecast five more times over the next twenty-four hours as heavy rain
lashed the valley. On the twenty-third, with the Ohio above seventy-two
feet and riverfront areas deep underwater, he started speaking of the flood
in the past tense, as if the worst had passed. "I don't think there will be
much change in the river for a few days," he told local officials. An approaching cold snap should slow the flood and end the rain cycle.[14]

Ferocious storms broke over Cincinnati on the twenty-fourth, the day
known as "Black Sunday." Devereaux lifted his estimate from seventy-
three and a half feet to seventy-eight. It is remarkable that he offered a prediction at all, because he was operating blind. His teletype machine had
malfunctioned, and his office had only sporadic telephone and telegraph
service. Using the fragmentary data available, he then called for a seventy-
seven-foot crest and declared that "the damage has been done." Devereaux
reversed course the next day with a projection of eighty-one feet. The Ohio
topped on January 26 at 79.99 feet, twenty-eight feet above his forecast of
a week earlier.[15]

"There [are] not sufficient words in our English to condemn, by me,
the stupidity of the United States Weather Bureau," one critic complained.
Born of understandable anger, his comment nevertheless ignored the limitations hindering meteorologists. Although better forecasting could have
saved lives and property, upgrades such as enlarging the nation's rain gauge
network required the political determination to increase the bureau's funding. Other improvements demanded the institutional will to pursue new
weather-prediction techniques. To some extent, the flood marked a human
failure to anticipate rather than react to natural disasters. At the same
time, observers did the best they could in an era where weathermen closely
resembled fortune-tellers. "Without some Divine power for foreseeing the
future," one Evansville, Indiana, meteorologist remarked, he and his colleagues could have done no better during those January days.[16]

A BRIEF DRY SPELL over the Missouri-Arkansas border depressed the
St. Francis and other swollen rivers. Vigilance nevertheless remained the
watchword. Volunteers and WPA patrols had orders to shoot anyone tam-
pering with protective works. The respite ended when five inches of rain
fell on the day after FDR's inauguration. Rain turned to sleet as temperatures dipped below freezing. Although milder than the previous week's

Workers clad in improvised storm gear sandbagging a levee near Gates Landing, Tennessee. Photo courtesy of the Franklin D. Roosevelt Presidential Library.

storm, this second blizzard rendered streets impassable, draped trees and power lines in ice, and crippled electrical services.[17]

Overworked crews battled the rising waters. Lucky workers had hip boots and warm coats. Others wore threadbare jackets and wrapped socks around their feet. Sandbaggers whispered "more water than 1927" as makeshift barriers groaned. The faithless started abandoning the lines for high ground. Levees on Mississippi tributaries failed at dozens of points, inundating hundreds of thousands of acres of rich farmland and forcing tens of thousands out of rural communities. They ran from Arbyrd, Cardwell, and Senath, Missouri. They ran from Lester, Osceola, and Trumann, Arkansas. Adding to the panic was the possibility that the untested barriers along the Mississippi itself might prove inadequate. Army engineers assured the public that the walls would hold even as they shifted personnel and supplies to riverfront areas in case they did not.[18]

Cold weather compounded the suffering. Skins of ice too thin to walk on but too thick for boats to break formed over flooded acres. Ax-wielding saviors chopped paths, some of them miles long, to reach backwoods cabins. One pregnant woman waded through three miles of jagged ice before rescuers picked her up, her legs bloody from dozens of cuts. Many farmers sent their wives and children to safety but stayed behind with the livestock, agreeing to board relief barges only after the water reached their cows' bellies. Their stubbornness meant extra work for exhausted boatmen, who made multiple trips to the same location to check whether a holdout was ready to admit defeat.[19]

Sharecroppers and tenant farmers joined the small-town refugees huddled in boxcars and unheated public buildings. Cases of pneumonia and influenza multiplied, and contaminated drinking water elevated the odds of contracting cholera. Boats were in short supply. Roads were impassable, and shivering flooders wandered hillsides with no destination in mind. Venerable Tin Lizzies sputtered past overloaded mule-drawn wagons that passed people on foot carrying their meager possessions through the muck. A fierce wind blew snow into eyes and whipped waves across lakes of backwater. Artist Thomas Hart Benton, who was in the area searching for subjects to paint, found himself unable to portray the tragedy. "Description can give no sense of the dread realities of flood misery," he finally decided.[20]

These people lived a threadbare existence even in good times. Their diet of beans, cornbread, and fatty pork caused malnutrition and pellagra. Malaria stalked their hovels every summer, and few had access to professional medical care. Poor nutrition, harsh living conditions, and a shortage of doctors made infant mortality so common that the death of a child merited little attention. Most sufferers had no electoral outlet for their frustrations because Jim Crow laws and other discriminatory legislation stripped them of their voting rights.

Plantation owners and overseers dominated the area's politics, economy, and society, their primary goal being to raise as much cotton as possible at the least expense. Cotton, as much a way of life as a crop, was a relative newcomer to the region. When insatiable lumber companies deforested the countryside in the early twentieth century, they exposed alluvial soil perfect for cotton. Penniless workers descended from Crowley's Ridge to the west or crossed over from Mississippi hoping to find better lives as sharecroppers or wage laborers. The Depression crippled small-town textile mills, sending many recent migrants back to the land, where they exacerbated a labor surplus. Farm laborers toiled from dawn to dusk— or from "can to can't," as in "can see" to "can't see"—for a few hundred dollars a year. Landowners dictated their lives. One observer wrote that "the cropper is so completely subjugated and at the mercy of the planter that he is unequivocally the most exploited worker in America."[21]

The plantation system demanded a docile labor force. Supervisors either disregarded their charges' material needs or convinced themselves they had none. "All that a sharecropper needs is a cotton patch and a corn cob," one planter reasoned. Neither Missouri's nor Arkansas's government worried much about poor farmers, and New Dealers' attempts to improve conditions did more harm than good. Roosevelt's farm program aimed to reduce supply and boost prices by subsidizing planters who withdrew acreage from cultivation, but few owners respected the administration's insistence that they share those federal dollars with employees. Many planters spent the windfall on tractors that drove additional farmworkers from the land.[22]

Official neglect inspired the formation of an organization dedicated to uprooting the entrenched social hierarchy. Its zenith came at the very moment that rising waters threatened to wash away its strongholds in the bootheel and the delta. Socialist leader Norman Thomas deserves much of the credit for creating the Southern Tenant Farmers' Union (STFU). The renowned and reviled labor organizer's tours through the area acquainted him with the appalling inequities sharecroppers endured. Frightened laborers whispered stories of capricious evictions, physical intimidation, and vigilante justice. Thomas preached collective action as the best way to improve their status. His unionist message horrified planters accustomed to silencing croppers' political opinions. Marked Tree, Arkansas, for example, passed an ordinance in 1935 declaring it illegal to "make or deliver a public speech on any street, park or other public place" without permission from local authorities.[23]

Thomas's words resonated with a shy, skinny dry cleaner from Tyronza, Arkansas, named Harry Leland Mitchell. Natives considered Mitch, as his friends called him, an outsider because he grew up in Tennessee before moving west in the mid-1920s. His radical streak set him apart from the town's conservative ethos. Mitchell avidly supported Wisconsin senator "Fighting Bob" La Follette and socialist writer Upton Sinclair. He denounced segregation and white supremacy and shared his views with everyone he encountered. Henry Clay East, an opinionated gas station owner from a prominent local family, was one of the few who welcomed Mitch's observations. East's socialism stemmed from his conviction that unscrupulous capitalists had caused the Great Depression. He became such a fervent convert that he forced salesmen seeking his business to subscribe to the socialist newspaper *American Guardian*, then quizzed them on its contents before renewing purchase orders.

East and Mitchell drove to Memphis in 1932 to hear Norman Thomas speak. He so impressed them that they decided to start a Socialist Party chapter in Tyronza. After recruiting some fellow merchants and some skilled workers, plus a handful of tenant farmers, they invited Thomas to inspect their progress. Over lunch Thomas suggested that they instead create a sharecroppers' union committed to overthrowing planters' dominance. From this conversation sprang the Southern Tenant Farmers' Union, an organization destined to be a major player in the region during the flood.[24]

The biracial union of croppers, tenant farmers, and day laborers claimed a membership of 30,000 in 1937, with strongholds in Oklahoma, the Arkansas delta, and the Missouri bootheel. It came of age during a great era of unionization that arose from the economic desperation of the Depression and the benevolent policies of the Roosevelt administration, the first to assert workers' right to organize and bargain collectively. STFU recruiters appealed to economic self-interest through demands for more equitable work contracts, lower interest rates on store credit, and federal oversight of year-end settlements. Membership also reflected a growing desire for independence and self-respect. Union officers denounced tenancy as "destructive of the most sacred and fundamental of all values: human beings and the land which sustains them."[25]

Mitchell and his associates, including STFU president J. R. Butler, ran a shoestring operation that as of winter 1936 had just $319 in its coffers. Visitors to its headquarters in the disreputable fringes of Memphis negotiated a dark hallway as they approached a grimy door with "Offices of STFU" scrawled across it. Butler himself ushered guests into the small room beyond. Tubs on the floor caught the water that poured through the building's leaky roof whenever it rained. A bare bulb flickering from the ceiling lit the sparse furnishings: a table, two rickety chairs, and shelves piled with organizational literature. Crudely painted slogans decorated the walls. One artist featured a verse from the book of Isaiah: "What mean ye that ye crush my people and grind the faces of the poor?" Another chose the more modest yet more direct "Land for the landless." Butler ignored the squalor as he drowned visitors under a wave of agrarian rhetoric. His cosmopolitan air and learned recitations of Marxist dogma surprised guests taken in by his hillbilly appearance, unruly blond hair, and careworn face.[26]

Powerful local interests mobilized to crush the ragtag union. Harahan Bridge, which spanned the Mississippi at Memphis, became a frequent escape path for STFU organizers fleeing Arkansas. An angry mob beat, then imprisoned a black minister who founded a chapter. Organizers canceled one gathering after opponents mounted guns across the road from their meeting place. Planters either evicted troublesome tenants or battered them with ax handles and pistol butts. Authorities denounced the group to nosy reporters who dared traverse the region. "The sharecroppers are better off today than they have been in years," one attorney told the *Nashville Tennessean*, "except for some shiftless ones who have gone on relief to avoid working." Dire warnings of miscegenation and allegations of "Russian schemes" followed STFU members wherever they went. Union leaders parried these charges as best they could while raising as much hell as possible.[27]

January 1937 found members of the STFU gathered in Muskogee, Oklahoma, for the union's annual convention. An optimistic air pervaded the hall. A series of strikes over the past growing season had shaken the planter establishment, and union leaders promised to resume the offensive that spring. Mitchell predicted a bright future for tenants who recognized their common interests. King Cotton sat on "a toppling throne," he told delegates, and planters were defending "a dying social order." Attendees created a revival atmosphere as they punctuated speeches with "amens" and sung hymns between addresses. A "Ceremony of the Land" served as the convention's emotional climax. Representatives from seven states mixed grain from their native soil in a cup as readers cataloged the inequities of the tenant system. "Land to the landless," the crowd chanted throughout.[28]

Unionists left Muskogee primed to battle planter autocracy. First, however, eastbound travelers had to battle fierce rainstorms. Delegates plodding along muddy roads heard of terrible hardships ahead. We are "absolutely up against it," one member wrote Mitchell. Rumors spread that relief organizations were rejecting tenants' requests for assistance. "Stay on the job," Mitchell urged one correspondent. "Report all discriminations. Have every Union man in need to apply to all agencies for help." The destitute group could not afford to care for flooded-out members and doubted that outsiders would help. One farmer insisted that because the

"Big Boys" dominated local Red Cross chapters, "us unions wont get anny-thing at all."[29]

Antagonistic forces were colliding. Planters wanted to exploit cheap labor in the name of profits, while the STFU promised a brighter future for families trapped in subhuman conditions. The flood inserted itself into this power struggle, carrying with it the power to topple the unbalanced social pyramid. Landowners understood the dangers carried in the rising waters. Their workers had become "a people in exodus," a ill-dressed army retreating before an implacable foe. Sharecropping might become obsolete should the Harahan Bridge to Memphis became a one-way avenue out of tenancy. They feared that "if we get away we won't go back," one cropper explained. Unionists fielded reports of planters turning back field hands at gunpoint and of loading their mules onto trucks but refusing to help their tenants evacuate. "Let the union move you," one planter sneered.[30]

Croppers in the Missouri bootheel began their own exodus when the Corps of Engineers finalized plans to employ for the first time the 1928 Jadwin Plan's most controversial element, the Bird's Point floodway. Somewhere around 3,500 tenant farmers occupied shanties within the 131,000-acre tract. No one had an exact head count. Many of these rootless, transitory people had arrived the previous fall to harvest cotton, then stayed because they had nowhere else to go during the fallow season. Now they needed to get out fast or be washed away when engineers detonated the levee restraining the Mississippi.

Army engineers advised floodway residents to seek safer ground when they concluded that the Ohio would hit fifty-seven feet at Cairo. Although the town was supposed to be secure up to sixty feet, the Corps chose to siphon surplus water through Bird's Point to drop the Mississippi and Ohio to more manageable levels. Highway patrolmen sped down country roads with sirens blaring, shouting "Get out of this spillway and get out quick" at everyone they saw. Messengers trekked to isolated farmhouses. Army planes dropped leaflets from the sky. A sense of haste bordering on panic descended on the floodway when stiff winds started blowing water over the frozen crown of the levee. Each encroaching wave increased the likelihood of a major crevasse rather than a controlled break. Lines of miserable people trudged through temperatures in the teens and a hard sleet storm to find refuge in one of the camps erected outside the flood-works. Mules, wagons, and rickety trucks groaned under whatever possessions flooders could salvage. A fleet of fifty cars and trucks swept the area for holdouts. Missouri Pacific railmen shoved livestock aboard a special train bound for Charleston, Missouri. Workers allowed the train to clear an opening in the setback levee before swarming in to sandbag the last gap in the now-unbroken line of earthworks. Bird's Point was a bathtub waiting to be filled.[31]

MANY RETREATING CROPPERS FOUND warmth, food, and shelter in facilities operated by the American Red Cross, an institution that made its reputation by caring for flood victims. Its first major relief effort occurred when an 1889 dam break near Johnstown, Pennsylvania, killed 2,200 people. The agency also shone during the 1913 Ohio River flood, a relief effort that encompassed a huge area and cost far more than the Johnstown tragedy. Although at the time the Red Cross boasted over 14,000 members in sixty chapters, its national staff operated from a single room in Washington, DC, in the Second Empire–style State, War, and Navy Building (now known as the Old Executive Office Building). Its volunteers' exceptional performance solidified the group's status as America's premier relief organization. Its renown grew with its handling of the 1927 Mississippi flood, a competent effort marred by pervasive racial discrimination. Volunteers drawn from local communities herded black refugees into substandard tents and fed them worse food than whites received.[32]

The 1937 crisis proved far more challenging than 1913, 1927, or any other natural disaster. Weather Bureau meteorologists conveyed word of impending trouble several days before most communities experienced severe conditions. The Red Cross's Washington-based Disaster Service advised hundreds of branches to prepare to evacuate and provide for flood sufferers. Emergency kitchens, hospitals, and refugee camps sprang up along the Ohio and as far down the Mississippi as Memphis. Nurses packed their bags for duty. Record keepers at headquarters logged the high water in their files as disaster number 2,128. It was destined to become the largest, most expensive peacetime crisis the agency had ever handled.[33]

The national headquarters—a twenty-year-old neoclassical building that marked a dramatic upgrade over the agency's previous home—buzzed. Disaster Service staffers hired temporary help and commandeered the facility's spacious assembly hall. A constant din of pounding hammers, ringing phones, clacking typewriters, and hurried conversations suffused the room as craftsmen rushed to convert the auditorium into a modern office. Desks covered the lavish parquet floor. Electrical and telephone wires snaked up the walls, obscuring the rich velvet drapes and glorious stained-glass windows. Thinner lines dangling from the ceiling delivered power and phone service to individual work stations.[34]

It seemed as if every electrical impulse coursing down those lines carried a plea for nurses. Signs of an impending epidemic, untreated wounds, elderly evacuees with pneumonia or hypothermia, unsafe drinking water—everyone needed nurses. Malinde Havey, director of public health nursing, had the immense job of providing them. Havey was one of the wonders of the flood, an anonymous bureaucrat who managed a vast life-saving empire. She ran her operation with minimal drama and optimal efficiency. Her files bulged with documentation on 15,000 professionals ready to serve at a moment's notice. She dispatched these caregivers with the skill of a general, sending her troops into the areas most needing reinforcement and relentlessly pressing the offensive against the enemy. Competence among her subordinates was a given, as was obedience. They should follow her orders without question and otherwise run their bureaus with nominal supervision, for they had a clearer view of affairs on the battlefield. Regional offices drafted plans specific to their areas of responsibility, conferred with local officials, and arranged for accommodations and supplies. Havey coordinated the overall effort and made the final call on contentious issues and broader policy questions.[35]

The 2,500 Red Cross nurses who served during the crisis were for the most part able, efficient, and image conscious. They usually wore wool sweaters, hats, and rubber boots appropriate to the conditions but donned authoritative dress whites whenever photographers dropped in. Havey insisted that nurses keep quiet around reporters. They should instead feed "interesting reports" to supervisors, who sifted their stories for emotional tales of heroism worth forwarding to the Red Cross's Public Information Service, which offered the cream to the press.[36]

By January 23, Red Cross facilities sheltered about 300,000 people, a figure sure to swell in coming days. Chapters from Pennsylvania to Arkansas scrambled for tents, cots, and food. They also attempted with varying success to delineate lines of authority with local officials. Some areas ran smoothly, while others sank into chaos. Officials in Washington found the Portsmouth, Ohio, chapter's executive secretary "absolutely unqualified" and thought its chairman a status-hungry hack. Inexperienced personnel in Cincinnati opened just seven kitchens for tens of thousands of refugees. They had to set up sixty more canteens to catch up with demand. Chapters in Paducah and Louisville reported massive confusion and duplication of effort. No one had expected the crisis to become so severe.[37]

Volunteers entering Missouri and Arkansas confronted additional problems. Those assigned to counties without hospitals had to build a medical infrastructure from scratch. Newcomers were shocked at widespread illiteracy and abysmal living standards. Dispatches to headquarters lamented that Red Cross tent camps equaled or exceeded the comforts families had before the flood. Sympathy sometimes bled into condescension; one observer deemed the slow evacuation of the delta "consistent with the regular thinking and moving of the Arkansas sharecropper."[38]

This vast operation demanded an unprecedented fund-raising campaign. On January 23, chairman Cary T. Grayson announced a $2 million target. FDR, fulfilling his ceremonial role as the organization's president, seconded his request, adding that he expected "this great national relief agency to act as our representative in this emergency." Grayson upped his call to $5 million two days later, then to $10 million the day after that. Americans eventually donated over $25 million for flood relief and rehabilitation, equaling the Red Cross's combined take during its two largest earlier disasters.[39]

Mass media outlets, a far more pervasive force in 1937 than during the previous decade's Mississippi flood, boosted this mammoth endeavor. Editorial writers around the country begged readers to give. Radio stations paired vivid descriptions of flood-torn communities with appeals for aid. Filmmaker Pare Lorentz, still thrilled with the acclaim for his documentary about soil erosion, *The Plow That Broke the Plains* (1936), rushed to the flood zone to shoot footage for an upcoming release about human mistreatment of the Mississippi basin. Cameramen from commercial newsreel studios braved frigid and often dangerous conditions to capture graphic images of devastation, then rushed the celluloid to dry ground for distribution to the country's 17,000 movie screens. Together their labors made the flood a national event, a shared experience relevant to all Americans.[40]

Grayson's office was a two-hundred-yard stroll across the Ellipse from the White House, a physical proximity that symbolized the government's close ties with the relief agency. Grayson knew the Roosevelt administration would help the Red Cross in any way possible once the president got past the distraction of the inaugural festivities.

The Coast Guard was among the first federal bureaus to come to the Red Cross's assistance. Officials dispatched half a dozen surfboats to Evansville, Indiana, and prepared scores of additional vessels stationed on the Great Lakes and the eastern seaboard for overland transport. The laborious task of hoisting boats onto railroad cars delayed their arrival by a few days. Officers could do little more, since the Coast Guard had just one base on the affected waterways, at Louisville. Crews in that city battled treacherous waters to ferry thousands to safety. This was hazardous duty; one boat was knocked out of action when a floating house smashed into it.[41]

Federal involvement in rescue and refugee care mushroomed over the following days. WPA chief and trusted presidential adviser Harry Hopkins assumed the brunt of the responsibility. A few thousand WPA workers were already on the scene before the Red Cross summoned the Coast Guard. Tens of thousands more arrived over the next few weeks. Operating under a presidential directive empowering federal employees to perform "necessary emergency work when danger to life or grave risk to property is engendered by flood or thaw conditions," WPA crews strengthened levees, evacuated refugees, hauled emergency supplies, delivered potable water, protected utility lines, and repaired washed-out roads, essential tasks that otherwise might not have been done.[42]

Hopkins and WPA chief engineer Colonel Francis Harrington disregarded regulations and budgetary restrictions on the grounds that the magnitude of the disaster trumped the need for prudence. "I want that job done right," Hopkins informed an Indiana WPA official. "You will probably have to break all of our rules down there, but it is all right." Hopkins told the president that money would not influence his decision making. He promised supplementary budget requests that "should receive prompt action, in order that operations may not be impeded." FDR never blinked when his right-hand man authorized local officials to hire anyone they needed regardless of whether they were jobless, a precondition for WPA employment in normal times. "You don't have to stop and scrutinize each one to see if they are [on] relief," Hopkins told subordinates. WPA recruiters in some places simply hired people off the street.[43]

Hopkins's WPA men toiled alongside Civilian Conservation Corps (CCC) enlistees. Created during the hectic first hundred days of Roosevelt's presidency, FDR's "tree army" sent unemployed young urbanites to work in hundreds of rural camps. Now the president ordered the CCC to set aside its irrigation, reforestation, and park improvement duties in the name of flood relief. Over 22,000 enrollees fanned out across the flood zone, with responsibilities paralleling the WPA's. CCC camps in the Ohio valley went

WPA workers assisting in the evacuation of Newport, Kentucky. University of Kentucky Goodman-Paxton Photographic Collection.

on a state of alert, readying their personnel to leap into emergency situations. Red Cross workers repurposed dozens of camps as refugee shelters. CCC brigades outside the valley loaded supplies and transported them to places in need.[44]

When Roosevelt created the WPA and CCC, he never imagined a disaster on a par with the 1937 flood, but it was fortunate that they existed at that moment. Without them the death toll would have been higher, the suffering greater, and the damage more extensive. Countless individuals would have lost everything if not for the federal workers who carted their goods to safety. In addition, Depression-racked communities would have faced insurmountable financial difficulties once postflood reconstruction began. State and local governments had no money for operating refugee camps, cleaning up private and public property, or rebuilding. No comparable labor force existed when the Mississippi went wild in 1927—a few communities assembled volunteer rescue units, but they rarely matched the effectiveness of the later New Deal brigades. For the most part, individuals trapped in that flood had to save themselves and whatever posses-sions they could carry.

FDR engaged the deteriorating situation within a few days of his second inauguration. His friend Cary Grayson walked regular updates to press secretary Stephen Early, who passed them on to the president. Roosevelt sought to aid the Red Cross without hindering or duplicating its efforts. He endorsed Grayson's appeals for donations and left Hopkins in charge of the details of crisis management. Hopkins wrested supplies from public sources, set up meetings with Corps of Engineers officers, and calmed Ohio valley leaders in Washington for the inauguration while Roosevelt kibitzed with Paramount Pictures head Adolph Zukor and newsreel com-pany executives. To be fair, the president could do little at this point be-yond ginning up public awareness, instructing cabinet secretaries to co-operate with the Red Cross, and clearing bureaucratic obstructions to federal rescue and relief efforts.[45]

"No sign of anxiety is evidenced anywhere at the possibility of a major flood," the *Paducah Sun-Democrat* declared in what turned out to be its last edition printed in Paducah for several weeks. Hopkins and his asso-ciates struck a more cautious tone. Colonel Eugene Reybold, chief of the Corps of Engineers' Memphis District, worried that the Mississippi might go berserk once the Ohio overflow emptied into it. Engineers in New Or-leans feared that "a first-class flood" was coming. Cairo's fate also hung in the balance. "I don't think the water will go over Cairo; do you?" Hopkins asked longtime friend and WPA administrator Howard Hunter.

"I think it will go over Cairo," Hunter asserted.
"They are going to dynamite this dam so it won't," Hopkins responded.
"I still think it might go over."

Prospects looked even worse upstream.

"What about Evansville?" Hopkins inquired.

Hunter paused for a moment. "That's pretty damn bad," he replied.[46]

Officials already anticipated a postemergency cry for improved flood protection. WPA's Indiana head Wayne Coy reminded Colonel Harrington that whenever the Corps built new levees, "we speed the waters up a little.

Make it flow faster and it does more damage." Coy warned that flooding would worsen unless Washington showed unusual wisdom. "The public is a little alarmed now," he told the engineer, and "thirty days later they will be building up more [levees]."[47]

THOMAS JEFFERSON IMAGINED GREAT things for Jeffersonville, Indiana, another town that was "pretty damn bad" in 1937. Standing opposite the hamlet of Louisville and commanding a sharp S curve on the Ohio, it seemed a natural place for a successful settlement. Jefferson laid out the city as a grid of streets that framed alternating squares of vacant and developed blocks, a monument to his love for order. He believed the plentiful green spaces preserved man's connection with nature and mitigated the lowland territory's worst attribute, "the miasmata which produces yellow fever."[48]

The Founding Father never realized his utopian vision, never even saw the village he designed in his drawing room. This was probably a good thing, since the actual town bore scant resemblance to his tidy sketch. Nor did it, as Jefferson had hoped, challenge Louisville's economic dominance over that stretch of river. Jeffersonville briefly hosted Indiana's territorial government because an ailing governor wanted to live near his Louisville-based physician. Its great moments were otherwise few and far between. Jeffersonville survived because its location at the junction of three railroad lines made it a pivotal transshipment point for goods traveling throughout the region. Its exceptional river and rail access led the Union government to place a military hospital there during the Civil War. This relationship solidified in 1874 when the army opened a giant Quartermaster Depot. The depot's spacious stone-and-brick quadrangle encompassed dozens of storage buildings and workshops. Sitting on an almost imperceptible rise on the town's northern edge, the depot was one of Jeffersonville's largest employers and its most important reason for existing.[49]

Jeffersonville's riverside location justified its creation but became less important once railroads supplanted steamboats. It also left the town vulnerable to overflows on the Ohio. Devastating floods in 1883 and 1884 prompted agitation for the federal government to build a levee. Washington agreed on the grounds that a wall would protect federal property stored in the depot. After the structure repelled the 1907 flood, an enthusiastic local historian declared that "Jeffersonville today is the safest and driest river town from Pittsburgh to Cairo."[50]

Jeffersonville's low land prices and its reputation as a flood-proof community attracted settlers and new businesses. About 15,000 people lived there in 1937. Well-heeled residents lived in large, century-old brick homes. The less fortunate occupied riverfront shacks. Poor vastly outnumbered rich, since average family income sat well below $1,000 a year. Major industries had closed or were running on skeleton crews. Jeffersonville's two lingering claims to fame, and its leading enterprises, were love and gambling. Amorous Kentuckians eager to capitalize on the community's indifference to waiting periods and residency requirements patronized marriage parlors along Court Avenue, a dense commercial tangle a few blocks from the Ohio and, not coincidentally, near the bridge to Louisville. After tying the knot, couples spun the roulette wheel at the Antz Café or one of the other seedy casinos lining the road back to the bridge.[51]

Few residents expressed much interest in the Ohio's climb until steady rains pushed the river into basements on inauguration day. Gas-powered pumps churned in a futile effort to lift water over the impregnable levee. Three shifts of WPA crews hoisted sandbags to the top of the wall. Local Red Cross workers organized an emergency kitchen and refugee centers. Their inexperience was obvious. Personnel shortages and confusion over responsibilities hampered every move. Merchants hurried their stocks upstairs after Louisville radio station WHAS broadcast warnings of worse to come. Block by block, water crept farther into town.[52]

Imperiled cities throughout the valley begged the Quartermaster Depot for emergency supplies. Army brass suspected that relief groups exaggerated the need for supplies. "It has been frequently found that conditions are not as bad as local authorities reported," one officer remarked. Doubtful military personnel nevertheless joined the WPA enrollees in loading railroad cars bound for destinations across the valley. Heavy sleet battered them as they sent tons of mess kits, kitchen utensils, heaters, stoves, pillows, garbage cans, towels, soap, and tables out of town.[53]

The War Department's inability to grasp the magnitude of the crisis left the depot's commanding officer, Colonel M. G. Holliday, without clear orders. Operating on his own authority, Holliday shipped goods as best he could with an ever-shrinking workforce. Civilian staffers who lived in Louisville either moved with their families to safety or found themselves unable to reach the depot. Those who did show up pitched tents, set up cots, and erected camp stoves for the anticipated rush of flooders. Having no option of fleeing, military personnel endured round-the-clock duty that confined them to the depot. Whenever he could spare a few men, Holliday dispatched rowboats to rescue marooned civilians.[54]

Army chief of staff General Malin Craig finally clarified Holliday's mission when he granted the colonel authority to lend military property to the Red Cross. In contrast to Harry Hopkins's open-ended commitment, the army demanded precise record keeping during a chaotic time. "Issue only a minimum of supplies necessary" was the order of the day, and be sure to get a receipt to ensure future repayment. Washington insisted that Holliday send no food without specific directions from the War Department. Feeding refugees was the Red Cross's job, not the army's.[55]

Floodwaters covered the roads out of town on January 22. Railroad tracks were under impassable depths a few days later as 95 percent of Jeffersonville sank beneath the waves. Silence fell over the city's streets, interrupted only by an occasional group of canoers. Ten feet of water sloshed around the iconic Colgate-Palmolive-Peet plant, an imposing pile of arches, turrets, and columns that in a former life had served as a state prison. Doctors evacuated the local hospital. Citizens Trust Bank, strategically located between the casinos and the marriage parlors, closed its doors. Bank executives later discovered that the company they hired to seal the vault forgot to close an air vent, allowing water to soak the currency and documents inside.[56]

Holliday encouraged his personnel to settle their families in temporary quarters in the administration building, but his superiors gave him no clear authority to accept flooders. It took days of haggling before the War Department granted permission to take them in, issue cots and blankets, and allow the Red Cross to feed them. Over 3,000 refugees soon overwhelmed the slipshod tent city. Late arrivals resorted to squatting in buildings around the campus.[57]

Depot personnel herded their guests onto the slight ridge underlying the facility's eastern edge because the west side was already a swampy mess. The few extra feet of altitude proved inadequate. Water reached the graceful arch fronting the main gate within hours of the exiles' arrival. It breached the administration building and the textile, leather, woodworking, and motor repair shops soon afterward. Electricity failed when the Ohio outpaced sandbaggers shoring up the power plant. Neat rows of army tents sank deeper and deeper until, reminiscent of some bizarre Egyptian tableau, only their pyramidal peaks broke the surface. Water jostled desks and office chairs, upset neat stacks of storage crates, and sent lumber drifting.[58]

Holliday dismissed his WPA workers and browbeat the civilian doctors administering typhoid shots to work faster. With the town nearly empty and the Ohio standing ten feet higher than its 1913 record, there was little else he could do. Jeffersonville's mighty levee was intact but useless, its top invisible in the depths below the river's surface. The twenty-six-foot cruiser *Peggy K* patrolled the streets looking for survivors or looters. Holliday's men lifted the sick into ambulances that sped cross-country to waiting trains bound for Red Cross camps. They loaded up the last civilians just as the flood lapped the flagpole in the center of the quadrangle.[59]

Soldiers settled into the administration building's second floor to wait out the storm. Briefly a source of comfort, the Quartermaster Depot was now just another set of roofs poking above the water. A single precarious Western Union telegraph line linked it to the outside world. Jeffersonville's silence prompted wild rumors. "People are dying there like flies," one unnerved state legislator claimed.[60]

Fear was spreading. Refugee camps in Memphis strained to accommodate tens of thousands of flooders. Backwater contaminated wells and invited disease. Certain the worst was yet to come, Louisville mayor Neville Miller advised constituents to "think about moving." Meteorologist J. L. Kendall concurred that "the prospect for Louisville can certainly be termed alarming." Similar sentiments prevailed 250 miles downstream. "Paducah is doomed," one Tennessee Valley Authority officer told state health director A. T. McCormack. Acting Kentucky governor Keen Johnson recalled Governor Albert "Happy" Chandler from a vacation in Virginia. "This is the most frightful disaster in history," Johnson cabled Senator Alben Barkley.[61]

Water had also swamped Portsmouth, Ohio, an industrial town of 45,000 that locals touted as the "dry city." After suffering through the 1913 flood, private donors had contributed funds for a seventeen-foot concrete wall that kept out the river for nearly twenty-five years but proved helpless against the current deluge. With the Ohio creeping toward its crown, city manager Frank Sheehan made the awful decision to sacrifice his own home. Fearing that a sudden crevasse would send a massive wave smashing into town, Sheehan chose to open the sewers and ease in the flood. "The people knew better than to argue with the river," a journalist later explained.[62]

Jeffersonville, Indiana, near the crest. The inundated Quartermaster Depot appears at top center. University of Kentucky Goodman-Paxton Photographic Collection.

Boy Scouts and American Legionnaires alerted inhabitants. Factory whistles screamed a warning that the sewers would open in six hours. Overloaded trucks jammed the roads. Many Portsmouthians ran to Hill Top, a wealthy neighborhood occupying high ground four miles away. Early on the morning of January 22, crews spun the wheels that invited torrents of water into the city. Portsmouth's business district went under first, followed by the working-class residential neighborhoods clustered along the riverfront. The town filled until it became one with the river, its vaunted floodwall no more than an underwater impediment to navigation. The Ohio had conquered the third-largest city in its path.[63]

Optimism prevailed in many places even as the Ohio topped flood level along its entire 981-mile run. River rats ignored the dead animals and bits of houses floating past as they insisted that 1913 and 1884 had this one beat. Mayor Miller predicted the return of normal conditions within a week or so. "Louisville can come through this with less trouble and damage than many believe," he declared. Cairo's civic leaders exhibited similar confidence. "Cairo hasn't had, doesn't have and will not have any flood water in its streets," the editors of the *Evening Citizen and Bulletin* boasted. Cincinnati meteorologist W. C. Devereaux predicted that "the end is in sight. . . . The weather is changing for the better." His projection appeared in newspapers on January 23, twenty-four hours before the day Ohio valley inhabitants came to remember as "Black Sunday."[64]

BLACK SUNDAY

~~~~~~~~

"I HAVE BEEN AROUND THE river a long time and never saw anything like this," one Louisville wharf rat said as he stared at the Ohio. "This old river has just gone wild." The second-largest city in the flood zone stood on the verge of an unprecedented crisis. Cold winds hurled angry waves against buildings. Snow blanketed highland areas. Panicked residents jammed the few usable roads, clogged switchboards with frivolous telephone calls, and gouged customers with inflated prices. Supplies of drinking water ran low owing to inundated pumping stations and widespread hoarding. "Unless chiseling stops immediately," the *Courier-Journal* warned with unintentional irony, "there may be no water at all before the emergency is passed." Workers at Louisville Gas and Electric Company's Waterside Plant caulked walls and windows, sandbagged doorways, and manned pumps in a last-ditch bid to prevent the Ohio from entering.[1]

Reverend W. O. Ulrey looked to a higher authority for relief. The spirit moved him to splash through hard rain and piles of slush to the building housing Louisville's two major newspapers, the *Times* and the *Courier-Journal*, and its most powerful radio station, WHAS. Ulrey climbed the narrow iron stairs and strode into the station's office. He found his friend, WHAS general manager Joseph Eaton, scanning dispatches by candlelight. "Joe," the preacher said, "I want to lead the Christian people in prayer. I want them to join me in asking God to stop this rain, and I believe he will answer prayer." Eaton saw little downside in Ulrey's request. They stepped over exhausted staffers wrapped in blankets on the floor as they walked to the larger of the station's two studios. A technician handed the minister some headphones. Ulrey intoned a fervent plea for dry weather into the microphone. Not long after he finished, the clouds parted and warm sunshine bathed the besieged community.[2]

The clouds closed a few hours later as sheets of rain again pelted the streets. This latest squall was part of a weeklong storm system that carpeted Kentucky and Tennessee with the heaviest precipitation of the four-week weather cycle. It dumped fourteen inches of rain on some places before climaxing on the day Reverend Ulrey spoke: January 24, or "Black Sunday." Frozen, saturated ground sped this new precipitation into rivers. Engorged lower tributaries such as the Cumberland, the Tennessee, and the Green submerged wide swaths of land before colliding with the wet wall raging down the Ohio. A colossal hydraulic battle played out as water crashed into water. Repelled by the higher, superior stream before them, tributaries spilled onto surrounding lowlands until the liquid roadblock dropped enough to allow them to resume their path to the sea.

Black Sunday changed a crisis into a disaster. It also marked the moment when President Roosevelt assumed more direct control over the situation. FDR began his Sunday with services at St. John's Cathedral. Afterward he ordered the heads of federal agencies involved in flood work to convene at Red Cross headquarters for the first of a series of daily meetings in Chairman Cary Grayson's office. Roosevelt wanted the principals to clarify lines of authority and draw up a program for averting epidemics. At his urging, the task force dispatched U.S. Public Health Service officers to the flood zone and stockpiled reserves of chlorine and biologics. FDR ordered the Federal Surplus Commodities Corporation to ship food and clothing from its warehouses to distribution points across the valley. Millions of pounds of eggs, evaporated milk, and canned beef rolled toward desperate refugees. Rural communities received mountains of prunes and grapefruit—items unfamiliar to most flooders, who tossed them in the street or used the grapefruit in improvised ball games. Government-owned trousers, jackets, caps, and mattress ticking supplemented distributions from private relief organizations.[3]

The next several days were a blur. Harry Hopkins ran laps between the White House and the Red Cross building, gathered information from local WPA officials, and fielded calls from innumerable elected officials seeking federal assistance. He ducked into FDR's office whenever possible to update the president on weather and river conditions. Press secretary Stephen Early stayed late into the night to relay messages from Hopkins and Grayson and satisfy reporters' demands for the latest news. He presented the flood campaign in a favorable light both for political reasons and to maximize relief contributions. Americans were more likely to donate if they believed the situation was both urgent and in competent hands.

White House switchboard and mailroom operators maintained a furious pace as correspondents bombarded the president with unwanted advice. "Suggest that you appoint Herbert Hoover administrator flood relief," wrote one man who remembered the former president's performance during the 1927 disaster. "What those people [flood sufferers] need is whisky," opined another letter writer. "Schenley's Distillers has it for them." A representative from the Women's International League for Peace and Freedom counseled Roosevelt to divert "all the military budget under your control" to flood relief.[4]

Ohio and Mississippi valley congressmen besieged the White House for up-to-the-minute information. FDR sent a delegation to quiet their concerns. It met with fifty legislators under the titular leadership of Kentucky senator Alben Barkley in the Senate's luxurious Military Affairs Committee room on the second floor of the Capitol. Hopkins rattled off an efficient status report before dashing to another conference. Army chief of staff General Malin Craig blasted Governor Happy Chandler's refusal to mobilize the Kentucky National Guard and lauded the regular army's work in the valley. Red Cross manager Richard Allen grumbled that Craig gave his forces too much credit at the Red Cross's expense.

The gathering turned rowdy as frustrated lawmakers quizzed the commission and became downright ugly once chief engineer Edward Markham began his assessment. A square-jawed, no-nonsense soldier, the general insisted that the Corps of Engineers had the situation under control. Untested levees along the Mississippi River would hold. Pennsylvania senator Joseph Guffey interrupted the presentation with a pointed question about reservoirs. This was no random query, but rather a shot at the Corps's historic antipathy to headwaters dams. Markham's dark, heavy brow furrowed as he parried Guffey's thrusts. Reservoirs would not have helped in this case, he argued, because the rain fell so far downstream. Guffey countered by citing Markham's recent testimony before the Senate that dams along tributaries in Pennsylvania might suppress flood heights. They fenced for several minutes before the senator disengaged.[5]

People wanted scapegoats and were already thinking about the future. Hopkins fretted about the WPA's ability to manage the enormous cleanup job lurking ahead. He acted as if the New Deal itself were on trial and believed that a sterling performance might guarantee his agency's survival beyond the Depression. Interior Secretary Harold Ickes hoped to use the heightened awareness of natural disasters to realize his longtime dream of creating a Department of Conservation. Advocates of levees, reservoirs, and reforestation prepared to descend on Washington for the inevitable postflood flurry of legislation.[6]

Roosevelt himself cocked an eye toward the future. Although focused on immediate needs, he saw the flood as an event that might resurrect his faltering comprehensive rivers program. FDR tried out the idea during an off-the-record press briefing when he answered a generic question about flood control by noting that he "would rather put it on a broader basis" than rely on a piecemeal approach. Experts brandished their own "particular pet theory" whenever a disaster occurred, he explained. They advocated additional dams or levees or championed erosion control and other land-based measures. "I have come to the conclusion that we have to pursue all of these things simultaneously," he observed. "They all tie in in a general picture."[7]

As he had during the 1927 flood, Roosevelt immediately retreated from this advanced position by stating that this was not the time to design an enormous new federal program. More immediate issues demanded his attention. Black Sunday rains pushed flood heights above record levels. Flood fighters worried about what all that water roaring toward Cairo would do to the swollen Mississippi. Colonel Eugene Reybold, the Corps's top man in Memphis, warned that "the greatest flood threat in the history of the Mississippi Valley now exists." Unlike his superior, Markham, he was not sure the levees would hold. About 100,000 people, including thousands of convicts from prison farms, shored up barriers along the Father of Waters. One joker working near Helena, Arkansas, made a sign that read "Wipe your feet before leaving the levee—we need the dirt."[8]

General Craig told a closed-door meeting at Red Cross headquarters that emergency crews could probably hold back the water already in the Mississippi. Additional rain, however, might require officials to manage another 1927 flood on top of the current catastrophe. Grayson, anxious to avoid the suffering endured ten years earlier, directed subordinates to compose a plan to evacuate the Mississippi valley. Within a few hours his staff cranked out a rough outline of relocation points and transportation options. Red Cross workers could provide food, clothes, and medical care but could not force people to vacate their homes. Grayson needed FDR's approval for that. The chairman rushed his proposal to the White House, where Roosevelt initialed a confidential order validating the Red Cross's blueprint.[9]

FDR's signature empowered the army to declare martial law throughout the lower Mississippi valley in the event of a major levee break. Organizations performing flood work would do so under military rule. Roosevelt charged General Craig with fleshing out the details. Craig gave area commanders forty-eight hours to prepare for an evacuation. Overburdened generals rushed to fuse the army, the National Guard, the Civilian Conservation Corps, and the Red Cross into a unit. Subordinates identified towns and CCC camps that were immune to high water, able to accommodate an influx of flooders, and close to flood-proof highways and railroads.[10]

Organizers hoped to prepare state and local officials to participate in a major military campaign without alarming an edgy populace. With so many parties involved, it was inevitable that the secret plan would leak out. Inaccurate wire reports suggested imminent rather than potential action. "Army to evacuate Mississippi Valley—Cairo to New Orleans," screamed one dispatch. Tickers clacked out a confirmation four minutes later: "Anticipating a much more serious flood along the lower Mississippi than is now raging along the Ohio River."[11]

Fear spread throughout the South. Newspapers reported that "territory for 50 miles on either side of the Mississippi from Cairo to New Orleans will be evacuated." An operation of this magnitude would add 500,000 refugees to the million already under Red Cross care. New Orleans residents stampeded newspaper offices and city hall for information. Political and business interests blasted the "scare story" as a groundless rumor that endangered the Crescent City's reputation. Concerns lingered despite the Corps of Engineers' assurance that "there is absolutely no danger for the city of New Orleans." Southern Illinois's *Golconda Herald-Enterprise*, flooded out of its offices and distributing a four-page typewritten edition with a hand-drawn masthead, twisted the rumors in a different direction when it reported that "every city and town on the Ohio and its tributaries has been evacuated." Word of an impending exodus even spread overseas. The *London News Chronicle* claimed the Red Cross had issued a warning to "evacuate—or die like rats."[12]

Stretched to the limit on the Ohio, the Corps of Engineers handed off its Mississippi River rescue duties to the Red Cross. Agency workers coordinated their expansive new undertaking from an improvised head-quarters on the third floor of an old Memphis newspaper building. From there they assembled an eclectic fleet of military and private vessels to scour coastlines for endangered residents. A detailed map attached to one wall bristled with pins representing boats, dredges, active distress calls, and evacuated areas. Electricians installed a bank of telephones and radio broadcasting equipment. CCC enrollees lugged stocks of Red Cross sup-plies and military surplus goods to staging areas for distribution should the levees break.[13]

As of Black Sunday, FDR's administration was using all the tools at its disposal to prevent a major humanitarian crisis from becoming some-thing even worse. Its smooth relationship with the Red Cross permitted an efficient public-private response to an unprecedented natural disaster. Ironically, the Depression benefited flooders, since it provided the federal government with a ready army of CCC and WPA workers. Human misery would have soared had rescue been in the hands of ad hoc local groups. Washington made a few missteps, including its poor handling of the pub-lic relations side of the Mississippi valley evacuation plan. Otherwise, it excelled under dire conditions.

BLACK SUNDAY PROVED THE tipping point along the Ohio, the day when a major flood turned into a nightmare. Problems varied from city to city, with each scenario demanding flexible leadership and effective coordination between volunteers, private agencies, and the federal gov-ernment.

Hard as it is to believe, one major difficulty was apathy. Cincinnatians, proud residents of the Ohio valley's most populous city, scoffed at threats of high water. Much of the Queen City's residential district sat more than one hundred feet above the river. Its twelve miles of vulnerable riverfront, once home to an array of upscale homes, had become the kind of district respectable folk dismissed without a second thought. A motley array of railroad offices, wholesale grocers, transport companies, breweries, meat-packers, pawnshops, and saloons had taken over when the elite relocated uphill in the early twentieth century. Old buildings lined the streets, their narrow frontages blending into nearly unbroken walls of brick.

Social status correlated with altitude; neighborhoods improved in qual-ity as one ascended the hills. River rats scratched out a living through fish-ing and day labor. Tuberculosis and infant mortality stalked the waterfront hovels of people unable to afford decent housing. Above them stood a ten-square-block ghetto holding most of the city's 45,000 African Americans. Italians joined recent migrants from the Kentucky hills in the next stratum, followed by a pastiche of Polish, Hungarian, and German families. A few lower-middle-class districts dotted this low-lying landscape, most housing blue-collar laborers living near their workplaces. Nearly two-thirds of them took either direct handouts or work relief before the flood. All suffered from a deluge that left their wealthier compatriots untouched.[14]

Journalists and public officials downplayed the risk of damage. A *Cincinnati Enquirer* reporter noted with some derision that the rise inundated "some of the cheaper residential districts." Within a few days hotel owners were doubling up patrons and setting up cots in conference rooms to accommodate thousands of refugees. Electricity failed in the East End when water extinguished boiler fires in power plants. Ground crews hurried airplanes off Lunken Field's runway before the airport went under. Rescue workers plucked victims from rooftops and second-story windows. The Ohio's unexpected lurch prompted one merchant to attach a half-desperate, half-resigned caption to a picture of the city at the river's previous high-water mark: "1884, you old panty waist." Weather Bureau staff transferred water level markings farther inland several times, completing each move just before the Ohio engulfed the old line.[15]

Cincinnati's city council invested city manager Clarence Dykstra with emergency powers that amounted almost to a dictatorship. They could not have picked a better man. Family legend had it that one of his ancestors—his name meant "dweller in a dyke"—had saved Holland by plugging a leaking floodwall with his finger. More important, the tall, austere, graying Dykstra was a near-perfect technocrat, a dispassionate student of public policy with a mind like a machine. As a young man he embraced the Progressive Era's reverence for experts who imposed order on America's anarchic cities. After studying urban government at the University of Iowa, he taught political science at several schools, then moved to Chicago to preach city management in the era of Al Capone and corrupt mayor "Big Bill" Thompson. Dykstra served as secretary of Los Angeles's City Club before winning appointment as the town's commissioner of water power. He became Cincinnati's city manager in 1930.[16]

Dykstra revitalized a community rife with economic problems. Under his stewardship Cincinnati retired millions of dollars in bonds while cutting taxes and expanding services. His office in city hall set the tone for his administration. Dykstra's waiting room had eight inexpensive yet functional chairs and no decorations. His inner quarters contained a single flourish: a photograph of Albert Einstein. Although quick to take a phone call from a citizen complaining about a missed trash pickup, he avoided photo ops and restricted discussions with reporters to tight, direct sentences. He saw no point in wasting time saying things that did not need to be said. "This is an age of cities, of ever expanding growth and multiplication of functions," he explained in his terse way, and "the proper carrying out of these functions with the least possible expense, with the most efficient personnel and the most appropriate appliances is the task of municipal statesmanship."[17]

Dykstra became a different man once he put on his hat and left the office. Among friends he was an easy conversationalist with a warm smile and flashing wit who enjoyed discussing history, economics, and detective stories. He played golf in his few spare moments and was an enthusiastic singer and pianist who loved to attend operas with his wife. For the most part, however, his job was his life. Dykstra saw public administration as a noble art but preferred to let his audience admire his work from afar. During the flood he stayed at his desk rather than touring flooded districts or smiling for photographers. "This man is just about as maudlin as a Diesel engine," one observer marveled, and "as politically minded as the Gulf Stream."[18]

Dykstra imposed order on the terrified city. He squelched rumors of ragged evacuees marching toward wealthy neighborhoods and fended off demands that he impose martial law. The manager sat in his office twenty hours a day with no sign of exhaustion. His calm decisiveness settled unnerved citizens. Dykstra closed movie theaters to reduce the threat of disease, abolished on-street parking to clear lanes for emergency vehicles, and consolidated social agencies to prevent duplication of labor. He asked Cincinnatians to limit energy consumption to a radio and a single light bulb. They must avoid nonessential phone calls and conserve drinking water. He authorized police to enforce his edicts but depended more on the honor system and peer pressure. His faith in the community reflected his belief that government was a simple matter so long as "the public it is supposed to serve permits it to be simple."[19]

Dykstra asked constituents to shut up and get out of his way. For the most part they obeyed. "Consider yourself a soldier under strict military discipline," the *Enquirer* advised. A few stores and suburban movie theaters defied his orders until he sent policemen to shut them down. Price gouging and food hoarding occurred despite adequate supplies (with liquor stores closed, bootleggers sold moonshine from rowboats at ten dollars a pint). Otherwise, quiet prevailed over a city on the brink of calamity. Pumping stations delivered one hour of water a day. Power plants shut down, leaving Cincinnati dependent on the trickle of electricity passing through wires from Dayton and Indianapolis. Over 50,000 refugees, most of them poor, required care. For all this, many assumed the flood had crested—the *Enquirer*'s Sunday morning edition suggested ways to "establish man's mastery over the river" now that the worst had passed. Meteorologist W. C. Devereaux predicted quiet weather ahead.[20]

Over two and a half inches of rain drenched the sodden city that day. A laconic Devereaux deemed the downpour "most unusual." Black Sunday saw the Ohio rise four feet in twenty-four hours, well on its way to a crest nine feet above its previous record.

Black Sunday's greatest danger came from fire. Floodwaters smashed debris into gas lines, electrical systems, and oil tanks. Petroleum tanks wrenched from their moorings became floating bombs drifting with the current. Hundreds of thousands of gallons of gasoline shimmered on the water's surface. Refugees cooked on open fires and lit homemade kerosene lamps. Firehouses sat under several feet of water, and isolated crews could not reach blazes in flooded areas. Irregular public water supplies made firefighting even more uncertain. "A fire in Cincinnati at this moment would be too terrible to contemplate," fire chief Barney Houston worried.[21]

Sure enough, a fire broke out on Sunday morning when a short circuit ignited a lake of gasoline leaking from a Standard Oil storage yard. Flames rushed in every direction until they burned almost three-quarters of a mile long and a quarter-mile wide. Scores of families ran for their lives as gas tanks exploded and naphtha drums popped from the heat. Policemen from an adjacent patrol house rushed outside in time to see a thousand-foot tower of flame. They recoiled from the earthquake-like shock that hit an instant later. Officers hurried inside to summon all available firemen and policemen before fanning out through the district to evacuate residents to, ominously enough, a nearby funeral home.

Retired assistant fire chief Clem Beckman answered the call first, followed by scores of Red Cross volunteers and American Legionnaires who spent the day bringing firemen coffee and sandwiches through the slush. One awestruck veteran fireman told a reporter that this was "the first fire

I ever arrived at and didn't know whether to start in fighting it or turn back and go home." A burning tire warehouse turned the air toxic, belching noxious black smoke. Firefighters sloshing through waist-deep water hosed down the roof of a Crossley refrigerator assembly plant to prevent the volatile chemicals inside from exploding. Some of the five hundred firefighters on the scene peeled off to spray two 60,000-gallon oil tanks surrounded by blazing oil drums.

Police chief Eugene Weatherly, a hard-nosed professional with thirty years on the force, said the scene "looked like hell at its worst." His comparison grew even more vivid once the sun set. Flames reflecting off the dark water created viscid sheets of radiance tinged a deep blood red. Houses and office buildings smoldered until fire consumed everything above the waterline. Refrigerators and furniture bobbed on the waves. Trolley wires and power lines dangled, waiting to electrocute anyone who touched them. Shouts of "I want somebody to get those flames" occasionally penetrated the deafening roar.

The rest of the city knew little about the inferno. The Crossley company's radio station, WLW, went off the air the moment the blaze began. Area telephones had been out for some time. With no solid information available, rumors spread almost as fast as the flames. Refugees in Kentucky assured Red Cross workers that one thousand people perished in the fire. Miraculously, no one died and a mere handful suffered minor injuries. Firefighters gained control over the area as Black Sunday eased into Monday, but not before the fire destroyed or damaged dozens of buildings. Rather than extinguishing the fire, they simply allowed a few acres of tanks to burn themselves out over the next several days.[22]

Local newspapers finally acknowledged that "Cincinnati is in the midst of the worst disaster in the city's history." Stinking, poisonous fumes blackened the skies over Mill Creek, a once placid stream running through the middle of town that now flowed like a river itself. Gas, electric, and water service ranged from inconsistent to nonexistent. Tens of thousands of refugees clogged relief centers. Hundreds of Ohio National Guardsmen represented law and order's last line of defense.[23]

FIRE WAS ONE OF many terrors to visit communities already reeling from the high water. The weekend's most unnerving events occurred in Kentucky's capital city of Frankfort, where a nightmare played out inside the Kentucky State Penitentiary.

Built in 1802, the prison was the oldest one west of the Appalachians. It housed British captives during the War of 1812 and survived three fires in the nineteenth century. Although renovations and enlargements had replaced much of its original infrastructure, the institution resembled a medieval fortress. Twin turrets flanked an entrance arch studded with narrow gun slots similar to those that shielded English longbowmen. Beyond the gate lay a network of grim blockhouses bristling with rows of barred windows. Inmates whose windows let them see over the walls glimpsed the barren slopes of the rocky hills beyond. Those who looked south could see the Kentucky River a few hundred yards away.[24]

Every stormy day brought the river closer. Tensions in the prison mounted. Nerves were already on edge owing to a daring breakout staged a few months earlier. Six convicts had commandeered a truck, driven through three unmanned checkpoints—the guards had entrusted a lifer with gate duty so they could warm their hands around a fire inside—shouted a perfunctory "OK" at the main entrance, and sped to freedom. It took prison officials seven hours to determine who was gone. Most inmates knew the break was planned.

Even though police caught the escapees within a few days, the incident prompted Governor Happy Chandler to review the prison's policies. His assessment uncovered a regime so incompetent that "the operation of the institution to a large extent has been delegated to the convicts." Many guards were too frail to restrain unruly prisoners. They had no password system or other means of identifying themselves. No one bothered to monitor the prison hospital, which housed several long-term inmates, including one of the escapees, who had overpowered a sentry with a stolen butcher knife. Uninspected trucks hauled illicit liquor through the imposing gates. Built to house 1,500 prisoners, the decrepit prison now held 3,000 murderers, thieves, and rapists. Severe overcrowding crushed morale and opened gaping security holes. "This reformatory is a public nuisance and it is cruel and inhuman to confine even the most hardened criminals in it," state health inspector A. T. McCormack advised Chandler.[25]

The Kentucky River provided the final embarrassment for an already infamous institution. Warden James Hammond ordered prisoners to man pumps once water started trickling into the complex. The Kentucky swamped the power plant anyway, leaving the prison in darkness. Guards locked felons in their cells and left to tend their own homes. A few remaining staffers herded inmates from lower tiers to the catwalk ringing the upper floor. Convicts groped their way through the cold, black gloom. Panic grew as they discussed their chances of drowning in a pitch-black masonry cube.[26]

Icy water rose above the prisoners' waists. A couple of trucks bearing oil stoves, food, and blankets made it through the gates before the rapid current forestalled further supply efforts. Terrified prisoners took matters into their own hands. One intrepid band tried to float to dry land on cotton mattresses. Another group adopted the more direct approach of diving off the prison wall and swimming to high ground. Among the escapees, all of whom police recaptured, was one with fifty-six days left to serve and one with just five. For these short-timers the risk of a watery death outweighed the prospect of a longer sentence. Frankfort residents directed their fears of prisoners on the loose at Happy Chandler. One woman demanded the governor pay her seventy-five dollars after a fugitive ransacked her home, took a bath in her tub, shaved, and stole some of her husband's clothes before slipping off into the night.[27]

Conditions in the jail spiraled toward anarchy. Its guards had disappeared; its inmates had no electricity, food, or drinking water; and the river covered its lowest tier of cells. Prisoners whispered that a wall of water from a collapsed dam was headed their way. Their mood darkened by the hour. Detainees broke cell locks with iron bars and used metal bed frames to smash through doors. Inmates ran wild through the halls. One team chipped through their building's wall into the adjoining women's lockup. From there they scrambled to the roof to get arms from the guards' weapons cache. People blocks away heard gunfire. Old feuds, racial hatreds, and blind fear spawned brawls. Victors flung losers from the catwalk into the scummy, debris-laden water. "Everybody just went crazy," an inmate later said. National Guardsmen fired occasional shots from outside the walls in a pathetic effort to silence the convicts. "The prisoners are in a pretty good humor," one delusional colonel told the press.[28]

With communication lines cut, Governor Chandler had little information about what was happening a few blocks from his office. "2 cell houses—men locked in—have not eaten since Wed or had water—fighting among selves," read a handwritten note waiting on his desk when he returned from his truncated vacation. Within an hour of his homecoming he donned hip boots and an old sweater from his days coaching Versailles

High School's football team, boarded a boat with Warden Hammond, and motored to the prison. Disheveled prisoners scrutinized the governor from barred upper-story windows and crowded fire escapes. Chandler waved his hat in a display of jaunty camaraderie. "Get us out of here," the convicts yelled in response. "This is a hell of a mess," the governor shouted, "but I'm going to get you out and take care of you. Just sit tight and keep your chins up."[29]

Chandler dropped his cheerful pose as Hammond turned the boat around. "The most desolate place I ever saw," he remarked. Convinced that the situation was untenable, he ordered authorities to empty the prison. It took considerable time to set up a temporary camp and gather enough sturdy vessels to evacuate inmates, and prisoners assumed the governor had abandoned them. Rioting continued into the next day, Black Sunday. Estimates of casualties ran between a dozen and fifty. "I don't know how many were killed," one National Guardsman said. "There's been a hell of a lot of them."[30]

Families of prisoners begged the governor for news. Their handwritten missives reflected the heartbreaking poverty and ignorance surrounding many of the inmates' lives. "I am worried about my grand son that is in Frankfard Pentuary his name is James Bowman," seventy-two-year-old Mary Bowman of Kitts, Kentucky, penciled in an unpracticed scrawl. "I would Be glad to no if he is all Rite and safe." Labor leaders dispatched more polished letters asking after miners imprisoned for participating in the infamous Harlan County strikes. Chandler's office assured all correspondents that their son, grandson, father, or husband was safe, often with no evidence.[31]

Once the camp was ready, National Guardsmen ushered inmates across a rickety wooden bridge connecting a third-story window with the prison wall. They passed above the floating wreckage, down a ladder, and across a pontoon bridge, where they met another armed unit that marched them to Greyhound buses waiting to transport them a few blocks to a rudimentary tent complex studded with barbed wire and floodlights. As Governor Chandler watched the battered evacuees file past, he promised himself the flooded buildings would never again house prisoners.

Reports of widespread fatalities proved false. Although some prisoners suffered from gunshot wounds, a head count found all 2,906 present, minus seven soon-to-be-returned escapees. "It was a miracle," Chandler sighed. "How we managed not to have lost hundreds of lives . . . is a mystery to me." Considering the prison's feckless staff and the state's slow response, Chandler's words held more truth than he intended.[32]

THE FLIGHT FROM THE Kentucky State Penitentiary coincided with a smaller but more consequential evacuation two hundred miles downstream. Word of serious danger coming to Shawneetown, Illinois, interrupted at least one joyful moment. Nine-year-old Frances Dyhrkopp had resolved to enjoy her birthday party despite the pouring rain. She and her friends wolfed down cake and ice cream as water drummed a monotonous cadence on the windows. Her grandfather's arrival interrupted their celebration. Guy "Cap" Lambert had piloted the ferry to Kentucky for twenty years. He was well known around town, an affable jokester whose gnarled hands showed the wear from decades behind the wheel, though his kindly face lacked the toughness one might expect from a sailor.

Lambert looked worried. That river was about to go on a tear, he declared. Adults at the party assured him the levee would hold. Although the Ohio ran three miles wide that morning, its fifty-foot height flowed well below the apex of the wall. "It won't matter whether the levee holds or not," he shot back. "If it does hold, the water's going to come right over the top of it." Stop fearmongering, they told him; don't ruin Frances's big day. Lambert finally persuaded the Dyhrkopps to carry their furniture upstairs. Taking a cue from their parents, children ridiculed their timidity.

A few days later Frances sat next to her grandfather as he navigated his ferry between the roofs poking above the twenty feet of water covering Main Street. Cap Lambert was one of the few to see disaster coming, and the Dyhrkopps were among the few to heed his warnings.[33]

Overflow from the Wabash and Ohio Rivers topped a drainage ditch behind Shawneetown several days before Frances Dyhrkopp blew out her candles, rendering Route 13, the lone highway out of town, impassable. Backwater was common, so locals showed little concern that their village was now an island. Most guessed the river would stall at fifty feet, the level reached in 1933 and far below the high mark of 1913. We might get a little wet, they said, but the levee was strong. It would hold. Mayor William Brinkley could not afford such complacency. "It's a freak river and hard to figure," he told reporters. "We will have a hard fight." He set a twenty-four-hour levee patrol and recruited sandbagging teams in case the wall showed signs of weakness.[34]

Brinkley's fears intensified when the water roared past fifty-five feet.

Rainwater filled the poor neighborhoods occupying the lowest elevations. Refugees sheltered in boxcars, the Riverside Hotel, and the high school. Brinkley asked for help from the military and the Red Cross. He also took the prudent step of engaging a steamboat from Memphis to remove people should the Ohio keep climbing. Skeptics derided the mayor's common-sense actions, and most ignored his pleas to get out. Their forefathers never ran—Shawneetowners took whatever the river threw at them.[35]

Their bravado crumbled when water started pushing through the levee. Inhabitants stashed household items in the high school gymnasium before seeking refuge with friends or family or retreating to rural landholdings. Those with nowhere else to go settled into the eleven-room school. Panic gripped a town that had long concealed its social fractures. "People acted crazy," one flooder remarked after watching a neighbor abuse a balky mule. "The mule didn't want to go," he remembered, "and the man was beating him something terrible. He wasn't trying to make him go; he was just beating him. Everyone was acting like that." An attitude of every man for himself swept the streets. Families fled without considering their neighbors' plight. Truck drivers charged exorbitant prices to transport endangered goods.[36]

Cap Lambert defied this rampant selfishness. The captain of the *Margaret J* worked beyond exhaustion. He manned the wheelhouse for twenty-four-hour stretches without so much as a cup of coffee as he shuttled people, livestock, furniture, and grain to Kentucky. Navigating the field of floating debris required skill and lots of luck. Water covered Lambert's usual landing spot in Blackburn, so the captain picked through the forest behind the town until he located a drop-off site several miles beyond the Ohio's normal bank. He yanked the whistle to alert Morgantown, ten miles inland a few weeks ago. Volunteers in trucks followed the sound cross country until they spotted the boat. Lambert unloaded the *Margaret J*, then immediately turned around to repeat the hazardous journey. He held up as best he could against the stress. "Don't thank me, lady," he told one appreciative passenger. "I had my eyes closed the whole time. I was scared to death. I was praying."[37]

Lambert had plenty to look at when he wasn't dodging floating trees or gazing at his devastated hometown. Every trip carried him past a cow and her calf stranded atop the levee. The bovine sentries plodded as far as they could in one direction before turning to pace in the opposite direction. Several of Lambert's passengers suggested shooting the animals to put them out of their misery. Instead, a benevolent bargeman took them on board. A caregiver returned the cow to its owner weeks later; he said he didn't know what had happened to the calf. Lambert also was amused one night when he discovered a goat splashing alongside the *Margaret J.* The captain hauled the goat up by its horns. With temperatures hovering just above zero, its coat almost instantly froze into solid ice. Lambert brought the unfortunate beast into the engine room and pushed it near the stove to thaw it out. He kept his new friend on board two or three days before depositing it on high ground. One observer swore the goat offered a bleat of thanks as it stepped off the gangplank.[38]

Rescuers had to literally drag resisters from their homes. By Black Sunday they had almost emptied Shawneetown. Local raconteur Rudy Phillips kept his barbecue joint open until the water reached his waist, then closed up and paddled out of town. Telephone operator Nell Awalt stuck to her post until the wires went down, then waded out of the switchboard office. Murky water lapped the top of the levee on both sides.[39]

Communities throughout southeastern Illinois shared the village's predicament. Harrisburg, the largest town in the area, sat twenty-two miles inland from Shawneetown, yet a combination of Ohio and Saline River floodwater reduced it to two small islands. Scores of hamlets—Equality, Junction, Ridgway—were accessible only by boat. A yellowish lake swirled above the undulating countryside, telegraph poles piercing its smooth surface. Furniture, animal carcasses, and homes spun with the current, each piece of drifting wreckage symbolizing an interrupted life. After touring the district, Governor Henry Horner pronounced the destruction "incomprehensible."[40]

Horner was aware of Shawneetown's misery but had no way to get there. His presence would have meant little anyway, because almost everyone was gone. A few dozen people huddled in the upper stories of the Riverside Hotel, the third floor of the bank, and a handful of private homes. They knew a repeat of the 1898 levee collapse would wipe the town off the map, to say nothing of the buildings sheltering them. Without any public discussion, without taking any votes, the town's elite decided to dynamite the wall and let the water ease in. Max Galt was among the instigators. His friends Harry Fred Hall and Ralph Harmon probably accompanied him. Captain Harry Frissell of the Corps of Engineers may have come along.

Someone rowed to Gus Blair's saloon, the last open store on Main Street, to purchase whiskey. The group reassembled on the village's downstream edge and sipped from the bottle as they looked over the Ohio, pausing to dabble their fingers in the chilly stream. After stalling as long as possible, the conspirators placed the charges. They paddled upstream along the levee until they reached a safe distance, then someone—exactly who remains a mystery—depressed the plunger. A terrific roar rippled across the empty landscape as the dynamite tore a gap in the wall. An even more terrible sound followed as the water rushed in. Melancholy consumed the friends as they watched their town disappear. Outbuildings and sheds popped to the surface like corks in a bowl of water. Their work complete, the men rowed off into the night.[41]

THE NATIONAL PRESS PAID little attention to Shawneetown's evacuation. Larger population centers like Paducah drew its focus. Once a major steamboat landing, that city of 35,000 huddled close to the Ohio's intersection with the Tennessee River. It had no flood protection. High waters, in fact, were a major component of Paducah's self-image. Paducahans had survived deluges in 1882, 1883, 1884, and 1913 with minor damage. These escapes bred a sense that the town had taken the river's worst, overconfidence that betrayed them in 1937. "Everybody knew the water was rising," Dulcie Lee Burns Bell remembered decades later, "but they didn't think it would flood." Nothing could top 1913.[42]

Paducah seemed on the cusp of a bright future. Industry had rebounded to pre-Crash levels, and residents saw the sooty, smoky air hanging over the town as evidence of prosperity rather than as a nuisance. Even the weather promised better days, as warm December temperatures kept chrysanthemums blooming well beyond their usual life span.

When the Ohio crept into the riverside industrial and wholesaling district, Mayor Edgar Washburn and city manager L. V. Bean summoned a Coast Guard transport vessel and asked the army for cots, blankets, and mess kits. Nobody expected the inconvenience to last more than a few days. When water infiltrated the basement of city hall, police chief William Bryant ordered twelve men jailed for misdemeanors to come back in two weeks. Boxing fans grumbled because organizers postponed the Golden Gloves tournament for a few days to let Hook's Arena dry out.[43]

"Heavy rain and colder tonight," stated the inauguration day forecast.

Over three inches of rain fell that night and the following day, equaling the average rainfall for January, and more came the next day. Red Cross chapter chairman Schultz Riggs burst into the *Paducah Sun-Democrat*'s offices at ten o'clock that night with dire news. He waved a telegram from Louisville to get the room's attention and read in a loud voice: "Prepare for the worst flood in history of the Ohio Valley." Most Paducahans never heard his warning. The river surged three feet over the next few hours. Stunned by the sudden rise, the *Sun-Democrat*'s editors got out a few copies of a single-sheet edition before retreating twenty miles south to the offices of the *Mayfield Messenger*. A skeleton crew of reporters who stayed behind took up quarters in a small gas station on the western edge of town, but swollen creeks isolated them from downtown. Refugees crowded hotels. Unable to find open roads, frustrated motorists ditched their cars—boatmen later reported seeing dome lights from submerged vehicles glowing several feet below the surface.[44]

Staffers from the Red Cross's national headquarters marveled at the Paducah chapter's ineptitude. Confusion reigned as city, county, and private organizations floundered through the unanticipated emergency. With official agencies paralyzed, some locals seized authority. Two lawyers and a minister exercised dictatorial powers over the elevated district of Avondale, not far from where the *Sun-Democrat*'s reporters set up. Friends Tom Waller, W. F. McMurry, and Reverend Fred Olert bumped into each other at a drugstore soon after bloated creeks divided the city. They lamented the city's slow response, then decided to take matters into their own hands. They hopped into a car and inched along the icy highway to Mayfield. The town's telephone service was down, but the group found a functioning telegraph line and dashed off a wire to Senator Alben Barkley, a native Paducahan. Next they shocked a local baker with an order for six hundred loaves, all he could make by the following morning. They signed a purchase order for the bread even though they had no authority to do so. Finally Waller, McMurry, and Olert gathered Mayfield's leading citizens to discuss housing for refugees.

On their return, the self-appointed community leaders gathered their neighbors at the Standard Oil station housing the remnants of the *Sun-Democrat*. So many showed up that they relocated across the railroad tracks to the Twinkling Star Club. A show of hands ratified their status as an emergency executive committee. The triumvirate's first act was to occupy the club in the Red Cross's name, without informing the Red Cross. Sub-committees arranged evacuations, procured equipment, and opened hospitals. Based on their self-granted authority, the troika commandeered additional buildings, broadcast calls for doctors and carpenters on radio station WPAD, and ordered schools to shelter flooders. Waller, McMurry, and Olert signed thousands of dollars in IOUs. Avondale's impromptu government finally made contact with Red Cross representatives, who assumed its promissory notes and advised it to carry on.[45]

Black Sunday sealed the town's fate. A warm southern breeze that day dispersed floating ice chunks but ushered in another downpour. New water entering the Ohio and Tennessee Rivers pushed the flood several feet higher. "Except for a few high spots here and yonder," one refugee reported, "there is no Paducah. It is a swirling, muddy, distressed and dangerous lake." Residents evacuated at the very moment when prisoners rioted in Frankfort, Galt and his friends discussed blowing the Shawneetown levee, and firefighters battled flames in Cincinnati.[46]

Red Cross volunteers ran their evacuation campaign from a dock built at Twenty-eighth and Broadway, a few blocks from the Twinkling Star Club. A steady flow of eastbound boats fought a vicious current as they dodged submerged cars and other obstacles to answer rescue calls. Ambulances and trucks waited at the dock to speed off-loading of refugees to a processing center for registration, medical care, warm food, and dry clothes. Medical cases went to George Rogers Clark School. Everyone else either went to stay with friends or family or boarded trucks for Mayfield and other dry spots.[47]

More than 20,000 Paducahans trudged across the wooden gangplank during the next ten days. Except for a few thousand immovable holdouts, the city was empty. City manager Bean presided over a shell of a government. Hundreds of vessels canvassed for survivors. With seven-eighths of Paducah underwater, pilots had plenty of places to look. Hundreds of National Guardsmen, American Legionnaires, regular army troops, policemen, and special deputies exercised near-total power. Military men gave those found in the flood zone ten minutes to collect their belongings and accept relocation. "All possible courtesy was shown," the *Sun-Democrat* noted in a feel-good retrospective, "but the relief workers had orders to brook no opposition in their tasks." Citing the health risks of staying, army officers authorized the use of force against disobedient civilians. "It's not martial law," local officials insisted. They defined the situation as "civil authority, almost completely superseded by military rule," a razor-thin distinction intended to preserve Paducah's reputation postflood.[48]

DISASTERS SUBJECT COMMUNITIES TO extreme pressure that can expose their true colors. This was certainly true in Cairo (pronounced KAY-ro), Illinois, the town commanding a triangle of alluvial soil past which water flowed from twenty-five states. With the Ohio valley surrendering to the flood, it came to symbolize man's last outpost against nature, a modern-day Rome besieged by barbarians. Newspaper readers and radio listeners around the nation interpreted its fight as a yardstick for the nation's overall response to the crisis. In the excitement, observers neglected to examine how the flood revealed divisions within a fractious city that should never have existed. Cairo's past travails bred a tradition of cynicism, suspicion, and apathy that laid the foundations for the town's lackluster response to 1937 and its aftermath.

The junction of the Mississippi and Ohio seemed an ideal spot for development. Thick forests of cottonwoods, sycamores, maples, and boxwoods offered abundant construction material. Buffalo and smaller game abounded. "There is no place in Louisiana [Territory] more fit, in my opinion, for a settlement than this, nor where it is of more consequence to have one," argued one eighteenth-century missionary. France coveted the intersection as a buffer against Britain's westward expansion, but its attempts to occupy the area failed, as did later British efforts. Hostile natives resisted the intruders, and yellow fever and malaria flourished in the saucer-shaped swamp between the rivers. Cairo's future location was a miracle of geography undermined by regrettable topography.[49]

Baltimore merchant John Comegys purchased 1,800 acres of area lowlands in 1818 and named his holdings Cairo because he thought they resembled the fertile Nile delta (some still call southern Illinois "Little Egypt"). He aimed not so much to create a community as to profit from land sales and the steamboat trade. His City and Bank Company of Cairo littered the country with promotional literature. "A single glance over the map of western America," one pamphlet read, "must convince the most superficial observer of the superior eligibility of this position for a great and commercial city over any other that could be found between New Orleans and the sources of those majestic streams which unite their waters at this point." Comegys dismissed rumors of miasmic conditions and promised that a low levee built with the proceeds from land sales would secure

Cairo against any possible flood, freeing it to become "the emporium of Western America."⁵⁰

Comegys died soon after launching the venture. His fellow proprietors lost interest in the settlement, which consisted of a ring of shacks surrounding a lumberyard, and returned their holdings to the federal government. Within a few years only a few frame houses, a tavern, and a store marked the site. Even those living there forgot its name. They referred to the forest clearing simply as "Mouth of the Ohio."⁵¹ This desultory settlement seemed to be another casualty of a catch-as-catch-can era of land rushes, shady speculators, and busts, one more decrepit reminder of young America's restless drive for profit at any price.

One generation and one land boom later, another group of capitalists took a shot at realizing Comegys's dream. The Cairo City and Canal Company bought the squatter settlement in 1835. Like Comegys, Boston mover and shaker Darius Holbrook, the company's leader, imagined himself as the mighty overlord of an inland empire built on a thriving river trade. Holbrook launched a branding campaign worthy of any modern promoter. Steamboats, fences, and buildings on both sides of the Atlantic displayed four-color posters proclaiming "the World's Greatest Manufacturing Mart and Emporium." Holbrook's salesmanship netted a $1.25 million loan from London's Wright and Company and a charter from Illinois granting him absolute administrative, executive, and judicial authority over his enterprise.

Holbrook erected a shipyard, stores, hotels, saloons, warehouses, brickyards, and lumberyards. He lured immigrants with promises of plentiful jobs and high wages. Newcomers discovered that the town in no way resembled the utopia described in its promotional material. Summer brought flies, mosquitoes, and an unbearable stench of decay. Winter brought chilly winds and muddy streets. Holbrook neglected to inform prospective migrants that he retained title to the land. Cairo was a city of serfs toiling under a feudal master. Holbrook knew that the best way to protect Cairo from inundation was to elevate it with packed dirt. Instead, he installed low levees, a faster and cheaper flood control option befitting his desire to turn a quick profit. As a consequence, disease-ridden groundwater often pushed to the surface and collected in stinking pools.⁵²

Frontier Cairo was less a community than a collection of individuals. No one but Holbrook had a stake in its survival. Inhabitants saw themselves as short-timers hoping make a buck before departing for greener pastures. The only thing uniting them was their shared hatred of the proprietor. Their displeasure, along with an economic downturn, demolished the second Cairo. The Panic of 1837 bankrupted Wright and Company. Holbrook, his main source of money gone, let the town fall into ruins. Outraged townfolk seized whatever valuables they could and destroyed everything else. One captain had to cut his steamboat's mooring lines when a mob tried to commandeer the vessel for a drunken joyride to New Orleans. Holbrook fled in 1841, his grand venture reduced to a few taverns and hovels populated by two hundred roughnecks happy to be rid of him.[53]

An English traveler named Charles Dickens passed Cairo the next year. Legend has it that the novelist lost money in the Wright and Company debacle. Whether that was true or not, he saw nothing to recommend the failed town. "At the junction of the two rivers," he wrote in *American Notes for General Circulation*,

on ground so flat and low and marshy, that at certain seasons of the year it is inundated to the house-tops, lies a breeding-place of fever, ague, and death; vaunted in England as a mine of Golden Hope, and speculated in, on the faith of monstrous representations, to many peoples' ruin. A dismal swamp, on which the half-built houses rot away: cleared here and there for the space of a few yards; and teeming, then, with rank unwholesome vegetation, in whose baleful shade the wretched wanderers who are tempted hither, droop, and die, and lay their bones; the hateful Mississippi circling and eddying before it, and turning off upon its southern course a slimy monster hideous to behold; a hotbed of disease, an ugly sepulcher, a grave uncheered by any gleam of promise; a place without one single quality, in earth or air or water, to commend it: such is this dismal Cairo.

Dickens took another shot at Cairo when he dispatched the title character of *Martin Chuzzlewit* to Eden, a decrepit scrap of swampland under the thumb of the corrupt Eden Land Corporation, an obvious stand-in for Holbrook's group.[54]

In spite of Dickens's fondest wishes, Cairo refused to stay dead. In the 1850s another team of speculators purchased the Cairo City and Canal Company's assets. Cairo was a phlegmatic phoenix reborn from the muck, a patch of real estate at once intriguing and useless. Most of the new Cairo City Property's trustees lived in New York City and never deigned to visit their land. Their negligence left effective power in the hands of the only investor who made the trip west, a lawyer and former bank director named S. Staats Taylor. An aloof man with aristocratic pretensions, Taylor became the town's new czar. He evicted squatters from "his" property when he arrived, exiling them to houseboats and floating stores until he finally consented to sell lots two years later.[55]

Notwithstanding his unpopularity in some quarters, Taylor served five consecutive terms as mayor. His leadership rooted Cairo in place. Darius Holbrook, who rebounded from his earlier disgrace to purchase a stake in the new company, contributed to the town's permanence. A major stockholder in the Illinois Central Railroad, Holbrook badgered the state legislature into locating the line's terminus at Cairo. Among his chief backers was United States senator and future presidential candidate Stephen Douglas, who persuaded Congress to hand the company two million acres of public land. Railroad jobs attracted hundreds of transients who had little interest in creating a cohesive community. Filled as it was with salts, vagabonds, and thugs, the settlement justified its reputation as the "Sodom of Southern Illinois." Its many saloons overflowed with brawling drunkards. Respectable citizens huddled in a few elm- and magnolia-lined neighborhoods and conceded the riverfront to the seedier element. Town leaders compounded the chaos by delaying construction of a jail and failing to create an effective police force.[56]

In exchange for generous land grants, the Illinois Central agreed in 1854 to build levees high enough to protect against any flood yet experienced. The Mississippi had buried the city five years earlier when it flowed through a leaky barrier no one had bothered to plug. Railroad officials hired a contractor named Dutcher to improve the levee. Unknown to Taylor, Dutcher was in cahoots with boosters from Mound City, a budding settlement five miles upstream that hoped to discredit Cairo and snare the railroad's terminus for itself. His workers undermined the wall's integrity by filling it with sand and stumps. In a less subtle move, they also left large gaps along the line.

The town fathers panicked when, as if on cue, the Mississippi rose. Dutcher's corrupt employees kept up a snail's pace in the face of pleas to work faster. Taylor hired three hundred men to bolster the levee during the crew's off hours. The contractor objected that the city's squad somehow interfered with his operation. His men stole their rivals' tools, then walked off the job. Taylor had little choice but to satisfy their outrageous demand for a salary of three dollars a day. Dutcher's men then threatened to either blow up the wall or burn down the town unless the trustee paid even higher wages. Taylor instead stationed armed guards along the wall and dismissed Dutcher, who got the last laugh when his Swiss cheese levees buckled during a mild inundation a few years later.[57]

Cairo City Property trustees bickered with Illinois Central officials over responsibility for this latest fiasco. The railroad finally agreed to repair the damage but did such a poor job that the city had to go into debt to fix the fix. This debacle fed Cairo's negative self-image. Town trustees shirked necessary improvements because they saw little hope for profits. Private citizens were similarly indifferent. In the 1880s merchants killed a plan to fill in low areas because they assumed Cairo would never be big enough to justify the cost of flood protection. Elected officials later passed an ordinance requiring property owners to fill low lots, then repealed it after objections from local elites, including the trustees, who owned many of the lots in question and would therefore bear the brunt of the expense.[58]

Ethnic and sectional tensions deepened these rifts. Recent arrivals from the North quarreled with native southerners. Both sides distrusted the clannish Germans, and not even the Germans liked the Irish immigrants who came seeking railroad work. Local newspapers caricatured Irishmen as "Popish . . . ignorant . . . worthless as niggers."[59]

Cairo's racial divisions further undermined the community. Two major rivers and a proximity to slaveholding states made Cairo a natural destination for free blacks and runaway slaves. Their presence outraged the white majority. Our town is "almost entirely overrun with free niggers," the *Weekly Times and Delta* complained in 1856. The following July saw four days of race rioting as a mob tried to carry free blacks to Missouri to sell them into slavery. Rioters eventually contented themselves with marching them out of town at gunpoint.[60]

Cairo's racial ugliness peaked with the 1909 lynching of William "Froggy" James, a burly coal hauler accused of strangling a white department store clerk named Anna Pelly. Policemen hustled James onto a train just as a gang of whites stormed the jail. Finding James's cell empty, the outraged crowd hijacked another train that overtook the first locomotive. They returned James to Cairo, then hanged him from the metal arch spanning Commercial Avenue. When the rope broke, ringleaders decided to drown him in the Ohio. Excited bystanders filled him with bullets before they could drag him the two blocks to the river. Onlookers burned his corpse, shredded his body, and staked his head to the ground. Opportunistic entrepreneurs sold popcorn and peanuts to gawkers.[61]

White Cairoites settled into a mood of sullen apathy. "The colored people are here to stay," a local historian lamented soon after the murder. African Americans, who accounted for one-third of the population, clustered in all-black neighborhoods near the town center. Their children attended segregated schools and watched movies in segregated theaters. The public library and swimming pool were off limits. Cairo's only hospital turned them away. "I wondered what the colored people used for restrooms," a white resident commented decades later; "Where did they get a drink of water?" The city directory put asterisks next to African Americans' names. Cairo was a racial powder keg.[62]

The same rivers that justified Cairo's existence limited its growth and discouraged any sense of civic unity. Prospectors who developed the muddy peninsula for profit viewed building levees and filling low areas as unnecessary extravagances. "If Cairo had been filled up before any lots were sold, there would now be a city of a million people, and St. Louis would be only a small city," the *Cairo Evening Citizen* remarked in 1916. "Because the founders of Cairo promoted a city instead of building one, Cairo is today a city of less than twenty thousand people." Successive waves of strangers clambered onshore in search of escape, personal gain, or a good time. Each new arrival stirred the city's festering hostility. Decades of violence, apathy, and corruption tarnished Cairo's national reputation. Declining river traffic transformed the unofficial capital of Little Egypt into a relic. Vacant buildings crumbled. Gaudy neon signs and overwrought Victorian facades along the Washington and Commercial Avenue business districts spoke more to the past than the future.[63]

Cairo limped into the 1930s, saddled with the burdens of its outstanding location. Its population sagged to 12,000. Police and public alike turned a blind eye to widespread bootlegging, gambling, and prostitution. Mayor August Bode, an insurance salesman and owner of a disreputable local eatery, may have profited from the corruption. Residents' penchant for evading taxes proved crushing when the Depression hit. Industrial failures compounded the town's pervasive defeatism. Rather than pulling together, the community disintegrated. One cheerleading editorial published a few days before the flood claimed that "old Cairo has a way of standing together and fighting grimly, showing the finest kind of sportsmanship and civic spirit whenever a real crisis arrives." Its troubled history suggested the opposite was true.[64]

Confident that the fuse-plug levee at Bird's Point offered total protection, the relentlessly buoyant *Evening Citizen and Bulletin* assured readers that the wave rushing toward them represented, at most, an "inconvenience." Mayor Bode put a handful of men on sandbagging duty even though the city could not afford to pay them. His prudence paid off when the engorged Ohio unexpectedly split into two parallel currents just upstream of Cairo. One followed the river's usual path, while the other swept through its prehistoric channel, a slight valley snaking one to fifteen miles to the north. These twin streams buried obscure southern Illinois towns close to the shore, such as Mounds, Mound City, and Brookport, as well as those far from the river's normal course, including Alexander City, Dog-Tooth Bend, Karnak, Olive Branch, Ullin, and Unity. They also forced the eastward flowing Cache River that formed the northern leg of the triangle of land containing Cairo to run backward, transforming the area from a peninsula into an island surrounded by a lake fifteen miles across.[65]

It was time to invoke the last line of defense. General Jadwin had promised that the Bird's Point floodway would knock six feet off the crest at Cairo, and engineers needed every inch they could get. The Mississippi would soon top the fuse-plug levee whether engineers acted or not, and corpsmen preferred a controlled break to a catastrophic collapse. Three small crevasses already threatened to widen into major gaps.[66]

Colonel Eugene Reybold wired from Memphis to an assistant in Cairo at 1:50 p.m. on Black Sunday: "You are authorized and directed to place floodway in operation at once." Reybold's decision attracted widespread attention. "This Order May Save a City," blared a *Memphis Commercial Appeal* headline. Although towns from Pennsylvania to Illinois were losing their battles with the rivers, mankind might claim a victory over nature if the city at the confluence of waters stayed dry.[67]

It took hours to implement Reybold's order. Demolition crews halted several times to conduct rescue missions inside the floodway. Work ceased at one point so engineers could shoo away a frostbitten elderly couple carrying two crates of chickens. Engineers summoned several companies of regular army troops to suppress a "levee rebellion" of shotgun-wielding farmers desperate to save their property. An old trapper named "Budge" Cobb caused yet another postponement. Cobb, an experienced hunter, figured that small game animals would run for the safety of the levee, and he

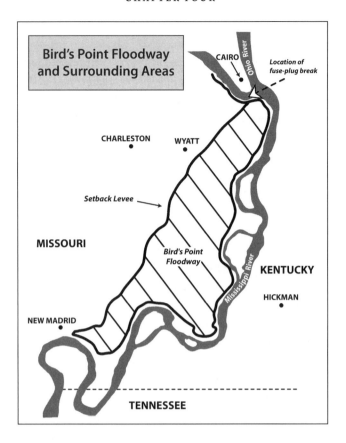

planned on being there when they arrived. Approaching dynamite crews encountered what appeared to be a crazy man randomly firing a shotgun. They sent to Cairo for reinforcements. By postponing the planned inundation, Cobb inadvertently gave a few more people time to escape the floodway.[68]

Engineers eventually overcame their fears, terminated their rescue missions, and completed their tasks. After years of theorizing, they were about to learn whether Jadwin's calculations were correct. National Guardsmen depressed plungers that detonated thousands of pounds of dynamite buried six feet under the hard-packed clay. Blast waves shook windows and collapsed chimneys ten miles away. Gushing water crushed barns and farmhouses as circling airplanes photographed the carnage. A handful of desultory stragglers sat atop the muddy levee to wait for the Coast Guard.[69]

No one could guarantee that Bird's Point would lower the crest at Cairo.

Floodway residents might have lost everything for nothing. Engineers even questioned whether the setback levees that guided the flow back into the Mississippi near New Madrid could withstand the millions of gallons of water barreling toward them. Thousands of WPA men kept sandbagging the setbacks. Additional Missouri towns faced a watery doom should they fail. Another concern was the five hundred people who from either ignorance or stubbornness stayed in Bird's Point. Pilots from the Missouri National Guard's 110th Observation Squadron spotted flooders on rooftops, on tiny islands, and in rowboats. One unfortunate man got trapped in his hayloft when water filled the barn. Thinking fast, he kicked a hole through the roof and signaled a passing airplane whose pilot radioed his location to rescue boats.[70]

Lines of slow-moving people plodded to safety through water too shallow for boats and too deep for trucks. Exhausted cattle lowed hungrily as they shuffled along icy roads; tenders had to halt their entire herd whenever one fell. Croppers drove overloaded mules through the night. A full moon lit their way, casting eerie reflections of their pathetic figures on the ice.

Engineers needed time to determine the floodway's impact on Cairo. Initial signs were bleak, for the Ohio jumped eighteen inches the day the charges blew. Forecasters estimated that the crest would lap or top the crown of the levee. An *Evening Citizen and Bulletin* editorial nevertheless claimed that "the old floodtime spirit of Cairo has reawakened in the breasts of those valiant souls who have fought other floods in Cairo and, in spite of the fact that this is the greatest of all time, there is a general feeling of confidence." Red Cross officials, on the other hand, sensed "great apprehension" on the streets. Muddy tap water inspired fears of unsafe or diminishing drinking supplies. Rumors that the floodway had failed and that the levees faced imminent destruction flew from house to house.[71]

Many Cairo residents doubted the community could outlast the crisis. When Mayor Bode urged all able-bodied men to report to the levees, legions of them instead motored to dry settlements in the north. Sheriff Lloyd Oller's troops arrested a few hundred would-be escapees on dubious charges of vagrancy, and Oller sentenced them to serve on the wall. Bode shuttered all stores except restaurants, groceries, and pharmacies and again ordered male citizens to register for duty. His actions prompted widespread resentment. One of the many bars he shut down had a sign in its window reading We Never Close. A rejected patron scribbled under-

Water pours through a break in the Bird's Point floodway. AP Photo.

neath, "Liar!" Citing the uncertainty regarding the eventual crest, Bode advised women and children to seek safety elsewhere, though he emphasized that there was no immediate threat.[72]

In keeping with the city's tradition of discrimination, public officials neglected to warn African Americans of the severity of the crisis. "There is an old saying that white folk don't let Negroes know what's going on," Hattie Kendrick remembered. Kendrick had spent the past few days glued to radio broadcasts from flood-ravaged Louisville. Suddenly a different voice broke in to advise listeners that the mayor was evacuating Cairo's women and children. "I was never so stunned in my life," Kendrick recalled, "I didn't know my own town was in danger."[73]

Hundreds of white people gathered at Safford School to board Greyhound buses that ferried them under the massive steel floodgate at the north end of town to the Cairo Junction train station. African Americans waited a few hundred yards away at the all-black Sumner High School to make the same trip in different buses. Brakemen waded in front of the crowded trains to check the track for debris. Passengers inching north had plenty of time to marvel at the ocean around them. "There was more water than I ever seen, and I've been in the world a long time," one awestruck rider thought as she looked out the window.[74]

Sheriff Oller's cordon on the edge of town proved as leaky as Dutcher's stump-filled levee. Women looking to rejoin their men sneaked back in after dark or presented forged passes. One intrepid wife donned men's clothes and a false beard to slip past the guards. Authorities also had a difficult time corralling men for the levees. Knowing that the nation's eyes were on the city and that visiting reporters hungered for news, the *Evening Citizen and Bulletin* offered heroic visions of "the banker, the truck driver, the merchant, [and] the clerk" toiling side by side on the riverfront, their "cheerful banter and wisecracking" reflecting the confidence Cairoites exuded during this unnerving time. In reality, local officials issued appeal after appeal for men to report for work. Endangered businesses compelled employees to head to the levees, then refused to pay them for their time. Police denied able-bodied men the right to leave without a pass even though, as the newspaper claimed, "Cairo cannot be said to be under military law."[75]

Emergency workers demanded compensation for saving their own homes. Bode might have accommodated them, if he'd had any money. He contended that the Corps of Engineers should finance the fight, but army officers agreed only to furnish materials and equipment. Bode turned next to the WPA, which was already paying thousands of enrollees toiling in Cairo, many of them shuttled in from elsewhere. In the rush of events the WPA failed to definitively answer the mayor's request, so no one really knew who was going to reimburse the muddy, exhausted men halfheartedly battling the Ohio. Officials issued work cards to some with the promise of future payment. They told others that their employers would foot the bill or that another agent would jot down their vital information later.[76]

Even engineers who trusted the levee worried the Ohio might surmount the wall despite the opening of the floodway. Local lumberyards churned out pine boards for mudboxes—parallel walls atop the levee filled with sandbags or dirt. Long wooden braces on the city side absorbed the pound-

Workers constructing mudboxes atop the Cairo levees. Corbis.

ing from the waves. The grimy, grueling work continued through the night. Tired men lugged heavy sacks of mud up the embankment, deposited them between the twin ramparts, then stumbled downhill for another load. Whenever possible they grabbed sandwiches delivered from American Legion and Salvation Army posts. Bonfires along the forty-block front provided some respite from the cold.[77]

Weary laborers hobbled home on muddy streets speckled with frozen backwater. The river raced high above their heads, invisible but not forgotten. Imported workers collapsed in warehouses converted into barracks, cots on the fourth floor of the Board of Trade building, or, for the fortunate few, in the teeming but comfortable Halliday Hotel, a five-story masterpiece whose tin roof offered a fine panorama of the campaign. Anyone standing on the roof could see the hundreds of filthy men packing mudboxes below. Their squalor contrasted with the pristine snow mantling the housetops. From there the river almost looked placid; opening Bird's Point slowed the current by several miles an hour. The same full moon that illuminated floodway refugees threw a warm orange light over the boats assembled in case of an emergency evacuation. From that high up, one could enjoy a quiet serenity, a feeling of peaceful solitude.

Another look around transformed that tranquility into a paralyzing sense of isolation. A peek downstream brought the Mississippi into focus, running heavy with the Ohio's excess as millions of gallons thundered toward hundreds of unseen communities to the south. A glance upstream beyond the flotilla's lights revealed an unbroken stretch of pitch darkness. Mound City, normally visible from here, had gone black. Its leaders had refused offers of assistance from outside WPA crews out of a misguided sense of town pride. Without sufficient manpower to save the town, civil and military authorities quit their battle, and exiles fled to refugee camps. So observers atop the Halliday Hotel might conclude that their tiny spot of lowland was all that humanity had saved from the river.[78]

Water hammered the levee top by the time crews finished bulkheading the Ohio and began working up the Mississippi River side. Any further rise or any windstorm strong enough to whip up waves might pierce the thin line separating Cairo from the flood. Yet a curious sense of complacency pervaded the town, at least for those not breaking their backs on the wall. Women strolled the streets in defiance of Bode's orders. Few people seemed concerned, at least in public, that the only thing separating them from almost certain death was a makeshift barrier of wood and mud three feet high and two feet wide.[79]

Although far from a model leader, Mayor Bode genuinely worried that the Ohio might force a chaotic flight. His meetings with representatives from the army, Coast Guard, Red Cross, and Corps of Engineers convinced him he needed a plan in case the worst happened. On the same day that the local paper labeled the situation "well in hand," he sent a telegram to Governor Horner asking that "advance preparations be made immediately for placing city of Cairo under martial law immediately upon my appeal for such assistance." Bode decided to emulate Portsmouth by easing in water through sewer lines should a levee collapse appear imminent.[80]

Horner relayed Bode's request to Major Harry Bolen of the 130th Infantry, Illinois National Guard, who crafted a rudimentary "Plan A" within a few hours. According to his sketch, a small-scale version of the scheme the army devised to evacuate the Mississippi valley, the military would assume positions within Cairo the moment the governor declared martial law. National Guardsmen, sheriff's deputies, and state policemen would herd 9,000 people to deportation centers and occupy the emptied city. "LOOTING WILL BE PREVENTED," the secret orders emphasized. Bolen did not say how his men would prevent looting, nor did he need to—his typescript said enough to convince anyone reading the document that he meant business.[81]

BLACK SUNDAY'S RAINS REVERBERATED from sunny Washington, DC, to waterlogged Cairo, to terrified New Orleans. About one million Americans had fled their homes. Vast stretches of the Ohio and Mississippi valleys stood virtually empty. Cairo's defenses held by the thinnest of margins. Floodwaters were spilling into the Mississippi. "The worst is yet to come," Colonel Reybold told a packed press conference in Memphis. Over 100,000 people were putting in twelve-hour days on levees from Cairo to New Orleans. Army units prepared to implement evacuation plans should their efforts and Jadwin's untested flood protection system prove insufficient.

What is the more pressing need, a reporter asked Reybold, more sandbags or more men? Neither, he replied. What he needed most was "the help of God."[82]

CHAPTER FIVE

SEND A BOAT!

~~~~~~~

FRANKLIN ROOSEVELT WAS NOT one to lament his birthday as an omen of time's relentless march. A social animal who craved attention, the president surrounded himself with close friends every January 30 for an evening of drinking, storytelling, and reminiscing. Associates who had dedicated years or even decades to his political advancement spun tales of old battles while FDR prepared wretched martinis and old-fashioneds.

Besides reveling in the fellowship, the president recognized the public relations value of his special day. Beginning in 1934, a privately run National Committee for Birthday Balls sponsored annual events to honor FDR and raise money for polio research. About five thousand communities hosted parties in 1937. Sara Roosevelt, the president's mother, headlined the gala at New York's Waldorf-Astoria, one of nine held in the city. Jean Harlow and Robert Taylor led a troupe of film stars who chatted with FDR before visiting the seven balls staged in the capital's hotels.[1]

Roosevelt's birthday meant extra work for everyone invited to his private party, for tradition dictated that they entertain the president with songs, poems, and skits. Any topic was fair game. Previous performances had mocked the League of Nations, the Republican opposition, and FDR himself. Guests spent days polishing their contributions and ghostwriting material for Eleanor Roosevelt and other humor-challenged attendees. This year they had to work around the time-sucking flood crisis. Press secretary Stephen Early drafted amusing ditties between meetings with Red Cross chairman Cary Grayson and army chief of staff General Malin Craig. Harry Hopkins bundled both the latest flood reports and his outline for a one-act satire into his briefcase when he made a lightning trip to New York to speak at Brooklyn College.[2]

Hopkins returned in time to join twenty other guests for a 7:30 dinner in the State Dining Room. Early, advisers Edwin "Pa" Watson and Marvin McIntyre, secretaries Grace Tully and Missy LeHand, Eleanor, the president's son James, and other intimates saluted FDR for another momentous year. A festive mood prevailed as attendees finished their meals and arranged themselves in comfortable chairs to watch the performances. Eleanor offered a glorious disquisition on her (actually ghostwriter Missy Le-Hand's) chosen text: "Old Father Franklin, he went to the cupboard / To get his poor dog a bone." Following a straight-faced inquiry into the significance of "the cupboard" ("not one of the cupboards, nor the right hand one or the left hand one or the one above or the one under the floor but just *the* cupboard"), she reasoned with the dogged intensity of a Talmudic scholar that, had there been "a little surplus commodity or some National Youth Administration cake or some WPA ditches . . . poor old Father Franklin and his dog might have found themselves a living."[3]

Conviviality spread as the drinks flowed. Marvin McIntyre's ode to "His Royal Majesty Roosevelt the First" chided critics who portrayed FDR as a potential dictator. Speechwriter Samuel Rosenman's poem derided the Supreme Court's opinions that the National Recovery Administration and the Agricultural Adjustment Administration, two key elements of the New Deal, were unconstitutional. "The farmers were in gravy (which came not from pork or beef)," Rosenman read, "Until the black-robed bozos laid the whole thing cold in grief."

Another high point came when guests dived into a farcical trial of Eleanor Roosevelt titled "Mis-Trial by Per-Jury." A prosecutor charged the first lady with suggesting that "the innocent, fragile, flowerlike womanhood of America should soil itself by knowing what happens in the wild and wicked world outside of her second home." FDR chortled when he heard her sentence. "You are to abstain from being interviewed or photographed," the judge declared, "from receiving delegates of patriotic societies, labor unions, peace advocates, war advocates, and middle-of-the-road advocates, winners of spelling bees and hog-calling contests, as well as from accepting gifts of 1,000-pound cheeses, pincushions embroidered with the American flag, crocheted bed-socks . . . , or poetic tributes to yourself as wife, mother, and First Lady of the Land." Eleanor thanked her jailer for going to such trouble on her behalf and for making "such *interesting* charges." She then linked arms with the judge, bailiff, and prosecutor and danced off the stage.

Early and Hopkins then unveiled their masterpiece, a faux radio drama about the flood. Earlier performers had engaged the tragedy. Eleanor's close friends Marion Dickerman and Nancy Cook mentioned it in their odes to the president. "I smiled up at the downpour / Knowing—My Hero would save me soon," Cook's tribute concluded. In contrast to this fawning treatment, the exhausted press guru and relief czar saw great humor in the disaster. An outside observer might view their skit as mean-spirited. Those present understood that their black comedy came from a sense of frustration.

The scene opened with an announcer from station FDR promising an inside view of the White House. His exposé reveals an administration at odds with the competent organization depicted in the press. Kentucky-born Marvin McIntyre plots to use the disaster as a springboard to the governor's seat. He blasts the "blankety-blank-blank" Happy Chandler and the "blankety-blank-blank" mayor of Louisville, Neville Miller. "If there are any mistakes which they haven't made," McIntyre says, "I will hear about them soon enough. For the first time in my life I am renouncing the State of my birth and claiming residence in Cincinnati." This attack on Chandler stemmed from Hopkins's conviction that the governor underestimated the desperation in Kentucky. "I want you to check up on the situation for me," was the constant refrain Hopkins heard from Frankfort. The administration's disgust lingered well past the emergency. A White House memo written a year later complained that "at the time of the 1937 flood, Happy Chandler put on rubber boots and rain coat and stepped into a rowboat to be photographed. This is his sole connection with rescue work."[4]

McIntyre got off lightly compared with the ribbing other administration members received. Secretary of War Harry Woodring planned to ride "the highest horse in the Army" to the flood zone just as soon as he finished distributing patronage jobs in his native Kansas. A clueless Missy LeHand divided her days between reading *Gone with the Wind* for the third time and sneaking out to swim in the pool owned by U.S. Maritime Commission chairman Joseph Kennedy. "I think the flood is very exciting," she says, but the sight of fatigued White House staffers napping in the Cabinet Room repels her. "I think all sleeping should be done in one's own office," she snorts. When the announcer arouses a slumbering Hopkins for a comment on the flood, the self-deprecating WPA chief says that "if there is anything to be done to make this flood worse, someone around here will think of it." Why, just now, Hopkins continues, Ohio governor Martin Davey invited him to take a trip down the river "in a nice, leaky boat."

No one in the fictionalized White House acknowledges the refrain of "Louisville calling the White House, Louisville calling the White House" ringing throughout the fifteen-minute comedy. According to the play, Pa Watson was off drinking in Louisville's exclusive Pendennis Club and Treasury Secretary Henry Morgenthau was tied up in a closed-door meeting—someone informed the secretary that the gold in Fort Knox had depreciated, so he was huddling with experts to learn what "depreciated" meant. Stephen Early staged a nonsensical press conference before disappearing for a round of golf and a four-hour lunch. The comedy reached a charming yet grim conclusion. "The reason the President keeps his health is that he is able to laugh," an announcer informed the audience. "Well, this mess certainly is funny."

Hopkins and Early's humor worked because the parodies captured their victims' essence even if, as everyone present knew, the play misrepresented their actions. It worked as a kind of team-building exercise, an opportunity for a close-knit bunch squeezed tighter by the pressing crisis to share a moment where they could look at each other and say, "Yes, that's you, all right." Their inside jabs and equal-opportunity ridicule must have tickled the good-humored Roosevelt.

After the performances the group presented FDR with an engraved sterling silver plate and a new chair. By then it was time for the president to give his birthday address. An attendant rolled him to a microphone waiting in the Diplomatic Reception Room. A small audience of movie stars and admirers rose when he arrived. FDR quietly reviewed the speech Early had written for him while an estimated five million birthday ball attendees waited for his broadcast, as did many more listening at home.

At 11:24 p.m., his back to a curved window framing the South Lawn, surrounded by a century-old wallpaper mural depicting America's natural beauty, he began talking to the "friends of crippled children" tuning in around the nation. He thanked the volunteers who organized birthday balls and everyone who paid to attend before shifting his attention to the Ohio valley crisis. Precisely enunciating each word in his crisp patrician voice, he asked Americans to donate not only to polio research, but also to the Red Cross. The agency has done a magnificent job so far, he said, "and I know that every dollar necessary to help the flood sufferers will be forthcoming from the rest of the Nation." Declaring this a moment of "high emergency," he demanded a "national effort on a national scale . . . to decrease the probability of future floods and similar disasters."[5]

FDR devoted about a minute to the flood before returning to the evening's main topic. His first nationally broadcast comment on the disaster was therefore a modest one that still managed to touch on several important points. In a rare fit of humility, the president minimized the federal government's service in order to highlight the Red Cross's rescue and relief funds. He also depicted the Ohio-Mississippi crisis as relevant to all Americans, not just those living in the valleys. This inclusive approach echoed the New Deal's emphasis on national interconnectedness and its desire to strengthen America's weakest links. As he had done numerous times over the past four years, Roosevelt urged listeners to recognize their common environmental interests. What was happening on the Ohio was more than a freak incident, more than a random act of nature. Rather, it marked a combination of unusual weather with two centuries' worth of human decisions. As he had during the 1927 disaster, FDR planted a vague notion of "national effort" into public rhetoric without articulating specific policies for editorialists and politicians to dissect. His obscurity did not conceal the fact that he viewed the crisis as a means for realizing his long-standing goal of instituting a national waterways program.

With his work completed for the evening, Roosevelt asked his aide to return him to a party that continued well into the night. He cleared his schedule for the next morning, making no official appearances until the French ambassador dropped by with his family for a late lunch. As the president enjoyed his slumber, tens of thousands of tired, dirty men piled sandbags along a score of rivers and a million people adjusted to life in refugee camps.

Roosevelt's address served its intended purpose. Contributions to the Red Cross spiked over the next several days. By February 1, donations approached $10 million, double what the agency had collected at the same point in the 1927 flood. "It would have been impossible to raise so large a fund in so short a time without radio's splendid aid," the Red Cross concluded.[6]

Franklin Roosevelt was the first president to exploit radio's power to mold opinions, advance political agendas, and mobilize popular support. His plea for donations did more to help flood victims than anything else he could have done. Widespread outrage might have ensued had the country known about his boozy, boisterous party, with its contempt for flood-area officials and jaunty disregard for the administration's handling of the crisis, but his unqualified endorsement of the Red Cross's efforts more than compensated for the unseemly moments in his private celebration.[7]

Radio played a limited role during the 1927 flood. As an infant industry it had a narrow reach beyond metropolitan areas and scattered amateur operators. Outside New Orleans few in the impoverished Mississippi Delta owned a radio receiver. Stations nevertheless publicized the plight of victims and ginned up support for relief efforts. Herbert Hoover, President Coolidge's point man in the emergency, used the radio to describe conditions on the ground and ask Americans who might otherwise feel disconnected from a faraway disaster to aid their countrymen.[8]

A decade later radio was an essential element of American life. A huge majority of people tuned in daily for news, music, and entertainment. Broadcast stars Jack Benny, Eddie Cantor, and Ed Wynn were household names. Besides having a far wider reach than in 1927, the medium also had a greater impact on Americans' understandings of this emergency because the populous Ohio valley had so many stations available to transmit up-to-the-minute news to the rest of the country. Their broadcasts guided rescue efforts, alerted individuals to impending danger, and shilled for the Red Cross. This "modern miracle conceived by man," gushed *Popular Mechanics*, "concentrated all its facilities in a grim battle with the most disastrous flood in American history. And radio won the fight."[9]

Radio reached its maturity in 1937, demonstrating for the first time its ability to cover a major disaster for days on end and proving its use as an informational tool in a time of crisis. Thousands of lives would have been lost without it. At the same time, it continued fusing the sprawling United States into a nation of shared experiences. A twist of a dial brought the flood roaring through your living room no matter how far you lived from a river. It became everyone's crisis as audiences everywhere experienced the woes of its actual victims.

Radio's local and national impact showed most clearly in broadcasters' coverage of Louisville, one of the hardest-hit towns on the Ohio. There more than anywhere the radio wove itself into the fabric of a community quite literally battling for survival. One contemporary account predicted that "for a considerable number of years to come Louisvillians . . . will speak of radio station WHAS and God with something of the same reverence." Fifty years later survivors still believed that WHAS's floodtime broadcasts represented "God's wonderful gift to man[,] the brightest hue in our rainbow."[10]

After fifteen years on the air, WHAS had become a local institution. As with many early stations, its birth resulted from a combination of commercial and idealistic impulses. Herbert Hoover's Commerce Department awarded Louisville's Robert Worth Bingham a federal radio license in 1922. Bingham was a well-connected plutocrat, a former mayor and judge who later served as Roosevelt's ambassador to the Court of St. James. His ownership of the *Louisville Times* and *Louisville Courier-Journal* made him the city's primary media mogul. He hoped his leap into radio would consolidate his dominance. Bingham also saw radio as a powerful weapon in his lifelong crusade to expand access to education. "I want a radio station that will reach into the farthest confines of the state," he said, "where a man may string an aerial from his cabin to the nearest pine tree, and sitting in his chair before the fire, have a pew in a church, a seat at the opera, a desk at the university."[11]

Bingham put his friend Credo Harris, a newspaperman with no experience in the radio business, in charge of WHAS. Bingham gave Harris a simple directive: "It must be a radio station which above all else is built on character and conducted with unvarying good taste." On July 15, 1922, Harris spoke the first words ever commercially aired in the state. "This is WHAS, the radio telephone broadcasting station of the *Courier-Journal* and *Louisville Times* of Louisville, Kentucky," he intoned in a serious, tenor voice to the handful of people listening on crystal sets. His operation was by today's standards a shoestring affair. WHAS's aerial broadcast with a mere 500 watts of power from atop the Courier-Journal and Times Building, a four-story limestone-clad structure four blocks south of the Ohio in the heart of downtown. A three-person staff oversaw its small office, primitive control room, and burlap-padded studio during the station's two and a half hour broadcast schedule. Harris himself played "My Old Kentucky Home" on a set of chimes before shutting down the station for the night.[12]

Rudimentary as it was, Harris's outfit had an innovative spirit that enhanced its popularity. WHAS mingled live performances of so-called hillbilly music with baseball games recreated from wire reports and remote broadcasts transmitted over telephone lines. Audiences in 1924 thrilled to Harris's on-air conversation with screen queen Mary Pickford. The following year brought suspense-packed updates on the travails of Floyd Collins, an amateur spelunker who became an international media sensation after getting trapped, and eventually dying, in a cave in central Kentucky. A few months later Harris perched in the cupola above Churchill Downs to provide live post-to-pole coverage of Flying Ebony's victory in the Kentucky Derby. WHAS's weak signal did not prevent far-off listeners from tuning in; fan mail arrived from as far away as London, Honduras, and Sydney.[13]

WHAS enlarged its capacities as it matured. A transmitter installed in 1928 increased its output to 5,000 watts. Four years later it boosted its strength to 50,000 watts, making it one of the most powerful stations in the United States. At night its signal reverberated across the eastern two-thirds of the country. Its growing staff moved into larger, plusher surroundings on the second floor of the Courier-Journal and Times Building. By 1937 the station broadcast eighteen hours a day. WHAS supplemented local programs with CBS network feeds of the New York Philharmonic, Al Jolson, and Benny Goodman's orchestra, along with several beloved soap operas and children's serials.[14]

WHAS first acknowledged the rising waters on January 21 when an announcer inserted a brief advisory between *Melodies and Moods* and *The Romance of Helen Trent.* "A warning just received from the Louisville weather bureau says: the Ohio Valley is facing the most alarming flood we have ever had on the Ohio River," he read. "If this rain should continue another twenty-four hours—which it doubtless will—the greatest flood in the history of the Ohio River and its tributaries is imminent. Warning! Hold yourselves in readiness to move to higher ground on a moment's notice— and if the water is near any of your houses in lowlands, move out before nightfall!"[15]

Louisville, constructed on loose alluvial sands and glacial gravels deposited millennia ago when the Ohio's channel ran through the present downtown area, had always been prone to inundation, but few people anticipated anything worse than a mild wetting. Most believed the river had reached its ultimate peak when it hit 46.7 feet in 1884. Utility companies built power plants and water pumping stations against a forty-seven-foot crest, ten feet below the river's final 1937 mark.[16]

It was easy to ignore the water soaking the riverfront, home to about three thousand drifters and river rats occupying shotgun shacks sided with unpainted pine boards. Indoor plumbing in the Point, the sliver of land between Beargrass Creek and the Ohio, was as rare as prostitution was common. Shippingport, an island carved out during the early nineteenth-century construction of the Louisville and Portland Canal, was similarly disreputable. Its inhabitants' disregard for overflows had changed little since Anthony Trollope observed them during the 1862 high water. "The men who were not at work in the boats stood loafing about in clusters, looking at the still rising river; but each seemed to be personally indifferent to the matter," the amazed novelist wrote. "Surely there is no other people so passive under personal misfortune!"[17]

Fueled by its surging tributaries, the Ohio jumped six feet higher on the day of WHAS's initial report. Harris dispatched half a dozen announcers wearing hip boots, raincoats, and sturdy hats to interview stranded flooders. Mayor Neville Miller, who had just returned from the inaugural, phoned in his assessment from a soon to be evacuated grocery store. Clad in waterproof boots and a rubber coat, he assured listeners that relief efforts were under way. He had assembled an emergency flood committee, and the Kentucky National Guard and Jeffersonville Quartermaster Depot could provide all necessary support. The situation warranted caution rather than concern. Louisville's street cleaning department made plans to relocate 250 families to hotels. Studio announcer E. A. Jonas took a lighthearted tone toward the overflow in his nightly report. "Water, water, everywhere, and not a drop to drink," he joked after reading a warning to boil or chemically treat tap water. He explained that receding waters can pollute the drinking supply, so the potential for typhoid was high now that the worst had passed.[18]

Jonas entered the building at nine that evening. When he left at eleven, water blocked his streetcar journey home. He made multiple transfers around the expanding flood zone before finally reaching his door. The next morning he hailed a taxi to drive him through a sleet storm to the studio and arrived to find that water had infiltrated the building. His colleagues watched from the windows as umbrella-wielding pedestrians rushed to Kaufman-Straus and other stores to buy lamps, candles, coal oil, and groceries. WHAS interrupted normal programming throughout the day to read official warnings to evacuate low ground. Employees sensed a long battle ahead. "Getting ready for siege," Jonas noted.[19]

Confusion spread as the Ohio shot past its 1884 crest. Refugees from Jeffersonville, Kosmosdale, Medora, and elsewhere searched a shrinking circle of dry streets for shelter as cars clogged the few passable roads out of town. A few drivers caught in the snarl gaped at the sight of a stolid group of habited nuns hitching a ride in the back of an Oertel's beer truck. Train and bus service came to a halt. Mayor Miller closed filling stations to save gasoline and shut off streetlights to conserve electricity. Movie palaces concluded afternoon screenings of *Bulldog Drummond Escapes*, *Fugitive in the Sky*, and *Smart Blonde* before closing their doors. Frustrated citizens jammed city hall demanding information from anyone who looked important. "Everyone is asking questions," one police officer said, "and since we wear uniforms we are supposed to know the answers, but we don't. No one knows the answers. No one knows where anything is or who to take orders from."[20]

Skeptical Louisvillians doubted the danger until the moment malodorous water spewed from nearby manholes or burbled up through their basement drains. "Everything happened so fast," WHAS employee Catherine Steele remembered. An evacuee who returned home to collect warm clothes for his wife and children discovered when he tried to leave that the water had trapped him. He phoned the radio station in a panic. "Lady, the water is around my waist now," he cried. "Which way can I get out of here?" Families called their neighbors to ask whether they thought the water would reach them. They tracked the flood's progress against stationary objects, watching as it consumed a mailbox, a tree, a car across the street.[21]

WHAS's telephones rang often enough to convince studio executives that this was no ordinary flood. They decided to forgo normal programming in favor of an all-flood schedule. Rather than introducing the next show, announcers read from a growing stack of news bulletins and calls for rescue. They advised callers seeking dry routes to "go home and stay home." The sheer number of pleas for deliverance spawned confusion. There was no clear chain of command, no real organization, and great duplication of effort. Multiple teams of boatmen arrived at the same address. WHAS unwittingly forwarded spurious aid requests from concerned individuals who wanted boats sent to a friend's or family member's house because they heard reports of flooding nearby.[22]

Most station employees spent the night in the office, either from a sense of duty or because they could not reach their homes. Those who left returned through a cold, gray dawn obscured by a sleet storm. Inside the building there was chaos. Southern Bell crews installing additional telephones dodged WHAS staffers rushing messages to the announcer's booth. Volunteers from the newspaper side supplemented the station's score of engineers, clerical workers, salesmen, and directors. Employees brewed coffee, answered phones, and relayed reports without regard to hierarchy. Everyone pored over topographical maps spread across the floor, straining to determine how the latest river predictions affected specific neighborhoods.[23]

Credo Harris posted a team on the nineteenth floor of the Kentucky Home Life building, two blocks to the west, and scattered other announcers and field engineers around the city. Reporters climbed telephone poles to catch a better view of their surroundings. Their eyewitness dispatches enlivened the steady stream of announcements: the next streets to be flooded, calls for boats, requests for supplies; public health experts asking listeners to boil water or get typhoid shots; broadcasters urging the city to be alert to the chance of fire. Open gas lines were likely to rupture, and a glistening layer of oil from riverfront refineries presented another obvious threat. Exhausted station workers feared a spark from the oil lamps, gasoline heaters, and diesel generators around the studio might start a blaze. Typists kept emptying wastepaper baskets in case someone got careless with a match.[24]

On the morning of Black Sunday, WHAS warned everyone west of Fifteenth Street to evacuate. Water had trapped tens of thousands of people downtown and in the city's East End. The Ohio's current ran so fast and deep that some believed it would cut a permanent new channel through the heart of town. "Truly it seems that nothing is impossible," one bewildered member of the mayor's inner circle responded to the rumors of a realignment.[25]

Authorities knew that Louisville's power generators and telephone exchanges would soon succumb. An executive from Louisville Gas and Electric called WHAS at four in the afternoon to report that its power supply would fail sometime after eight that night. His message sent technicians scrambling for a way to stay on the air. Lead announcer Pete Monroe shared the ominous news with listeners. "All electric current will be cut off," he said. "There will be no current for light nor heat nor for broadcasting our bulletins." Executive Lee Coulson sent a blunt teletype to Harry Stone, manager of WHAS's greatest rival, Nashville station WSM. "Our power goes out at eight tonight," Coulson wrote. "We want your transmitter." Stone wired a response minutes later. "She's yours, immediately, if you want her. And as long as you need her."[26]

WHAS could not capitalize on WSM's offer unless it also secured electrical and phone service. Battery-powered generators could keep the station

Carrying equipment borrowed from Philadelphia station WFIL, WHAS announcers Pete Monroe (*left*) and Foster Brooks (*right*) report on the rising waters. © The Courier-Journal.

going for the moment, but engineers needed a stronger, more dependable power supply. Linemen from Louisville Gas and Electric started stringing a cable from the Courier-Journal and Times Building to the Dix Dam hydroelectric plant, forty miles to the southeast. This was a dangerous job. "Switches will be closed at midnight," the crew heard over its portable radio. Power would start coursing through the line at that time regardless of their progress, bringing with it the possibility of electrocution.[27]

WHAS's off-site transmitter would lose power even if the station's offices remained electrified, so Harris's troops needed a telephone connection to carry their signal to WSM's facility. The Salt River had submerged eighteen miles of telephone poles along the Louisville-Nashville line, rendering the circuit inoperative. Southern Bell promised to restore service as soon as possible. An unknown electrical wizard hurried to the point where the poles went under, joined all forty phone lines into a single cable, and boated across to do the same at the other end. Technicians tested each line in the mass until they found a combination strong enough to transmit a voice to Nashville. The sound popped and whistled and went dead for brief spells. A piece of debris or a surge of current could cut Louisville off from the rest of the world. But it would have to do for now.[28]

Louisville Gas and Electric's Canal Station plant went silent at 8:30, leaving its Riverside plant as the city's sole source of electricity. Its fate lay in the hands of thirty-eight-year-old oiler William Thomas, who spent the evening of Black Sunday in a condenser well one hundred feet below the water's surface. His job was to operate the pumps that kept seep water from infiltrating the station's remaining generators. Working five stories above him, seventy-five of his colleagues shored up the well with timber and sandbags. Thomas refused to give up even after it became clear that the battle was lost. "I'll be damned if I'll come [out] until the walls cave in," he shouted into the blackness above him.[29]

Louisville's telephone exchanges started failing once the Ohio reached Southern Bell's low-lying offices, not long before the Riverside plant's general superintendent persuaded Thomas to abandon his post. Water knocked the city's last electric generators out of commission at 11:39 p.m. The Riverside plant was a local landmark whose thirty-foot sign proclaiming Louisville the Gateway to the South was one of the first things visitors saw as they crossed the bridge from Indiana. Now it was a useless hunk of brick and stone erected too close to the river to survive the emergency. Radios, except those running on batteries, went dead. Louisville plunged into darkness.[30]

WHAS personnel fired up their generators to begin broadcasting through WSM's transmitter. CBS plugged the WHAS feed into its network, turning Louisville's plight into a subject of national interest. WLAP in Lexington, WCKY in Covington, and WFBM in Indianapolis hooked into the relay. Eventually about two hundred stations and five thousand shortwave operators rebroadcast WHAS's flood messages on what radio men called the Volunteer Inter-City Network. Federal Communications Commission officials waived regulations prohibiting stations from picking up a competitor's feed on the grounds that the improvised radio web encouraged donations to the Red Cross. Washington also OK'd the BBC's request to carry WHAS's signal.[31]

Radio listeners sat on the edges of their seats as Pete Monroe, Joe Eaton, and young Foster Brooks, who later enjoyed a long career as a comedian, spent hour after hour reading from a stack of cards:

"A boat is needed immediately at 229½ South 18th Street. There is a confinement case [pregnant woman] at this location which must be removed to City Hospital at once."

"Send a boat at once to Eighteenth and Main. Six people there. Two old people and a baby. Water rising rapidly."

"Owner of hardware store at Twelfth and Maple authorizes relief workers to break in store for flashlights and batteries."

"Cancel call for powerboat to take nurse to Fontaine Ferry."

"Police department calling. Urgent. Fifty refugees must be moved immediately by boat from 1023 West Madison Street. This is imperative."

"Carrolton, Kentucky, is in desperate need of 1,000 cc's of typhoid vaccine, 1,000 blankets, and all possible coal. The city is completely isolated and almost totally submerged. Will someone having a large powerboat or a plane capable of making this trip please get in touch at once with the County Medical Officer? This is a desperate emergency."

"Embalmers are urgently needed at Waverly Hills Sanitarium. The situation there is critical. All embalmers please report to Waverly Hills."[32]

The signal crackled and dipped as emergencies piled up. Each diminuendo sent hearts fluttering as the sound—and the tens of thousands trapped in Louisville—threatened to disappear from the ether. Fatigued announcers ignored the surrounding turmoil as they plowed forward. More than anything, what kept Brooks, Monroe, and the rest of WHAS going was knowing that they were saving lives. Even Louisvillians with dead radios heard their broadcasts from a fleet of sound trucks patrolling the edges of the flood zone.[33]

WHAS afforded a crucial outlet for Mayor Neville Miller, who became one of the most prominent voices emanating from the valley. His broadcasts assumed an upbeat tone without sounding naive. Louisville will survive with aid from the state, the federal government, and the Red Cross, he told listeners. Miller had to row the three blocks from heavily sandbagged city hall to WHAS until phone company workers installed a direct wire between the two buildings. Linemen drove wooden pegs under the receiver hooks to ensure that no one accidentally hung up. In city hall a police sergeant and a newspaper reporter took turns dictating messages, passing the telephone to the mayor whenever he needed to talk on the air. Whoever was handling WHAS's side at that moment faced an interesting problem: needing to keep both hands free to type. One creative mind solved this dilemma by taping the earpiece to her head and hanging the mouthpiece from a belt looped around her neck.[34]

Miller's calm public persona concealed massive confusion inside city hall. A viscous scum of oil, gasoline, sewage, and river water pounded the sandbags surrounding the seventy-year-old building. Kerosene lamps threw a shaky light over the hungry flooders packing the hallways. Exhausted, unshaven officials wobbled under the strain, hands quivering and voices trembling as they tackled an endless series of crises. A relentless litany of appeals for help added steam to the pressure cooker. "Only the mayor preserves his marvelous cheerfulness," one awed observer noted. Indeed, Miller appeared unaffected by the emergency. Accustomed to putting in eighteen-hour days since assuming office at the bottom of the Depression, he took a business as usual approach, catching catnaps when he could and performing his cheerleader role to perfection.[35]

Mayor Miller's steady leadership made him one of the heroes of 1937. He expected no less of himself. A tall yet unimposing man with thinning dark hair, he had a piercing gaze conveying a deep self-confidence tempered by compassion for the downtrodden. His father, a respected judge and an outspoken Democratic politician, raised his son to love the law and public service. After earning degrees from Princeton and Harvard, Miller came home to work in his father's firm and join the faculty of the University of

Louisville's law school. He left private practice in 1930 to become dean of the school, then resigned his post after winning the 1933 mayoral election.

Miller ran as a New Deal Democrat who also glorified rugged individualism. He saw no contradiction in arguing simultaneously that real men raised themselves by their bootstraps and that the government should assist victims of the Depression. Miller tried to transcend party lines, committing himself above all to good government. Like Cincinnati's Clarence Dykstra, he eliminated corruption, rooted out wasteful spending, and used an influx of federal relief funds to slash the city's budget while expanding services. His largesse extended into a black community that not coincidentally played a major role in his narrow victory. The mayor appointed African Americans to low-level government positions and improved recreational facilities in black neighborhoods. Yet segregation in Louisville remained intact—ushers roped off the left side of Memorial Auditorium's balcony for blacks attending his inauguration.[36]

Miller was a confident, levelheaded man who embraced leadership. "Regardless of others' advice," he told a friend, "the final decision must always be yours, and the responsibility yours." His flood committee assembled three times a day to update him on rescue operations, transportation, and vital supplies. Miller ordered members to cut bureaucratic corners whenever lives were at stake. If refugees need food—go get it. If rescuers need boats—confiscate private vessels. At first he froze out the incompetent local Red Cross chapter, then he gave it space near his office once experienced operatives from National Headquarters took charge. More important than any concrete actions, Miller's authoritative voice provided a constant companion for an isolated city. His frequent radio appearances left no doubt that Louisville was in able hands.[37]

WHAS's special report continued hour after hour. Announcers replaced their animated radio patter with a hushed monotone that preserved their voices while disguising their emotions. After a few days, that faded into what one listener remembered as "a dead singsong." Children caught in upper stories, babies requiring medical attention, and elderly folks facing starvation blurred into meaningless strings of words scanned through eyes heavy from sleeplessness. "Merely a set of figures," WHAS staffer J. Kenneth Jones later wrote, "figures of which we had long grown weary but with which we forced ourselves to be accurate." A few reports hit the crew hard, including one notifying medical personnel that the mayor of Philadelphia had sent four thousand gallons of embalming fluid, but for the most part exhaustion trumped emotion. Monroe, Eaton, and the other readers just wanted to reach the bottom of the pile of typewritten notices.[38]

WHAS's office resembled a refugee center, which in a sense it was, because few employees could go home even if they wanted to. Candles and oil lamps cast uncertain shadows on the walls. Dozing staffers wrapped in blankets covered the floor of Studio B. Others tried to nap on tables. Although exhausted, many of them were too wound up to sleep unless they soothed their frazzled nerves with bottles of smuggled whiskey. Occasional voices pierced the gloom: "Take your typhoid shots." Even Barry Bingham, Robert Worth Bingham's son and the effective head of the *Courier-Journal* and *Louisville Times*, took shifts at the microphone. His time on the air allowed him a respite from fretting about his hospitalized wife, who gave birth two days before Black Sunday.[39]

As if worrying about the whole city were not emotionally draining enough, studio workers also had to consider their own futures. A few escaped confinement for a few hours to visit their waterlogged neighborhoods. "I think I left the window open," technician Carl Schmidt deadpanned as he paddled between rooftops to view his inundated home.

Most excursions involved gathering supplies rather than tourism, as when engineer Carl Nielsen joined the manager of a Sears store on an arduous quest for batteries. They rowed down Third Street until they reached the YMCA building, then turned west onto Broadway, where they saw the legendary Brown Hotel on their right. Hundreds of refugees jammed the building. Red Cross nurses had converted the tenth floor into a command center. It "seemed as if the whole world had decided that this was a sort of Gibraltar and flocked here for safety," one tenant remembered. Conditions inside resembled those at WHAS. Several families crowded into each room. Dogs roamed the hallways. Bellboys delivered a glass jug of iodine-flavored water, courtesy of the Oertel Brewery, to each room daily. Bucket brigades relayed sewer backwater to flush toilets. Cooking was a nightmare. There was no shortage of food, as guests supplemented the hotel's ample reserves with fish caught in the lobby. The real issue was substandard equipment; the smoke from the oil-fueled emergency stoves was so foul that Mr. Brown permitted employees to dull their discomfort with one shot of whiskey every hour.[40]

Nielsen and his companion paddled past the Chesterfield Hotel, the federal courthouse, and the small stores lining Broadway. The imposing Sears building lay ahead on the corner of Eighth Street. Its fifty-foot tower rose well above the waterline, but its first floor lay beneath the waves. They rowed through the main entrance, navigating the aisles until they procured the battery-powered radios, dry-cell batteries, and storage batteries WHAS needed. Creature comforts came next as they rowed over to the apparel department for winter clothes. With their boat dangerously full, they turned homeward to share their bounty with the station's staff.[41]

Water covered about three-quarters of Louisville. Although many inhabitants had evacuated, tens of thousands still occupied pockets around the city. The Highlands district southeast of downtown sat above the waterline, as did a few other middle- and upper-class neighborhoods. All were vulnerable to communicable disease, and Mayor Miller believed the public health threat merited drastic action to clear out stragglers. Fatigued policemen and National Guardsmen were unable to evict bitter-enders without assistance. "Our greatest need is for fresh manpower," Miller told the national audience listening to WHAS's feed. Off the air he asked Governor Chandler and federal officials to declare martial law so they could dispatch regular army troops to relieve his force.[42]

Chandler urged FDR to send infantrymen. The situation in Louisville was "so serious that the National Guard is taxed to its capacity and cannot handle it," he reported. Secretary of War Woodring and army chief of staff Craig demurred, citing the heavy demands on soldiers in the area and ongoing negotiations with Miller over how to use troops. An outraged Miller fired off telegrams to Chandler, who was busy dealing with the prisoners trapped in the state penitentiary, and to Kentucky's United States senators, Alben Barkley and Marvel Logan. "Flood situation here desperate imperative need for at least two regiments of infantry," his wire read. "Eliminate all formality and give us action. . . . Have already lost 20 hours in trying to get action at Washington and do not know how many deaths have resulted." Factions within the military agreed with Miller. Brigadier General G. L. McClain of the Kentucky National Guard begged General Craig to dispatch troops "regardless of regulations," as "you may be assured that this request [would] not be made unless positively necessary."[43]

On the evening of January 25 the governor issued an executive order putting the mayor "in supreme charge and direction of all civil and military authorities and agencies in the city of Louisville." Army brass finally consented to send in troops and trucks. Chandler publicized his decision on WHAS the next morning, explaining that "civil officers are unable to protect the lives, health, and property" of Louisvillians. Only federal soldiers could guarantee the "preservation of peace, protection of lives and the health of all citizens." Miller took to the air later to alleviate fears of a federal takeover. "The army is not running the city," he noted, and "neither is the National Guard." Civilians were in charge even though armored cars were scouring the East End for holdouts, rifle-wielding soldiers barred anyone without a pass from the flood zone, and police departments from fourteen states had answered Miller's request for additional men. Martial law in fact was not martial law in name.[44]

With most of Louisville underwater, WHAS's flood coverage moved into a new phase. Announcers no longer needed to list neighborhoods in immediate peril. "Send a boat" messages grew rarer once rescue teams evacuated critical cases. WHAS evolved into a logistical hub connecting a patchwork of local, state, and national agencies. The station cooperated with city hall, the Red Cross, and the military to direct men and supplies around the outskirts of the inundated area. It also retained its role as a morale booster by giving Mayor Miller a platform for his hopeful updates.

WHAS's ongoing presence buoyed hopes for Louisville. Shawneetown was silent, as were Jeffersonville, Mound City, Paducah, Portsmouth, and scores of other communities. Louisville had a voice. So long as WHAS kept talking, victims could believe the Ohio had not closed the Gateway to the South forever. Normality would return. "Our people began to realize that Louisville was not cut off from the outside world, but rather that people all over the United States were sharing our difficulties and straining every resource to help us," Barry Bingham later said. "It was then that we began to realize the great power of radio."[45]

WHAS performed another service the day after Governor Chandler declared martial law, when it guided refugees trapped downtown to a pontoon bridge leading over Beargrass Creek to safety in the Highlands. In normal times the stream separated the former wetlands the central city occupied from the elevated area to the east. Floodwaters transformed it into a fast-flowing channel of the main river that neither truck nor train nor streetcar could span. Debris-filled whirlpools covering Broadway cleaved Louisville into two isolated halves.

Fire department mechanic Jack Britt devised a means of crossing the gap. "Why don't they take the barrels at the distillery on Lexington Road and build a pontoon bridge?" he asked his chief. Britt's inspiration may have come from watching children collect floating barrel staves for the one-cent bounty distillers paid for each returned piece. The mayor's committee sat on his idea until Black Sunday, when a team of engineers and architects hashed out the details by lantern light in the Broadway Street Federal Building, two blocks east of the Sears store that Carl Nielsen later plundered.[46]

After making their final plans the mayor's men asked WHAS to broadcast an appeal for workers. A motley group of three hundred craftsmen, bankers, clerks, and lawyers answered the summons, studied the blueprints, and started hammering. Architects fashioned a bare-bones proposal appropriate to the improvised workforce and substandard conditions. Carpenters nailed lumber from local mills into cages capable of holding three empty fifty-gallon whiskey barrels, then anchored the frames to telephone poles. Crews toiling in waist-deep water laid a walkway of planks and affixed handrails. Electricians placed lights every six feet along the course. By the end of the day the squad had lashed fourteen hundred barrels into a two-thousand-foot span. Their shaky but serviceable bridge began downtown on Jefferson Street, ran above the raging Beargrass, and terminated at the Highlands.[47]

Hordes of people rode anything that floated to the foot of the bridge. Soldiers, policemen, and WPA enrollees formed the crowd into a long line. One by one flooders tottered between parallel rows of half-submerged billboards and telephone poles. The bridge held steady for the first third of its length, then began pulling with the current. Crossers instinctively stuck to the middle of the walkway; stepping too close to the edge tilted the bridge enough to send water over the top. Then they rushed to the other side to compensate, swaying it the opposite way. After seesawing for about a minute, the line rediscovered its collective center of gravity. Its slow crawl toward freedom resumed, at least until someone threw the whole thing out of whack again. On reaching the far shore, one agitated woman fell to her knees and cried, "I don't care where you take me so long's you take me away from this water."[48]

At its peak the whiskey-barrel structure delivered 35,000 exiles a day to buses and trucks that carried them to camps throughout central and southern Kentucky. Thirty-six corpses also made the crossing. The bridge was a one-way passage; Mayor Miller wanted everyone out. No one got back in without one of the mustard yellow passes his committee issued to a handful of people with official business in the flood zone.[49]

The emptying of Louisville again shifted the station's coverage. A growing proportion of bulletins aimed to reunite separated families or reassure friends and relations that loved ones had escaped harm. "Calling W. F. Gardner, calling W. F. Gardner," ran a typical message, "your sister is safe at Union City." "Calling all relief stations, all relief stations," went another. "James Cross, age five, separated from family in evacuation. Where is James Cross? Find James Cross. Advise, please. We will inform mother." One can imagine frantic searching through Red Cross tents, the panic in the parents' hearts, listeners leaning in a little closer to their sets. WHAS finally delivered the good news that the boy had turned up in a relief camp in Richmond, Kentucky.[50]

Happy news momentarily eased the tension in the dark, stuffy studio. Frustrated telephone operators struggled to verify statements they passed to announcers. Tangled chains of command made it difficult to know where to refer messages. WHAS cleared up most of the snarls once it started transferring calls for boats to city hall rather than reading them over the air. And along with all the uplifting items the office broadcast, staffers endured persistent rumors of widespread death. Mayor Miller spun these dire reports as best he could. "So far as we have been able to ascertain, there have been no mass drownings and no great number of casualties from the flood itself," he informed listeners. Louisville had perhaps two hundred dead, he argued, far below the wild estimates gaining traction in the press.[51]

Station employees worked in conditions approximating World War I trenches. With their blank stares, they looked like shell-shocked soldiers. Walls closed in on staffers who had spent a week inside the building, breathing air reeking of gasoline, sweat, and sewage. Many did not know whether their homes were standing or where their families were. People broke under the pressure. One punch-drunk announcer could not stop giggling as he lamented the fate of "remooned" Louisvillians—his conflation of "removed" and "marooned." On another occasion an employee suddenly unleashed a shriek that shocked the noisy rooms into silence. Colleagues delivered her to an emergency hospital for medical care. This incident led station executives to replace the frenzied, "go on until you collapse" routine with regular twelve-hour shifts. They secured a few unheated rooms in nearby hotels so their weary crew could sleep in beds instead of on the floor or on tables. Although they lacked running water, the accommodations at least provided a respite from the Courier-Journal and Times Building.[52]

Overworked employees cherished the few moments of levity during their marathon. They laughed for hours about the man who burst into the studio shouting "This is urgent!" He started babbling about a fire at a local varnish plant. Then he fixed his gaze on the microphone and realized he was screaming into a live national hookup. His eyes widened as he backed out of the room, alarmed to discover that the whole country had heard his rant.[53]

Even more memorable was the tragicomic arrival of poor Rabbi Solomon, whose determination to make his weekly broadcast produced a scene fit for a Hollywood farce. An acquaintance agreed to row the rabbi to the station, but his boat capsized in Beargrass Creek. Solomon insisted on continuing once rescuers fished them out. He arrived at the Courier-Journal and Times Building freezing and bedraggled. Employees dried him off, wrapped a blanket around his lower half, and handed him a dry shirt. Herb Cook, a studio organist who had been on duty for seventy-two sleepless hours, delivered the news that Solomon had arrived. "I've got the rabbi out here with no pants and some whiskey to keep him warm," he told his co-workers. Solomon collected his dignity as he sat down before the shadow-shrouded microphone. Wearing a ratty Dizzy Dean sweatshirt reading "Me and Paul," he launched into his service without a hitch in his voice.[54]

WHAS went off the air at 2:30 a.m. on February 1 after 187 hours and 30 minutes on the air. Its announcers had read 115,000 messages during the run, an average of one every six seconds. Barry Bingham, grimy and hollow-eyed from a week of catnaps on his office couch, made the final announcement. "The situation has now been brought under control to the extent where it is possible for this station to leave the air for a few hours," he said. "WHAS is now preparing to sign off with a final word of gratitude to all who have helped us in this crisis through which we have passed. From our hearts we say, 'we thank you, and good night.'"[55]

Telephone operators unwound the tape holding receivers to their heads and peered through the gloom at the oily yellow waves caressing the walls below. For the first time in days no sirens disrupted the eerie silence. The Ohio rode at 52.5 feet, well above flood stage but down from its crest of 57.1. It showed every indication of continuing its decline. Louisville had taken the flood's worst.

WHAS returned to the air several hours later. A few downtown store owners swept muck from their doorways and hung Open signs. Curious pedestrians wandered into districts that had been deep underwater a few

Abraham Lincoln appears to walk on water outside the Louisville Free Public Library soon after the crest. University of Louisville Special Collections.

days earlier. Mayor Miller lifted quarantine restrictions on some neighborhoods. Stragglers stuck their heads out from upstairs windows to ask passing boatmen for news of the outside world.[56]

Cynics including University of Louisville sociologist Robert Kutak saw WHAS's performance as typical of a society built on entertainment rather than introspection and entranced with the notion of constantly updated news, or what we today call the twenty-four-hour news cycle. For him WHAS offered a vicarious thrill, the broadcast equivalent of experiencing a disaster by watching *San Francisco* or reading *Gone with the Wind*. "The radio audience enjoyed a ring-side seat without leaving the comfortable arms of the living-room chair," Kutak asserted. Red Cross bureaucrats complained in an internal report that WHAS's unauthorized appeals for aid and supplies created unnecessary duplication of effort and generated widespread panic. Most took a more generous perspective. "WHAS stood like a stone wall," one aspiring poet rhapsodized, "Rendering, perhaps, best service of all; / Working untiringly, counting no cost; / Without them, thousands had been lost." Another would-be Keats wrote, "Their messages brought prompt relief / To thousands in distress / So let us not forget the boys / of WHAS."[57]

WHAS saved countless lives, and by keeping morale high and broadcasting word of the city's survival, it set the stage for Louisville's postflood revival. The station's story serves as a microcosm of radio's contributions to rescue, supply, and fund-raising efforts across the Ohio and Mississippi valleys. Along a thousand miles of river, in villages and cities across the United States, radio transformed what a decade earlier would have been a regional disaster into a global event. Broadcast journalists risked their lives to keep audiences informed. WBBM Chicago broadcast from an airplane circling besieged Cairo. NBC reporters in Portsmouth, Ohio, sent shortwave transmissions from a boat floating outside the abandoned Uptown Lunch café. Listeners sent the Red Cross $100,000 in response to requests from Memphis stations WMC and WREC. "Radio Priest" Father Charles Coughlin, one of America's most powerful on-air presences, contributed an impassioned prayer to the chorus of voices. "I have never stood before a microphone to beg for money for myself," he told his audience of thirty million, but "in this instance a sin of omission is as serious as a sin of commission."[58]

Behind the networks and local stations lay a web of ham radio operators. For a time attorney Warren Middleton's shortwave station W9CXD provided Paducah's sole means of radio communication. A phone company employee strung a line from the Red Cross's local headquarters to Middleton's house. The agency then called in messages that he, with his wife and three other radio enthusiasts who took turns at the microphone, transmitted to other ham operators. W9CXD stood down after 175 hours on the air. An amateur in Dyersburg, Tennessee, relayed broadcasts from WMC in Memphis, a center of refugee activity. The weary man sounded apologetic when a friend asked several days into the crisis how he was holding up. "I haven't had but three hours of sleep since Friday," he replied, "an' I'm gettin' kind of tired. I can hold on here a while yet, but if you can get me a relief operator I'd sure appreciate it."[59]

Rising waters forced a million people to flee for their lives. Whether famous or unsung, these radio staffers were among those who stayed behind. They shared the valley with a smattering of other residents who for various reasons chose to remain in their homes.

CHAPTER SIX

THOSE WHO STAYED

〜〜〜〜〜

Louisville Courier-Journal REPORTER Edward Neil imagined he would see a watery wasteland when he joined the crew of the Coast Guard launch *Port Huron* on a rescue and supply mission. He boarded from the new dock at Eighteenth and Broadway and set off into the churning river that was Louisville. Lookouts on the prow scanned for submerged cars and hollered Duck! when the vessel approached trolley lines. The westbound craft chugged past twelve blocks of silent distilleries, cigarette factories, and mud-smeared frame houses, then turned to port for a two-block cruise to collect supplies stashed in boxcars standing in three feet of water at Thirtieth and Garland. Neil marveled at the incongruity of the landscape. "It was the weirdest sight I've ever seen," he wrote. "There was nothing but a vast world of water. . . . You had to see it to believe it."

Contrary to expectations, Neil spied signs of life as the *Port Huron* bore north to the inundated West End. It was a bright, sunny day, the kind of January afternoon that inspires dreams of an early spring. Fishermen dangling lines from second-story windows were hoping for a warm breeze as much as for a fish. People living downstream from grocery stores snared floating food with baskets on ropes. The boat attracted attention because it carried provisions, the possibility of escape, and a distraction from the monotony. Sailors tossed bread into waiting arms and promised to alert rescue craft. All in all, Neil thought, stepping back onto the pier as the sun went down, it had been the strangest day of his life.[1]

Cities such as Louisville, Paducah, and Shawneetown hummed with life even after officials emptied them. Thousands of people, for reasons ranging from logical to foolish, chose to remain in their hometowns rather than to flee. Some who stayed remember those weeks as tolerable, even enjoyable. For others they marked a low point in their lives. The only commonality linking their diverse experiences was the river, that raging, savage force of nature whose potential for transport, military use, and commerce had inspired their ancestors to plant communities in its path.

MAYOR NEVILLE MILLER'S SOOTHING broadcasts on WHAS did not squelch the horrific rumors flying around inhabited pockets of Louisville. With normal communication systems underwater, newspapers nearly nonexistent, and radio reception erratic, most holdouts had only a tenuous connection with the world of facts. Many of the self-proclaimed FFV— filthy flood victims—trapped in houses and apartments believed the city had suffered up to 15,000 casualties. Stories of mass graves rang true to people living through a monumental catastrophe. News photos of workmen digging burial pits validated their fears. "They had pine box after pine box stacked up at a funeral home over on [Bardstown] Road & over in Cave Hill [Cemetery] they dug a trench & buried lots of bodies," one flooder wrote in early February. "The officials won't tell how many deaths," she continued. "Guess they want to keep it from the public [as] long as possible." These tales took weeks to quiet, as did gossip about various epidemics. An ill-informed Western Union operator reported that 2,500 Louisvillians had died. Newspapers in Vicksburg, New Orleans, and elsewhere reprinted his spurious claim.[2]

This imagined carnage seemed distant to the Hammer family, who rode out the flood in their modest two-story brick home near the corner of Twenty-sixth and Slevin, three-quarters of a mile from the Ohio on Louisville's west side. Anna Hammer's clan lived on a gentle rise that kept the water at their front gate. They had no electricity but were otherwise comfortable, a stark contrast to the scene in the *Courier-Journal* building a mile and a half to the east. "We have not suffered from the flood," they agreed.

Anna knew suffering, having in 1921 lost her thirty-nine-year-old husband George. His passing left her in charge of ten-month-old Bill, five-year-old George Jr., and fourteen-year-old Naomi. Friends in Louisville's sizable German Catholic community helped her raise the family. Soon after George's death Anna moved the kids two blocks north from their house on Cecilia, the house where their father died, to Twenty-sixth Street. They still lived there fifteen years later, surviving on George Jr.'s salary as a clerk and Naomi's wages as a finisher.

The Hammers had known the Reynards, who would be their guests during the flood, for at least a dozen years. Louis and Margaret Reynard lived two doors down before moving around the corner to Slevin Street in 1926. They later relocated a mile southwest to a two-story rental in a respectable neighborhood on Thirty-eighth Street. Louis was a modest success story whose Swiss-inflected French accent betrayed his foreign origins. He grew up in the tiny village of Savièse, Switzerland. In 1913, as an adventurous eighteen-year-old, he left for the United States by way of Le Havre. He came to Louisville from New York and worked his way up to foreman in a bakery. He and his wife Margaret had a sixteen-year-old daughter named Maggie. Margaret's mother, Ella Fleitz, and Margaret's stepfather Edward, an assistant foreman at a tobacco company, lived with the Reynards. Margaret's older brother Johnny lived near the train yard, a ten-minute walk to the west, close to his job with the Kentucky and Indiana railroad.

Although the Reynards and Fleitzes lived farther from the Ohio than the Hammers, their house sat at a lower elevation. The water rose so fast that they just had time to grab a few items of clothing before running to the Hammers' house. The nine of them—George Jr. was battling tuberculosis in Waverly Hills Sanitarium—joined periodically by other visitors, waited out the deluge in what they called the "Life Savers Hotel."[3]

Days were long in the "hotel." Occupants stared at the A&P across the street, watched the boats from the water's edge, and listened for word of the outside world. They had a good grasp of what was happening in Louisville but little sense of the valley beyond. They believed Black Sunday's fire in Cincinnati had obliterated half the city. Friends dropped in bearing news and supplies. Insignificant details of day-to-day life assumed great significance because they filled empty time. The families staged a grand debate on the best way to grind coffee beans that Bill, now a precocious sixteen-year-old, liberated from a deserted store. Crack them with a mallet, Edward suggested. No, crush them under the rockers of the chair, Ella countered. Mrs. Hammer severed the Gordian knot—perhaps too soon, considering their boredom—when she produced a food chopper. Hotel residents pecked out a few issues of a flood newspaper on the Hammers' typewriter. Needless to say, their sheet dealt with parochial affairs. Since none of them had seen a real paper in days, anything was better than nothing. At least it gave them something to talk about.

Guests and crew at the Life Savers Hotel never considered leaving town. They felt so secure on their elevated location that they even found their aquatic environment charming. "We have beautiful nights, with the moon shinning on the water," Margaret Reynard wrote. "It makes you feel as if you were in Venice. If only we had Gondiliers!" They cheered when Lee Ballard, a yardman for a petroleum company who lived around the corner, caught a fish in their front yard. But Ballard was outdone by the man who snagged a fifty-pound catfish half a mile away. An uncertain supply of drinking water and lack of working plumbing were the only real impediments to their comfort. A young woman marooned a few miles away with her parents and two stranded medical students acknowledged "the obvious fact that five people using one non-flushing toilet created problems. One precious pail of water was kept in the bathroom, to be used *very carefully*." The Hammers also had a hard time locating an open drugstore when Naomi took ill. An expedition had to hike through a mile of water to buy medicine at the Miersch Pharmacy.[4]

Floodtime realities sometimes forced their way through the lighthearted mood. A stroll downhill from the hotel led to an inundated neighborhood where people cried out from their rooftops and starving dogs howled for their masters. Errand runners inevitably returned with evil tidings—three corpses floating down Broadway after a funeral home flooded, an acquaintance who buried his dead infant in the basement.

The Reynards and Fleitzes carried the extra burden of not knowing whether their own home was intact. Determined to resolve this nagging question, Edward Fleitz and his stepson-in-law Louis Reynard got hold of a boat once the water started retreating. They found their house in bad shape. A ring of scum circled the walls. Water had ruined their furniture, including their pride and joy, a new baby grand piano. Their hardwood floors were warped beyond repair. The canary had died. They estimated it would take about a year to repair the damage. To make things worse, Louis had to rescue Edward when he tumbled into the icy water.

These worries aside, the group found plenty to be happy about. Mother Hammer cooked delicious meals in the fireplace. They had plenty of food because the police deputized Bill Hammer and Louis Reynard to protect the grocery store across the street, a duty that brought enviable privileges. "We got to take all the groceries we wanted," Bill told his brother George.

The younger deputy dropped off armloads of bacon, ham, bread, cigarettes, soda, and cheese at the house. He also lifted some choicer goods but refused to say what because, he explained in a letter to George, "Mom is afraid you will show this to someone else." To their credit, Bill and Louis also distributed boxes of groceries to hungry flooders.[5]

Bill enjoyed sharing his good fortune. One day he trudged through knee-deep water to see whether his Aunt Mamie needed food. He discovered her house dry but empty. A neighbor told him she and her daughter had decamped for Bloomington, Indiana. "Boy did I cuss," he wrote, not so much for the wasted effort as because his relative had forsaken Louisville. "Scare crows," he groused. Mamie lived a block from the railroad tracks and could have escaped had the water reached her. After all, he complained, his clan stayed even though they lived ten blocks from the tracks. "The best thing that I know for them is that they ought to make them stay [in Indiana] because they were so anxious to go away," he huffed in teenage pique.

Bill and Louis hung up their armbands for good after an incident-free night protecting "the Jew store," as they described Emil Hochstrasser's establishment on Slevin. "I really enjoyed what I did for ourselves and for every body else," Bill concluded. His one lingering concern was that he might have to return or pay for the felt-lined hip boots authorities issued him on his first day of work. "I am going to keep them until they call for them," he told George. Just to be sure, after scrubbing the mud from the $6.50 boots he boxed them up to hide them from anyone seeking restitution.

Bill Hammer's actions may not deserve to be labeled "looting," but plenty of other Louisvillians crossed that line. City merchants estimated that thieves cleaned out about 750 businesses, with groceries and drugstores hit the hardest. These numbers are difficult to confirm because water rather than looters carried away some goods. It is clear, however, that the combination of desperation and an overtaxed police department pushed many budding Jean Valjeans to commit acts alien to their usual natures. "This was my town," an astonished policeman mused. "I'd been born here and raised here. I couldn't *believe* it was happening."[6]

Stealing bread to feed a famished family was understandable and perhaps acceptable. The actions of brothers Jack and Tom Byrne went beyond decency. In an egregious act of looting, the two piloted a motorboat toward a liquor store at Twenty-sixth and Portland, eight blocks north of the Hammer hotel, with malice in mind. They made sure the place was deserted before draping a tarp over their heads, ramming their vessel through the window, and packing the boat with booze and cigarettes from shelves above the waterline. The Byrnes crashed through a different window on their way out. Not having much taste for alcohol, the brothers gladly shared their haul. They were far stingier with their purloined cigarettes, which were in their minds the real prize of the heist.[7]

Overmatched policemen and National Guardsmen fought back as best they could. The *Courier-Journal* reported in its little-read Black Sunday edition that police had orders to "shoot down looters." Director of safety Dunlap Wakefield issued a stronger statement two days later. Not only would police shoot looters, authorities would also pardon store guards who shot anyone caught breaking in or carrying stolen property. WHAS rebroadcast his message several times a day for the duration of the crisis. Yet the pilfering continued. "Attention all police in the vicinity of 18th Street and Broadway," one announcer intoned in an all-too typical message, "looting is being attempted at this location. This is an order from the Chief of Police of Louisville. You are instructed to shoot to kill if necessary."[8]

Mayor Miller needed help. An appeal for out-of-town policemen garnered quick responses from Boston, Chattanooga, Chicago, Philadelphia, Phoenix, Toledo, and elsewhere. So many officers either boated or flew into town that Miller broadcast a second statement asking cities to stop sending aid. Getting the army's assistance proved harder. District commander General Daniel Van Voorhis refused to put his troops on patrol without orders from above. Miller's office cleared the assignment with Marvin McIntyre at the White House, who promised that army chief of staff Malin Craig would telephone the order to Van Voorhis. The generals spent most of a day trying to establish a connection, a delay that drove the cool-headed Miller to distraction. "Can't the federal government get hold of their own brigadier-general?" he complained to his staff. "If they can't, the Mayor of Louisville will help the federal government get in touch with the federal army." In an extraordinary breach of military protocol, Miller had Craig dictate orders to him over the phone, then repeated them in a late-night radio broadcast for Van Voorhis to hear. "Take the load off the shoulders of the mayor by relieving his officers and guards on patrol and similar duty, and give these men a chance to rest; and use everything you have to accomplish the wishes of the mayor," he read. Van Voorhis, who was listening to

WHAS but had no functional telephones, moved his men into position. "And the army finally condescends to help," one of Miller's aides griped.[9]

POLICEMEN, SOLDIERS, AND SPECIAL deputies did a better job of cordoning smaller communities such as Paducah. City manager L. V. Bean had enough armed men to ring the flood zone with minimal outside assistance. Several incidents nevertheless occurred in the days surrounding the crest, when fast currents and floating debris made nighttime patrolling unsafe. Officials incarcerated a score of suspected looters in a stockade at Thirtieth and Broadway. Among them were three employees of the Federal Materials Company who stole six hundred pounds of oil, tires, and other wares from their employer. A *Sun-Democrat* editorial recommended harsh consequences for such crimes. "Any person caught stealing should be shot if he does not immediately surrender to officers," it declared. "This is no time to be lenient with criminals." Large numbers of guards and the arrival of patrol boats with powerful prow-mounted spotlights eventually brought looting under control, but police were still stumbling upon caches of stolen goods weeks after the waters receded.[10]

One of the approximately 1,500 people who defied the health department's order to evacuate was Charlie Jackson, a middle-aged machinist and foreman at the family-owned Jackson Foundry and Machine Company, on the corner of Kentucky Avenue and First Street, just across the Illinois Central tracks from the Ohio. Jackson was working on Owen's Island, a teardrop-shaped spit of low ground peeking above the waters adjacent to downtown, when word came to get out. His crew piled into a decrepit Ford coupe and wound through several detours around flooded blocks before arriving at the shop. He found his parents, Samuel and Evelynn, hurrying business records and other valuables upstairs. Jackson rushed to a nearby store to buy hip boots. He paid ten dollars for the only pair available, a considerable markup from a few days earlier, then grumbled about the inflated price while he boarded up his shop's first-story windows. Nasty weather complicated his task; nails froze to his wet fingers when he tried to drive them into the wall.[11]

Jackson decided to build a boat even though he believed the inundation would fall short of the 1913 disaster. It took five hours of sawing and nailing lumber salvaged from the shop and from the Petter Supply Company next door to create a rickety but seaworthy johnboat. Water covered the

Charlie Jackson. Courtesy Sam Jackson.

floor by the time he floated out the door. He tried to drive his car uphill only to have the Ford's brakes freeze up outside the Irvin Cobb Hotel. Jackson left the car to the river. He retrieved his craft and set out on the six-block trip to his rented house. A heavy buildup of ice in the streets frustrated his efforts to row, so he dragged the boat through the persistent drizzle. His wife Violet, whom he called Vi, and his one-year-old son Sam were waiting at the door. Water sloshed a few inches below their floor.

Jackson downed several shots of whiskey. Thus fortified, he led his family through knee-deep water to his parents' house, which sat on higher ground a few doors down. His parents had left the shop at the same time as Jackson but were nowhere to be seen. Puzzled, Jackson set off to find them. He spotted Evelynn coming down the street just as she broke through the skin of ice covering the sidewalk. Her clothes started freezing within seconds. Jackson asked after his father as he guided his shivering mother home. She answered that Samuel had decided to stay in the courthouse. Jackson cursed under his breath while he plodded back toward the river to retrieve him. He arrived at the courthouse wet and miserable—again—and found his father, but Samuel had no intention of leaving. Jackson stalked out of the building, stomped home, where his wife and son were waiting for him, and collapsed in his own bed well after midnight.

Jackson awoke to the sound of water lapping at the floorboards. He herded his family back to his parents' house, where he discovered his father waiting for them. Samuel explained that conditions at the courthouse had deteriorated overnight. Hundreds of refugees jammed the building, with more coming all the time. The place stank because the bathrooms had no running water. After a group discussion Jackson elected to deposit his wife and son at the courthouse despite the abysmal sanitation. At least it was dry, he reasoned. They joined about five hundred other flooders, segregated by race, roaming the airless, stench-ridden halls. Jackson persuaded a Red Cross worker to give him a pitcher to fill from a fountain. "Don't give anybody any water," he told Vi, "we will need it later."

The Jacksons nursed their precious water for several hours before Vi decided she could endure the squalor no longer. Charlie tried to persuade her to stay, but Vi was unmoved. I will leave without you, she warned. Charlie caved in. He loaded everyone into the boat and started rowing. On the way home they made a snap decision to occupy a vacant two-story building until the flood ran out. He dropped Vi and Sam with his parents, grabbed some tools, and paddled back to his find. His vessel swayed with the current as he sawed through the door facings, rowed into the gap, and tied up to the staircase. After testing the structural soundness upstairs he introduced the family to the place some of them would call home for the next six weeks. The Jacksons had a cold but dry night.

The next morning, Black Sunday, brought new problems. Sam, Vi, Samuel, and Evelynn woke up hacking and wheezing. Jackson set out to find food and coal. He helped a store owner row his equipment to safety in exchange for canned goods, flour, eggs, and other groceries. For coal he paddled to the inundated Illinois Central railyard. His journey took him through one of Paducah's flooded black neighborhoods. People there believed no one would ever come to rescue them. They prayed and screamed for help from snowcapped rooftops. Panic-stricken refugees pillaged stores for anything of value, regardless of its current usefulness. "Things are now getting out of hand," Jackson muttered. "Not enough boats for rescue work."

Jackson ferried his wife, son, and father to the Red Cross emergency hospital in the western suburb of Avondale Heights when their health worsened. He left Samuel with the nurses, handed Vi the few coins in his pocket, and loaded her and young Sam onto a bus for Mayfield. Sam's cold had deepened into pneumonia, and Vi was not much better off. Jackson talked his way past a guard blocking the way back to the flood zone and his ailing mother, who remained bedridden with a fever. He later obtained a pass, an identification tag for his boat, and a license to carry his pistol. Everyone left in town had a gun. "If you didn't[,] you lost your boat" to someone who did, Jackson later remembered.

Jackson spent the next few days nursing Evelynn. Mostly he provided moral support, since the only medicines he could find were some Vicks VapoRub and nosedrops. A visit to the Irvin Cobb Hotel netted a more useful commodity. Sculling over his abandoned car, through the open doors, and into the liquor store in the lobby, he discovered a cache of booze that he loaded into the boat. A nearby grocery store offered a wealth of mysterious canned goods. Jackson had no idea what he took because the labels had disintegrated. As it turned out, many of the cans contained floor wax, shoe polish, and other inedible goods. He completed his rounds by appropriating another load of Illinois Central coal.[12]

Jackson's dismay grew when he visited Avondale Heights to see his father and get medicine for Evelynn. His wife and child's fate weighed on him as he watched flooders who had lost everything but the clothes on their backs shuffling toward buses bound for refugee camps. Haggard, despondent women stood with dirty children in their arms. Many of them had spent the past few days in some church or school, waiting for deliverance without food or running water. They stared blankly, their faces red with cold, as officials herded them toward an indefinite future. Red Cross representatives issued dirty mattresses. Blankets and food were scarce. "What are they going to do with the mattress and blanket?" Jackson wondered. "Can't eat them." The hospital in George Rogers Clark School further depressed him. "Lord what a mess," he wrote. "White, black, male and female all mixed up in large room. There were some signs of [organization] but not much."

Evelynn's health improved over the next few days. Jackson rowed back to the Cobb Hotel, crammed with nearly eight hundred refugees, in search of news and another boatload of liquor. A group gathered around a short-wave radio shared the latest updates, and the same store he had plundered earlier yielded more whiskey. He later swapped a bottle for five loaves of bread.

Jackson's trip did bring a few negatives. The first came when the sheriff deputized him. "Thanks for the badge," Jackson said. ("Nuts," he thought about the unwanted duty.) The second came when he visited his family's shop. He knew the damage would be bad— the Ohio, usually half a mile across, now flowed seven miles wide—but the magnitude of the devastation shocked him. Their heavy equipment was wrecked. Everything that could float was gone.

"Charlotte," the *Sun-Democrat*'s writer-about-town, summarized the mood among Paducah's holdouts. Sitting in a dim room, typing on an ancient machine resting on a cardboard box, she wrote, "The flood turned out to be a disaster instead of a novelty, and puddling around in a boat is no longer fun." By now Jackson was one of about fifty stragglers in the quarantined area. They shared the town with house pets imprisoned on upper floors and a menagerie populating a small island in Oak Grove Cemetery, where former city commissioner Charlie Rieke tended to a pack of dogs, cats, mules, cows, horses, quail, and rabbits clinging to life in that place of the dead. There was no government in the flood zone, and the few dry neighborhoods verged on anarchy because Mayor Edgar Washburn refused to set aside his hatred of L. V. Bean, the city manager, for the duration of the crisis. Ensconced in competing headquarters in Avondale Heights, they published conflicting orders and invalidated passes from the opposing camp.[13]

Jackson knew nothing of this dispute. With only about thirty working telephones in town, almost no one understood what was happening in Paducah. He was not the kind of man to take an excessive interest in other people's business anyway. Even so, the bizarre sights must have raised questions in his mind. He saw one unusual thing on a tree-lined street in a middle-class neighborhood about a mile north of his house. "Cow on second floor porch with hay and water," he observed. "It was doing o.k." Jackson did not stop to wonder how Bossie ended up on the balcony of a two-family house on Sixth Street. Almost everyone else who saw her did. Today her story remains one of Paducah's most cherished pieces of lore, as any visitor to the Stranded Cow Restaurant, the building's current occupant, soon learns.[14]

Bossie was there because of Jimmie Huston, a recent graduate of Tilghman High School—Charlie Jackson's alma mater—who lived in the Sixth Street house with his mother and sister. Huston was a polite, humble, good-humored young man with a big smile and a rakish tilt to his hat. Still seeking his path in life, he held down a steady if unexciting job at the Unique Cleaners up the street. Huston viewed the flood as one might expect from a twenty-two-year-old: he drove up to Cairo for a look. "What a sight!" he enthused. His mother's home rested on relatively high ground, so he saw no reason to fear for his own family's welfare.[15]

Once back in Paducah, Huston split his time between puttering around in a rescue boat and cooking for refugees, including Charlie Jackson's father, in George Rogers Clark School. One day his Uncle Frank called to ask a favor. He was trapped at Union Station, where he worked in the icehouse, and feared the river would catch his milk cow. Would his nephew retrieve her for him? Huston was happy to help but faced a daunting journey. He could not drive the mile and a half to his uncle's because of closed streets and official disapproval of nonessential motoring. So he set out on foot, bearing south as best he could until he reached the Lassiter home on A Street, a short thoroughfare linking Guthrie Avenue with South Twenty-first.

Huston found Bossie in the back, tied a rope around her dark brown neck, picked up a sack of feed, and set off for home. He followed Sixteenth, keeping the waterlogged Illinois Central yard on his right, until they hit Monroe Street. Tugging Bossie to the right, toward the Ohio, he took Monroe for a few blocks before jogging over to Harrison. With the sun setting behind them and the water in front, man and cow passed through modest residential neighborhoods, then traversed the few blocks of junkyards, whiskey warehouses, and industrial plants straddling the railroad tracks before returning to more pleasant surroundings. The sun had long disappeared by the time Huston, wet and shivering, made it home.

Huston stashed Bossie in the wooden shed behind the house and called it a day. Climbing waters forced him to move her to their latticed back porch the next morning. As the family stacked furniture upstairs, he realized that Bossie and their flock of a dozen chickens needed to be even higher. Moving the chickens was easy. Bossie presented more of a challenge. Huston coaxed her inside, weaving among the twenty friends and relations already packing the building. Another refugee helped him lead the cow through the kitchen and front hallway, onto the flooded front porch, and up the stairs to the second story. Bossie navigated the first flight without complaint but refused to pivot on the landing to ascend the last set of steps. Huston pushed on Bossie's rear while his companion yanked the rope from above. The stubborn beast dug in her heels. A gathering crowd shouted support and ideas, but she refused to budge from the narrow platform. After fifteen futile minutes, Huston tried a more aggressive approach. He cleared the steps in front of him, grabbed Bossie's tail, and crimped it as hard as he could. The animal uncorked a tremendous bellow as she bolted upstairs. She submitted as Huston led her onto the wide upper balcony spanning the front of the house. He surrounded her with feed, some coal, and a gaggle of clucking birds.

The group spent the next few weeks dining on fresh milk, eggs, and an occasional chicken. Huston's fun ended when he contracted double pneumonia and had to be ferried to a hospital. His housemates evacuated soon after. Coast Guardsmen fed and milked Bossie until Uncle Frank retrieved her. Huston swore that Bossie's tail never recovered from its twisting. "Kinda hung at an angle," he laughed.[16]

For Charlie Jackson, not even a cow on a balcony could enliven what was becoming a tedious flood. He justified his deputy's star by aimlessly steering his johnboat around the empty town and pulling a few shifts at the Avondale Heights jail for looters, where he downed the occasional slug of hot rum to keep warm during his duty. His time at the prison brought a bit of excitement. One day a gunshot interrupted his preparations for heading home. He rushed inside the office to find police chief William Bryant writhing on the floor with an ankle wound. A National Guardsman who needed a refresher course in shotgun safety stood over him with a guilty look. Otherwise, each day brought more of the same. Jackson had nothing to do but wonder when the water would go down and his family would come home.[17]

He rowed for hours without encountering anyone. Chance meetings brought awkward nods, muttered greetings, and unspoken questions about what the other was doing there. Jackson doubted the city would ever recover. Either waves or looters had smashed the plate glass windows adorning the Broadway storefronts. Telephone poles jutted from doorways like giant spears. Floating railroad ties snagged against houses, and trees snared enough debris to create logjams that blocked entire streets.

City manager Bean insisted that "a new city is going to rise out of the wreckage." Few shared his conviction. State health director Dr. A. T. McCormack believed Paducah would remain uninhabited for weeks or even months. "These water-soaked homes are poison," he informed residents. "They will breed tuberculosis, dysentery, pneumonia and other malignant diseases. . . . The future of your city depends upon staying away from these homes." Although more optimistic, Happy Chandler doubted the community would rebound anytime soon. Not even his experience at the state penitentiary prepared the governor for what he saw during his mid-February boat tour. "This is the worst blow to any city in the state of Kentucky I have visited," he gasped.[18]

Jackson would have agreed with Chandler's sentiment had he heard it. With no newspaper or radio access, he had little idea of what was happening beyond the tidbits he picked up during visits to Avondale. His limited contact with the outside world did provide some evidence that Paducah might recover. Locals threw up temporary structures and commandeered existing ones on the corner of Thirty-second and Broadway, just across the waterline, to house a hive of essential services. Pine shacks containing a post office, hospital, and police headquarters jostled for space among the filling stations, Coca-Cola bottling plant, and cathedral that made up the area's usual occupants. Although still printed in Mayfield, the *Sun-Democrat* established quarters nearby, as did the phone company, the WPA, and city manager Bean. The Reed Lumber Company building hosted a racially segregated morgue and a dozen other businesses. The nearby Twinkling Star confectionary housed four more.[19]

Rather than the beginning of a new Paducah, this ramshackle outpost might represent the city's last gasp. Its inhabitants had scattered. Retailers told a roving *Louisville Courier-Journal* reporter that they would not restock their shelves because major industries were leaving the area for good. Even if people came home, they still faced the daunting tasks of sanitizing their contaminated houses and restarting a wiped-out local economy. A feisty sign outside the city's last surviving hot dog stand applied equally well to the restaurant and to Paducah. "Love to all / Credit to none," it read. "We love you all / But we need the mon."[20]

FLOODERS UPRIVER IN SHAWNEETOWN pondered the same long-term questions. But while Paducah's future depended on the decisions of thousands of individuals and families, Shawneetown's fate lay in the hands of a small coterie that spent the flood in and around the village's most prominent landmark. Max Galt's First National Bank bustled as the rest of the town fell still. The justice of the peace and police magistrate abandoned their offices in the bank when water covered the ground floor. Mayor William Brinkley deposited everything he could save upstairs before sending his family to Morganfield, Kentucky, and moving in with a friend who lived in one of the town's few high spots. Galt directed employees to remove the money from the second-floor vault as a precaution— even though he doubted the Ohio would reach its heavy steel doors. In fact, water dampened the currency before they started the transfer.[21]

Galt returned to finish the job a few hours after he helped blow up the levee. He and his brother-in-law Carroll Goetzman piloted a skiff past the soda fountain lodged against the bank's front steps, through the main doors, and behind the tellers' windows to the vault. The room was too small to accommodate their craft, so Galt extended a plank to the shelves and scrambled across to retrieve the bank's records and a small stack of bills. On his way back he wobbled when the board shifted, then lost his balance and plunged into four feet of icy water. "Get out of there," Goetzman yelled, "you'll freeze to death." "Might as well finish the job while I'm here," his shivering friend replied as he handed over papers. Their mission complete, the duo clambered to the third floor to dry Galt's clothes, the documents, and the eighteen one-dollar bills in his pocket.[22]

Galt saved some of the few local records to survive the flood. Shawnee-town's book of ordinances drifted off to parts unknown, leaving the community, in a sense, lawless. The Ohio also carried off the *Gallatin Democrat*'s morgue. Both would have been lost forever if not for a vast collection of back newspaper issues belonging to Ida Coyle of Equality, a hamlet fourteen miles up the highway. WPA workers spent weeks recording notices of changes in the local legal code that they found in her hoard of newsprint.[23]

Galt and Goetzman's aquatic escapade marked a rare moment of interest in an otherwise dull time. Life on the bank's third floor settled into a quiet if surreal monotony. Nothing to see but water and rooftops. Visitors paddled from the Riverside Hotel to chat and play a few hands of cards or boated in from hilltop farmhouses to share news and check on their property. The stairway ascending the rear of the building provided a convenient mooring post and entry point. More athletic guests crawled in through the third-story windows.[24]

The third floor resembled an impromptu Kiwanis meeting. Max and Marie Galt moved in after water destroyed their home. Max pressured his wife to stay on their farm until her relentless complaints about the arduous journey to visit him wilted his resolve. They ended up living in the bank for a few years. Marie was happy to be with her friend Pauline Harmon and Pauline's husband Ralph, who spent hours gazing at their inundated grocery store next door. They could also see their recently remodeled home, with its new bathhouse, furnace, and living room set—all ruined.

Carroll Goetzman lay on a mattress, panting from a respiratory illness that was sliding toward pneumonia. Harry Fred Howell, who stayed to look after his father's store, wandered the rooms with a dozen or so other

Shawneetown's First National Bank about a week after the crest. From the collection of the Harrisburg District Library.

members of the social elite. Butch Day, a former steamboat engineer who now worked as the bank's janitor and jack-of-all-trades, was the only social and racial interloper.[25]

Generations of tenants had occupied the third floor, so sheltering there was not so much uncomfortable as inconvenient. Lanterns provided adequate if shaky light, and an oil stove sufficed for heat and cooking. A lack of running water prevented the refugees from filling the oversized marble bathtub, so they used it for seating. A table and a few chairs completed the bathroom's transformation into a rudimentary dining room. Sleeping space in the four bedrooms was luxurious compared with the overcrowded hotels and refugee camps.[26]

Combating boredom was a larger problem. Galt and his fellow flooders spent hours staring at the water. The men amused themselves and irritated the women by rescuing dogs clinging to debris. "My goodness," Pauline Harmon complained, "we haven't got enough trouble and all these men to feed and all [of] them have to have those darn dogs." Her husband Ralph and the other men laughed off her protests as they filled the attic with stranded animals. When not acting as Good Samaritans to the local animal population, the bank dwellers worked their way through a case of whiskey they had squirreled away before the flood reached critical levels. Together the river and the holdouts made a most incongruous symphony. Water lapped outside the windows with a monotonous, almost soothing rhythm, its regular tempo interrupted by the cymbal crash of an outburst from the drunken card games on the other side of the glass.[27]

Talk inevitably turned to the future. Although few of them remembered 1898 or had participated in 1913's abortive relocation talk, their current predicament convinced them the river was unmanageable. New businesses and prosperity would never come unless Shawneetown achieved complete security. Some later claimed the idea to move originated with Mayor Brinkley, including Brinkley himself. It would be more accurate to say that the idea was in the air—or in the water—and that several people reached the same conclusion at the same time. With the village's most active citizens locked together, surrounded by twenty-five feet of water, it would have been surprising had such a resolution not emerged.[28]

William Brinkley recalled 1898 and 1913 well. At fifty-five, he was older than the other boosters but nevertheless an integral part of the dominant clique. Locals swapped stories at his hardware store and drugstore. Shawneetown's business elite kibitzed at his Silver Moon Tavern. Brinkley liked Galt and his young cohorts, who respected his sense of civic responsibility. Then completing his fourth two-year term as mayor, Brinkley had also served as a tax collector, master in chancery, town alderman, and school board president. No relocation scheme could get off the ground without his endorsement. "Now's the time to get the town moved," the bank refugees told him, and "you're the one to do it." Brinkley had watched the Ohio conquer his home three times. He was ready to cede the lowlands to the river. Either on his own initiative or at the behest of his peers, Brinkley contacted Congressman Claude Parsons, who hooked him up with officials in the WPA.[29]

Few residents were aware of these momentous decisions. Existing barriers shut Shawneetown's poor whites and African Americans out of these conversations. Except for Butch Day, who mostly kept to himself, an unspoken social segregation discouraged the lower sorts from seeking refuge with local elites. The high school three miles west of town represented their shelter of last resort. Before late January, four people lived in the basement of the eleven-room, two-story brick school: principal Henry Packett, his wife, their young daughter, and janitor George Weber. Its population ballooned to nine hundred almost overnight. This invasion overwhelmed Packett's ability to maintain order. Victims were hungry, and Packett had no food to share. Cramped, unsanitary conditions offered breeding grounds for communicable diseases. The principal relied on two overworked nurses to handle emergency cases after the only doctor on the scene fell ill and left. Packett needed help.[30]

Reinforcements came in the form of Red Cross disaster worker Sophie Foote. Foote was a Red Cross lifer, a twenty-five-year veteran devoted to the corps and willing to take on tough responsibilities. The agency had sent her to Italy during World War I to run a tent colony for tubercular children. After the war she directed child welfare programs in the new country of Czechoslovakia. She gained additional disaster experience when in 1926 she assisted relief workers coping with a terrible hurricane in Florida.[31]

Foote boated into Shawneetown during a sleet storm so severe it encased her clothes in ice. The levee was still intact, but water covered the lowlands. She expected to find the town preparing to evacuate. To her horror, she found that no one had laid in supplies or drafted a coherent escape plan. Anticipating a deteriorating situation over the next few days, she bought up the town's food stocks and transferred them to the high school. Her decisive action saved many from starvation.[32]

Foote's portfolio expanded as water engulfed Gallatin County. She spent countless hours begging people marooned in isolated farmhouses to come to the high school so the Red Cross could transfer them to refugee camps. Most preferred to stick it out despite the obvious danger. Tales of armed holdouts determined to repel would-be rescuers swept the area. Local law enforcement was too occupied with other matters to aid the Red Cross's evacuation. One of Foote's colleagues deemed county sheriff Dutch Jones "as effective as a tail light on a baby carriage."[33]

Tireless as she was, Foote needed additional support. Two days before Galt's company blew up the levee, she enlisted amateur shortwave enthusiast Bob Anderson to radio for help. Anderson, a native of Harrisburg, had endured much just to make it to Shawneetown. He left his home with vague intentions of helping flood victims, then became one himself when he got stranded miles from anywhere. A chance encounter with the crew of a flat-bottomed scow brought him closer to his destination. Anderson staggered into town with an acute stomachache and symptoms of hypothermia, but he plunged into relief work despite his ailments. Foote met him as he was helping a group relocate to the high school and soon employed his radio talents.[34]

Operators in Harrisburg forwarded Anderson's distress call to the Red Cross office in St. Louis, where it reached nursing director Lona Trott. Radio men may have embellished the message as they relayed it west. Trott read of widespread panic. Refugees were running out of food, medicine, and clothing. Pneumonia and influenza were rampant.[35]

Trott packed some warm clothes and a few other possessions before catching a bus for Illinois with two other nurses. It took seven hours to cover the 140 miles to Harrisburg, where they hired a car to get them as close to Shawneetown as possible. Their guide spent several hours searching for passable roads. Occasional radio cries for nurses underscored the importance of their mission. With telegraph lines down and no working telephone within thirty miles, Shawneetowners had no idea that help was on the way. The car sheared through water that topped its running boards. Chances of getting stranded in the middle of nowhere were high. Trott ignored the driver's nervous babbling as she watched the passing landscape with a mix of fascination and dread. Tresses of ice on the trees created a beautiful yet terrifying scene, a shimmering wonderland that carried the potential for freezing to death.[36]

The nurses' driver plowed northeast for several hours before losing his nerve. He dumped them at Omaha, a crossroads town almost as far from Shawneetown as was Harrisburg. At a filling station Trott flagged down a truck driver who consented to take them on the next leg of their harrowing trip. Five more frustrating hours brought them to Ridgway, about eight miles from Shawneetown. The trio fortified themselves with hamburgers from a lunch wagon before setting out to find lodging for the night. Because Ridgway's tiny hotel was bursting with flooders, local Red Cross members took the visitors to the home of a charitable woman with a vacant living room. The nurses collapsed into an exhausted sleep, interrupted only by an attention-deprived dog who was determined to horn in on Trott's couch.

New adventures came the next morning, Black Sunday, when the weary group commandeered a small motorboat to ride the final miles to Shawneetown. Its two-man crew navigated past animal carcasses and between submerged houses. Ice floes thudded into the prow. A slow drizzle pocked the water's murky, swirling surface. They saw no sign of life except a pitiful cat on a barn roof. Their launch nearly foundered when the pilot got hung up on a fencepost. He bickered with the motorman as the craft heaved in the current. Eyes agape and hands gripping the rails, the land-loving nurses feared the worst. The intrepid sailors managed to dislodge the boat and pressed on until they spotted land two miles west of the high school. Atoning for his earlier ill temper, the chivalrous pilot carried the women ashore. Forbidding as the landscape was, Trott and her companions celebrated the end of their two-day trek. "I felt like hanging up a flag and . . . claiming the country for the good old U.S.A.," she exulted.

A passing local gave them a lift to the school in his beat-up car. "We found between 600 and 700 people packed into a building designed to hold about two hundred," Trott wrote. "Hardly elbow room to get through the crowd. Men, women and children—and babies! . . . Poor, tired, hopeless, pathetic creatures, milling around, waiting—for they knew not what. . . . No beds, except about a dozen cots for the sick, and a few cotton blankets. But there wouldn't be space for beds if we had them." One doctor and five fatigued volunteer nurses operated a makeshift hospital in the upstairs auditorium. About twenty pneumonia patients groaned on tables and pallets.

Shawneetown High School looked like a war zone. Jumbled heaps of furniture filled the gymnasium. Elderly flooders slumped in chairs, clutching bundles of treasures. Sleeping children sprawled on the floor. Mothers with careworn faces clung to howling babies. People wandered the halls searching for a space to sit or lie down. They had to keep the windows closed against the pounding sleet and howling wind, so a nauseating combination of stale dampness, sweat, and cigarette smoke permeated the stuffy air.

Trott and her companions began their quest for order in George Weber's improvised basement canteen. The janitor was doing the best he could with the three pressure cookers and fifty sets of plates, cups, and spoons at his disposal. After cataloging the limited stores Sophie Foote had gathered, Trott ordered Weber to serve two meals a day instead of three. She dispatched scouting parties to acquire milk, eggs, meat, and other essentials from area farms, then organized a bucket brigade to draw water of dubious quality from a well. With little time or fuel for boiling, she had to hope the water was potable.

Trott and her nurses tried to respect the community's social conventions—they made no objection to the segregation of black refugees in two rooms apart from the white quarters. Even so, persuading suspicious locals to accept their authority was a challenge. The interlopers posted guards outside toilets to ensure that Shawneetowners whose homes had no running water knew to flush them. They organized sleeping shifts to conserve floor space, a sensible plan undermined by exhausted or selfish people who refused to move when their turn ended. Trott did as much personnel management as nursing. Flooders drifted from their assigned tasks unless someone supervised them. Two female volunteers spent most of their time yelling at each other until Trott threatened to expel them. They stalked off the job, sulked in opposite corners, and snapped at anyone who crossed their paths. "They are out from under foot at least," Trott sighed.

Their days devolved into a blur of catnaps and coffee-fueled toil. Conditions worsened as rising water encircled the school. Sharp coughs and wheezy gasps punctuated the steady buzz of muttering refugees. A large pack of dogs roaming the island barked, growled, and fought. A canary, one flooded-out woman's last possession, brightened the atmosphere. Its insouciant singing broke through the moans, yowls, and cries like a ray of sunshine bursting through clouds.

Stress from the emergency unhinged some locals, whose quirks intensified the eerie mood. A gaunt woman wearing a black shawl and battered sunbonnet entered the building once a day. She roamed the corridors from top to bottom, examining every detail of the Red Cross's setup. After a thorough inspection, she meandered back outside without a word, her whereabouts unknown until she returned the next day. Then there was the gray-bearded man from the countryside with no name and a glassy look in his eyes. Nurses kept putting the addled patient to bed only to discover him minutes later standing in a corner. "I got ter feelin' kinder hungry," he mumbled as an attendant returned him to the infirmary.

Boredom gripped the dispossessed. People stopped at the back windows to watch the water creep toward them. If they stood outside and looked east they could see the trees lining the Ohio's usual banks. Shawneetown itself was invisible. They had no means of communicating with the outside world. Water covered the roads, and boats were in short supply. Choppy waves made it too dangerous for small craft anyway. Food and medicine were running low.

A measure of relief arrived when the whirring of a motor penetrated the racket of howling dogs and human voices. People rushed outside to see an Illinois National Guard plane circling overhead. Its pilot dropped a small tube containing a message asking whether the adjacent cornfield was frozen solid enough for landing. A group of men tramped over the plot before writing yes in the snow. Refugees crowded around as the soldier landed. He told them to run a strong cord between two ten-foot poles spaced about twenty feet apart. They could attach a list of their needs, he explained, and tomorrow morning another plane would snag the line with a hook.[37]

The next day's plane whisked away a satchel of messages. "It was like writing a letter to Santa Claus," Trott thought. "Not much hope of getting anything." Her fragile hold over the place was disintegrating. Tired refugees either abandoned their chores or did slapdash jobs. Slipping sanitation standards elevated the risk of epidemic. In a cruel twist, the first supply drop further demoralized the group—it hit the ground so hard that most of the cans of soup and fruit juice exploded.

Grueling work, inadequate nutrition, and sleep deprivation wore down the threadbare medical staff. Nurses hacked and panted. Blisters covered their feet. Pneumonia spread. Aged refugees collapsed on the floor after days of privation. Discouraged mothers hugged their children as if they could ward off infection through closeness. "Please come," Mrs. Bernard Roberson wrote to her husband in Harrisburg. "Our baby is very bad sick. So please come soon." To make matters worse, nurses had to waste time and energy visiting rural refugees who refused to come in. Their attachment to the land, deep mistrust of outsiders, and sense that the high school was falling into anarchy caused them to hold tight to their farms. "Why can't we get these people to leave?" a frustrated Trott exclaimed.[38]

Red Cross regional disaster director Walter Wesselius ordered the evacuation of Shawneetown proper just before Galt's cadre dynamited the levee. A Memphis-based steamboat, the *Patricia Barrett*, arrived in response to Mayor Brinkley's calls for assistance. Its captain moored in midstream to avoid being sucked into the breached levee. Foote and other Red Cross workers herded evacuees onto ferries that took them to the steamer. Bob Anderson set up his equipment atop the pilot house to air appeals for help as the *Patricia Barrett* fought its way upstream. Anderson finally located safe harbors in Mount Vernon, Indiana, and Henderson, Kentucky. The crew unloaded its two hundred passengers, then went back for another load.[39]

With the town nearly empty, attention turned to the overcrowded high school. Ferryboat captain "Cap" Lambert transported critically ill refugees from the building to the *Patricia Barrett*. A few days later a Major Smith ordered everyone else out of the school. No one knew who Major Smith was or whether he had the authority to give such a command. Doctors refused to move their patients until Smith convinced them that plunging temperatures would soon freeze the water surrounding the school and make the building inaccessible to boats.[40]

Trott complied without enthusiasm. She did her best to prepare her confused charges for their voyage. Yes, the Red Cross would take care of them. No, she didn't know where the boat was headed. Already suffering from a throat ailment, by day's end she had full-blown laryngitis. News that refugees had to leave their possessions behind compounded the hysteria. Mayor Brinkley threatened to cut off supplies if they stayed. This show of authority won over the protestors. Falling into a sullen silence, they wrapped themselves in blankets and plunged into the inclement weather.[41]

Packed with exiles, Lambert's *Margaret J* chugged over cornfields to the waiting steamer. Pneumonia, influenza, and respiratory cases mingled with the healthy. Women and children enjoyed the warmth of the engine room, but Shawneetown's men huddled on the deck in three inches of snow. Lambert steamed back to the high school for a second load. This trip proved more eventful, and tragic, than the first: a ninety-nine-year-old woman died just as the *Margaret J* shoved off. Her fellow passengers shivered from both cold and dread as nurses removed her corpse. Lambert revved the engines again only to spring a leak. His craft bobbed helplessly in the water. The captain helped Red Cross workers transfer the exhausted, frustrated evacuees to another boat. Just as that boat prepared to depart, a patient suffered an epileptic seizure. It was a rattled group of passengers that finally reached the *Patricia Barrett*.[42]

The mysterious Major Smith planned for the passengers to disembark thirty miles downstream at Golconda. When the *Patricia Barrett* arrived, the doctor on board determined that the flood had so disrupted the town's unloading and transportation facilities that it was unsafe to leave them there. The boat plowed upstream, passing the remains of Shawneetown, until it reached Mount Vernon. Two more passengers perished on the way. Ambulances drove the weary survivors to an emergency hospital in the Posey County Coliseum. From there officials scattered them among camps throughout Illinois.[43]

Shawneetown High School assumed a funereal air. Trott, Foote, two other nurses, and a doctor cared for a few refugees who could not squeeze onto the boat. With help from a handful of volunteers, they scrubbed the building in anticipation of more flooders coming down from the hills. Yowling dogs pierced the silence. The canary sang through the night, either not knowing or not caring that its audience had departed. A bearded refugee stalked the halls with a gun on his hip, threatening to shoot anyone who dared try to evict him. "We shall see that he is treated with proper consideration," Trott concluded.

Once a bulwark against the horrors outside, the building now became a revolving door as people drifted in from the countryside and out on launches bound for Red Cross camps. Foote divided her time between visiting farmhouses and enforcing discipline at the school. There was plenty of work to do, she told refugees, and anyone who wanted food and shelter had best pitch in. Trott supervised a growing staff of assistants who converted sleeping quarters into the office space needed for processing casework. A shortwave radio transmitter on the roof represented a considerable upgrade over the aerial "snag a bag" method of communication.[44]

Work continued at a punishing pace. One doctor toiled with a 103-degree fever. A variety of symptoms left Trott bedridden; an errant short-wave broadcast announced that she had died. Food was plentiful but repetitive, largely prunes and canned hamburger. Trott almost leaped out of bed with joy when a farmer brought her a bucket of chicken broth.

By early February the school quieted down. Flooded-out residents either had evacuated or had ample Red Cross supplies. Boatloads of cots, mattresses, pillows, and clothes made life easier for the country folk dribbling in. Shipments of typhoid vaccines alleviated the risk of a major epidemic, although Principal Packett spent some time in bed after an adverse reaction to his shot. Foote welcomed caseworkers who started shifting the Red Cross's mission from relief to rehabilitation.

Lona Trott left for St. Louis a few weeks later, stopping in Equality, Illinois, to broadcast a status report that quashed rumors of her demise. Her colleagues still oversaw about one hundred patients, most of them respiratory cases, but they had the situation under control. Sophie Foote stayed until late March when the Red Cross transferred her to supervise rehabilitation in Cincinnati.[45]

Before she left Trott finally found time to consider Shawneetown's future. With the river receding and her illness fading, she persuaded the Coast Guard to take her into town. Feeling an attachment to the community even though she had never seen it, the nurse grieved as the boat passed empty windows with sodden curtains flapping, houses flipped upside down, and detached roofs drifting with the current. The scene brought to her mind a stanza from Minot Judson Savage's "The City of Is":

In the weird old days of the long agone
Rose a city by the sea;
But the fishermen woke, one startled dawn
On the coast of Brittany,
To hear the white waves on the shingle hiss,
And roll out over the City of Is,
And play with its sad débris.

Trott could not imagine people living here again. "The oldest town in the State," she lamented, "rears its historic head above the water as if struggling with its last breath against the fate which is trying to overwhelm it."

AS PADUCAHANS SPOKE OF a comeback and Shawneetowners talked relocation, Cairoites still hoped to save themselves from inundation. Opening Bird's Point helped their cause. The floodway "has undoubtedly prevented a catastrophe to Cairo so far," reported Colonel P. S. Reinecke of the Corps of Engineers' St. Louis office. He gave the city a fifty-fifty chance of survival. Fifteen million gallons of water tore past it every second, one-third more than during 1913's record flow. A brackish brown ocean extended as far as one could see. Two thousand men reinforced the mudboxes straining to repel the heaving river.[46]

The Missourians across the river also felt the danger. Residents of New Madrid left in droves for fear the floodway's setback levees would collapse and send the Mississippi their way. Stores closed. Proprietors hoisted stocks onto scaffolding and boarded up windows to ward off floating debris. New Madrid's women and children left for safer ground. Its physically able men were among the five thousand people, most of them WPA enrollees, piling lumber and sandbags against the setback. "First it was announced as a precautionary measure," a local newspaper said of the work. "Now it's an emergency." Workers from Mississippi City, Charleston, East Prairie, Anniston, and other endangered towns joined them atop the revetments.[47]

Rescuers in the spillway picked dozens of stragglers from roofs, second floors, rickety rafts, and treetops. One man who paddled to shore in a hog trough insisted he would have stayed had his tobacco supply held out. A handful of farmers marooned on Sugar Tree Ridge, the highest point in the area, refused to abandon their animals and food stocks. Looters operated even in this inhospitable place, an unfortunate reality reflected in Mississippi County sheriff Walter Beck's "shoot to kill" order for deputies operating in Bird's Point.[48]

On occasion the decision to defy the flood proved fatal. Black sharecropper Gene Brown thought he could ride it out with his wife and his baby daughter, Mary Jean. Once the levee blew, the fast-rising water and vicious current convinced him of his terrible mistake. A storekeeper named Nelson drove up to save them, only to have a surge wipe out a small land bridge before they escaped. Abandoning the truck, they boarded a skiff to pole themselves the mile and a half to the floodway's edge. Brown, holding Mary Jean, took a false step in the dark and splashed into the water. Nelson and Mrs. Brown stared as father and daughter both drowned. The river swept their bodies and the couple's meager life savings, which Brown had stuffed in his pocket, through the southern fuse plugs and into the Mississippi.[49]

A barge accident in Bird's Point claimed twenty-six more victims, most of them transients earning thirty-five cents an hour to reinforce setback levees under Corps of Engineers supervision. These exhausted sandbaggers were eager to return to their encampment after their shift. They stamped their feet against the cold as they waited for a towboat shoving a barge to deposit the night gang. The weary workers hurried on board the moment the deck cleared. Tired from their own labors, the tugboat's crew focused on speed rather than safety. "How many men can this boat hold?" one sandbagger asked. "All that can get on it," someone replied.

About two hundred people packed the unsteady craft as the tug pushed upstream. A violent lurch ten minutes later threw the men to the deck. A snag had ripped through the barge's hull, and water bubbled through the hole. Panicked laborers fell or jumped into the floodway as the barge started settling into twenty feet of icy water. Others rushed to the stern, further destabilizing the vessel. Someone yelled "Sit down, it won't sink!" in a futile bid to calm the group. Crewmen desperate to keep their tugboat from foundering kicked away terror-stricken passengers clambering aboard the ship. The captain cut the ropes linking the two boats, then backed up to the levee and blew his whistle for help. Another tug hauled the crippled barge to shore, leaving survivors in the water and on the levee to fend for themselves. Sailors yelled that a rescue boat was on its way. Shivering, sullen laborers waited several futile hours with their clothes frozen against their skin. Small groups started peeling off to search for help. The rest sat until the next morning when a barge arrived.[50]

The Corps of Engineers' botched response infuriated an already angry district. Eyewitnesses contradicted Lieutenant Colonel E. C. Kelton's assertion that "we have found no evidence that any were drowned." Government dredges recovered the first bodies soon after. Complicating their task, no one knew how many men had died. Several victims had no family in the area, and the survivors had scattered. Searchers eventually raised twenty-five bodies and found another wedged in a treetop. Officials identified some from the meal tickets in their pockets. Unidentified corpses went to a funeral home in New Madrid for claiming. A coroner's jury found the tugboat crew responsible for the deaths but decreed its actions excusable under the circumstances. No one was ever punished.[51]

Broken-down trucks and tractors littered the roads out of the floodway. Lines of sharecroppers trudged along, their hands folded into their coat sleeves and rags wrapped around their heads to fend off the cold wind. Merging with exiles streaming from other parts of southeast Missouri, they overwhelmed local relief capabilities. Charleston, population 3,000, cared for 6,000 refugees. Tiny Hornersville took in 500. Kennett, facing high water on both sides of town, accepted 2,500. Dunklin City somehow accommodated 10,000.[52]

Cairo fought on, a beleaguered island in a frothing lake. The Ohio stood a hand's width beneath the top of the levee. Gusts of wind tumbled water into the mudboxes above the wall. Even with three feet of freeboard, additional rain or a structural weakness would unleash a cascade onto the streets below. Cairo could do no more to defend itself than it had already done. Mayor August Bode's often-ignored proclamations had persuaded everyone who was going to leave. Nothing short of martial law could move the rest.

Cairo as the crest nears.

Utilities still functioned, making Cairo almost unique in the lower valley. Water company employees delivered five-gallon glass jugs of drinking water and trucked more to towns desperate for supplies. Company officials also filled a 200,000-gallon elevated tank and piped water from artesian wells to the second floors of hotels. Mistrustful Cairoites undermined these efforts when they left their taps open for fear of frozen pipes or a sudden interruption in service. Wasted gallons flowed into the overloaded sewer system, further taxing the pumps lifting wastewater back into the river.[53]

Destructive sand boils kept the city on edge. Sand boils—local leaders preferred the more benevolent-sounding "sand springs"—resulted from Cairo's location and its founders' refusal to elevate the town. They occur when water seeps through a levee or when rising rivers push groundwater to the surface, where it explodes skyward at hundreds of gallons a minute.

These geysers can flatten buildings or rip holes in levees, leaving behind the distinctive ring of silt that gives them their name.[54]

Several sand boils erupted as the Ohio and Mississippi pushed Cairo's high water table upward. One knocked down half a dozen houses in a black neighborhood on Poplar Avenue. Another spurted through an abandoned well that no one had bothered to seal. That gusher sucked enough sand from beneath the Cairo Ice and Coal Company to collapse its chimney. The surrounding pavement sank by several feet. Crews circled the boil with sandbags, allowing gravity to press down on the water confined in the cylinder until its force equaled the pressure from underground. Workers sighed in relief when they saw the water was clear, meaning it came from the aquifer. A muddy boil meant the river had eaten into the levee. Despite this silver lining, many assumed the Ohio would burst from the ground or punch gaps in the wall at any moment.[55]

Even though the *Cairo Evening Citizen and Bulletin* declared victory on February 1, Mayor Bode asked constituents to continue the war. "This is no time to quit," he said. "The danger today is as great as it was yesterday, and it may continue for many days before we reach a breathing spell." Worrying that complacency might lead to disaster, he chastised Cairoites for allowing outside WPA laborers to do their work. "This is the business of Cairo citizens," he fumed, "and is not to be left to workmen sent here from out of town. Our own people . . . should be looking after their own interests and the interests of their neighbors, without being forced or shamed into it. We prefer to have them volunteer their services, but if they are content to shirk, we intend to see that they do not get away with it." He hammered home his point with another order for all able-bodied men to report for work. This directive proved as ineffective as earlier ones.[56]

Governor Henry Horner joined Bode to welcome a delegation led by Harry Hopkins. The WPA chief looked exhausted as he stepped from the *Inspector*. After a twenty-four-hour trip from Washington to Memphis, Hopkins had spent the morning touring refugee camps in eastern Arkansas and scrutinizing levees along the Mississippi. Major General Edward Markham accompanied the relief czar. Markham pronounced the barriers "in excellent shape and ready for the water in sight." His carefully worded statement suggested that all bets were off should the rain resume. The dignitaries retired to the Halliday Hotel, where Bode no doubt presented them with a list of needs and desired projects. They negotiated the sticky question of how to pay non-WPA levee workers without reaching any definite conclusions. Hopkins cheered the city's performance during his subsequent press conference before boarding a speedboat for Paducah. The affable Horner seconded Hopkins's praise.[57]

In contrast to today, when presidential tours of disaster sites are an obligation shirked only at great political risk, no one expected Roosevelt to personally survey the damage. Hopkins, however, wanted to see the flood at its crest in order to gauge public sentiment, monitor the WPA's performance, and design the administration's rehabilitation program. "I want to be sure that our job is well done," he said, "and I can't do that over the telephone." His conversations with valley officials confirmed his belief that the administration needed to move fast to control the postflood debate. "It is just a matter of days until [flooders] will be right on our necks" demanding action, Ohio governor Martin Davey warned him. Hopkins used his tour, which took him to Paducah; Owensboro, Kentucky; Evansville, Indiana; Henderson, Kentucky; Louisville; Carrollton, Kentucky; and Cincinnati, to assure elected officials and Red Cross chapter heads that the WPA would clean up private property deemed a health risk, an enormous undertaking that stretched the boundaries of the agency's mandate to build and repair public facilities.[58]

Hopkins also wanted positive coverage of Washington's performance. After consulting press secretary Stephen Early, Hopkins's subordinates decided to speak to local reporters at each destination rather than allowing a literal boatload of newsmen to accompany them throughout the trip. "If we used the same reporters they would write up the first stop very vividly and then get bored with it," decided Colonel Francis Harrington, Hopkins's right-hand man. Talking to new people every day meant more enthusiastic stories that showed the administration in a positive light. Roosevelt insisted that only Hopkins, whom he trusted to stay on message, make public statements and cautioned against saying anything specific about future flood control programs.[59]

Cairo's situation brightened after Hopkins visited. Mayor Bode finally exhaled when the Ohio held just below the mudboxes, ran steady for several days, and then dropped. A severe storm or levee breach might still devastate the city, so the mayor fought the impulse to celebrate too soon. To try to staunch the illicit influx of women and children, he issued yet another proclamation barring entrance or departure without a permit.[60]

Bode relented after the Ohio fell several more feet. The first passenger train in weeks huffed into town, and Coast Guardsmen heaved their boats onto flatcars for the journey home. Cairo, a city that should never have been built, overcame confusion, internal dissent, and indifference to survive the greatest flood ever to strike the Ohio valley. Workers had protected the apathetic city at the expense of floodway sharecroppers and scratch farmers. "S. E. Mo. Sacrificed for Cairo," read one angry headline from across the Mississippi. One sarcastic newspaperman remarked that "the families of these men whose lives were lost [in the barge accident] will find solace and comfort in the official statement: 'Cairo was saved! The spillway is a success!'" The only way to justify Missouri's sacrifice was for Cairo to parlay its miraculous deliverance into a renaissance for a city long down on its luck.[61]

Even those who stayed experienced the sorrow of parting. In Louisville, overcrowding in the Life Savers Hotel became so acute that the families decided to go their separate ways. Matriarch Ella Fleitz moved herself, husband Edward, daughter Margaret, and the other Reynards to her son Johnny's house by the railroad tracks. "We hated to break up our swell hotel," Margaret wrote. Painful as it was, their relocation was far easier than the ordeals a million other valley residents endured. Rather than establishing quarters in a relative's house, those who fled often found themselves in an alien world as dehumanizing as it was strange.

THE EXILES

JOHN ROBINETTE NORMALLY SPENT his days working as a pump operator for one of the Louisville-area oil refineries lining the Ohio. Each night he returned to a home humming with activity as six children dashed from room to room while his harried wife struggled to preserve order. It was much quieter outside. The silence was near total around Valley Station, a swampy outpost a dozen miles southwest of town. Here nature crowded close—from their yard the Robinettes could see the wall of hills rising from the Indiana shoreline. Close by but hidden in its valley, the Ohio flowed past on its way to Cairo and the sea.

Now Robinette steered a rowboat through a cold wind and strong current to rescue his neighbors from that river. His temporary job as an emergency worker demanded constant vigilance. Inconsequential features of the landscape had mutated into deadly hazards. Fences and trees clutched at his craft as the current carried him past, and every so often an obstacle captured him. As frightened passengers waited for a passing motorboat to tow them to safety, they prayed that the waves would spare their fragile boat. When not dodging these threats, Robinette had to worry about his own future, for every moment water drew closer to his front door.

Robinette came home from a long day of relief work to discover that the Ohio had encroached on his property. Wet and chilled, he nudged his sleeping wife. "The water's about two foot along our garage, Ma," he said. "We might even have to git ourselves." He rolled into bed and dropped into an exhausted stupor. His wife was too scared to sleep. After a few hours of fitful tossing, she arose to check the water from the bedroom window.

Shaking her husband awake, she told him, "Hon, I don't want to scare you none, but the garage is gone." What had been a modest pool in their yard was now a deep lake. Charged with adrenaline, they roused their kids and gathered household items before reaching the sober realization that they had no way to get the family through the water and that, even if they did, they could carry few of the possessions they hoped to save. The only thing to do was to wait for dawn.

Water splashed their front steps as a rescue boat arrived soon after sunrise. The Robinettes' savior carried the couple and their excited, terrified children six miles north to the small community of Riverside Gardens. They fled again when the Ohio threatened this refuge too. John elected to remain behind to aid rescuers. He put his seven loved ones on a truck for Louisville and, from there, who knew where. They arrived at the armory, the city's main refugee check-in point, long after sundown. The children clutched their mother while Red Cross agents jotted down their vital information, handed them numbered identification tags, put them in the line for typhoid inoculations, and showed them to their cots. From there on their path becomes unclear. Workers may have put the Robinettes on a truck bound for some remote location, or perhaps Mrs. Robinette and her children held hands as they crossed the swaying pontoon bridge to safety.[1]

Hundreds of thousands of families shared the Robinettes' fate. They repeated their conversations—to stay or to go, to stick together or to separate—and replicated their feelings of confusion, determination, and fear. Floodwaters prompted an exodus from one of the United States' most populous regions. People from Pittsburgh's Golden Triangle to Cairo's alluvial triangle, from Bird's Point in Missouri to Friars Point in Mississippi ran for their lives.

One can make few generalizations about those who fled. They left home in luxury cars, trains, jalopies, rafts, and wagons, on horses and on their own two feet. They came from every race and social class, although poor whites and African Americans tended to live closer to the river and suffered disproportionately. Sharecroppers, businessmen, the unemployed, housewives, and children took flight. Some left of their own volition, others at the point of a gun. Some sought refuge with friends or family, others trusted in the kindness of strangers. Some ended up in refugee camps that offered living conditions better than anything they had ever known, others found squalor and discrimination. All of them would have understood the sentiment of the Kentucky hilltop philosopher who proclaimed, "Noah had a drought compared to this." That sense of shock, the feeling that they were part of something unprecedented, resonated in all of them. No one had ever seen the river go on such a tear.[2]

One million Americans depended on the Red Cross for food, shelter, and clothing. An additional quarter million relied on it for food and clothing but took shelter outside its relief camps. There is no way to know how many more survived on their own but they certainly numbered in the hundreds of thousands. Nor was the Red Cross the lone source of assistance. The Salvation Army, Boy Scouts, and American Legion also aided victims. So did the WPA, the Civilian Conservation Corps, the National Youth Administration, and the Resettlement Administration, which cared for thousands of hapless farm animals.[3]

Red Cross workers shouldered most of the relief load and earned the bulk of the attention from politicians and the press. Agency officials liked it that way and dismissed other groups' efforts as a potential liability. Every hand reaching for donations diluted the available money supply. Every voice talking to reporters amplified the cacophony. Richard Allen, the group's top man in Kentucky, fretted that "the [American] Legion wants definitely to go before the American people as the organization handling the emergency period of the disaster." One southern Illinois representative reveled in the rival Salvation Army's shortcomings. "As usual," he laughed, its contributions proved "most insignificant."[4]

A well-oiled public relations machine ensured that the Red Cross dominated the country's attention. Personnel developed relationships with reporters and editors to ensure that newspapers emphasized their work over that of their competitors. Dutiful bureaucrats fed canned stories to harried journalists and recorded how many column inches papers devoted to the Red Cross. Members lobbied to speak before Kiwanis, Rotarians, and any other gathering of area leaders. Close bonds with local elites paved the way for more contributions, larger membership rolls, and increased prestige. The flood also marked an opportunity to consolidate ties with Washington. General headquarters advised subordinates that, with the Roosevelt administration trusting so much in their efforts, "it is more than ever necessary for Red Cross representatives in the field to cultivate the acquaintance . . . of all the governmental groups."[5]

Despite its self-awareness and its sharp elbows, the Red Cross deserves credit for managing an intolerable situation. Or, more accurately, for managing a series of intolerable situations, since each locality presented unique difficulties. National headquarters did not have a blueprint stashed in a file cabinet for responding to an unprecedented Ohio-Mississippi River flood. Instead it asked local chapters, most of them lacking clear disaster plans themselves, to improvise. Ironton, Ohio's, tiny branch was supposed to care for 16,000 victims. Evansville, Indiana's, division supervised 30,000. In Louisville, a thirty-member brigade cobbled together a program to feed 230,000 victims. Chapters swelled with volunteers—about 1,600 in Louisville alone—most of them ill-qualified, undertrained, and, in the words of one frustrated regular, "incompetent."[6]

Chapters, volunteers, nurses, and imported Red Cross experts hastened to shore up relief infrastructures. City governments sometimes hampered their efforts, as in Louisville, where the Mayor's Flood Committee dickered over jurisdictional boundaries. The two groups transmitted conflicting calls for nurses and argued over supplies. This miscommunication almost produced a catastrophe when civil leaders informed an unsuspecting Red Cross that the warehouses holding confiscated supplies the administration had charged to the Red Cross's account were nearly empty. Elected officials threw up their hands and dumped the problem on the Red Cross. Startled aid workers had to find food for 150,000 refugees in short order.[7]

Cincinnati did a better job of integrating public and private relief. W. Howard Cox, the president of Union Central Life Insurance, offered the company's headquarters, a thirty-eight-story tower capped with a distinctive pyramid, as a temporary Red Cross operations center. It only took a few hours to convert the main floor into a supply warehouse and canteen for relief crews. Other floors served as dormitories, financial offices, and communications hubs. Round-the-clock pumping crews and teams of craftsmen who laid brick bulkheads around boilers and switchboards prevented the Ohio from interrupting phone lines, heat, or electricity.[8]

Maurice Reddy, assistant national director of the Red Cross Disaster Service, ran the charity's Pittsburgh branch during the 1936 flood. Nine months later he undertook the challenge of merging Cincinnati's local chapter with city, county, and federal bureaus. City manager Clarence Dykstra maintained public order and cut red tape, mundane tasks sometimes neglected elsewhere. Dykstra also negotiated a crucial shipment of rescue boats from Cleveland. The Federal Surplus Commodity Corporation trucked in food, clothes, and bedding for the city's 50,000 refugees. Hundreds of clerks in the Union Central building coordinated shipments to relief stations. Cooks in the sixth-floor lunchroom fed 500 boatmen, volunteers, policemen, truck drivers, and National Guardsmen an hour.[9]

Although Cincinnati was the largest city affected, the Red Cross's work there constituted a tiny fraction of its total effort. It opened more than 1,500 refugee camps—ten times as many as in 1927—and 300 field hospitals. Kentucky hosted half of the camps and one-third of the hospitals. Most of the rest were in Ohio, Illinois, Indiana, and Tennessee. "Camp" was a broad term that encompassed St. Peter's Cathedral in Cincinnati, a Masonic temple in Louisville, the Booker T. Washington School in Memphis, a cluster of boxcars near Cairo, a CCC facility near Booneville, Indiana, Earl's Café in Corinth, Mississippi, and a tent city in Natchez. Camps housed anywhere from a few dozen to 50,000 flooders.[10]

Workers arriving from outside the valley struggled to comprehend the misery. Widespread poverty, ignorance, and sickness appalled battle-tested relief officials. Barefooted children with "cough-racked little bodies" stood beside parents whose rotting teeth attested to a life without dental care. Rural victims suffered from malnutrition and respiratory ailments. Doctors in southern Illinois determined that one in six patients had syphilis. Caregivers sometimes interpreted privation as evidence of laziness. "This section of the country is 'top heavy' with people who have not learned or gained the gift of doing things for themselves," remarked one Red Cross observer near Shawneetown.[11]

Refugee status actually improved many flooders' living conditions. Hundreds of sharecroppers poured into the town of Caruthersville in the Missouri bootheel from their tumbledown shacks in such devastated crossroads as Black Island, Fourteen Bend, and Tomato Point. "They represent the ultimate in poverty," a reporter wrote. "They had nothing before the flood. Now they have less." Unable to handle the crush, the local Red Cross housed refugees in drafty boxcars and a dilapidated laundromat, where fifty men, women, and children, most of them wearing the mud-caked clothes they left home in, shared four hundred square feet of floor space. They slept on filthy straw mattresses. The air in the windowless room grew thick and stuffy but, as one survivor explained, "It's better than the cold on that river." At nine every morning they shuffled to the commissary for a tin plate of oatmeal, hash browns, fried sow belly, and canned milk. They returned at four in the afternoon for beans and more sow belly. Few complained about the meager fare, which cost a mere fourteen cents a day per person to prepare, because it marked a vast improvement in both quantity and quality over what they ate at home.[12]

Epidemics could easily sweep refugee camps. Many victims arrived with pneumonia or influenza. Cramped conditions offered plenty of chances to infect others. Contaminated drinking water might touch off a wave of typhoid. Chronic malnutrition raised the odds of contracting contagious disease. The physical exertion of evacuating in harsh weather strained weak hearts. Under these tense conditions and with normal lines of communication down, hazy rumors of illness morphed into authoritative reports of devastating outbreaks. A plague of smallpox in southern Missouri turned out to be several children with itchy but otherwise harmless cases of chicken pox.[13]

The Red Cross's bond with the federal government proved pivotal in countering the threat of epidemic. U.S. Public Health Service crews shipped millions of units of vaccines, serums, and antitoxins to camps. Supplies generally came on trucks or boats, but some arrived through more exotic means, including one hundred pounds of typhoid serum that descended into Paducah on the back of a parachute jumper. Rural and small-town refugees who rarely saw doctors hesitated to let a stranger plunge a needle into their arms. A nurse in Rockport, Indiana, found a way to shame them into compliance. "I usually contacted the head of the house, who would refuse at first," she said, "but I usually selected the wife or a small girl and gave them a shot without any trouble. After seeing how brave they were the father would finally consent." Hundreds of thousands of right arms ached for days after receiving shots, particularly of the dreaded typhoid vaccine, which saved countless lives.[14]

Even though disease killed more flooders than drowning, the expected epidemics of pneumonia, influenza, and typhoid never emerged. A rash of meningitis cases in Jonesboro, Arkansas, was the deadliest outbreak to strike a refugee community. Meningitis, a potentially fatal inflammation of the membranes covering the spinal cord and brain, haunted rural northeast Arkansas long before the flood, and an unhealthy concentration of refugees increased its reach. Jonesboro officials crammed flooders into churches, hotels, the police station, the courthouse, and the junior high school gym. Conditions were awful, particularly in the gym, where 110 families combated influenza and pneumonia in an overheated, poorly ventilated space. Many who had never seen a toilet urinated and defecated on the floor.[15]

Horrified Red Cross workers moved the filthy, hungry refugees to a tent city on the campus of Jonesboro Baptist College. Between thirty and forty people huddled around the blazing army funnel stove inside each tent. With rain and sleet turning the outdoors into a morass, there was little else to do.

A small boy was the first to present the fever, stiff neck, and nausea that are the hallmarks of meningitis. Aid workers rushed him to a nearby hospital, where he died two days later. Another boy and a girl, both nine years old, had similar symptoms the next day. Hospital officials informed the Red Cross and state health officials that they had neither the facilities nor the expertise to care for them, so Red Cross volunteers constructed an isolation tent. Nurses scoured the town for terrycloth bathrobes to use as doctors' gowns, gauze for face masks, and the special needles used to draw spinal fluid for diagnosis. A handful of National Guardsmen prevented wandering flooders from entering the quarantined area.[16]

Additional cases arrived over the following days. Most sufferers were under ten years old, with the youngest just four months. They lived hard lives in small, impoverished communities such as Tulot, Trumann, Bunny, and Black Oak. WPA enrollees erected a larger meningitis ward out of wooden tent floors to accommodate the growing caseload. The disease ultimately killed twelve people. Medical workers heaved a sigh of relief that the toll was so minimal. "It is hardly conceivable that patients with such general low resistance and suffering from undernourishment and exposure, and who were so desperately ill could make a complete recovery," one nurse marveled.[17]

Camp officials in Arkansas and elsewhere hoped to use the flood crisis to improve exiles' long-term prospects. Nurses offered classes in personal hygiene and provided tips on maintaining sanitary households. Facilities offered courses in basic nutrition that often proceeded from the faulty assumption that refugees had bad diets because they were ignorant of nourishing foods rather than unable to find or afford them. Related to its interest in fostering good health habits was the Red Cross's debate on whether to hand out cigarettes and loose tobacco. Executives initially classed tobacco products as unworthy of emergency expenditures before relenting and shipping Camels, Lucky Strikes, Old Golds, and other "generally accepted standard brands which will meet the widest range of smokers' tastes." Flood disaster head DeWitt Smith acknowledged that economics motivated the switch. "Some of the tobacco and cigarette manufacturers have already contributed to the flood relief fund," he noted. Left unspoken was that camp mood would have soured had the Red Cross prevented strung-out survivors from indulging their habit.[18]

Camp operators boosted morale using programs designed to amuse as well as enlighten their charges. They tapped into the notion, prominent since the early twentieth-century Progressive Era, that structured, supervised recreation engendered a sense of teamwork and fair play crucial to molding effective citizens. On a more pragmatic level, camp leaders needed to give refugees appropriate ways to channel their energy and forget their sorrows. Sensible leisure also defused some of the tension inherent to any situation where strangers have to coexist in uncomfortable circumstances.[19]

Representatives from the Red Cross's Recreation Division enlisted local gym teachers, WPA enrollees, and National Youth Administration staff to design programs to perk up dispirited young people. National headquarters assigned the one-million-strong Junior Red Cross to collect toys and games. Warehouse workers in St. Louis sorted, packed, and distributed these donations to hundreds of camps. Pens, pencils, crayons, scissors, puzzles, board games, and athletic equipment poured into regions unfamiliar with organized leisure beyond the family level. Junior Red Cross members walked rural kids through the rules of baseball, read stories to toddlers, and taught handicrafts. Camps supplemented these activities with rudimentary schools that imposed structure on children who might otherwise run wild.[20]

Relief workers hoped to offset the tendency for families to isolate themselves from the strangers surrounding them. Events for adults therefore concentrated on forging a spirit of kinship rather than on individual amusement. Crowds gathered by firelight to hear glee clubs and singers of spirituals recruited from their ranks. At least one community sing-along failed because evacuees from backwoods homesteads did not know any of the tunes. Recreation coordinators advanced their twin goals of strengthening morality and nurturing community when they invited dislocated preachers to preside over revivals.[21]

Recreation programs flopped in some places, including the all-black Camp Peay, a converted National Guard outpost in Tullahoma, Tennessee. Tullahoma was a railroad village best known for its nearby whiskey distilleries. A long-standing joke around town held that "Tullahoma" was Greek for "mud and more mud," a reference to the abominable weather conditions during Confederate general William Hardee's 1863 occupation of the area. The town lived up to its reputation in 1937, as persistent rain forced the 1,200 Arkansas sharecroppers housed there, many of them suffering from respiratory illnesses or other communicable diseases, to cram into quarters designed for 200.

Camp recreation director William Jacobs faced daunting challenges. Days of foul weather precluded outdoor fun. Ailing flooders overflowed the four hospital buildings. Able-bodied men and women spent long hours cooking, cleaning, and chopping wood to keep the camp going. Donated books offered little respite because few of the refugees could read. Jacobs grew frustrated at his inability to interest exhausted sharecroppers in wholesome activities. "Where one is dealing with an ignorant type of people, such as I was," he fumed in a private message to a superior,

I would advise that no complicated type of recreational program be tried. These people understand the simpler things best, and are happiest when they can have little things that are novelties to them. Because they are not accustomed to a rigid schedule of any sort, it is best to let them think they are having a free rein in their play. Although they are used to taking orders, they are not quick-thinking and reasoning enough to want to take orders about recreation and play unless there is an ultimate view immediately in sight.

The Tennessean's bewilderment about why flooders ignored his orders to have fun and his contempt for their character suggests the cultural gap separating destitute refugees from their middle- and upper-class overseers.[22]

Eastern Arkansas's hard-up sharecroppers and scratch farmers endured more than most flooders. Communities in this poor district lacked the resources to care for hundreds or even thousands of indigent outsiders, many of them African Americans. With area elites often in charge of local Red Cross chapters, the relief corps's policies on the ground, as opposed to its official guidelines, often reflected the region's racist, classist mores.

Nearly two million acres flooded in eastern Arkansas, where few towns interrupted the expanses of rich, black soil that provided abundance for a few while locking most of the region's 140,000 inhabitants, half of them black, in poverty's grip. Those driven from their shacks could either head east by boxcar or take Highway 70 to Memphis or travel west toward Crowley's Ridge, a 150-mile upland looming over the otherwise flat district. The ridge is neither broad nor high, reaching a maximum of fifteen miles in width and rising an average of two hundred feet above the lowlands, but it offered ample protection for displaced delta farmers. Fossils of enormous mastodons and caches of relics from a succession of Quapaw, Osage, Cherokee, Crow, and Choctaw inhabitants suggest that both man and beast have taken shelter amid the ridge's oak and hickory forests since time immemorial.[23]

Benjamin Crowley, a veteran of the War of 1812, gave the outcropping its name. The federal government rewarded the Kentuckian's military service with a 160-acre plot near the Mississippi. He brought his wife, eight children, slaves, and livestock on the arduous trek west in 1821 only to discover that the New Madrid earthquake had sunk his claim beneath the river. He pushed south until he found a suitable homestead on high ground that he named for himself.[24]

Future migrants capitalized on the hills' moderately fertile soil and abundant timber stands. Former Confederate general Nathan Bedford Forrest opened the ridge to commercial development when he secured a contract to cut a groove deep enough for the Memphis and Little Rock Railroad to pass over. Irish laborers spent months hacking at weathered crags before producing a grade that trains could manage. Forrest himself opened a commissary that became the nucleus of a settlement called Forrest City. Farmers brought cotton, corn, soybeans, rice, apples, and peaches there to load them onto trains that delivered them to a national market.[25]

With 5,500 inhabitants, Forrest City was one of the largest communities on Crowley's Ridge. Its stately brick-and-stucco business houses and two-story yellow brick-and-fieldstone courthouse topped with an impressive clock tower on its northwest corner suggested pockets of affluence. An enormous cotton compress on the west end of town hinted at the source of this wealth. Jonesboro, an agricultural center with twice the population of Forrest City, dominated the high ground to the north. The smaller town of Marianna stood to the south. These were insular communities where strangers felt stares on their backs. Except for Forrest City's annual Peach Festival, not much happened there. Visitors from Little Rock merited newspaper notices, and the construction of five homes constituted a "building boom."[26]

An armada of Missouri Pacific boxcars, battered trucks, and creaky Model T Fords dumped about 50,000 refugees from the Mississippi, St. Francis, Cache, and Little Rivers, plus a menagerie of chickens, dogs, and other animals, on this sleepy, inward-looking region. The Red Cross sent 1,000 flooders to Jonesboro. Marianna absorbed 3,500, equaling its preflood population. Forrest City, a favored destination owing to its superior railroad access, somehow accommodated 12,000. These were ignorant, impoverished folk. Along the way some of them sold their precious animals for pennies on the dollar to con artists who claimed the levees were about to break or said that camps would not accept livestock.[27]

Their troubles continued once they arrived in camp. Housing on the ridge proved abysmal. Officials guided many of them to cotton compresses, generally the largest buildings in town. These refuges provided a solid roof but little privacy. Flooders heaped their meager possessions against a wall in either the white or the colored section, marked out a spot on the floor to sleep, and held a sharp vigil against possible thieves. Authorities stashed the others in sixteen-by-sixteen pyramidal tents. People assigned to the tents had a more defined personal space but were vulnerable to the rain and sleet. They slept on straw-filled ticks laid on rough lumber floors. Temperatures inside alternated between frigid and stifling depending on the mood of the wood-burning stove in the center of the tent.

Thomas Hart Benton claimed that refugees accustomed to cornmeal, molasses, and fatback ate so much nutritious food that they grew sick to their stomachs. In reality, Arkansas exiles thought the twice-daily ration of three or four spoonfuls of gruel and a few thin slices of bread so inadequate that they considered hunger marches or bread riots. Complaints about conditions elicited little sympathy. "The average refugee thinks that he should be fed, housed and adequately taken care of without turning his hand toward helping himself," snorted one National Guard colonel.[28]

Exiled flooders often did work for their sustenance. Guardsmen conscripted over a thousand Helena-area refugees to bolster nearby levees. Black sharecroppers camped around Marianna gathered wood and cleared land under orders from local soldiers and Red Cross officials. Authorities never paid the dollar-a-day salary they promised. Supervisors told workers the wood was for their camp, but when the sun set they received a mere armload of what they had cut that day. Drivers trucked the rest into town. Soldiers admitted to taking a "rather hard and positively firm" approach with refugees who lay around the tent city rather than earning their keep. Angry victims claimed that firmness included clubs, pistols waved in faces, and overnight lockups for anyone who refused to comply with labor demands. Inhabitants of the tent city in Wynne, about fifteen miles north of Forrest City, who staged a mass sick-out to protest the forced work detail caved after the camp director issued a simple threat: "No working, no eating."[29]

Long reviled by the elites who dominated the local relief hierarchy, the Southern Tenant Farmers' Union was the only group to demonstrate genuine concern for exploited refugees. Floodwaters scattered the organization's members. "We are in a very bad situation here," cofounder H. L. Mitchell informed a contact in the Roosevelt administration. "All of Union territory is underwater or soon will be[.] There [are] already reports of discrimination in matters of relief but all our work is at a standstill—we are completely out of money and also cut off from our membership. . . . I do not know just what we will be able to do."[30]

Union leaders answered members' pleas for assistance as best they could. STFU lawyers hassled the Red Cross about inadequate food supplies in Forrest City and cried foul when planters pushed sharecroppers to commit to another year of work in exchange for Red Cross feed for their mules. President J. R. Butler's men solicited assistance from the American Civil Liberties Union, a better-funded outfit with powerful allies, to help monitor local groups that might discriminate against unionists.[31]

Recent clashes with planters left Butler feeling feisty. He kept on the offensive despite the STFU's financial and organizational difficulties. Butler probed the Red Cross's safety net for frayed cords, determined to ensure that his people got everything they deserved under the agency's rules. He told members who wrote for advice to ask the Red Cross for help, and to tell him if anyone gave them trouble for being in the union. Butler was spoiling for a fight, eager to find enough examples of discrimination to build a case against the lords of the soil. He dispatched trusted associates to the scene the moment he caught wind of malfeasance. Some accusations turned out to be misunderstandings. At other times his efforts reversed actual cases of abuse. In Forrest City, for example, the Red Cross defied its own guidelines when it limited assistance to people in its camp rather than helping the needy wherever they resided.[32]

Anti-unionists saw STFU outsiders as unwelcome intruders. Tensions already simmering after months of strikes and bullying threatened to boil over every time an investigator stuck his nose into a tent or wandered through the doors of a cotton compress. Harsh travel conditions benefited those seeking to shut the union out of the camps. Butler's men found that high water closed the roads into many places reporting discrimination. Locals pressed their advantage by prohibiting STFU representatives from entering relief facilities. Snoopers risked violence—armed thugs nearly lynched two attorneys who entered the Forrest City tent colony to check out allegations that planters denied food to farmers who refused to sell their land to them at discount prices.[33]

Conservatives hoped the inundation would destroy the nettlesome organization as completely as it had demolished the hovels housing its members. "I have heard that the flood washed away the Southern Tenant Farmers Union," a gleeful correspondent wrote to the pro-establishment *Memphis Commercial Appeal*. "Since I haven't heard anything about them lately, I wonder if it is true." As soon as he saw the letter, Butler fired off an angry reply. "Instead of being washed away by the flood," he retorted, "the Union has increased its membership by reason of the fact that new thousands have been reached in the refugee camps by union members."[34]

Butler exaggerated, but the flood did augment his rolls. Refugee camps brought close together sharecroppers who saw the STFU as an alternative to poverty and injustice. Organizers accustomed to speaking individually with farmers who lived far from their nearest neighbor now discussed common experiences and shared goals with large groups of potential members. "We can put the program over now is the time i need to work while we have the people to gather" one excited correspondent told Mitchell. Butler sent application cards and bundles of the *Sharecroppers Voice* to camps containing a cadre of union hands.[35]

STFU members from the Bird's Point area targeted Washington as well as local landlords. It was, after all, the federal government that had sent them running by dynamiting the levee. A group of black spillway croppers warned that they would not return unless planters raised their allotted share of the crops, lowered interest rates on seed loans, and improved housing and schools. Their agitation boosted interest in the union, especially after the Resettlement Administration agreed to give the farmers tents and seed packs. Black preachers who had held aloof began extolling the movement in sermons.[36]

"We must absolutely stick together now," Butler advised a unionist from a scattered local chapter. A revolutionary fervor flowed down Highway 70 from Memphis into the waterlogged delta, up the heights of Crowley's Ridge, and into the depths of Bird's Point. Continued planter dominance rested on launching a counteroffensive strong enough to crush the insurgency.[37]

WASHED-OUT ROADS TRANSFORMED THE 47-mile trip from Forrest City to Memphis into a 246-mile expedition. For imperiled west Tennesseans and Arkansans who chose to put Crowley's Ridge at their backs, the rollicking city atop Chickasaw Bluffs represented a haven worthy of an arduous trek. Memphis offered total protection from floods, except for low-lying suburbs along the Wolf River on the city's northern edge and in the Nonconnah River Basin to the south. It therefore became the primary refugee center for the lower Mississippi valley. "Residents of the Mid-South have come to look upon Memphis as a source of succor," the *Commercial Appeal* declared. "Memphis will not disappoint them."[38]

American Legionnaires prepared the county fairgrounds, Memphis's main refugee depot in 1912, 1913, and 1927, to again accommodate the suffering. Relief groups and public officials stockpiled supplies for the 5,000 flooders they expected. Their preparations fell far short of actual need, as some 80,000 miserable victims flowed through the city's gates in an exodus that drew comparisons to the Israelites' departure from Egypt. Trains, trucks, buses, cars, mule-drawn wagons, and foot traffic clogged every path into town. Lowing cattle, clucking chickens, and barking dogs on the roads made Memphis seem like Noah's ark. "If the movement into Memphis continues at the present stride," remarked a chastened *Commercial Appeal*, "the Mississippi will find only a deserted area on which to exp[e]nd it[s] wrath by the time its crest is scheduled."[39]

Mayor Watkins Overton recognized that the influx posed tremendous health and humanitarian dangers. "Vitally essential that they be moved to points further inland as rapidly as possible," he wired military and congressional leaders. Overton urged Carl Bailey, the brand-new governor of Arkansas, to divert eastbound traffic before it reached the Mississippi. Bailey stationed a handful of apathetic state rangers near the Harahan bridge.[40]

Still the exiles came, passing submerged cotton, corn, and rice fields as they followed the rising sun toward the promise of shelter from the storm. Many were without shoes and wore improvised headgear against the chill. Their hacks and wheezes heralded the contagion coming Memphis's way. Near the crossing they passed the Corps of Engineers' West Memphis headquarters, the nerve center for the army's fight against the lower Mississippi. Ringed with strong levees, the complex was an embattled island whose denizens alternated between organizing relief shipments and reinforcing their own defenses.

Rural émigrés carried few possessions. A few clung to things with no apparent use. One man brought a paddle to Memphis. He had no boat but, he told befuddled relief staffers, it might come in handy anyway. An elderly lady arrived with an iron. "I doesn't like wrinkled clothes," she insisted. A family of Arkansans refused to surrender a butter churn smashed into three pieces. S. A. Denison, a part-time Corps of Engineers employee who worked in a saloon in the West Memphis bottomlands, brought the most unusual item. Red Cross volunteers stopped his battered truck when they spotted a steel coffin in the bed. Denison claimed it contained the corpse of the Spanish explorer Hernando de Soto. He had acquired the body several months earlier and made a decent living charging admission to see it. After what must have been a remarkable discussion, the Red Cross agreed to let Denison and the cadaver occupy a vacant building.[41]

Railroad employees dumped refugees at Grand Central Station. From there authorities trucked them to Municipal Auditorium, on the corner of Poplar and Front. Those arriving by foot or car came over the Harahan Bridge, a cantilevered nest of iron trusses that deposited them on the south side of the city. Arrows pointed the way from there to the auditorium. Arrivals who either had caught wind of conditions in the refugee center or preferred to strike out on their own ducked into buildings and alleys whenever their military escorts looked the other way. Those who stuck to the official path and walked along Front Street passed towers in the commercial district taller than any building they had ever seen. Mud Island, a vast pile of sediment that had sprouted from the river in the early twentieth century, hunkered down below the bluffs.[42]

After hiking a two-mile course teeming with confused livestock, exhausted refugees, and the mud-caked detritus of thousands who had passed before them, flooders gathered at the south doors of the auditorium, a massive, squarish edifice that combined clean lines, arched windows, and terra-cotta flourishes into a perplexing jumble of function and form. Besides hosting concerts and sporting events, the hall provided space for a hodgepodge of civic and charitable agencies. Employees of the New Deal's short-lived Temporary Emergency Relief Administration canned millions of pounds of meat there; Memphis's PTA chapter kept an office inside; a

WPA band used smaller rooms for practice sessions and for storing instruments. Out-of-work Memphians had lined up in the west hall to visit the underfunded municipal free employment bureau when it was headquartered there. Volunteers had stuffed the hallway with clothes and other supplies during the 1927 flood.[43]

Another group of needy people now jammed that same corridor. Harried officials handed out identification tags bearing numbers assigned to each family, its luggage, and its livestock. Cafeteria workers distributed sandwiches and coffee before pointing refugees toward the north hall, where WPA enrollees took their names at the registration desk. National Youth Administration workers led visitors from the hall to the Red Cross's medical department for typhoid and smallpox vaccinations. Ailing refugees went to hospitals and clinics. Volunteers loaded the healthy ones onto buses bound for the county fairgrounds, for schools, or for camps in Chattanooga, Tullahoma, Birmingham, and elsewhere.[44]

The agencies staffing the auditorium oversaw an efficient system that processed and transported tens of thousands of bewildered people in just a few days. A team of forty workers organized registration cards that helped the Red Cross find families and reunite them with their possessions. Other squads lugged bundles of wet and muddy goods, precious and useless, to a warehouse to await their owners' return or shipment to a refugee camp, assuming the city's health department did not condemn them as unsanitary. Chickens, ducks, and other animals went to the Resettlement Administration. Donated items landed in an eclectic pile that included old corsets, evening dresses, bathing suits, sandals, ice skates, and derby hats. The Red Cross turned over the most ridiculous handouts to the YMCA to use as costumes in plays.[45]

Sitting a comfortable seventy-five feet above the Mississippi and four miles inland from the auditorium, the Tri-State Fairground offered what seemed an ideal destination for dispossessed east Arkansans and west Tennesseans. During the 1912 inundation, its 124-acre lot had provided a sanctuary for black refugees held under close supervision by white police officers. It replayed that role the next year when it hosted about a thousand African American women and children—Memphis conscripted able-bodied black men for levee work. Its focal point, the majestic Shelby County Building, slept hundreds beneath the curving ribs outlining its graceful ceiling. A spacious Women's Building hosted movie screenings, quilting bees, and community sing-alongs. Unfortunately, the weather and the season kept children off the Zippin Pippin, the wooden roller coaster anchoring the fairgrounds' amusement park.

American Legionnaires exerted authority over what came to be known as Camp Legion. They hired three hundred laborers to clean the grounds, connect electric circuits, and knock together temporary dining halls. The National Guard contributed five hundred cots it had stored on the site. Army quartermasters sent five thousand more, and legionnaires pried another few hundred from the Shelby County prison farm. Red Cross officials agreed to cover the cost of feeding refugees. Camp Legion had five nurses on duty, with a hundred in reserve, all unmarried and under forty years old.[46]

These careful preparations collapsed as upward of ten thousand people crowded into the fairgrounds. Hundreds suffered from influenza contracted during their icy journey. "They were poorly clothed, hungry and chilled from exposure," one caregiver wrote. "Many were not well when they left home; little crying children, the aged, the chronically ill, mothers about to be confined; all requiring nursing care." Camp Legion's unheated buildings swelled the ranks of the infirm. Most refugees slept on straw rather than mattresses and did not have enough clothes to keep dry through the rainy days.[47]

Flooders stood on the brink of mutiny. Among other things, they despised the camp's paternalistic policies. Sentries banned automobiles and demanded a pass to get in or out. Married couples resented the restriction on men's entering the women's quarters after four in the afternoon. Camp officials locked away victims' personal belongings as a public health measure. Refugees said the practice unfairly prevented them from getting clean clothes out of their bags.

City officials argued that "many of the refugees were better cared for and clothed than they have ever been before in their lives." Even so, exiles objected to the fairgrounds' subhuman living standards. Muddy, churned-up paths linked the few available washing facilities. Trash piled up everywhere. Camp operators had enough food but few stoves, so mealtimes were erratic and the cuisine was poor. Unheated buildings forced residents to light fires inside. Most galling, no one could leave without showing evidence that a friend or relative would take them in. Camp Legion was more a prison than a sanctuary.[48]

The first death sent a wave of fear through camp. Early one morning

C. H. Barrett, who farmed a few yards from the Mississippi near the destitute crossroads of Luxora, Arkansas, found Nat Wheeler, his sixty-seven-year-old father-in-law, dead on his cot. Wheeler had arrived the previous evening suffering from exposure and a severe cold. Owing to a shortage of beds in the emergency clinic, camp officials assigned him a berth in the general men's quarters among two thousand other people, hundreds of them seriously ill. Constant coughing and the moans of ailing croppers filled his final hours.[49]

Another disturbing incident occurred in the same building a few hours earlier. Hard-pressed legionnaires compensated for the lack of chimneys by venting cooking stoves through broken windowpanes, a shortcut that obliged them to place the stoves far closer to the wooden walls than was advisable. Sure enough, one of the walls caught fire. If not for the quick action of the Memphis Fire Department, the blaze might have spread to the entire building and killed hundreds.[50]

Camp Legion was a death trap in the making, a terrible embarrassment for Memphians who had boasted about their community's generosity. Machine boss Ed Crump, the most powerful politician in town, could not believe his eyes when he visited to check on the flooders. He had spent the crisis encouraging sandbaggers on the Nonconnah levee south of town. They were, after all, his constituents, except for the conscripted workhouse inmates toiling in leg irons. Crump must have felt a tinge of pride as he watched the waves beat against the wall, for he was largely responsible for Memphis's current floodworthiness. Crump had been the mayor in 1913, when a rickety levee allowed the Mississippi to flood much of north Memphis. He championed the subsequent campaign for levee improvements and a north side pumping station that drained groundwater into the river. The boss also raised vulnerable streets and strengthened the Nonconnah barrier.

Crump had been too busy to give much thought to his city's guests. "Think we have the situation in hand," he wrote to Walter Chandler, his flunky in Congress, on the day the men's quarters caught fire. His composure turned to rage as, wobbly with the aftereffects of the flu, he stumbled across the campgrounds. He gaped as refugees dressed in rags shuffled through the rain to far-off dining rooms and swallowed hard when he toured clinics packed with cases of tuberculosis, pneumonia, and measles.[51]

Crump was still seething when he return to his office at the investment banking house that provided cover for his political activities. He dictated an outraged letter to another of his cronies, Mayor Watkins Overton. "It is criminal on our part to pack all of those people—men, women and children—like sardines in a box at the fairgrounds," he thundered. The boss ordered the mayor to convert school buildings into temporary shelters that would ease the strain on Camp Legion. "Please let's not postpone this another hour," he closed, his tone somewhere between a humble request and a barked command. "It is too important—not only for the poor sick people, but for the citizens of Memphis."[52]

Overton, who had postponed his honeymoon to oversee Memphis's fight against the flood, had no time to deal with Crump. Anyway, he was already laying plans to relocate flooders when the boss's letter arrived. Truck and bus drivers transported nine thousand people out of Camp Legion within twenty-four hours. Sensitive to the city's public image, the *Commercial Appeal* dismissed reports of mayhem in the fairgrounds as "another flood rumor." An almost unbelievably sunny letter to its editor bolstered the paper's case. "The sanitation is beyond criticism," Alexander Carmack Cartwright (fairgrounds refugee #401) wrote of his temporary home. Cartwright asked readers to ignore whiners who focused on a few negatives. "Memphis is surely a city of charitable acts," he concluded.[53]

As the fairgrounds emptied the skies cleared, as if to confer nature's blessing on the evacuation. A warm sun dried the mud, while WPA trash-removal teams swarmed over the grounds like scavengers picking a carcass clean. WPA carpenters followed close behind. Hammer blows rang through the deserted complex as crews erected a cluster of eight barracks, four bathhouses, kitchens, mess halls, an administration building, a clinic, and a post office. Crisp new Red Cross flags flapped over a refurbished camp that quartered several thousand flooders over the next several weeks.[54]

Although improving, the situation in Memphis was hardly settled. Sanitary conditions in the segregated schools rivaled those of Camp Legion's hectic first days. Relief workers calculated how many refugees a school could hold based on its square footage. They ignored details such as the number of toilets, a foolish decision that caused severe crowding and sanitation problems. According to one condescending health inspector, "The low mental age of the refugees as a whole . . . resulted in the use of the floors by refugees, both in the toilets themselves, and at times in the sleeping quarters, for the purpose of relieving themselves." Poor ventilation compounded the heavy stink hanging over the buildings. School employees charged with running the centers despite having no experience in such matters strained to enforce discipline and sanitation standards.[55]

Planter greed compounded the humanitarian nightmare. Fearing the natural disaster might permanently disperse their workforce, landowners stashed their laborers in cheap rental homes and abandoned buildings. Caseworkers found 124 black men and women living in a two-room apartment leased to a planter. City health officials tried without much success to corral these stragglers into supervised housing.[56]

Considering the terrible health problems plaguing refugees, the Red Cross, American Legion, and Overton administration deserve credit for holding the death rate well below epidemic levels. About 150 flooders died in the city, most from pneumonia contracted before they arrived. It is of course impossible to determine how many would have perished had they never left home or had there never been a flood, for a sharecropper's life was likely to be nasty, brutish, and short. This held especially true for African Americans.

BEALE STREET WAS THE CENTER of Memphis's black community, a cultural whirlpool that drew people in regardless of their social status. "Everybody comes to Beale at least once or twice a day," explained the *Chicago Defender*, a nationally distributed African American newspaper. Black Memphians shed their inhibitions in its theaters, poolrooms, and juke joints; sated their hunger at swanky restaurants and downscale hot dog stands; and swapped stories at drugstores, shoeshine parlors, and hotels. It was both respectable and seedy, a place where upstanding black-owned insurance companies stood shoulder to shoulder with disreputable saloons. Beale Street anchored a loud, fast, and vibrant district bearing little resemblance to today's sanitized tourist trap. "It seems that the devil left hell on a vacation, stopped over at Memphis, sat down on Beale Street and rewrote the Ten Commandments leaving the NOT out of each commandment," thundered one outraged black preacher.[57]

Flood-driven Arkansans who followed the arrows to the Municipal Auditorium noticed an odd thing as they walked past Beale Street: silence. Deserted sidewalks. No piano music. Craps rooms without gamblers. The threat of kidnapping, not flooding, emptied Beale Street. When Memphis faced a labor shortage during the 1912 flood, Mayor Ed Crump had conscripted African Americans. Twenty-five years later police vans again trolled black neighborhoods for physically able men to dump before a pile of sandbags.[58]

Everyone on the levees endured tough physical labor, but African Americans got the worst of it. Policemen nabbed sixty-two-year-old Charles Hurse from a Beale Street billiards parlor late one night, tossed him in a paddy wagon with eighteen other men, and dropped them at the Nonconnah levee, where rifle-toting overseers forced them to hoist sandbags onto the wall. White workers stopped to warm themselves at bonfires, but a guard swung a two-by-four at a black man who broke ranks to enjoy the same privilege. Officers beat black laborers whose pace lagged.[59]

Even in normal times, segregation pervaded Memphis's public transportation, eateries, and hotels. Black Memphians generally received little education, lived in substandard housing, and held low-paying jobs. Boss Crump welcomed them into his political coalition without granting them much of a political voice. Discrimination intensified during the Depression. In 1932 Crump, fearing a white backlash against his interracial alliance, ordered policemen to destroy the camera of anyone photographing black voters entering polling stations. Local National Youth Administration officials refused to train African Americans for anything other than domestic work. Leaders of the city's Civil Works Administration branch assigned black women to serve as domestics for their friends.[60]

Racism was a national scourge. President Roosevelt, who needed the votes of white southerners and could at times be insensitive to African Americans, resisted calls to push antilynching legislation and tolerated differential pay rates and segregated workforces in government work-relief programs. This was the era when the radio exploits of *Amos 'n' Andy* amused millions while dancing on the edge of racial mockery. Hollywood cast black actors as porters, mammies, and comic relief. Nationally syndicated comic strips featured bug-eyed, gape-jawed "darkies" whenever they depicted African Americans at all. Cities around the United States segregated housing and education by custom if not by law.

Memphis was one of many places where African Americans faced extra hardships during the flood. As a destination for thousands of black refugees, it drew a disproportionate amount of the scrutiny given to race at that moment. African American organizations remembered Red Cross officials' standing mute as white refugees received preferential treatment in 1927. They fumed about the planters who had forced black flooders to bolster the levees at the point of a bayonet. The National Association for the Advancement of Colored People, the National Urban League, and the black press were determined to prevent similar injustices in 1937.[61]

Floodwaters struck African Americans especially hard. Although just under one in ten Americans were black, they accounted for over one-quarter of those seeking Red Cross aid. African Americans made up a majority of the victims from Arkansas and Mississippi. This disparity resulted in part from the flood's assault on alluvial farmlands associated with share-cropping and from the fact that urbanized African Americans clustered in undesirable neighborhoods hard up against the riverfront. Ohio water crushed the Bottoms, one of Cincinnati's primary black districts. Half the city's black population went into exile, compared with about 4 percent of its whites. Although nearly everyone in Louisville fled, black neigh-borhoods in Cabbage Patch and West End suffered the most damage. The black shantytown of Villa Sites in Evansville, Indiana, as well as black areas in Gallipolis and Portsmouth, Ohio, and in Wheeling, West Virginia, all went deep underwater. Victims were not just disproportionately black but also poorer than their white counterparts. To use one measurement, while almost 30 percent of white victims owned their homes, fewer than 10 per-cent of black victims did, against a national homeownership rate of about 45 percent.[62]

Black leaders expected trouble. Roy Wilkins, editor of the NAACP's *Crisis*, fired off a telegram to Harry Hopkins demanding that he instruct local administrators to avoid racial prejudice. The *Pittsburgh Courier* sent a similar note, then fixed a suspicious eye on the valley even after the White House insisted it would not tolerate discrimination against flood-ers. Unsubstantiated reports that the Cincinnati Red Cross rejected qual-ified black volunteers led the *Courier* to accuse the city of permitting "the grim spectre of discrimination to outrank human need, suffering and want." *Chicago Defender* writers leveled several charges against the Louis-ville chapter, none of them backed by much evidence. Articles blasted "Jim Crow tactics" in housing refugees, foul conditions in camps for black refugees, and a reluctance to rescue African Americans. "The ugly spec-ter of Race hatred has reared its head above the angry waters in the flood," staff writer Lonnie Moss proclaimed.[63]

Because the Red Cross needed local chapters to run operations on the ground, it was impossible to enforce the national office's colorblind guide-lines. National executives dealt with "realities rather than theories," and the reality was that integrating camps might provoke conflicts that ham-pered relief and rehabilitation. In this moment, when every hour counted and decisions were made on the fly, the organization acknowledged the

African American refugees wait for food in Louisville as a billboard mocks their plight. Courtesy Getty Images.

unfortunate fact that many communities would not accept black flooders. Washington kept quiet about segregated camps and hospitals because its central mission was to ease suffering, not to create laboratories for racial experimentation.[64]

While acceding to segregation with barely a whimper, the Red Cross took accusations of preferential treatment toward white refugees seriously. It invited representatives from the National Urban League, the STFU, the black press, and other organizations to tour tent colonies. Investigators checked out all charges of discrimination, most of which proved false. At the same time, the Red Cross stonewalled against pressures to hire additional black caseworkers, medical workers, and camp officials, assuming a reactive rather than a proactive position on what should have been an obvious concession on behalf of overall refugee morale.

NAACP officials stressed the employment issue on the grounds that only African Americans could "interpret properly the problems of Negro refugees." Roy Wilkins complained that the Red Cross maintained "a steadfast refusal to employ trained Negro case workers." His wife Aminda, an experienced New York–based social worker, led a drive to overwhelm the agency with applications from qualified African Americans. Her effort had little impact, since the Red Cross preferred to employ locals. It therefore had to hire whites because there were not enough properly trained blacks in Kentucky and elsewhere in the flood area to fill available positions.[65]

The Red Cross did not officially discriminate against African American refugees. It did tolerate inferior pay rates for its black doctors and nurses, a practice the Washington bureau justified as "following the customs of the community." White doctors in Paducah earned ten dollars a day plus hotel accommodations and restaurant vouchers. Black doctors made sixty-five dollars a month with no living arrangements and stood in line at soup kitchens for their meals. White nurses in the Memphis area earned five dollars a day. Black nurses made three.[66]

National headquarters refused to crack down on these inequalities for fear of complicating its mission. "It can readily be understood that the Red Cross cannot pay the same rate in these sections without stirring up local trouble," the organization told concerned correspondents, and "the less that is said about this matter the better." Staffers seemed happy to sweep the issue under the rug. An executive in the Memphis office who discussed discrimination with representatives from the Urban League was more interested in limiting the public relations fallout than in changing policies. "Nothing unpleasant has come from it," he informed his superiors afterward. Its official history of the flood also sidestepped volatile racial questions.[67]

Reporters from mainstream papers gravitated toward dramatic flood stories, not hard-nosed investigations of discrimination in affected areas. The Red Cross's cozy relationship with the media further discouraged journalists from peering too deeply into its racial practices. White reporters who did discuss race generally fueled the offhand bigotry of the era by stereotyping African Americans as lazy, ignorant, and comically inept. Papers printed several variations of one narrative that featured an overweight black woman who entered a vaccination clinic asking to be "assassinated." Another persistent theme was the assumption that African Americans' childish, easygoing manner enabled them to adapt to the emergency "with a minimum of discomfort." One Red Cross officer asserted that "pickaninnys" were too indolent to keep their camps clean. Mainstream newspapers extended segregation all the way to the grave when they separated casualties into white and "colored" columns.[68]

Few white journalists paid much attention to the plight of black refugees. Their black peers took the opposite approach, focusing almost exclu-
sively on African American flooders and dwelling at great length on what
the disaster said about race relations. *Chicago Defender* correspondent Dan
Burley, who later became an associate of Malcolm X, interpreted the disaster as divine retribution for America's racial misdeeds. "Old Man River was
mad," he explained, "because God's law of 'do unto others as you would
have them do unto you' had been disdainfully flouted and sin and corruption was rampant in the land." An anonymous contributor seconded
Burley's assertions in verse:

Men, who'll abuse subjective races
With fiendish brutality in "places,"
Must remember: that God seeth all
And will o'er their misdeeds, cast a deep pall;
Striking at the things nearest their heart,
Hence, the loss of money has played a great part
For some white men, worship things monetary;
Thinking of humans as secondary;
The black man's loss is of small consequence;
For God has shown him his munificence.

These writers concluded that white men bore responsibility for the deluge.
In their eyes the crisis proved that God held black Americans in special
favor, for he sent this flood to raise awareness of injustices against them.[69]

Once the black press confirmed to its satisfaction that the Red Cross
distributed supplies without regard for race, it initiated a fund-raising
campaign aimed at demonstrating that African Americans could play a
vital role during national crises. Their effort provided invaluable publicity
for black newspapers, which plastered their sponsorship of benefit performances and donation drives across their pages. The *Chicago Defender* adver-
tised its office as a drop-off station for cash and supplies intended for the
Red Cross. It also staged benefits in theaters, dance halls, and churches, including an all-night blowout at the legendary Savoy Ballroom. Louis Arm-
strong shook off the effects of a recent throat operation to headline the
show. Tiny Parham's Orchestra, Nat King Cole and his Syncopators, and
other local entertainers made it a must-attend event for Chicago's black
elite.[70]

Pittsburgh Courier writers highlighted the absurdity of differential treatment through its features on African Americans who performed heroically in the flood zone. Verna Green, a casework supervisor in Cincinnati known to readers as the "Modern Joan of Arc," acted as its greatest exemplar of black competence. The paper represented her service in refugee camps and crowded canteens as integral to the city's ability to curtail contagious disease and prevent mass starvation. She garnered far more ink than meteorologist W. C. Devereaux, city manager Clarence Dykstra, and the other stars of mainstream press coverage. *Courier* writers molded her into an idealized model of black femininity. She was a hard-nosed yet compassionate humanitarian and a skilled organizer. Green "proved to Cincinnati and the world at large that our women can do anything anyone else can," the *Courier* concluded. It hoped her courage, dignity, and talent might shame whites into abolishing discrimination.[71]

Black leaders suppressed their outrage at unequal pay, conscripted workforces, and segregated campsites to present a cheerful assessment of race relations. Many seemed relieved that abuses were localized rather than systemic. "I sought for definite criticism of Red Cross administration," wrote Claude Barnett, head of the Associated Negro Press, after touring Kentucky, "but was unable to discover any." He could have found grounds for criticism had he looked hard enough, but he chose to emphasize the positive. With an unprecedented natural disaster drawing the country together and a modestly favorable administration in the White House, the deluge might become a teachable moment. "Perhaps a major catastrophe of this kind banishes Jim Crowism and lets in the Christian spirit," the *Courier* editorialized. Thomas Jordan, a ninety-two-year-old former slave and Civil War veteran, agreed. The resident of Joiner, Arkansas, who had survived the floods of 1913, 1927, and now 1937, believed this latest inundation would shock the nation into changing its racist ways. "I think Negroes will have better times in the South after the flood has gone away," he told reporters in Memphis's Church Park Auditorium. "The white people will learn to be more understanding. This is God's plan."[72]

Skeptics disputed these rosy views. Dan Burley expressed dismay at black apathy toward racial inequality in Memphis. Black Memphians, he claimed, "have allowed the Jew, the Greek, the Italian and the southern white man to invade their business sections," leaving them no way to make a living other than to become Uncle Toms. Although occasional voices from the pulpit or rostrum demanded respect from the white man, their calls never resulted in action. Nor, in Burley's estimation, had the flood changed the city's racial dynamic. The poor, ignorant, and humble refugees he met expressed gratitude to the whites who mistreated them.[73]

The survival of an economic way of life rested on their willingness to return to a devastated region and a brutal existence in the fields. "It was dark and it was rainin', / baby you could hear that howlin' wind," sang Big Bill Broonzy in "Southern Flood Blues," a track he recorded in Chicago that January. "If I get away this time," he concluded, "I will never come here again." If Broonzy was right, sharecropping was doomed.

WATKINS OVERTON UNDERSTOOD THE difficulty of formulating an effective response to a crisis rife with unknowns. Once he found time to answer Crump's badgering letter about Camp Legion, he vented his frustrations. "We all deeply appreciate that if we had known what was coming we would have been prepared," he wrote. But "sometimes in an emergency all that one can do is to meet the situation—not as one would like—but as the situation demands." Those who fled the rivers, whether from Louisville or Luxora, Parkersburg or Portsmouth, had to meet the situation before them and carry on with their lives as best they could.[74]

And life did go on for the flooders. They danced to the music of WPA bands, swayed to the words of hellfire preachers, and clapped to the beat of community sing-alongs. Some fell in love, some died, and some began their lives. One couple in a Forrest City camp named their new son Highwater. New parents outside Paducah welcomed Wadelle Floodina to the world. A mother in the Marianna colony named her twin girls Mary and Anna. For many refugees the flood marked the first time strangers had lavished attention on them. It seemed Americans were willing to go to any length to help people they had never met. "My husband and I would like to know how to go about getting a little flood victim girl, left without parents, with a clean body and of good blood, to take her home with us," Lenah Brock Anderson of Mishawaka, Indiana, wrote to Governor Happy Chandler. "I am desirous of one with good features and curly hair if possible," she continued, "but if the family slate is clear, I would forego the curly hair."[75]

More than anything, the exiles wanted to know when they could go home. People thrown into an alien world yearned for the familiar. They had no idea whether their houses stood or their possessions had survived. Dense newspaper listings of missing persons and forwarding addresses testified to the valleywide angst. A mass exodus from the camps was the last thing the Red Cross and government officials wanted. Hundreds of flooded communities posed health risks. Backwater polluted wells and drinking supplies, caked walls with slime, and washed garbage into the streets. Water damage weakened hundreds of thousands of homes and buildings. For those who fled, each day away seemed an eternity. And as the exiles watched the ground dry, the country began the laborious process of cleaning up.

CHAPTER EIGHT

COMING HOME

～～～～～～

CHARLIE JACKSON SAVORED THE warm weather that settled over Paducah in mid-February. Everything else disappointed him. He yawned at the spectacle of a three-house blaze. "They were a mess anyway," he sighed. A starving dog with its ribs outlined under its fur drifted past on a wooden gate. A half-dead black man with no food and only river water to drink cried for help through an air vent in his attic. Nothing grabbed Jackson's attention. He saw few people other than his mother, now recuperating in the upstairs apartment they had appropriated weeks earlier. The city was desolate. He did not know where his wife and son were or when they would be home. He wanted his world back.

Although the flood never endangered Jackson's life, it almost stole his livelihood. One night the sound of shots jerked him from a doze. Interpreting it as the signal for fire, he put on his wet clothes and rowed to the Irvin Cobb Hotel, where a fire barge crew told him that the Petter Supply Company, the business next door to Jackson's foundry and machine shop, was ablaze. River water had reached containers of carbide, setting off a chemical reaction that produced heat, then fire. Spraying more water on the blaze only fueled the flames. To Jackson's relief, the fire exhausted itself before spreading to neighboring buildings, including his own.

Violet and Sam, his wife and infant son, returned in late February after a month at a camp in Mayfield, twenty-five miles to the south. Their house was still uninhabitable, so they squatted in their borrowed upstairs quarters until the city dried out enough for them to move back in. Jackson could finally inspect the family business. Located at the corner of

Kentucky Avenue and First Street (now Water Street), just yards from the Tennessee River's junction with the Ohio, the building had been deep underwater. Overflow from the two streams had destroyed the foundry, but Jackson believed he could salvage the machine shop on the other side of the building. He did in fact restore it to profitability and worked there for the rest of his life.[1]

The thousand-year flood had exhausted itself by the time it reached the picturesque bluff community of Vicksburg, Mississippi. Its demise resulted largely from topographical differences between the Ohio and Mississippi valleys. Hills paralleling the Ohio River produced a high, narrow inundation. Once the water cleared Cairo it was free to spread out over the flatter Mississippi valley, covering a broader area but at lower depths. The effect was like an ostrich swallowing a grapefruit—obvious and painful as it passed through its thin neck, then disappearing once it entered the more capacious stomach. Hundreds of miles of expansive floodplains siphoned off excess volume until the riverbanks could contain the remaining flow.

The Mississippi carried about the same quantity of water as it had in 1927, yet it flowed ten feet lower at Vicksburg. Relieved engineers credited the twelve cutoffs built under the Jadwin Plan. These projects to straighten the twisting Mississippi lopped one hundred miles from the river's length, speeding it to the sea before it piled on top of itself. Their success validated tests conducted on a scale model of the river at the new Waterways Experiment Station, whose creation the Army Corps of Engineers had opposed. Unlike 1927, when many Mississippi levees crumbled, the mainline barriers strengthened under the Jadwin Plan held this time, saving countless riverside areas from inundation.[2]

City fathers in New Orleans, the scene of great panic in 1927, anticipated smooth sailing in 1937, at least once they confirmed that rumors of a military evacuation of the Mississippi Valley were untrue. They did little to guard against a possible flood. For the first time, engineers opened the Bonnet Carré floodway, a major element of the Jadwin Plan. Army officers saw the operation as a rare opportunity to test the equipment, more a practice exercise than a safety measure. A portion of the Mississippi was diverted away from New Orleans and into Lake Pontchartrain, where it eased into the Gulf of Mexico. So many curiosity seekers turned out to watch water ooze through the marshy floodway that the highway patrol assigned a squad to direct traffic.[3]

Detritus from flooded communities, some of them fifteen hundred miles upstream, poured into the Gulf. Uprooted trees, shattered buildings, telephone poles, clothes, photographs, animal carcasses—the material accumulation of a million lives now reduced to fish food, pollutants, and waterborne landing spots. Birds devoured toads, snails, crickets, and other small animals riding the wreckage. Chief engineer Edward Markham and Mississippi River Commission president Harley Ferguson exulted as they watched debris-filled water pass down the spillway. "Flood control is here!" Markham exclaimed in triumph, and the Jadwin Plan "stands completely vindicated" despite the dire predictions of amateur engineers who had predicted devastation along the Father of Waters. Ferguson used this opportunity to chide advocates of reservoirs and other flood-control tools. "Build your levees high and strong enough, clean out your channel, give the necessary outlets on the sides, and keep the current moving out to sea in a steady, orderly fashion," he told reporters, "for the Gulf of Mexico is the only reservoir big enough to hold this river."[4]

"The greatest flood in [the] recorded history of the Mississippi Valley came to an official end yesterday noon," the *Memphis Commercial Appeal* enthused almost three weeks after Black Sunday. This pronouncement had no hydrological significance, since rivers exceeded flood levels at many points in the Ohio-Mississippi valley for days to come. It did, however, serve as a symbolic declaration of the end, for the odds of additional serious damages had dwindled to near zero.[5]

The *Commercial Appeal*'s turning of the page underestimated the catastrophe's long-term reverberations. Mid-February marked the end of the first chapter of an epic tale. Physical reminders of the flood abounded. Dark mud smeared buildings. Passers-by craned their necks to marvel at high-water lines. Homes lay toppled in the streets. One Cincinnati school hung from the treetops. Returnees to the James Bayou in Bird's Point discovered that their school was also gone. Its superintendent later received a telegram from Caruthersville, one hundred miles down the Mississippi, that explained the mystery. "Found—one schoolhouse," it read. "Now tied to a tree. Owner can have it by proper identification." River water fouled drinking supplies and dismembered roads, bridges, and railroad tracks. A dead mule at the corner of First and Broadway in Paducah—one block north of the Jackson family's machine shop—was among the tens of thousands of decaying carcasses littering the region. Receding water stranded an untold number of fish that suffocated in fields and city streets. Their rotting compounded the stench over the Ohio valley.[6]

Then there was the question of what to do with the million or more displaced persons. They represented a humanitarian nightmare, a rootless, shifting horde vulnerable to hunger, exposure, and communicable disease. Getting them home, and ensuring that their homes were safe to occupy, posed enormous challenges to cities, the Red Cross, and the Roosevelt administration. Authorities coming off weeks of rescue and relief operations had no time to catch their breath before turning to complicated problems of rehabilitation. Too much was at stake for them to slow down now. Their handling of the massive humanitarian issues would define public perceptions of their overall performance, a matter of great importance to status-conscious politicians and charitable organizations. Beyond that, their ability to not just restore but improve the Ohio valley represented a measure of the merits of active government and the New Deal.

Governments and relief agencies urged most exiles to stay put until they received the all clear. Thousands of sharecroppers in Memphis, Forrest City, and elsewhere heard the opposite message. Head for the fields, their employers said, and do it now. "We must get the farm families back on the farm," one Tennessee planter told a reporter. "If we don't get them back, they are going to the city to live and bring about a shortage of farm labor." Landowners drove pickup trucks into Memphis to recapture their charges before they got ideas of leaving. Fearing an invasion of impoverished, unskilled workers, Memphis was happy to be rid of them.[7]

Red Cross officials proved willing partners in the campaign to repatriate sharecroppers. Planters badgered local relief heads—many of them property owners interested in restoring the preflood status quo—into providing transportation back to the fields and tents to replace obliterated shacks. Washington did nothing to discourage the premature return to areas speckled with ponds of river water. Apathy in the capital left sharecroppers' fate in the hands of individual chapters that had little incentive to resist powerful elites. "All refugees under Red Cross care should be returned to their homes as soon as the recession of the water permits," decreed a Little Rock–based director. His counterpart in Memphis agreed that "it is imperative that flood refugees return to their own land [the land they rented] for spring plowing and planting."[8]

J. R. Butler's Southern Tenant Farmers' Union opposed this semiforced reintegration of crop laborers. Butler worried that dispersing the agricultural workers housed in tent colonies would doom the union's best chance of breaking the cycle of agrarian poverty. He urged croppers to stay off the land until planters improved their contract terms. Building on negotiations initiated in Bird's Point, STFU officers advised correspondents to demand a larger share of the produce they raised, the right to own livestock and to plant vegetables for their own consumption, houses with screened windows and doors, and access to schools.[9]

Planters panicked when sharecroppers hunkered down in tent camps. The rebels planned to stay put until after May 15, or "furnishing day," the traditional date for croppers to purchase goods for the year on credit from planter-owned stores that charged ruinous interest rates. But the STFU's bid to sow revolution failed. Croppers lacked the money to hold out, and the bankrupt union could not carry them long enough to provide much bargaining leverage. Planters' aggressive moves to herd laborers back to the land further undercut efforts to force systemic changes. Sharecropping continued much the same as the previous season.[10]

The flood proved disastrous for the STFU, whose star had been ascending before the waters climbed. Its Memphis office lost contact with members who fled the Mississippi. Reports from scattered chapters were few and far between. It took months to re-form some units, in many cases as shadows of what they had been. New privations that hampered sharecroppers' ability to pay the union's modest dues compounded the STFU's persistent money woes. Butler could not afford postage for mailings, furthering his office's distance from local branches.[11]

The sight of STFU recruiters among refugees redoubled planters' resolve to destroy the troublesome group. Forrest City stood at the center of what Butler called "a new wave of terrorism" aimed at stifling members. Authorities there jailed two organizers on charges of "enticing labor" and stepped aside when a planter-organized mob attacked Butler outside the courthouse. Another crowd brutalized an attorney defending three union members. Armed vigilantes in nearby Mississippi and Crittenden Counties, as well as in Caruthersville, Missouri, interrupted union gatherings, smashed furniture in meetinghouses, and confiscated STFU literature. One tenant in Blytheville, Arkansas, overheard a deputy sheriff from a prominent planter family telling a friend he would kill anyone who interfered with his laborers. A few days earlier a different deputy had shot at a black man who refused to work for less than union wages.[12]

Unrest also continued in Bird's Point over the next few years as organizers strove to convert sharecroppers' fury into a sustainable reform movement. Landowners answered the STFU's demands for better working conditions by expelling ringleaders and perceived troublemakers. Hundreds of dislocated farmers set up camps along the highway to draw attention to their plight. Police crackdowns on the roadside communities demoralized unionists, who found themselves imprisoned in concentration camps erected in the floodway's swampiest sections. Planter unity and internal disorder eventually cracked the resistance, but periodic violence continued into the early 1940s. In 1942 landlords orchestrated an attack on an STFU member as he left a meeting in Caruthersville. An unknown assailant beat the unionist over the head with a pistol butt and fired two bullets at him, but missed. This assault followed an incident the previous week where a planter-run mob disrupted another meeting and threatened to lynch the organizer if he ever came back.[13]

Fractious leadership and an inability to raise funds kept the STFU weak even after physical attacks against it waned. The flood played a key role in preventing the union from changing cotton country's sociopolitical structure. High waters broke up cohesive chapters and taxed the resiliency of impoverished sharecroppers. A well-organized campaign to hustle farmers back to shattered homes blunted the union's efforts to use the crisis as a recruiting tool. Planters' brutality and intimidation cowed many who would have listened to its message. Destitute and dispirited, the STFU plodded on well after mechanization, the rise of wage labor, population shifts, and the civil rights movement combined to end the exploitive sharecropping model.

Sharecroppers and tenant farmers proved an exception to the Red Cross's overall goal of keeping exiles from their homes until public health officials could ensure their safety. Exactly how long that took varied by location. Pittsburgh and other upper-Ohio communities returned to normal before the crest passed Cairo. Cincinnati city manager Clarence Dykstra reopened downtown businesses in early February. Liquor store sales exceeded all-time records as residents replenished their depleted supplies.[14]

Officials farther downstream kept people out of their houses for weeks or even months. Tent cities stayed open into the summer as flooders exchanged their old lives for something approaching permanent refugee status. A few of them enjoyed their new existence so much that they defied efforts to push them off the relief rolls. "We've got plenty of food. We've got plenty of water. We've got a place to live and we do not have to work," one contented survivor noted.[15]

This group constituted a small minority of the exile population. A vast majority of refugees chafed at official strictures keeping them from their homes. Many did not know whether their loved ones had lived through the deluge. Red Cross representatives and local missing persons bureaus fielded hundreds of thousands of requests for information. One of these came from Willie Mae Leglet, who fled when the water engulfed the home near Hughes, Arkansas, that she shared with her husband, Mose. They ran to Memphis with their five-year-old son, then Mose headed north to Illinois to find work. Willie Mae had not heard from him since. Frightened that something terrible had happened, she borrowed a pencil and wrote to one of Illinois governor Henry Horner's aides for help. "I have no one to depen on my HusBon left just a little Before the water com up he told me to com up to my sister House an He was goning to try to find sum work to do and I Haven Heard from Hem sence," she wrote.[16]

Although records do not say whether Willie Mae found Mose, separated families generally did reunite in time to prepare for the trials ahead. Returning could be more wrenching than leaving. Many who found their dwellings intact had to break a window to get inside because water had made the doors swell shut. An aura of unfamiliarity fell over hundreds of hometowns. Newspaper publisher Bessie Smith shook her head after touring the streets of Greenup, Kentucky, where the Ohio had covered nine out of ten homes. "There is little left of Greenup but its name," she lamented. In Vanceburg, fifty miles downstream, city court clerk J. C. Knapp declared, "We're all socialists. Everybody's broke and equal, if that's socialism." Flooders reentering Portsmouth got a visual reminder of Knapp's quip when they passed the city elites' colonial-style mansions. Lines of scum encircled their magnificent second stories. Ruined mahogany furniture lay jumbled on front porches. Water was clearly no respecter of class.[17]

But at least they had homes. Raging rivers created thousands of vacant lots. Buildings sat in broken heaps or had simply vanished. Lost houses sometimes turned up, leaving their owners to wonder how to restore them to their places. One Cincinnati man found his garage perched on the roof of another house. A *National Geographic* essayist reprinted a conversation between a boy and his father, who had sent him looking for their missing domicile: "Pop, I've found our house," the son reported. "It's three miles down the river, against some trees, and upside down. Everything's in it, but what a mess!"[18]

Floodwaters ruined paper, one of modern man's most important yet most fragile treasures. Libraries across the region staggered from the impact. Wet books in the Louisville Free Public Library swelled so that the pressure snapped the cast-iron stacks. Thousands of sheepish patrons handed in damaged volumes checked out weeks or months earlier. Courthouses and law offices trashed tons of mud- and mildew-covered records. Banks scrubbed muddy coins and dried soiled currency on commercial mangles. Treasury Department officials shipped carloads of clean new bills in exchange for soaked dollars.[19]

Rural areas were a mess too. Depending on their location, farmers returned to discover either fine white sand or a packed layer of clay covering their fields. Rushing water slashed deep grooves into the earth and washed precious topsoil into the Gulf of Mexico. Government scientists estimated that the disaster relocated sixty-four million tons of soil. Mississippi valley farms sometimes benefited from the flood, which in places deposited a fertile layer of nutrient-rich silt that produced excellent corn and cotton harvests that summer. But even those lucky cultivators contended with extensive property damage and huge losses of livestock and crops.[20]

For those who still had homes, cleaning them took immense effort. Water discolored carpets, buckled linoleum, stained upholstery, and destroyed mattresses. Pockmarked walls needed replastering. Electrical systems required thorough drying and testing. Residents threw out 150,000 tons of contaminated food. Mud was everywhere, soft and gooey, pressed into every crevice and squeezed into every piece of machinery. Aching homeowners spent days scrubbing red and gray stains. Stores could not keep up with the demand for trisodium phosphate, a popular cleaner. Chloride of lime, used to purify water, was also hard to find.[21]

Claude Harris, a paperhanger in Paducah, demonstrated the dangers of housecleaning. Harris's home suffered extensive water damage. He lit fires in three stoves to begin the drying before taking his wife and child to a neighbor's for lunch. They returned ninety minutes later to find the building in flames. It collapsed before firemen arrived. Harris must have felt a bitter twinge of déjà vu, since he had lost a house to fire a few days after the 1913 flood.[22]

"Hercules had nothing on my department," Louisville superintendent of sanitation Al Rosenberg said, because "the task of Augeas was nothing compared to Old Man River's." It would have taken destitute, depopulated cities months if not years to scour the valley's metaphorical stables without help from the WPA. Harry Hopkins's vast pool of laborers proved crucial during rescue and relief operations, and it did so again during the rehabilitation period. An army of 200,000 attacked debris piles like ants raiding a picnic. Understanding that his primary responsibility was to prevent epidemics, Hopkins had laid plans to help the U.S. Public Health Service decontaminate thousands of artesian wells and dispose of dead animals long before the rivers retreated. WPA workers either burned carcasses or buried them in lime-covered trenches. They also helped Department of Agriculture agents persuade farmers not to feed the bloated corpses to their livestock.[23]

Hopkins directed subordinates to work fast and ignore red tape. Besides approving repairs to public buildings such as schools and courthouses, projects well within the WPA's portfolio, he told federal crews to clean private residences on the grounds that filth endangered public health. Authorizing this task required a broad interpretation of the WPA's legal foundations. "We are taking the lid off," Hopkins told subordinates, who proceeded on the assumption that workers should accept rather than reject requests for help.[24]

This top-down, almost authoritarian approach to recovery was combined with the bottom-up ethos necessary for any action covering such a huge territory and involving so many communities. Hopkins cleared the bureaucratic hurdles to a successful cleanup while the WPA men who wielded brooms, shovels, and mops from Pittsburgh to Cairo and deep into Dixie acted according to local needs and obeyed local officials as they dumped an inconceivable quantity of mud, wreckage, and carcasses into the Ohio and other rivers. Enrollees used saws and crowbars to demolish "strays"—runaway buildings that blocked roads. They crawled underground to replace collapsed sewer lines and tended fires that extracted moisture from courthouses and libraries. Fleets of WPA vehicles trucked massive garbage piles from streets to freshly dug landfills.[25]

Hopkins, who was acutely aware of the value of good publicity, made sure that WPA photographers captured representative scenes of the cleanup. Pathé News, as part of its production contract with the agency, contributed a gripping newsreel titled *Man Against the River*. Released to screens throughout the United States, it is an exceptional piece of salesmanship that portrays the New Deal as an effective, efficient, and compassionate answer to America's problems. Replete with attention-grabbing shots of trapped victims, stranded animals, and devastated buildings, it lauds the White House for orchestrating "the best organized and most effective campaign against such a disaster in the history of the country" and lionizes the WPA as the nation's savior. Viewers learned that the flood was a freak occurrence, a one-time invasion of "man's domain." In so arguing, *Man Against the River* wandered off message, since scientists and the administration alike hoped to convince the public that humans bore some responsibility for these events. Americans could not rest on their laurels and assume this was an isolated incident. The picture got back on track when it evaluated the importance of federal relief efforts. Pathé's cameras caught WPA sewing rooms churning out clothes and bedding, WPA enlistees assisting Red Cross nurses, WPA heroes rescuing desperate women, and WPA "shock troops" strengthening levees. Its sound track, ominous and foreboding in earlier scenes, turns gentle, almost pastoral, as the relief corps ministers to the nation's needs.

Man Against the River was right to assert that the WPA prevented epidemics and saved lives. Entire cities might have vanished had the New Deal not made this resource available to local governments. This was true for Paducah, which was 93 percent submerged at the water's peak. WPA workmen there filled a nine-acre U-shaped hole with trash from streets and yards. Scavengers picking through the rubble occasionally stopped to tinkle the keys of one of 872 pianos, the ultimate symbol of middle-class respectability, strewn around the dump. Other crews spread 25,000 tons of gravel over damaged streets. They dried, replastered, and repainted schools and other public buildings and replaced 100,000 square feet of warped wooden floors.[26]

Work continued for months before communities reached the point where they could compose official applications for projects. Bureau files groan with records of repairs to streets, bridges, sidewalks, drainage ditches, airports, sewers, prisons, parks, schools, libraries, firehouses, police stations, and levees. Millions of federal dollars created jobs where the river once ruled and enabled cities to continue educating, governing, and serving citizens. This was the promise of the New Deal writ large, a living advertisement for an efficient, activist government, especially one dependent on periodic votes of confidence from the people it served. Unlike previous administrations and unlike previous emergencies, it insisted on providing security for all citizens facing hard times. Whether it could uphold its promise to effect long-term changes in mankind's relationship with the environment remained to be seen.

JURISDICTIONAL LIMITS RESTRICTED THE work of the WPA and other New Deal organizations such as the Resettlement Administration, which repaired damaged croplands and distributed thousands of seed packets. By law the WPA could not help individuals, as opposed to cities or states, no matter how much they had lost in the flood. The Red Cross, flush with gifts from around the world, could. Red Cross caseworkers began processing rehabilitation awards before Black Sunday. They adhered to the principle established after the 1913 flood of compensating victims based on need rather than loss, meaning the agency reimbursed flooders unable to replace losses of whatever amount rather than those who lost the most but had enough money to rebuild.[27]

Determining an applicant's level of need entailed an intensive review. Caseworkers, each responsible for about two hundred files, gathered information on a family's history, health, income, savings, and assets. Researchers double checked statements and ensured that the flood had caused the damage claimed, then passed their recommendations up the bureaucratic chain. With each worker closing about twenty-five claims a week, it took months for the Red Cross to satisfy the 258,604 families that requested aid.[28]

The organization dispensed grants to cover debts incurred during the flood, restore ruined equipment, and rebuild water-damaged homes. It even replaced lost artificial limbs. In all it spent $25 million settling claims, matching donations almost to the dollar. Almost everyone who applied—87 percent—received an award. Many who did not either withdrew their applications or disappeared before the Red Cross completed their cases. Just over 2 percent of claims proved fraudulent, in that the family had not in fact suffered from the disaster.[29]

Critics attacked the Red Cross despite its efficiency and thoroughness. Returning exiles grumbled that they received less than their fair share or that their neighbors got more than they deserved. Staffers fielded charges that they favored the poor and minorities at the expense of hardworking white people. "They help nigers give them something to eat they sell at and by some to drink moon shine so please get them to give me some furniture fer my home I got no money to get eny thing," one aged Louisville woman complained in a letter to Governor Happy Chandler. Much of the anger arose from a widespread failure to grasp the Red Cross's policy of "need not loss." Wealthy people who received no compensation for their extensive flood damage cried discrimination after learning about payments to social inferiors.[30]

Hostility ran hottest in Louisville, where well-to-do residents calling themselves the West End Crusaders launched a movement to get the checks they believed they deserved. They accused the Red Cross of discriminating against the wealthy—or the thrifty, as members labeled themselves—and of spending more on overhead and administration than on relief, a ridiculous charge considering that the agency's nonrelief expenses totaled a mere 7.4 percent of overall costs. Richard Allen, the Red Cross's lead man in Kentucky, dismissed the crusaders as symbolic of the "decided change of thinking taking place throughout the country . . . due to many of Mr. Roosevelt's announced policies and to the extensive governmental relief given." In other words, an undeserved sense of entitlement.[31]

Mayor Neville Miller had to at least pretend to sympathize with the West Enders because he was locked in a bitter primary contest for reelection. After meeting with the group's leaders, he offered platitudes that the press interpreted as support. "The Mayor did not take the trouble to verify any of their charges," Allen seethed. When the Red Cross and several prominent Louisvillians pressured him to retract his statements, Miller blamed reporters for misquoting him. He set the record straight in a second meeting, this time with Allen present. Allen explained the "need not loss" policy without convincing the crusaders of their error. "Do you think that some people should be rewarded for being spendthrifts and shiftless and others penalized for being saving and hard working?" one crusader countered. Allen reviewed their cases but found no reason to overturn the original decisions. "Clearly your financial condition even after the flood is stronger than that of many if not most of the contributors to the relief fund," he concluded.[32]

In response to this latest denial, the crusaders ran ads decrying the Red Cross's malfeasance. Over the next few weeks the group gathered two thousand testimonials from others who felt ill-used. Leaders carried the letters to Washington in a trunk and conferred with members of Kentucky's congressional delegation. Red Cross national headquarters tried to mollify the congressmen with another explanation of the "need not loss" policy. Hoping to end the dispute and preserve the organization's good name, investigators again reexamined the documents. Officials refused to open their files to the crusaders on the grounds of confidentiality, a consideration Allen neglected when he showed those same records to important Louisvillians to win their support.[33]

Crusaders and their allies either misconstrued Red Cross rehabilitation policies or were ignorant of them. A large percentage had already received an award but wanted more. Others applied too late to qualify for relief or had not given caseworkers time to process their claims. Red Cross researchers determined that about two dozen of the two thousand letter writers merited further consideration. Not all of them got checks once the investigation wrapped up.[34]

The West End Crusaders incident fizzled by the end of 1937, leaving administrators with a few more gray hairs and souring the Red Cross's relations with the city. It exposed the strong passions the flood unleashed and the jealousies separating neighbors. These tensions were repeated on a larger scale once constituencies started lining up for federal waterways dollars. Although the Red Cross violated privacy rules and acted with a keen eye toward its public image, its resolution of the crusader imbroglio further testifies to the organization's thoroughness. Its caseworkers were right far more often than they were wrong, no small achievement for people operating under difficult conditions and facing intense pressure to pay up.

RED CROSS RECRUITS WORKED alongside federal employees to rebuild a shattered region. This private-public cooperation did not exist ten years earlier, when victims of the Mississippi River flood found Washington unwilling to answer their cries for help. Roosevelt's New Deal provided a large, mobile force of laborers and a bureaucracy nimble enough to help the Ohio valley to its feet far quicker than most observers expected. Rehabilitation, however, meant more than sweeping out schools and replacing windows. Depression-racked cities worried that the flood might damage their future prosperity beyond the actual destruction it brought. New businesses and investment dollars avoided communities with reputations for flooding.

Government and business leaders in New Orleans launched a vigorous operation to counter spurious claims that the flood endangered the city. Mayor Robert Maestri bemoaned the press's "careless use of words, lack of information as to the real facts, [and] thoughtless handling of situations."

Actual doomsday reports of a flood-prone New Orleans were few and far between. Maestri nevertheless assailed these straw men for committing "a grave injustice to a port and a community which today is probably as safe from the tragedy of a flood as any other city in America." The New Orleans Chamber of Commerce backed the mayor by sending upbeat memos to railroad companies, travel publications, radio stations, newspapers, and other chambers of commerce.[35]

From Maestri's perspective the risk of water damage paled beside the possibility that negative news coverage would depress attendance at the cash cow of Mardi Gras, held during the first week of February. This scheduling ended up working to the city's advantage, since guests saw that New Orleans was, if not high and dry, at least low and dry. Civic groups kept pushing this cheerful message. "Our City Is *Safe* from Floods," screamed a full-page ad welcoming the National Education Association conference later that month. Organizers encouraged guests to visit Bonnet Carré to watch the Mississippi flow harmlessly to the sea.[36]

Memphis had a tougher time rehabilitating its image. Flood coverage in the national press convinced some readers that the city either was inundated or had narrowly escaped disaster. Photo spreads in *Life* magazine depicted masses of dirty refugees and showed long rows of cotton bales, apparently intended as emergency levees, stacked along Front Street. In reality, warehousing firms had piled the bales in preparation for shipping. A *Commercial Appeal* editorial chided gullible northerners who mistook storage for protection. "Audiences outside the South expect and demand cotton bales in whatever is going on down here," it joked. Such imagery was no laughing matter. The Depression had hit Memphis hard. Failing textile mills and a general industrial decline devastated its crucial transshipment trade. Thousands of dispossessed farmers who migrated to town stretched relief resources to the breaking point. Bad publicity would spook investors and further undercut shipping companies.[37]

The flood hit in the middle of a crusade by Mayor Watkins Overton and boss Ed Crump to reinvigorate the bruised city. Although reluctant to expend local funds for relief and infrastructure projects, Overton talked about parlaying federal largesse, including cheap electricity from the Tennessee Valley Authority, into better streets, schools, and public health programs. Crump mobilized businessmen behind this rebranding campaign. "Memphis has probably under-emphasized its location, natural advantages, short winters, railroad and river facilities, etc.," he observed. If they expected to attract jobs, economic leaders needed to advertise the city's advantages over such rivals as Dallas, New Orleans, and Atlanta.[38]

Crump was a hardball politician willing to do anything to get his preferred candidates elected. He saw no problem in hobnobbing with Memphis's seedier elements whenever it furthered his agenda. Crump also wanted the best for his city. His office stationery reflected his approach. The back of each sheet bore full-color scenes glorifying the "industrial capital of the Mid-South." An accompanying narrative trumpeted Memphis's outstanding access to transport and natural resources and invited recipients to contact the Chamber of Commerce for more information.

Local power brokers issued a steady stream of optimism during the levee battle, but the real work of image management began soon after the crest. Congressman Walter Chandler delivered an oration on the House floor demanding official acknowledgment of Memphis's service in the refugee crisis. Closer to home, the Chamber of Commerce compiled a slick circular titled "Here Is Memphis at the Crest," aimed at convincing peers around the nation that the Bluff City was a safe investment. "During the recent flood," read a comment from the Chamber's president, "Memphis received considerable unfavorable publicity throughout the country due to the false impression that the City was inundated by flood waters." Common sense demanded a strong reiteration of the town's advantageous business climate. Still playing the cheerleader, Mayor Overton contributed a celebratory piece. "Here Is Memphis at the Crest" observed that "Memphis" is Egyptian for "Good Abode." It ignored the good abode's problems with Camp Legion and misleadingly claimed that the flood neither wet the city nor interrupted normal industrial operations. In fact, the low-lying, reclaimed lands on the north and south edges of town experienced major disruptions.[39]

Prominent Memphians saw the annual Cotton Carnival as the most important step toward redemption. The Chamber of Commerce concocted the "South's Greatest Party" in 1931 as a way to raise interest in cotton, and thus its price. Although it failed to realize those goals, the carnival, along with its segregated cousin, the Cotton Makers' Jubilee, became one of the most important dates on Memphis's social calendar, the upriver equivalent of New Orleans's Mardi Gras. With the city's economic future in the balance, this year's festival had extra significance. "Nothing will restore confidence in the city's business so much as everybody co-operating to put on the best carnival we have ever had," remarked chief organizer Arthur Hale.[40]

City fathers promised to dazzle the tens of thousands of visitors arriving in mid-May with the greatest spectacle in Memphis's history. True to their word, they presented five days of events designed to demonstrate to guests that the town's spirit had survived Mother Nature's abuse. Out-of-town industrialists and politicians could see Memphis's intact infrastructure and dry buildings for themselves. National radio broadcasts of the festivities lauded the city's sterling health and pristine location. The Peabody Hotel, recently the site of tense flood meetings between federal and local officials, hosted boozy luncheons and grand buffets. Dancers whirled across the same auditorium where half-frozen Arkansans had eaten sandwiches as they awaited transfer to the fairgrounds.[41]

Memphis's good name survived the flood. Boss Crump's relationship with Mayor Overton did not. Although the mayor's political pedigree extended back to his great-grandfather, town founder John Overton, the boss was largely responsible for his rise to city hall. Crump, who served as behind-the-scenes head of Shelby County's Democratic Party, celebrated Overton's 1928 victory with an orgy of patronage appointments that consolidated his local power and confirmed him as a player in statewide politics. His machine paved the way for his two terms in Congress and a huge FDR majority in Shelby County in 1932.[42]

Despite their protestations of harmony, Crump had a rocky association with Overton, who was at times too headstrong for the boss's taste. Pressures from the flood widened the tears in their bond. Crump excoriated Overton for the mismanagement at Camp Legion. He never forgave him for endangering lives and threatening Memphis's reputation. Overton resented Crump's misguided attack. As temperatures warmed that spring, their correspondence grew chillier. Determined to escape from his patron's long shadow, Overton rarely checked in during the months Crump spent resting in a Michigan sanitarium. Their simmering feud boiled over the next year when the mayor claimed credit for brokering a deal to lower utility rates. Although Overton was in the right, Crump begrudged his former crony's refusal to share the glory. The boss made his displeasure public, blasting the mayor's "peevishness and insincerity." Overton dictated an overwrought response to a *Commercial Appeal* reporter. "Can his poison pen deceive the people always?" he asked. "I will never bow my knee to any tyrant," he continued. "I will never raise my hand in the Nazi salute to any dictator. I still believe in Democracy."[43]

Out of sync with the machine, Overton stepped down in 1940 to be replaced by none other than Crump, who engineered a complicated scheme whereby he immediately resigned in favor of one of his lackeys, Congressman Walter Chandler. Born from a disastrous first response to the flood, Crump's split with Overton forever weakened his political organization. His mayoral victory was its last hurrah. Chandler proved even more aloof than Overton, often going months without consulting the man who once held Memphis in the palm of his hand. Although he remained active in civic affairs, the aging boss never regained control over the town he had both loved and dominated.[44]

NO CITY WORKED HARDER to restore its reputation than Louisville. Unlike Memphis, which was already in bad economic shape before the flood, Louisville was in a boastful mood. It emerged from the Depression relatively unscathed to continue a period of growth begun in the 1920s. The Jazz Age saw new industries move in and modest skyscrapers replace Victorian-era brick-and-limestone buildings in the business center surrounding Fourth and Broadway. A new bridge to Jeffersonville, Indiana, increased commercial traffic, and a hydropower dam spanning the Falls of the Ohio transformed a scourge into a boon. Louisville's industrial output reached an all-time high at middecade. Americans' demand for tobacco, a commodity crucial to the local economy, outlasted hard times. Prohibition's end in 1933 revitalized local distilleries. Thick blankets of pollution from factories often blocked sunlight from reaching the city, but they were evidence of Louisville's financial strength.

"It's going to take Louisville a century to recover from this," one flooder wrote in her diary. "We thought for a while that all Louisville was doomed," another told a friend. Municipal leaders sensed the widespread despair. They knew the city's progress would stall if people thought it was flood-prone or damaged beyond repair. Mayor Miller pooh-poohed the need for serious postflood reconstruction even when three-quarters of the town sat underwater. Several days later he issued a statement that set the tone for the coming months. "We will build a better and a Greater Louisville," he asserted. "Louisville must have better homes, better churches, better schools, better courts, better streets, better sewers, better bridges; a better social, industrial, political and religious life." He offered similar senti-ments in his WHAS broadcasts after the emergency. "The flood has come and gone, but the things that produced Louisville's greatness were not washed away," he said. "This city . . . has experienced Indian raids, wars, floods and tornadoes, but after each adversity it has always marched on to better times." Local media outlets rehashed his upbeat assessments, drumming the idea of rebirth into citizens still scraping slime from their homes.[45]

Miller, hoping to restore public morale and a favorable investment cli-mate, tried to prove that Louisville had never been under martial law de-spite Governor Happy Chandler's explicit order. This semantic quibble was in a sense irrelevant, since the mayor reestablished normal lines of authority soon after the crisis peaked. Miller, however, thought the mat-ter so crucial that he split hairs to define as something other than martial law the presence of soldiers empowered to shoot anyone who disregarded their orders. He argued that Chandler issued his proclamation solely to skirt military regulations forbidding the use of troops as a police force ex-cept in martial law cases. At no point did the city curtail civil rights—de-spite using the military to enforce its quarantine order—and at no point did civil authorities submit to military rule. "Neither martial law nor extra-official authority superseded the elected authority for an instant," the *Courier-Journal* declared, not even when elected officials "temporarily abdicated to committee direction." Whatever label one used, Miller's ma-neuvering paid off, as the "no martial law" argument became a bedrock as-sumption in the community's memory of the emergency.[46]

Louisville's Board of Trade was eager to help Miller restore the city's image. In early February members formed a Business Rehabilitation Com-mittee to brainstorm a campaign to get their hometown back on its feet. Shivering in their hats and overcoats in an unheated room, the committee concocted a slogan that board president William Stoll of Stoll Oil unveiled on WHAS the next day. "Chicago had its fire, San Francisco its earthquake, and Galveston its tidal wave," he told listeners, and "all emerged as bet-ter and more beautiful cities. What other cities have done, Louisville can do, and will do." Posters shouting CHICAGO DID IT! SAN FRANCISCO DID IT! NOW WATCH LOUISVILLE! appeared around town. News-papers repeated the chant until a rise from the ashes seemed inevitable.[47]

Mayor Miller's new Committee on Morale, a group largely comprising Board of Trade members, took the lead in enforcing buoyancy. Volunteers distributed bright orange paper badges reading "I dare you to catch me not smiling" and pestered residents to pin the cards to their coats. "I will not complain," the card read, "I will not spread bad news. I will be encouraging, helpful, friendly. I will work unselfishly. I will give all I can. I will do my part toward building a better and a greater Louisville."[48]

The Board of Trade also hatched the idea of a morale-boosting rally at the Jefferson County Armory, a thirty-year-old edifice capable of seating 18,000 enthusiastic Louisvillians. Nearly 80,000 flood refugees, up to 15,000 at a time, had used the building as a temporary shelter. They filled the balconies, corridors, and basement, surviving on exotic foods such as quail, kumquat preserves, and imported olives donated by the Jefferson Meat Market and on water that arrived in galvanized iron cans filled from the well beneath Frank Fehr's brewery. Now the building would witness the rebirth of a city. Board members coordinated with the mayor's office, local newspapers and radio stations, and area businesses to line up speakers, arrange entertainment, and publicize the free gathering. Stoll promised that "optimism, good cheer and confidence are to be the dominant notes." He assured the city that the celebration would prove that "Louisville's doors are open and Louisville is marching on."[49]

About 10,000 people attended the gala—a number the press inflated. Most came from the middle and upper classes. The Louisville Male High School band preceded a vaudevillian parade of gymnasts, dancers, singers, and radio artists. New York actor Jack Pearl, best known for playing Baron Munchausen on NBC's *Jack Pearl Show*, headlined the affair. After an hour of performances, city judge George Burton called the assembly to order, then introduced Robert Worth Bingham, recently returned from London after a stopover in Washington to confer with FDR. Bingham promised "great spiritual gain" from the disaster, observing that "fire and flood and pestilence can destroy material things, but nothing can overcome the unconquerable spirit of our people." William Stoll took the stage next, boring the crowd with a turgid recitation of positive economic indicators before groping for a rousing finish. "We're ready for action," he declared, "and there's nothing in the way."

The crowd greeted the mayor with a tremendous ovation that echoed around the half-empty hall. Miller again insisted the city had escaped with minimal harm, noting that just four of the 429 people who died during the flood had drowned. He said nothing about those who died of tuberculosis, typhoid, and other causes directly or indirectly related to the disaster. What damage had been done might prove beneficial in that waters obliterated slum areas in desperate need of renovation or razing. Miller also restated his proposition that the flood had united Louisvillians into a stronger, more cohesive community. It marked a moment "when rich and poor labored side by side to rescue their fellow men, when executive and truck driver jointly operated a truck in carrying food to the homeless, when Protestant, Catholic and Jew filled sandbags to protect the homes of those they had never seen." Should they preserve and nurture this spirit, the thousands present tonight would lead the charge toward a greater Louisville. The party concluded with the crowd singing "My Old Kentucky Home."[50]

Bingham, Miller, and Stoll spoke the next day to a national CBS hookup arranged through WHAS. With millions listening, including potential investors, the dignitaries focused their half-hour show on discrediting the notion that Louisville occupied dangerous ground. "The flood has come and gone and will not happen again in a thousand years," Miller promised. Judge Bingham stressed the freakish amount of rain that fell and noted that many centuries might pass before a similar storm cycle occurred. Stoll contributed an invitation to visit. "Our people are back in their homes, business has returned to normal, transportation facilities have been restored; railroads, buses, and air transport services are operating, communications lines are clear," he insisted. WHAS's orchestra, silent during the emergency, provided an upbeat soundtrack and further proof that Louisville had moved on.[51]

The situation was gloomier than civic leaders suggested. Louisville faced a massive job of cleanup and rehabilitation, and no one was quite sure how to pay for it. Muck and debris covered streets and coated buildings. Sewage pipes, telephone networks, gas lines, and drinking water systems all needed extensive repairs. Most important, Louisville sat on the same floodplain it had occupied since its founding, hard up against the Ohio with no real protection and no immediate prospects for getting any. It had survived the deluge. Prospects for the future remained murky.

The upcoming Kentucky Derby represented the city's best chance to highlight its rebound. It is hard to overstate the importance of horse racing in Louisville, a place where vendors hawked the *Daily Racing Form* on street corners. A substandard Derby meant financial disaster. Churchill Downs, four miles from the Ohio on the southern edge of town, absorbed terrific punishment during the inundation. One of the most widespread photos from the emergency showed two jokers paddling improvised rafts across the flooded track. Hundreds of refugees took shelter in the twin spires capping the grandstand. *Life* magazine photographer Margaret Bourke-White's haunting shot of Jim Lawhorn, a white-bearded former slave who spent ten days in the building, became one of the flood's iconic pictures.[52]

Louisville needed to replace these images with scenes of glistening horses galloping past cheering crowds. Back when water still covered the track, the *Courier-Journal* insisted the event would go off as planned. Mayor Miller seconded the paper's confidence. "We are going to show our visitors that the old hospitality, the real Kentucky spirit is still here," he said. The Kentucky Derby Festival Association recognized the added pressure to perform. "We must produce concrete evidence that the courage, stamina, and fortitude with which we have been credited is not mere oratory but the real genuine article," the director of the local Retail Merchants' Association told the group. Lawrence Aronson, the race board's head, agreed: "There is no better way to tell the world that Louisville is emerging from the disaster as a greater city than ever than by staging a festival which will attract national attention."[53]

With the national spotlight fast approaching, the city had to show clear evidence that it had defeated the flood. Downtown was a wreck. Heaps of sand, piles of lumber, and mounds of rubble clogged streets along the parade route. Collapsed sewers and elevated groundwater levels thwarted efforts to repair sunken pavement. City workers joined WPA crews to pump out water, fill holes, and clear rubbish. Area businesses also spruced up, hoping to entice visitors with new landscaping and redecorated interiors. Newspapers featured examples of the community's fighting spirit and reports of record-breaking sales from stores. One bombastic *Courier-Journal* piece hailed Louisville's alleged passion for bowling as evidence of broader urban renewal.[54]

Workers completed essential street repairs and tidied Churchill Downs just in time to welcome guests arriving for the weeklong Derby Festival, an annual celebration Mayor Miller and a group of young businessmen had dreamed up in 1934 to encourage visitors to come early and stay long after the race. Crews festooned forty-six downtown blocks with bunting and draped hundreds of flags from lampposts. Storekeepers and homeowners decked out their property in shows of solidarity. Hotels ordered additional stocks of chicken, ham, and mint. This illusion of a quick recovery was perfect so long as one avoided the East and West Ends and the devastated riverfront, which most tourists were happy to do.[55]

A headline emblazoned atop the *Courier-Journal*'s commemorative Derby Week issue declared, "All America Hails Winner! City Puts Flood Far Behind!" Race organizers insisted that Louisville's rebound demanded national admiration. Red Cross area manager Richard Allen called Louisville's "phenomenal 'come back' . . . little short of miraculous." United States Chamber of Commerce president Harper Sibley deemed its recovery a "remarkable achievement." Mayor Miller seconded Sibley, writing that public services were up and running, tax revenue was streaming in, and epidemic disease was nonexistent. Meteorologist J. L. Kendall's declaration that Louisville would probably never suffer another disaster on a par with what it had just endured confirmed its long-term prospects.[56]

Louisville pulled off the occasion with admirable style. Festivities opened with the crowning of the Derby king and queen—a machinist and a stenographer—at a gala in the Rialto Theater. Neville Miller donned black silk knee breeches, silk hose, and diamond-buckled shoes for his role as lord mayor of Louisville. WHAS broadcast a mock-serious coronation that included a dozen trumpeters, a king's guard, eight pages, and the ninety-member Louisville Chorus. After the royal pair kissed a horseshoe allegedly worn by Aristides, winner of the first Kentucky Derby, Miller gave the new king the onerous responsibility of ensuring that "your people shall be merry—that the carnival spirit of your realm shall not languish—that refreshment shall be everywhere abundant and free—well, maybe not free—but anyway, cheap." Drumrolls and blaring bugles cued the audience to belt out "Happy Days Are Here Again."[57]

The week's keynote event, the Derby Parade, occurred the next evening. Participants followed a float bearing a twelve-foot, thousand-pound derby hat along a winding route through downtown. An intermittent rain depressed attendance without depressing the revelers. Each successive day brought more tourists, so many that Red Cross agents relocated from hotel rooms to a tent colony to clear space for them. Thick crowds on the sidewalks meant big money for businessmen. Sidings at Union Station filled with special trains. Visitors ambled through downtown seeking evidence of the wrecked city depicted in recent headlines. Most gave up after failing to spot spectacular destruction and elected to enjoy the party.[58]

As the week wore on, the disaster assumed an almost nostalgic quality. Tourists compared postcards depicting flood scenes with the current cleaned-up cityscape. With no heaps of sodden rubble to gape at, their talk soon turned from crest heights to horses. Ample numbers of celebrities walking the refurbished streets lent a stamp of approval to the reborn Louisville while giving the anonymous masses something else to chatter about. Babe Ruth, Jack Dempsey, and Gene Tunney represented the world of sports. Political figures including Happy Chandler, New York City mayor Jimmy Walker, and Kansas governor Alf Landon hobnobbed with the masses. A delegation of New Dealers headlined by Vice President John Nance Garner chartered a train from Washington. FDR's son James canceled at the last minute, but Mr. and Mrs. Harry Hopkins came, as did politico extraordinaire Jim Farley and Reconstruction Finance Corporation head Jesse Jones. Mayor Miller invited them to a private luncheon in his home, along with Philadelphia police chief Edward Hubbs and others who had helped protect the city. Lubricated with good liquor, they reminisced about the hardships they had surmounted and discussed the difficulties on the road ahead.[59]

Early race speculation focused on Pompoon, a sleek bay thoroughbred with a distinctive white star on his forehead, who had notched up big wins in the Belmont Futurity and the National Stallion Stakes. Local entries Reaping Reward and Dellor attracted gamblers banking on home-field advantage. The clear favorite at post time was War Admiral, the diminutive yet powerful offspring of Brushup and the legendary Man o' War. Betting surpassed the previous year's Derby but fell far short of its 1926 record take. More important was just that the nation's best three-year-olds had come to Louisville. Excited patrons filled every grandstand seat and all 20,000 boxes in Churchill Downs. Newsreel crews shot scenes of graceful horses, happy people, and a city on the rise.[60]

After months of doubts whether it would happen, the race itself offered little suspense. War Admiral leaped from the inside post position to an early lead that he never relinquished. Pompoon's valiant chase could not close the gap. The Admiral took the first jewel of his eventual Triple Crown with a convincing two-length victory. For Louisville the specific result was inconsequential, except to those with money on the line. Americans who listened to Clem McCarthy describe War Admiral's win on the radio or who saw the newsreel replays had no inkling that a calamity had wrecked the city. The illusion of restoration was complete. Louisville was back in business.

It seemed fitting for the city's elite to close Derby Week with a black-tie dinner at the Brown Hotel to honor Mayor Neville Miller, their face to the world. Guests dined on lobster bisque, boneless squab chicken perigour-dine, and potatoes margot as speakers competed to lavish the most praise on the mayor. Barry Bingham read glowing testimonials from federal officials, members of Miller's administration, and an assortment of mayors. Franklin Roosevelt interrupted a fishing trip off the Texas coast to write a congratulatory note. Happy Chandler extolled Miller's calmness and efficiency. Former mayor and political enemy William Harrison noted that "I sometimes believe in the secret recesses of my heart, that the reason I haven't agreed with him is he is doing some of the things I should have done." A humble Miller managed a brief speech thanking fellow citizens for being so gracious.[61]

Louisville's image makeover closed with a thud in the form of a scathing article in the September 1937 issue of *Harper's Monthly*. Author George R. Leighton's opening paragraph derided Louisville as "a museum piece among American cities . . . the city of let-well-enough-alone." He blasted the community's antilabor and antiblack biases and argued that its insular upper crust focused so much on preserving their own power that they ignored broader socioeconomic developments swirling around them. "That any genuine intellectual life could flourish in such an atmosphere was of course impossible," he laughed. This, after all, was a town that considered the trifling novel *Mrs. Wiggs of the Cabbage Patch* high literature. Leighton ignored the postflood narrative prominent in local circles, devoting few lines to the disaster itself and saying nothing of Louisville's rebuilding campaign. In his eyes the city had descended so far into "ossified dotage" that it was probably beyond saving.[62]

Leighton's article cut deep and hung over the city for years to come. Political and business leaders dismissed it as misinformed sour grapes. Adversarial as it was, the essay nevertheless helped jolt Louisville into a new era. Along with the flood, it dislodged ingrained traditions and inspired the city to modernize. There was much to do, but Mayor Miller and associates had begun pulling the Gateway to the South in a new direction.

Leighton's article suggested that recovery would be a long process marked by both successes and failures. Cleanup was well under way, thanks in large part to the activist Roosevelt administration. Refugees were coming home. Publicity campaigns sought to polish tarnished images and convince the outside world to forget the disaster had ever happened.

Simply forgetting the flood would leave a host of unanswered questions. Energetic Louisvillians believed their city stood on the brink of a new beginning, while bored Kiwanians killing time in the Shawneetown bank saw the end for their village as they knew it. Whatever their view of tomorrow, people everywhere understood that they could not move on until they first came to grips with why the flood had happened and figured out how to prevent another one. For answers they turned to Washington.

CHAPTER NINE

POLITICS

~~~~~~~~

"SIN IS THE CAUSE of all troubles and disasters of earth," thundered the Reverend B. F. Atkinson from his pulpit in Louisville's Hazelwood Methodist Church. "As the people of America have drifted from God into wickedness her disasters have increased in number and magnitude," he told his flock. An angry God answered our drinking, gambling, greed, cursing, and dishonesty with a wall of water. Now that the river has receded we must recommit to freeing ourselves from sin. Should we return to God, Atkinson said, "we may be sure we will have no more disastrous wars, depressions, earthquakes, drouths, floods or other disasters."[1]

Reverend Atkinson was not the only repentant who saw a divine hand in recent events. "An Angel said that the whiskey bottle . . . is a golden calf of today . . . bringing the wrath of God upon us," one man wrote, "and unless same is removed the rain will continue to get harder . . . and the State of Kentucky is to be wiped out." Charles Hoskins of Paducah expressed his moral disappointment in verse. "We failed to pay the Gospel cause / right in our home town," he stated in an unpublished poem. "So God with all authority / has surely brought us down."[2]

Most people blamed the flood on impersonal nature or blundering humans rather than on the Deity. Odd theories of causation nevertheless made their way into public discussions. E. H. Anderson asserted in a letter to the *Memphis Commercial Appeal* that "superagitation of the air by the criss-cross of airplane service" confused the atmosphere into unleashing an immense quantity of precipitation. Corps of Engineers spokesmen spent months denying rumors that Ohio River navigation dams had caused the overflow. Even if they could have affected flood heights, which they could not, crews had lowered them flat against the riverbed days before the storm cycle began. One angry correspondent insisted that the Tennessee Valley Authority monopolized the president's attention to the detriment of other waterways. "Like the fiddler Nero you have been so engrossed singing the praises of T.V.A. [that] citizens in other river valleys are left to drown," he wrote to FDR.[3]

These crackpots indicate the confusion pervading the chastened country. "There is no reason why Americans should suffer from the floods like the Chinese, when we have the wealth, the will, and the skill to control them," stated a widely reprinted editorial from the *Sandusky Register*. Anger centered on national politicians who failed to anticipate a major Ohio River inundation. These complaints made salient points even though they vastly overstated public support for dramatic changes in national water policy before 1937. Critics finally recognized that, despite decades of spending, the United States had a scattershot flood control network. Ohio valley residents believed that Congress lavished money on the lower Mississippi while ignoring its tributary because southerners dominated key committees. New Dealers took some heat for failing to commit public works programs to an expensive reshaping of the Ohio valley. "We had millions of idle men and billions of cold storage idle money and the two should have been brought together," argued one frustrated correspondent.[4]

Although no single action caused the 1937 disaster, the pioneers who settled the Ohio valley deserve a measure of blame. These hearty characters prized the river for its potential in trade, defense, agriculture, and mineral resources. It nurtured them during their early years and enabled them to thrive when fledgling settlements grew to maturity. Americans struck a bargain with the Ohio. It carried their steamboats upstream and downstream, provided drinking water, and acted as a sewer. In exchange, valley residents accepted that every so often the river would go on a tear.

Justifications for living along the Ohio faded when steamships yielded to railroads, but once rooted, cities are nearly impossible to relocate. River life defined Cairo, Louisville, Paducah, Shawneetown, and hundreds of other communities. It gave them an identity. So rather than moving out of the way when the river's importance diminished, residents dug in, building larger monuments to their own wealth and greater symbols of a rising nation's economic might. Americans constructed electrified, industrialized, densely populated cities without accounting for their silent neighbor's desire to stretch and move. They refused to adjust their lives to the river's inexorable will. Each triumph of civilization, every flag planted before the impassive river, exposed them to greater risks. "Floods are 'acts of God,'" geographer Gilbert F. White once wrote, "but flood losses are largely acts of man."[5] Damage estimates from the 1937 inundation approached $1 billion, including indirect expenses such as business interruptions and property depreciation.[6]

Choices made in the nation's capital sealed the flooders' fate. Engineers and congressmen favored Captain Andrew Humphreys's disastrous levees-only policy over Charles Ellet's multifaceted if flawed line of attack. Policymakers disregarded nineteenth-century naturalists' warnings that human development upset environmental balances and talked the recommendations of Teddy Roosevelt's Inland Waterways Commission into the ground. Narrow interpretations of the Constitution left flood control in the hands of state and local governments ill equipped to formulate a national program. Corps of Engineers officers obstructed innovative approaches to flood control, and their focus on restraining the lower Mississippi diverted attention from other dangerous streams.

Finally, there was Congress's failure to craft a comprehensive flood control program despite decades of talk. Roosevelt's halting efforts to produce one generated more heat than light. Even had one of the president's committees created a feasible plan, FDR would have had to convince governors they should allow federal intrusions on states' rights, ram a bill through a Congress ill disposed to endorse expensive projects that lay outside its supervision, and persuade voters in flood-free areas to help pay for it. And there is no way such a system could have been operational by 1937 no matter how fast he surmounted these obstacles. Congress had only recently claimed authority to create waterways projects intended for flood control rather than navigation, and legislators were still suffering from sticker shock after the 1928 Jadwin Plan.

Unprecedented devastation across the Ohio and Mississippi valleys ignited an intense debate over what to do next. Months of discussions in Washington and elsewhere raised fundamental questions about the nature of the national experiment in self-government. Politicians, editorial writers, and concerned citizens wondered whether it was best to dominate nature, run away, or adapt. They also asked whose job it was to defend against natural disaster. Was it the federal government's responsibility? If so, that required a redefinition of its constitutional prerogatives in environmental matters. Who got to define what protection meant? And what would protection cost? What was the proper price to pay for security?

Americans who rehashed arguments that predated the Theodore Roosevelt administration also called into question the purpose of the New Deal. If the New Deal's primary goal was to enhance security, then it could achieve this through overseeing an effective cleanup and building some flood protection structures. But if New Dealers aspired to create long-term change, reshape natural regions, and recreate the environment to maximize social and economic gains, then a far more ambitious agenda was required. National planning, erosion control, reforestation, expanded hydropower capacity, improved land use, and reduced waterborne pollution would have to accompany flood protection.

A chance to remake America presented itself at a delicate moment in Franklin Roosevelt's presidency. At times FDR himself doubted whether to seize the brass ring. His uncertainty, combined with bureaucratic turf wars, arguments over the balance of power in government, legitimate policy disputes, and the messy realities of legislating, ensured that the 1937 Flood Control Act would be a stopgap measure that solved few problems and set the stage for another round of politicking the next year.

SCIENTISTS, ENGINEERS, JOURNALISTS, AND amateurs vied to advance their preferred flood control schemes to the forefront of the national debate. One well-meaning educator with an eye for cheap labor suggested using beavers to construct thousands of dams in headwaters areas. Former railroad man Hugh Horn was one of many people to propose an enormous underground sewer paralleling the lower Mississippi. In a letter to presidential secretary Stephen Early, Horn noted that his project required a special kind of dredge that it just so happened he had designed. "It would be useless to refer this plan to the Army Engineers," he informed Early, "for they have already remarked that the proposition is ridiculous, that no nation on earth could afford to construct a new river half way across the continent."[7]

Politicians responsible for passing waterways bills limited themselves to more viable options that nevertheless redrew the blueprint established under the 1928 Flood Control Act. Realists understood that the cutoffs and continuous levees used to control the Mississippi would not work on the Ohio. Unlike the Mississippi, whose broad floodplain enabled the Corps to build levees far enough back from the riverbanks to hold crests to a man-

ageable height, the steep hills rising from the Ohio's banks forced engineers to construct levees close to the waterway, producing high crests.
Nor would cutoffs do much good, because the Ohio's channel was much
straighter than the twisting Mississippi's. There simply wasn't much to
cut off.

Pessimistic observers asked Americans to surrender lands that belonged
to nature. "Nature, when she looses her full fury, is still an antagonist unconquerable," declared one Kentucky newspaper. Scientists and colum-
nists suggested it was time to move uphill. Advocates of this approach
envisioned an age of limits. There were some things the country could not
do, some obstacles too large to overcome. This spirit of resignation echoed
the contemporary argument that the national economy had reached its
maximum prosperity. After eight years of depression, it seemed reasonable to assume that Americans would have to learn to make do with less.
They must abandon their naive conviction that the sweep of time inevitably led to progress and greater wealth.[8]

With absolute flood protection an unattainable dream, it made sense
to question the logic of spending billions to create an imperfect system.
The best way to stop flood damage was to live beyond the reach of rivers.
As when environmental thinkers such as George Perkins Marsh raised
this point in the mid-nineteenth century, few could stomach this defeatist ideology. The *Cairo Evening Citizen and Bulletin* acknowledged the argument's validity before rejecting it as unpatriotic. "Most human beings
are gamblers at heart, and gluttons for punishment," it explained. "They
always have been willing to take whatever Nature could hand them, and
come up fighting, providing they thought they had a chance to win."
Rather than initiating a serious discussion about man's intrusion into
dangerous lands, the flood unleashed another round of the can-do spirit
that had motivated Americans since pioneer days. "There is one thing that
is beyond question," declared an editorial in *Scientific American*: "we *will*
continue this fight."[9]

Americans wanted Ohio River flood control. Other than ordering Washington to take the lead, they were unsure how to achieve it. Proponents of
land-based methods that had been gaining supporters in recent years redoubled efforts to inject reforestation, erosion management, wise land
use, and improved water absorption into the debate. Soil Conservation
Service chief H. H. Bennett, a relentless backer of erosion control, led the
charge with an article in *Forestry News Digest* that restated the benefits of

modifying farming techniques, restoring depleted grasslands, and planting new woodlands. Bennett and his allies argued that the Corps of Engineers approached flood control backward. Rather than hastening water's
progress to the sea, a responsible program should focus on slowing its
path from the moment it hit the ground until it reached a river.[10]

Documentary moviemaker Pare Lorentz contributed the most lucid defense of this "slow it down" philosophy with his short film *The River*, released in 1938, near the apex of the flood control debates. Working under
the auspices of the Farm Security Administration, Lorentz created a self-
conscious call for environmental action that doubled as an advertisement
for New Deal conservation programs. Over its first fifteen minutes, *The
River* details the consequences of unplanned development. The camera
lingers on farmland slashed with plow lines, black smoke belching from
ships, forests denuded to fuel hungry factories. Lorentz uses the pro-
noun "we" throughout this barrage to imply collective rather than individual guilt. "We built a hundred cities and a thousand towns, but at what
a cost?" asks narrator Thomas Chalmers.

After establishing the woeful conditions in the Mississippi basin, the
film's second half considers floods and other stream-based problems. Powerful images return audiences to January 1937. Sirens wail and thunder
crashes as a rushing torrent fills the screen. Thousands of miles of levees
to hold. Lives in the balance. Radio announcers pleading for boats. Then
a sudden shift to scenes of rutted landscapes stripped of their topsoil.
Land and water fuse in the viewer's mind to become inseparable pieces of
a single puzzle. "We planted and plowed with no regard for the future,"
the narrator laments, and the Ohio valley is now tasting the bitter fruits of
that failure to plan.

But we can redeem ourselves. "We had the power to take the valley
apart," Chalmers notes as the music turns upbeat, and "we have the power
to put it together again." He explains that the Tennessee Valley Authority
provides a model for reconstruction. Smiling New Deal employees working on the Norris Dam and other TVA installations flash across the screen.
We can provide flood control. We can institute scientific farming techniques. We can generate hydroelectricity. We can weave a new social fabric. We can strategize our way to a better future. "You cannot plan for
water unless you plan for land," Chalmers intones, "but you cannot plan
for water and land unless you plan for people." Man and nature coexisting

in harmony, with man's guiding hand firmly on the tiller. There is no better, more succinct summary of New Deal conservationism.[11]

The Corps of Engineers swatted away the arguments of Lorentz and H. H. Bennett with a flick of the wrist. In an article for *Military Engineer*, Captain Paschal Strong expressed sympathy for erosion control and planting programs while cautioning that they were nearly useless as flood control measures. Army men dismissed calls for damming the Ohio on the reasonable grounds that preventing another deluge like 1937's required a storage reservoir larger than Lake Erie. Further, corpsmen expressed doubts about the *Little Waters* type of headwaters barriers. Like the reforesters, acolytes of H. S. Person's 1936 volume pounced on the crisis. Paul Sears, author of the 1935 soil erosion primer *Deserts on the March*, urged his countrymen to view flood control as "landscape architecture on an imperial scale," using thousands of small ponds and dams to retain water at its source. Former Forest Service chief Gifford Pinchot contributed a passionate endorsement of *Little Waters*. "A flood is like an epidemic," he wrote. "The time to stop it is before it begins."[12]

After arousing great interest when it emerged the previous year, the headwaters plan faded from the public imagination primarily because Person's agenda bore little relevance to the recent flood. January's disaster came from downstream rather than upstream, as heavy rains pounded rivers from Cairo to Cincinnati. Small check dams along the rivulets feeding the Allegheny and Monongahela would have had little effect on crests save perhaps in the Pittsburgh area, and the Steel City suffered minor damage compared with downstream communities such as Louisville. Americans were more willing to embrace a program that prevented another 1937 flood than to adopt a speculative approach that, while effective under certain conditions, would not have stopped the Ohio from flooding. They wanted to refight the last war rather than prepare for the next one.

There was no consensus on Ohio valley flood control. Gatherings of politicians, scientists, and engineers bickered over the size, scope, and particulars of a plan. Rabble-rousing valley congressmen more interested in shouting than specifics asserted that somebody should do something to prevent another disaster. Difficult questions of who should pay for a program that would doubtless be expensive remained unresolved as states' righters sparred with supporters of federal development and funding. Their theoretical and philosophical concerns contrasted with the tangible problems facing basin residents who paused in their scrubbing and hammering, or peeked out from their tent flaps, to wonder when the government would figure out how to protect them.

Authorities wanted to get waterways reform right this time. But ideological differences, petty rivalries, and honest disputes over how to protect Americans precluded a consensus definition of "right." Competing and to some degree incompatible proposals emerged.

FDR's National Resources Committee issued a long-term flood control agenda two weeks before chief engineer Markham declared victory over the inundation. Its blueprint eschewed the *Little Waters* approach of building hundreds of small dams on headwaters streams in favor of a series of reservoirs across tributaries. Roosevelt presented the report as a huge step toward the comprehensive approach he had advocated since his presidency began. The committee judged projects not just on their own merits, but also on how they related to other watershed improvements. FDR cited the board's work as further proof of the benefits of a permanent planning agency housed within the executive branch, responsible for articulating long-term plans and construction schedules without the parochial thinking that had hamstrung progress for decades.[13]

Ever the deft politician, Roosevelt added a wrinkle that co-opted a competing congressional plan. Inspired by the ability of TVA and the Miami Conservancy District to manage their rivers during the crisis, Senator Robert Bulkley and Congressman Robert Secrest, both of Ohio, proposed an Ohio Valley Authority vested with the power to build and operate dams and reservoirs, improve navigation, and oversee reforestation and conservation throughout the watershed. Governors from Illinois, Indiana, Ohio, and Pennsylvania endorsed the bill. In tandem with congressional allies, they lobbied the White House for approval.[14]

FDR sympathized with Bulkley and Secrest's goals but feared that a new authority might function independently of his cherished National Resources Committee. On a more idealistic level, he thought it represented another piecemeal attack on waterways problems. The crafty president sought to incorporate the Bulkley-Secrest bill into his vision of a unitary planning agency. Roosevelt set aside his preparations to unveil his court reform package (which proposed expanding the Supreme Court from nine justices to a pro–New Deal majority of fifteen) to share a leisurely lunch with TVA director Arthur Morgan. As they dined the two men discussed whether putting TVA on a national scale might "bring order into the flood control situation." FDR generously recounted the gist of their conversation for the press. The next day, a gaggle of reporters heard administration ally and TVA supporter Senator George Norris remark that the best way to handle water and conservation problems would be to create "enough TVAs to cover the entire country."[15]

With attention fixed on Roosevelt's surprise announcement of his court plan, Norris's trial balloon garnered little interest until FDR mentioned it a few days later in a press conference. Seeming to speculate out loud, the president suggested setting up new regional planning agencies to propose flood control, drought, and conservation projects through a permanent national planning board that coordinated the proposals into an overall agenda. This casual aside hinted at a revolution in American environmental policy, a dream come true for advocates of national planning.

FDR offered only hazy insight into how he wanted different levels of government to divide the expense of new river projects. Labeling the 1936 Flood Control Act's insistence that locals pay for lands, rights-of-way, and maintenance of levees and dams "a headache," he suggested that the federal government should assume a larger financial role in order to cut through bureaucratic snarls entangling state governments struggling to determine how to divide project costs. At the same time, he opposed calls for the federal government to bear the entire burden of improving rivers.[16]

Within twenty-four hours of the president's press conference, Senator Bulkley and Senator Alben Barkley of Kentucky introduced legislation to create seven TVA-style bureaus. Congressman Secrest initiated an identical bill in the House. That both senators had conferred with Harry Hopkins the previous day indicates that they acted with the administration's consent. In addition to an Ohio Valley Authority, the Bulkley-Barkley bill would establish agencies supervising the Atlantic seaboard and the Arkansas, Colorado, Columbia, Mississippi, and Missouri River valleys. As FDR had suggested, the proposed boards reported to a national planning committee under presidential control.[17]

The Bulkley-Barkley bill prompted outrage from power companies and their friends in the legislature, who believed it would grant the federal government control over hydropower resources. Their antagonism marked another chapter in a long battle between power interests and New Dealers. Ever since the Progressive Era, and particularly during the 1930s, reformers had advocated publicly owned hydropower as a means for uplifting impoverished regions. Utility firms blasted this idea as unconstitutional, economically inefficient, and communistic. FDR's enthusiasm for TVA reflected his position in the dispute. On this occasion, however, the mercurial president sidestepped the issue, equivocating when reporters asked whether he envisioned the proposed authorities' constructing hydroelectric dams.[18]

Roosevelt's end run around the Corps of Engineers in favor of his own board antagonized defenders both of congressional privilege and of the politically savvy Corps, which had spent years cultivating influential politicians. The Corps's strongest supporter in Congress was Mississippi's Will Whittington, who had assumed the chairmanship of the House Flood Control Committee just days before Black Sunday. A lawyer by trade, the graying, sleepy-eyed Whittington had focused on waterways issues ever since coming to Congress in 1925. His primary goal, one he spent twenty-five years pushing for, was to win federal appropriations for flood control in the basin of the Yazoo River, a tributary of the Mississippi that meandered through his district. Although he possessed a gift for legislative maneuvering, the tall, doughy attorney was a bland man prone to turgid prose. He was either lazy or self-confident enough to reuse large blocks of text in speech after speech. For all his oratorical shortcomings, Whittington lit up when he talked about streams. "There is a beauty and a charm about rivers to me," he told one waterways convention, "and I am devoted to the Mississippi Valley as I am to no other Valley in all the world." He fancied himself a historian of floods who sprinkled his talks with poetic, scriptural, and historical references to inundations. His tenacity and expertise made him a key player in passing the 1928 and 1936 Flood Control Acts.[19]

Whittington's almost reverential respect for the Corps of Engineers compelled him to resist any move that reduced its power. He perceived FDR's love for national coordinating boards as a misguided infatuation that would expand an already bloated federal government and impose "an economic and planning dictatorship" that robbed the army, and by extension Congress, of its right to select and fund worthy projects. Whittington also worried that new TVAs would concentrate on reforestation and soil erosion at the expense of what he considered real flood control. "I am interested in little waters, but I am emphasizing big waters," he told the Ohio Valley Improvement Association. "The digging of a few ditches, the building of a few dams will not suffice. The planting of grasses, trees and soil conserving crops is not enough." This child of the volatile Mississippi basin believed the best way to safeguard the Ohio valley was with strong levees and a smattering of reservoirs. He appreciated conservation for conservation's sake, but like his friends in the Corps, he saw no reason to complicate the pressing issue of reducing flood heights with such esoteric concerns as reclamation, pollution control, and hydropower. For him a comprehensive plan was one that covered as many rivers as possible, not one that sprawled into far-flung considerations of water and land use in general.[20]

His comments revealed the philosophical differences underlying the flood control debate. Supporters of a multifaceted approach carried forward a tradition of seeing the environment as something to be sculpted to fit human needs. That reshaping represented mankind's effort to accommodate and adapt to the natural world. It respected the power of nature by improving on it rather than conquering it. Whittington, on the other hand, saw the environment much as the Puritans had—as a dark, dangerous enemy, an enigmatic other. Rather than to sculpt it, he wanted to literally wall it off with an unbreakable barrier between man and river. He would not back away from nature. Neither would he try to meet it halfway.

Whittington's committee countered Bulkley and Barkley's "Little TVAs" bill with a resolution asking the Corps of Engineers to assemble a plan for Ohio and Mississippi River flood control. The Mississippian hoped to blunt momentum for the more expansive and intrusive alternative while preserving Congress's and the Corps's prerogative over rivers. He also knew that chief engineer Markham's proposal would focus on traditional flood control methods rather than more exotic measures.[21]

Whittington reframed the postflood debate around two distinct alternatives. If he and the Corps had their way, the federal government would provide the Ohio valley with a reasonable level of flood protection akin to that achieved along the Mississippi following 1927. Should Roosevelt and the Bulkley-Barkley forces prevail, Americans might see something much larger than flood control. A permanent national planning board and a well-funded, well-run group of waterways authorities could revolutionize the country's environmental priorities and its use of natural resources. If managed well—by no means a given—this centralized arrangement might mitigate wasteful soil and water use, ease pollution, protect communities from flooding, and create reservoirs suitable for recreation and tourism. It might also develop inexpensive hydroelectric power capable of fueling an expansion of industry in underdeveloped regions.

Roosevelt's silence left Congress and the public unsure of his desires and relegated his demand for a permanent planning board to the back burner. His inattention seems baffling until we recall that other matters held the White House's attention. "Three weeks ago we were working day and night because of the flood," Stephen Early wrote in his diary. "Now, it is the judicial reform program that causes midnight oil to be burned." Besides hoping to reinvent the Supreme Court, Roosevelt was also trying to reorganize the executive branch; balance the budget; manage the fall-out from the recently concluded sit-down strike at a General Motors plant in Flint, Michigan; monitor signs of renewed tension between China and Japan; and keep an eye on Adolf Hitler. The president hesitated to stir up more trouble with Congress, especially if it meant alienating conservative southern Democrats who objected to growing the federal government— except perhaps to attend to the lower Mississippi. With FDR distracted and Whittington promoting his alternative, Bulkley-Barkley languished in both houses, stuck in committee with no immediate hope of making it to the floor of either side of the Capitol.[22]

Chief Markham was not about to let the Corps of Engineers fall victim to legislative drift. His victory lap at the Bonnet Carré floodway kicked off a string of appearances intended to burnish the Corps's reputation and authority. Markham used a series of newspaper interviews and a turn on the lecture circuit to steer the army's agenda into the limelight.

By the time he addressed the Mississippi Valley Association's March 1937 gathering in St. Louis, he had his basic patter down. About two hundred delegates from nineteen states gathered to hear the general and other dignitaries speak in the Statler Hotel, a brick-and-limestone colossus looming near the current site of the Gateway Arch. MVA president and former Nebraska governor Arthur Weaver set the tone when he begged the administration to put its faith in "the most efficient governmental agency in the United States." The pro-army crowd burst into applause whenever one of the governors, congressmen, or experts on the slate praised the Corps's floodtime performance.[23]

Markham dominated the room like a Roman emperor. Alternating between his prepared text and extemporaneous asides, he opened with an assault on his critics aimed at establishing the Corps's unimpeachable wisdom. He encountered many nonsensical arguments on river management as he traveled the flood zone, the engineer said. False prophets voiced strong opinions that were "one hundred and eighty degrees in error." Never pausing to cite examples of such erroneous thinking, he ordered the gathering to insist on facts rather than speculation when dealing with water-ways. "And I assert that you will get from the Corps of Engineers facts and nothing else," he roared as the audience cheered.[24]

Markham next attacked those who claimed the Corps favored levees over reservoirs. We are not "anti-reservoir," he said, but evidence contra-dicted reservoir exponents—and, by extension, Corps detractors such as the National Resources Committee and *Little Waters* enthusiasts—who believed they could protect the Ohio valley without levees and local river walls. No reservoir complex could hold the Ohio, nor would headwaters dams have impeded the deluge. Adjusting his sights toward the conserva-tion crowd, he derided the notion that reforestation and soil conservation could prevent major floods as further evidence of the "misinformation" pervading the debate. "There is a large amount of brains wrapped up in a small package," Chairman Weaver gushed after the general sat down.[25]

Will Whittington seconded Weaver when he spoke a few minutes later. The congressman touted the Corps as the agency best suited to lead a na-tional flood control program. Like his friend Markham, he rejected the "superficial theories, lopsided plans, and fallacious remedies" offered over the past few years. He voiced particular scorn for "so-called scientists" and "alleged geologists" who suggested pulling back from the rivers. "I oppose retreat; I oppose the abject surrender of progress and advancement to the rule and reign of the beasts of the forest and of the jungle," he bellowed to great applause.[26]

Unlike the chief engineer, who preserved a veneer of political neu-trality, the congressman devoted much of his time to mocking the FDR-backed Bulkley-Barkley legislation. Repeating arguments rehearsed in previous talks, Whittington charged that the proposal created an out-of-control bureaucracy operating without input from the Corps or the public's congressional representatives. The authorities' mandate to tackle environmental issues would distract them from the more important goal of defending Americans from dangerous waters.

Whittington argued for the opposite of Roosevelt's comprehensive ap-proach. Instead of uniting land and water-based subjects within a single bureaucracy, he wanted to divide them among multiple agencies. Public Health Service investigators could handle pollution issues, and the De-partment of Agriculture, not some permanent national planning board or valley authority, could house expanded reforestation and erosion control programs. His vision seemed an invitation to redundancy and inefficiency.

Perhaps stagnation was his goal, a crude if effective way of ensuring that the Corps retained its power.[27]

After hearing Whittington and subsequent notables, the body adopted a resolution urging Roosevelt to keep the Corps of Engineers as the nation's primary flood control body. Although the group did not specifically consider the Bulkley-Barkley proposal, its vote of confidence for the Corps conveyed its perspective well enough. Its decision signaled that the flood control establishment accepted the need to extend protection beyond the lower Mississippi and favored a greater federal role in financing improvements but balked at bids to expand the definition of "flood control" or to make a bold break from traditional lines of authority.[28]

Few Americans understood the nuances of these competing proposals. They did, however, agree that Washington must move now, before memories of the disaster faded. Editorialists, civic groups, and congressmen beat the drum for action. They could not say how best to attack the problem, but, as Senator Alben Barkley explained, "a way must be devised."[29]

THE GOVERNORS, MAYORS, LEVEE board engineers, and esteemed citizens descending on Washington cared less about the exact means of winning protection than about ensuring that the river avoided their little corner of the world. Most congressmen felt the same way, agitating for their own states' defense while exhibiting scant interest in the particulars of a basinwide program. Quick to claim states' rights when they resented federal intrusion, now they all wanted Washington to pay. "There will be a whacking big appropriation for flood control programs," one newspaper correspondent wrote from the capital, "but there is also going to be a considerable sectional scramble for the money." Local concerns reacted to the prospect of cash on the loose like sharks to blood. "Whatever you're going to do, do it now, so that you can get your claim in and share in the appropriation that is to be made," the Kiwanis Club of Harrisburg, Illinois, advised the city's delegation to Washington.[30]

Visiting lobbyists all believed their cities deserved flood protection more than any other and insisted they could not pay for it themselves. Scores of communities enlisted powerful politicians to their cause. Boss Ed Crump of Memphis relied on Washington cronies Representative Walter Chandler and Senator Kenneth McKellar to win appropriations for enough walls and pumping stations to put north and south Memphis beyond the water's reach. The boss articulated as well as anyone the rationale for federal funding. "This is not Memphis water," he told reporters. "Some of it comes from New York State. It comes from all over the valley."[31]

Cairo, the survivor, the city that reveled in its invulnerability to high waters, also wanted to ride federal dollars to a brighter future. As soon as the danger passed, Mayor August Bode organized a committee to represent the city's interests. Members spent months arguing over what they wanted Congress to do for them. They all agreed, however, that "Cairo's name ought to be in the pot when those appropriations are made." Boosters backed their demand with a campaign of puffery intended to promote the laughable claim that Cairo's location made it the most important city in the United States, so it deserved special consideration in any future legislation.[32]

Paducah's business community tasked its delegation with selling a plan to construct a floodwall. For them, flood protection had become an absolute right on a par with life, liberty, and the pursuit of happiness. City manager L. V. Bean asserted that damages dwarfed Paducah's revenues, bolstering the case for federal responsibility. Without Washington's help, the city could never be safe.[33]

Bean's fiscal dilemma resounded throughout the valley. Floodtime expenditures imposed huge shortfalls on state and city governments. Mayors and governors advised Washington that the twin demons of Depression and high water destroyed any chance for significant local contributions to a national flood control agenda. They could not even scrape together money to meet the 1936 Flood Control Act's requirement that they purchase land and rights-of-way for flood works. Washington answered these protestations with a new Disaster Loan Corporation that lent $20 million to victims ineligible for Red Cross funds or WPA relief. Although a significant departure from Calvin Coolidge's tightfisted response in 1927, the sum was a drop in the bucket for the devastated region.

It is ironic that the intense fixation on national flood control increased the chances that Congress would fail to achieve it. Washington felt relentless pressure to pull a legislative rabbit out of its hat. Parochial politicians focusing on their districts' desire for immediate protection threatened to continue the practice of treating flood control as a hodgepodge of pork barrel projects. The 1928 act had corrected some earlier mistakes but could not prevent policymakers from returning to precedents in the name of constituent service and the path of least resistance. A new law based on who spoke the loudest and who carried the most political clout might worsen the situation on the Ohio. Raising walls in one place meant more water downstream. Misplaced reservoirs were expensive boondoggles that had little or no impact on water levels.

Roosevelt held to his insistence on a unified, comprehensive approach. He squelched rogue congressmen's pet proposals like a firefighter dousing a thousand blazes. But not even the master politician could keep the lid on forever. Flood control fever surged when General Markham announced in early April that the Corps of Engineers had completed its review of the watershed studies in its files and was prepared to tender a report. Leaked stories indicated that the Corps wanted to construct eighty-eight reservoirs and local protective works for 155 cities. Its program carried a $1.1 billion price tag, four times the amount authorized under the 1928 act. Most exciting for valley residents, rumor had it that Markham had reversed his opinion that local interests should finance floodwalls and was prepared to endorse federal funding.[34]

Roosevelt, just returned to the capital after six weeks at his retreat in Warm Springs, Georgia, intended to maintain control over the legislative process. Ignoring customary procedure, he intercepted the Corps's report before it reached Whittington's Flood Control Committee, the body that had requested it. He explained to an outraged secretary of war, Henry Woodring, that the magnitude of the flood issue and the need to connect it with other waterways problems necessitated his decision. FDR wanted the National Resources Committee to review the document before Congress saw it. Woodring objected to the breach in protocol. He forwarded the report under a huffy cover letter that proclaimed Markham's work "sufficiently comprehensive in scope to prevent a repetition of the disastrous flood of this year" and questioned the wisdom of undermining the Corps's authority, to say nothing of his own.[35]

Markham's proposal fulfilled Woodring's interpretation of "comprehensive" in that it employed levees, floodwalls, channel improvements, and floodways to defend a large portion of the country from inundation. Actually, Markham had appropriated Roosevelt's language without fulfilling his intentions. FDR clung to a broader definition of the term that echoed the visions of Charles Ellet, John Wesley Powell, and Teddy Roosevelt. The president imagined a sweeping policy that folded all land- and water-based problems within a river basin into one interconnected program that reflected the input not just of hydrological engineers, but also of the Interior and Agriculture Departments, the Federal Power Commission, and the Public Health Service.

Roosevelt's treasured National Resources Committee added to the public confusion when it unveiled a $4 billion package of erosion, anti-pollution, conservation, reforestation, hydropower, navigation, and water supply projects. Ohio valley communities still processing the differences between the Corps of Engineers' program and the Bulkley-Barkley bill now had a third option thrown into the mix. Angry editorial writers demanded a quick resolution. "Why can not a plan proposed by a group of engineers who have no peers in flood control work . . . be spared the fate of being jostled about by various committees and choked to death in red tape?" the *Paducah Sun-Democrat* asked. Everyone wanted to hear from FDR, who chose this moment to fade into the legislative shadows, refusing to say exactly what he wanted to pass.[36]

Roosevelt further obscured his objectives when he situated flood control within the context of an ongoing fiscal retrenchment. Upward-ticking financial indicators convinced the president that the Depression had run its course. Soon after his reelection he decided to slash federal spending in order to balance the budget. FDR dashed the hopes of waterways proponents who thought the public clamor for protection insulated river improvements from the budgetary ax. "I recognize the need for flood prevention and control," a presidential message to legislators read, but the current proposals before Congress were simply too expensive for his liking. FDR aimed to cut waterways spending rather than expand it. "Purse-Pinching Injures Flood Control Effort," screamed a *Sun-Democrat* headline.[37]

The National Resources Committee promptly contradicted the president's belt tightening when it dismissed the army's billion-dollar request as inadequate. Loaded with representatives from Interior and Agriculture and their ideological allies, the board's rebuttal alleged that the Corps of Engineers viewed hydropower, erosion, and pollution control as "incidental to flood protection." It further complained that Markham's stranglehold over waterways excluded other interested agencies. The general, who had a seat on the committee, refused to sign off on its recommendations. He showed little interest in its work and sent subordinates to most meetings rather than attending in person.[38]

FDR received the National Resources Committee's recommendations while on his way to New Orleans for another fishing trip. He agreed that the Corps had not satisfied his demand for a comprehensive approach, an objection he noted when he finally forwarded Markham's outline to Whittington's committee. He also rejected the Corps's suggestion that Washington pay for land, damages, and rights-of-way needed for new projects because the measure upset his budgetary priorities and undermined cooperation between local and national governments, an important element of national planning strategies.[39]

From the safety of his boat Roosevelt delegated Secretary Woodring to inform Markham that his program failed to meet the president's criteria for comprehensiveness and exceeded his fiscal limitations. Always a tough mind to penetrate, FDR appeared to be asking for a bigger bill that cost less money. Perhaps he was just stalling. He asked the secretaries of agriculture and interior to work with Representative Whittington to present a plan to Congress the following January. Turf wars and an inability to agree on basic terms had dragged progress on Ohio valley flood control to a standstill.[40]

Whittington could not fathom the president's objections. As he read the Corps's agenda he saw everything necessary to lowering crests. It had reservoirs, levees, and local floodwalls. It was a by-the-book strategy bearing a stamp of approval from the world's most talented engineers. "The proposed plan appears to be comprehensive for flood control," he wrote in a personal letter to FDR. It reflected the accumulated knowledge of decades of waterways studies. Its long-term benefits far outweighed its immediate costs. Whittington cast the issue as a political boon that dovetailed with the president's overall agenda. "You have stated that one-third of the nation is ill-housed, ill-clad and ill-nourished," he observed. "Many of these poor people are in constant jeopardy of floods." As if to conceal his anger and pave the way for fruitful negotiations in the future, Whittington closed with a jovial note wishing FDR good luck with his fishing.[41]

Other correspondents were less courteous. "It is inconceivable that the President and the Congress would fail to put through legislation to remedy the flood danger on the Ohio, when so much is at stake," the *Paducah Sun-Democrat* sputtered. A physician from Covington, Kentucky, complained to his congressman that FDR had pulled the rug from under them. "Perhaps if he had also had one good dose of mud and water in his own home with destruction of his property he would not be so glib on promises and so damn poor on fulfillment," he exclaimed.[42]

Reminders of what was at stake could be found throughout the valley, including Jeffersonville, Indiana, where four months after the crest many residents still lived in a tent community outside town. WPA crews scraped away six inches of silt from the Quartermaster Depot before flushing it out with high-pressure hoses. With most of the city's houses destroyed and local government in debt to its statutory limit, Camp Melville assumed an air of permanence. Each tent had an electric light. A half-mile of pipes delivered water for drinking, showering, and washing. Few homeowners had the resources to rebuild on their own. Overburdened Red Cross staffers faced thousands of unprocessed claims. Civic groups begged donations from sightseers and mailed circulars soliciting aid from undamaged towns that, regrettably, provided little assistance.[43]

Another pathetic scenario played out a few hundred miles to the west. Bird's Point farmers drifted back to the floodway, often with a shove from their landlords, to find they had lost whatever meager possessions they left behind. Sharecroppers' tents dotting the landscape represented a slight step downward from their obliterated shacks. None of the returning flooders received monetary compensation for their troubles because the government had purchased flowage rights for the property years earlier. Those payments, generally about ten dollars an acre, went to landlords, not tenants.[44]

Repairs began as water drained from the floodway. In a patch of timber, a levee patrol discovered the remains of the barge that had carried two dozen men to their deaths. Rotten corn strewn across the ground and mangled railroad tracks leading nowhere testified to how much had to be done just to return the area to its preflood squalor. Deep deserts of sand covered acreage near the levees. Corps of Engineers officers supervised teams that reconstructed fuse-plug levees and filled "blue holes," deep new lakes that the rushing water gouged from the earth.[45]

Landowners hustled the Red Cross from the floodway so they could concentrate on planting rather than rehabilitation. A spring rise almost buried the fragile seedlings. Engineers issued an order to abandon Bird's Point as the Ohio climbed against the blasted-out fuse plug. Local flood boards advised farmers to take their tents with them to ensure a quick resettling once the danger passed. Thousands of residents again trudged the sad paths to refugee camps. Over five thousand WPA and CCC enrollees manned tractors, earthmovers, and shovels to shore up the levee. This time the floodway stayed dry. Planters sent croppers back to their plots well before the river settled to a comfortable level, content with knowing their land was safe for now.[46]

Dramas like these impelled representatives in Washington to keep pressing for reform. In June Roosevelt crafted a message to Congress designed to refocus the drive for flood control. Instead, he frustrated representatives who already opposed his waterways plans and confused others who supported him but could not figure out what he wanted them to do. His much anticipated communiqué articulated the same environmental priorities he had expressed for years. Its suggestion that droughts and floods resulted from poor land management and its praise for headwaters dams and environmental solutions to waterways problems indicated that the president favored the *Little Waters* perspective. "Great works on main streams" could not solve America's ecological problems, Roosevelt stated in a slap at the Corps of Engineers. He reiterated that he wanted local interests to cooperate with flood control measures, a subtle way of telling Congress he did not want the federal government to pay. At the same time, he recommended greater federal authority through the creation of additional TVA-style entities under executive control. Roosevelt therefore wanted Congress to enhance the president's powers at its own expense while abandoning its relationship with the Corps of Engineers, long the ultimate authority on river matters. And still he offered no specifics.[47]

Opponents of his agenda, including many Democrats, rebelled. They chose as their weapon an innocuous resolution introduced during the flood by two Arkansas legislators, Senator Hattie Caraway and Congressman John McClellan. Senate Joint Resolution 57 asked the Corps of Engineers to produce a national flood control plan. Whittington's directive to Markham made S.J. 57 redundant and condemned it to legislative purgatory. Congress resurrected the bill after FDR's speech convinced detractors that he intended to centralize environmental policy within the White House. Hoping to comply with the letter if not the spirit of Roosevelt's desires, committees tacked on amendments empowering the Corps to update its report to include hydroelectric power, land use, and erosion. In a stunning power play, the Corps's congressional backers sought to invest the engineers with the powers the president wanted for the national planning board while simultaneously killing plans for additional valley authorities.[48]

Set against the multiple plans floating through the legislative ether, the ensuing debate was so confusing that not even Congressman McClellan could determine whether Roosevelt favored S.J. 57. Showing a stronger grasp of the bill's purpose, Secretary of War Woodring and Will Whittington lobbied for its passage. If they had their way, Congress would take up a comprehensive plan that marginalized hydropower development, forest and soil reclamation, pollution control, and recreation and exiled Roosevelt's planning board to irrelevance.[49]

Representatives from the Federal Power Commission and other agencies that saw S.J. 57 as an attack on their authority convinced the president that the resolution betrayed the goals of his June 3 address. FDR reacted with uncharacteristic glee when the proposal reached the White House after passing both houses without objection. "It is a Joint Resolution; it is on my desk, and I am going to veto it!" he told his uncle Frederic Delano.[50]

His veto message threw down a gauntlet to Corps defenders. He framed his rejection as a defense of the common man. The national planning board used a "thoroughly democratic process" that incorporated opinions from state and local experts. S.J. 57, on the other hand, handed control to a single agency that reported to Congress rather than to the president, the sole representative of the nation as a whole. Under his rather tortured logic, Roosevelt's plan to consolidate power within the executive branch actually decentralized power across the country. His reasoning made sense only to those familiar with theorists such as George Soule, who argued that a central board was the most effective way to coordinate planning agencies at all levels of society, guaranteeing maximum possible input from ordinary citizens. Roosevelt failed to explain this rather nuanced context.[51]

FDR offered to give Whittington a voice in the planning board's talks. The Mississippian accepted the deal while continuing to pursue his own bureaucratic priorities. He opened hearings to consider local protection projects along the Ohio. His Flood Control Committee did not have much to discuss because Whittington and Roosevelt had already agreed to authorize $25 million in new spending—nowhere near enough to provide for all 155 candidates Markham's report listed—and to let the Corps decide what towns received a slice of the pie.

Whittington's main objective for the hearings was to showcase the Corps and diminish Roosevelt's plan for little TVAs. He scheduled Markham's appearance for the first few days of hearings, when public interest was at its peak. The general sounded polished, well informed, and ideologically neutral as he explained the Corps's goals for the Ohio basin. Whittington dominated the questioning, lobbing softball inquiries that Markham answered with the skill of someone who knew what was coming. No, he responded to the congressman's innocent inquiry, reservoirs would have affected crests "in a very trifling way." Yes, local protection works were the sole means of guaranteeing a town's safety. No, reforestation and other conservation projects would not solve the flood problem. And no, states and localities could not afford the contributions that the 1936 Flood Control Act demanded. This last point was crucial for Whittington. Reversing his stance of a decade earlier, he now believed the federal government must shoulder the fiscal load. He knew that Mississippi could never finance the expensive levees and reservoirs he desired for the Yazoo basin.[52]

Congressman Orville Zimmerman of Missouri pressed the general to move Cairo to the top of the Corps's priority list to ensure that the army would never again open the Bird's Point floodway. Other committee members asked a few desultory questions before sitting back to watch the chairman run the show. Their meek probing reinforced their conviction that Markham knew best. "The Corps of Engineers is thoroughly satisfied that if the projects herein recommended are constructed, we would have flood control on the Ohio and Mississippi Rivers?" John McClellan asked. "I see no reason to doubt it," the general replied. Neither did the committee. Its members had no scientific training and no background in hydrology. And unlike the aloof scientists and bureaucrats on Roosevelt's planning board, the engineers had cultivated them for their entire congressional careers.[53]

Markham's two days of testimony marked the first act in Whittington's dog and pony show. A gaggle of high-ranking engineers confirmed their leader's testimony. After them came a string of what cold war–era inquisitors might have called "unfriendly witnesses." Soil Conservation Services chief H. H. Bennett's passionate recitation of the benefits of better land use failed to impress congressmen primarily interested in whether his ideas had flood control benefits. Bennett's tepid allowance that they might have some effect on reducing crests won him few friends. Committeemen lost interest in the Forest Service's Edward Munns once he admitted his department did not know whether reforestation could prevent major floods. Nor did they ask much of Clark Salyer of the Agriculture Department's Biological Survey Division, whose enthusiasm for the new wildlife refuges that headwaters dams might create far exceeded their own.[54]

Whittington welcomed these eager environmentalists because they gave him cover to argue that he had thoroughly investigated the president's demand for a comprehensive plan. In reality he conducted two hearings, one that counted and one that did not. Representatives from other departments could not change the fact that, no matter how compelling their presentations, Markham's men would determine the shape of pending legislation. Anxious as they were to have a platform, they did a poor job of connecting their ideas with a larger program of Ohio valley flood control. Committeemen agreed that soil and trees were important but saw no link between them and the committee's legislative portfolio.

The Flood Control Act stormed through Congress a few weeks after Whittington gaveled the hearings to a close. It was a stopgap measure that addressed some of the Ohio valley's most urgent concerns while shoving larger environmental questions under the rug. Under its provisions the Corps of Engineers spread a $25 million authorization for local protective works among fifteen communities. Costs ranged from $87,770 for Metropolis, Illinois, to $1,310,000 for Huntington, West Virginia. Cincinnati and Paducah made the list. Louisville, Cairo, and Memphis did not. No one had any clear explanation for why some towns merited protection and others did not.[55]

Although Whittington's Yazoo basin received no direct benefit from an act that centered on the Ohio River, the chairman did insert a clause that eased Washington closer to his goal of having the federal government assume the full cost of flood control. The law reaffirmed the requirement that locals pay for land acquisition, rights-of-way, and operating expenses required for projects, as well as for any property damages incurred during construction. Whittington's proviso, however, allowed the president to waive up to half of those costs if communities demonstrated they could not afford them. Roosevelt disliked the clause but saw it as too insignificant to justify a veto that Congress would override anyway. In fact, he applied the rule several times over the coming years.[56]

New Dealers did an exceptional job of handling Americans' short-term needs. They proved less able to realize their long-term hope of eliminating the weaknesses that made the region so vulnerable in the first place. The 1937 Flood Control Act marked a tentative stab at tackling problems that could have been solved long before. It forestalled rather than confronted the differences between Congress and the president, leaving the devastated Ohio valley to wonder whether this unique opportunity for protection might founder on political shoals. Even cities included in the act had reason to doubt the government's sincerity. Although the law authorized

$25 million for walls, it appropriated only $5 million. Congress still faced hundreds of millions of dollars in unfunded mandates from earlier river bills. Prospects for additional funds were hazy.

Residents of the Ohio basin kept cleaning their homes and rebuilding their towns as Washington debated, discussed, and delayed. "The country will demand a general flood control bill in 1938," Whittington told a gathering of the Mississippi River Commission. The chairman understood that lawmakers had to overcome their conflicting loyalties and philosophical differences to produce an act that was in some way comprehensive. Whether it would be comprehensive in FDR's sense or in the Corps's remained unclear. At stake was the notion that an activist, scientifically managed central government could coordinate improvements in American life. Also hanging in the balance was a golden opportunity to redesign the country's relationship with its soil, its forests, and its water. As Roosevelt's men saw it, this moment offered their best chance to install a long-term, rational approach to the national ecosystem. Anything less would simply push environmental problems onto the next generation.[57]

One small town reenacted in miniature many of the conversations taking place across the country. Shawneetowners debated whether to face the river or abandon it and wondered if their heritage meant more than their security. They asked whether the federal government was a partner or an enemy. They struggled to determine whether the old ways were good enough for them or if the flood had created a new world with new rules.

CHAPTER TEN

MOVING?

~~~~~~~~~

FEW PEOPLE HAD HEARD of Shawneetown, Illinois, before the 1937 flood. The ranks of those in the know grew only slightly after the catastrophe. Except for its many links with prominent figures from the past and its importance to the early republic, the old village was basically indistinguishable from a hundred other settlements lining the banks of a score of rivers. It was the tiniest of dots on the map.

Events in Shawneetown after the flood nevertheless raised issues central to New Deal era America. A movement to relocate the village transfixed federal officials eager to test whether enlightened bureaucrats could remake a devastated community. Their interest embodied the goals of the New Deal. The Roosevelt administration sought not only to provide economic and environmental security, but also to merge the central government with local interests to create a more rational and better planned nation.

A small project with big stakes ended up revealing some of the limits of the New Deal as Washington struggled to translate grand designs into reality. Idealism faltered in the face of grassroots actuality. Like the larger flood control debate, the new Shawneetown became mired in conflicting agendas as residents nudged relocation in unexpected and, from Washington's perspective, undesirable directions. Shawneetown was a proud, divided community ruled by go-getting elites who saw the flood as the start of a new chapter in their glorious local narrative. Officials in Washington agreed that a page had been turned, but neither they nor competing factions of Shawneetowners seemed to realize they were reading from different books.

RESIDENTS OF SHAWNEETOWN DRIFTED home far earlier than they should have. In mid-February African Americans ventured out of the segregated Red Cross camp in Marion, fifty miles to the west, to join whites coming down from highland farms and refugee camps. Ten feet of water still swirled through parts of the village. The river sat five feet higher inside the levee than outside.

"Any attempt to detail the losses sustained by the property owners of Shawneetown would be futile and fall far short of accuracy," the local paper gasped on April Fools' Day, its first edition since the evacuation. A decomposing pig swung from telephone wires in front of the courthouse. A cow dangled with its head wedged in the fork of a tree. People who had herded their livestock upstairs before the flood found the animals had starved or drowned. An awful stench hung over the community. Mud covered everything. Incoming water had leveled shacks in the south part of town, across from where Galt's crew dynamited the levee. Among the best-preserved structures were the rudimentary box-construction homes the Red Cross had erected after the 1898 and 1913 overflows. Although most remained intact, floodwaters had either flipped them over or shoved them off their foundations.[1]

Devastated Shawneetown became a popular tourist destination. On some Sundays 20,000 visitors poured through, creating miles-long lines of cars on the highway. The ruins assumed an oddly festive spirit as gawkers snapped photographs and gazed at the river. Alert National Guardsmen ensured that they respected property rights. Opportunistic store owners reopened well before the town dried out to capitalize on the once-in-a-lifetime crowds.[2]

A few hundred hardy, or perhaps foolhardy, souls set up in town despite the lack of electricity and the risk of disease owing to poor sanitation. When Rudy Phillips, the eccentric owner of Rudy's Barbecue, hitchhiked from his refuge to the water's edge, he discovered his boat tied up right where he left it. Dodging low-hanging power lines, he rowed around the village until he found his restaurant jammed against a tree a block from its original location, with Harry Harmon's house nearly on top of it. Phillips next visited his parents' muddy but livable home. He scooped muck there for several days before getting back to his business. A trip to the high school

A family kills time in the Shawneetown tent camp. Library of Congress Prints and Photographs Division, LC-USF34-010659-D.

garnered some Red Cross pork and beans. Phillips dragged his barbecue shack back to its original site, next door to Hoppy Venters's livery stable, and sold the donated food to tourists and relief workers.[3]

Few returning Shawneetowners inhaled the mingled smells of barbecue, stagnant water, mildew, and horse manure. Rather than moving into their homes—if they still had homes—most sheltered in the tent colony near the high school. Camp officials provided seven hundred flooders with bathhouses, laundry facilities, and hot and cold running water, conveniences rarely enjoyed before the inundation. Red Cross workers transported white children to school in shuttle buses and erected a tent to replace the missing black elementary school. Recreation was also segregated. People sat and waited, and waited some more. A kind of inertia fell over the community. Days turned into weeks with no sign of movement.[4]

Efforts to alleviate the boredom sometimes backfired. In March the Red Cross announced a big Easter party. Excited children spent days coloring hundreds of eggs before discovering on Sunday morning that thieves had stolen all but seventeen. This brazen larceny marked a low point; otherwise camp morale fluctuated from hour to hour. Weather shifts prompted wide mood swings. Sunny mornings brought good humor that evaporated whenever storm clouds darkened the sky.[5]

Uncertainty pervaded the colony. Some spoke of going home. Others sought a new direction. "There's no use looking back," Mrs. Fred Logsdon wrote to her sister. "Looking back only grieves everyone."[6]

This absence of direction offered a perfect opportunity for Max Galt, William Brinkley, and their friends to impose their relocation plan. Sensing the thirst for leadership, they posted notices announcing a meeting to discuss "the future of the city of Shawneetown." This open-ended mission statement implied that everyone's opinion mattered when in fact the dominant clique had already decided the town's future.[7]

Forty-one leading citizens answered the summons to the high school. Mayor Brinkley invited Congressman Claude Parsons, representatives from the Red Cross and WPA, and Harry Frissell of the Corps of Engineers to join them. Although the meeting had no formal agenda, at least so far as the general public knew, relocation backers carefully prearranged the results. "We had to make plans ahead of time for what we wanted to do at the mass meeting so that it would all seem spontaneous," one of the organizers recalled.

Mayor Brinkley opened the discussion by asking his friend Frissell whether raising the levee would provide complete flood protection. The engineer answered that the wall could go no higher unless the town razed Main Street to accommodate the wider base needed to support it. Even if we leveled our commercial center, he continued, the village's sandy soil would draw in seep water no matter how high the levee. Shawneetown would always be wet. Residents would not rebuild and new businesses would not move in.[8]

Having established that the status quo meant stagnation or slow death, someone in the cabal mentioned Charles Carroll's 1913 offer to donate land for a relocation. An old plat showing a tidy new town on the spot miraculously appeared. Congressman Parsons, who had discussed relocation with Brinkley in private, promised to wring funds from the WPA, the Public Works Administration, and other federal agencies. He claimed the Red Cross would contribute $150,000. Max Galt and Harry Howell speculated that the state might preserve Shawneetown's historic buildings and convert the rest of the site into a park. Their overwhelming, coordinated assault of logic goaded the assembly into voting forty to one in favor of relocation.[9]

Mayor Brinkley flourished the business class's endorsement at a second, larger meeting. Congressman Parsons stopped by the packed schoolhouse to repeat his assurances of federal and private support. A Red Cross representative confirmed that flood victims could still receive rehabilitation funds if they resettled. Lieutenant Governor John Stelle offered the sole cautionary note. Illinois could not legally appropriate funds for individual needs, he observed, and moving uphill might eliminate jobs because Shawneetown's industries required riverside locations. Once repaired, the existing levee provided sufficient protection against anything other than a thousand-year flood. Rather than diving in headfirst, the community should name a committee to discuss proposals with government officials and the Red Cross.[10]

Whether by accident or by design, the lieutenant governor's suggestion dovetailed with the Young Turks' plans. After hearing Stelle's speech, the assembly asked Mayor Brinkley to name a negotiating team. His handpicked commission consisted of Shawneetown elites who favored relocation over rebuilding. Sensitive to charges of denominational if not class-based favoritism, Brinkley appointed representatives from every church that had a predominately upper- or middle-class congregation. By placing relocation in the hands of a select committee, the audience gave the people who raised the issue in the first place the power to determine its course. To all intents and purposes, Brinkley decided the community's fate before most Shawneetowners even came home.[11]

Brinkley, Galt, Howell, and the rest of the relocation committee conferred with Governor Henry Horner and his advisers through the spring. Brinkley spun nightmarish scenarios of a community held captive, unable to defend itself from the mighty Ohio. He hammered at the idea that Shawneetown's best hope for survival was for the legislature to buy out its residents. Horner questioned the plan's merits. A hardworking, soft-hearted man who favored relief to the poor and grieved at the suffering of others, he nevertheless remained wary of big government, especially when that meant working with the WPA, as any town relocation program would do. He considered Harry Hopkins a patronizing bully and, as a budget hawk, resented the WPA's insistence that states match federal relief contributions. It took multiple tries for Brinkley's group to persuade Horner to support relocation.[12]

Despite Congressman Parsons's optimism, the Red Cross also cast a skeptical eye on relocation. DeWitt Smith, the organization's general director of flood relief, believed the price tag for a new town would exceed Red Cross rehabilitation payments. Rebuilding was more cost-effective than moving. Beyond that, Smith saw no reason to waste money on a community whose reason for being had evaporated decades earlier. "There is apparently little justification for a town at the present or proposed site," he told one confidant. Smith expected many property owners to take the money from their land sales and head for more prosperous cities, leaving the Red Cross and the government in charge of a ghost town. Agency executives decided to suspend rehabilitation payments until the town resolved the question of relocation versus rebuilding, a nondecision that enhanced the uncertainty in the tent colony.[13]

Shawneetown's plight intrigued the WPA, an essential ally for any relocation setup. The WPA was already paying 150 locals to clean public property, pump out polluted wells, and tear down or reposition displaced buildings. Transferring the town would put hundreds to work constructing public buildings, sidewalks, and roads. On a larger scale, Shawneetown offered a chance to win good press and congressional favor by revitalizing a downtrodden community through government planning. That the project offered a vast canvas for showcasing WPA efficiency and expertise appealed to Hopkins and his colleagues. Critics unfairly derided the WPA as a make-work bureaucracy that hired people to rake leaves or move piles of dirt. In contrast, Shawneetown required substantial technical know-how that would create lasting monuments to the WPA. A successful operation could silence doubters and convince legislators they should make the agency permanent.[14]

The *Gallatin Democrat*'s financial well-being depended on advertising revenue from the same businessmen who were organizing the relocation bid. Predisposed to favor the establishment, the paper emerged from its three-month flood hiatus as a weekly exponent of a new Shawneetown. Articles imagined tourists and employers flocking to a gleaming, flood-safe metropolis, sparking an economic boom that resonated throughout southeast Illinois. One fanciful piece imagined the village itself urging residents to head for high ground. "It is my desire," said the fictionalized city, "that I be moved bodily from my present location to one that would assure me of a chance to bloom and thrive."[15]

Democrat publisher W. W. Mattingly ran with the Galt crowd and was no doubt aware of the behind-the-scenes maneuverings in the relocation saga. His paper simplified these events into a narrative that emphasized positive developments and ignored or downplayed obstacles. *Democrat* writers concealed the frustrations of local, state, and federal officials and minimized dissenting opinions within the community. Removal assumed an air of inevitability as readers perused article after article extolling their leaders' triumphs over bureaucracy. This selective reporting further estranged ordinary citizens from decision making and diminished their emotional investment in the town's future. Exclusion heightened long-standing social tensions. "I don't trust the whole crowd of them," a detractor complained of Brinkley's team. "They're as crooked as a barrel of snakes. Why, you can't even find out what they're doing."[16]

The secrecy cloaking negotiations inspired fears that "outsiders" like Galt and Mayor Brinkley, considered an interloper by some despite his twenty-year residency, wanted to turn local troubles to their advantage. "They knew this was a flood area when they came in," one doubter informed Governor Horner. Now that the town had gotten wet, they planned to profit through business deals and real-estate sales associated with the move. A vocal minority revived hoary tales of the town's glorious past to support their argument that Brinkley's mad dash to move would destroy a cohesive, compassionate community. "If I could choose a heaven, it would be Shawneetown," one nostalgic villager wrote to the *St. Louis Post-Dispatch*.[17]

April's mayoral election attested that voters desired a heaven without a riverfront. Brinkley wanted out after eight years in the unpaid position. Still ailing from a bad chest cold he picked up in January, and fuming about his constituents' refusal to heed his flood warnings, he was eager to retire to his farm. Harry Howell and former mayor June Rowan vied to succeed him. Howell, a member of Brinkley's relocation committee, ran on a pro-move ticket. Rowan opposed relocation largely based on his deep roots in the area. He lived in a magnificent brick home his grandfather had built in 1832, a three-story masterpiece that had survived thirteen floods but was too old and too massive to be moved.

Rowan's campaign invoked Shawneetown's history and pioneering spirit, insisting that the community lived or died by the river. Even if the Ohio no longer served much of an economic function, forsaking it meant surrendering their heritage. Shawneetown without the river was not Shawneetown. This sense of place, this attachment to a waterway, resounded throughout the valley. On some level they could never quite articulate, the people of the Ohio basin identified with a river that had punished those who dared live near it. Its power excited them, enchanted them, held them to the spot against all rational arguments.[18]

On election day, voters, most of them living in the Red Cross camp, trudged through a driving rainstorm to put Howell in office by an overwhelming margin. Brinkley swore in the new mayor that evening. Howell's victory consolidated the Young Turks' hold on the town's public affairs. His opponents saw the election as Shawneetown's death knell. "Now we are told that we'll have to move whether we like it or not," Rowan lamented. "When they haul us out feet first—that's when we're going," his wife added defiantly.[19]

Pro-move forces received an additional boost when an ominous spring rise on the Ohio reminded everyone of the old town's vulnerability. A more dramatic event occurred at the high school, the scene of so much recent misery. Once the refugees left, principal Packett's family and new janitor William Brown had settled back into their quarters. Their peace lasted only a few weeks. Early one morning the principal woke up to the smell of smoke. He leaped from bed to find fire tearing through the gymnasium and licking its way into classrooms. Packett shook his wife awake and grabbed Brown to join the battle against the growing conflagration. Flames engulfed the building before a pumper truck arrived from Harrisburg. Volunteers dived for cover when the gymnasium roof collapsed in a smoking mass of metal girders and smoldering timbers.

The blaze probably started in the pile of goods refugees had left when they fled the flood. Eager to return his school to normal, Packett had recently distributed notices asking people to claim their possessions before the upcoming commencement ceremony. Few complied before the massive stack of clothes, furniture, mattresses, appliances, and pianos went up in flames. People still coping with the loss of a home now lost the rest of their belongings. It was a cruel blow to a shattered community. Some interpreted the fire as a final break with the past, a cleansing if destructive symbol of the need for a fresh start.[20]

Locals were reconciling themselves to moving. Officials in Springfield remained unsure whether they wanted to help. State director of public works Lynden Smith's office became the epicenter of the debate. Shawneetown's request for the state to convert the town site into a park put the relocation issue within Smith's bureaucratic domain, and the director did not like the way things were going. He objected to enlarging the park sys-

Max Galt, the driving force behind Shawneetown's
relocation. Courtesy of the Galt family.

tem during tight times and demanded more concrete answers from town
leaders before signing on to what could become a budget-busting fiasco.
Smith also wanted Shawneetown to replace Mayor Brinkley's slapdash
commission with a state-approved housing authority composed of impartial delegates with no stake in the city's property holdings or future.[21]

Mayor Howell agreed in principle, but the resulting Gallatin County
Housing Authority (GCHA) was neither impartial nor disinterested. Its
members—Max Galt, who emerged as the GCHA's point man; Harry Howell;
grocer Ralph Harmon; car dealer Earl Rich; and former mayor William Brinkley—were close friends and staunch pro-movers with important business
and real-estate interests. Few Shawneetowners had a greater stake in the
village's fate.

The *Gallatin Democrat* predicted smooth sailing and accepted at face value
Howell's proclamation that "the Housing Authority has no secrets." Journalists rarely questioned committee members' actions or provided insight
into their activities. They wrote vaguely sourced stories of outside indus-

tries yearning to set up shop on a new site and feel-good summaries of the GCHA's harmonious meetings with the WPA or State Housing Board. Their obfuscation echoed the traditional way of doing business in the fractured community. The upper classes ruled, and the masses stayed out of the way.[22]

Shawneetown's "outs" had little idea that the GCHA was in far over its collective head. Galt, Howell, and company were fine small-town businessmen who had no conception of how to transport, then renovate, 250 homes, build 175 more, lay miles of roads, install a sewer system, run water lines, and construct a courthouse and other public buildings. Overconfident committee members talked of easy money coming from Washington. They assured the WPA that they could contribute $1 million to the project even though the GCHA had almost no staff, no architectural or engineering plans, and no way to get the move off the ground. Its working capital consisted of a $500 gift from Kiwanis International. "There is some disparity between one million dollars and five hundred," one WPA wit observed when his agency learned of the discrepancy.[23]

The GCHA's formal proposal for a $2.5 million WPA grant reeked of amateurism. It contained no explanation of how the authority planned to finance its part of the operation, no evidence that people would buy the homes it proposed to construct, and no building designs. GCHA investigators had not determined which structures could be moved and which needed replacing. They had not acquired land for a new town. Galt's group asked the WPA to pay for $5,000 houses—far beyond most locals' means—featuring intricate detail work that would require skilled labor imported from larger communities. WPA administrators rejected the submission out of hand. Either ignoring the humiliation or unaware of it, the *Democrat* informed readers that the WPA's check was practically in the mail just a few days after officials laughed the proposal out of Washington.[24]

"That project's in pretty bad shape for us to try to handle," observed Harry Hopkins's deputy Francis Harrington. WPA officials, however, refused to relinquish their dream that Shawneetown could become an economic anchor for southern Illinois and a model for future social engineering projects. Believing there were too many cooks in the village, Washington wanted to push the state out of the picture to enforce a more top-down structure on the project. WPA officers thought the Illinois Housing Board, another piece of Lynden Smith's bureaucratic empire, was too cautious. Its delays eroded confidence that the move would happen. As months passed without evidence of activity, homeowners started rebuilding. Each hammer blow of new construction sapped impetus from relocation.[25]

A parade of WPA officials trooped through southern Illinois seeking to overcome the GCHA's shortcomings and impress their stamp on the project. They wanted Shawneetown to move in spite of itself. WPA laborers cleared space in the bank to accommodate an army of technicians, draftsmen, and architects that it hired to design houses and fix a definite price tag. WPA hires decided what to salvage from the old town. They rewrote the GCHA's grant application so thoroughly that the WPA was essentially asking itself for money. Washington also prodded Galt's team to hire Lincoln Rogers, an experienced project manager in the Public Works Administration's housing division, as the relocation's general manager.[26]

Washington wanted to give Shawneetowners tangible evidence that the move would happen, so WPA officials hired Mary Long Whitmore, a landscape architect from Metropolis, Illinois, to construct a miniature of the community. She built a 225-square-foot model in her garage that the GCHA trucked in for exhibition in the historic Peeples Building, just up the street from the bank. Residents could now imagine themselves in one of the 484 tiny houses. Viewers admired the ample green space, gracious central mall, and striking juxtaposition of square blocks in the city center with semicircular roads delineating the outer rim. They unconsciously invested the design with their own prejudices, replicating in their minds the divisions that marked old Shawneetown. "One thing I like about the new town is that we will be able to select the neighbors we desire," an admirer noted. "While no segregation of our colored population is shown on the map," a *Gallatin Democrat* writer added, "it is believed they will be offered a section to themselves."[27]

The model revived interest in the move without speeding actual progress. Heavy lobbying from area representatives and the WPA finally convinced the Illinois legislature to authorize $150,000 to purchase lots in Shawneetown. Lynden Smith's State Housing Board refused to release the money until the GCHA acquired options to sell from property owners, a labor-intensive responsibility the authority shirked. The GCHA's empty treasury meant the board could not meet the local-contribution requirement demanded of any WPA project. Even if it somehow raised the cash, it did not yet own a site for the new town. "Not at all encouraging," remarked Arthur Lord, the WPA's chief liaison with the GCHA.[28]

Whitmore's creation sat on display for six months before the GCHA finally struck a deal with the WPA. A realistic assessment of Shawneetown's housing requirements halved the authority's $2.5 million request. Under the revised application Washington contributed about $700,000 for labor, supervision, and materials. The GCHA promised nearly $600,000 for its share of the work.[29] On paper the proposition transformed a dying river community into an economically diverse regional showplace. New Shawneetown featured a grand courthouse, a multipurpose public building, a history museum, a host house for curious visitors, and a crafts center. This was New Deal optimism at its audacious best, a glitzy example of the good that came when local dreamers cooperated with the central government's social planners.

Galt assured Washington that the move could start within two weeks of approval. Lincoln Rogers arrived to assume his duties soon after Roosevelt signed off on the proposal. Despite these positive signs, the one-year anniversary of the flood passed with no signs of activity—no ground broken, no streets graded, no homes transferred. Louisville had staged its Derby and Congress passed a stopgap flood control act. Shawneetown was still a ragged array of tents and tumbledown houses tucked between cornfields and the Ohio. Blame for the delay rested largely on the GCHA. WPA officials refused to start construction until Shawneetown proved it would pay its share of the costs, and the impoverished community simply could not do this. Its only hope for raising money was the Disaster Loan Corporation, the relief agency created in the wake of the flood. It needed to have the federal government lend it money it could then leverage into additional federal aid.[30]

DLC representatives agreed to lend the GCHA $450,000 if the authority first collected binding commitments to relocate, a precaution designed to ensure that people actually occupied homes constructed with DLC funds. Rather than fulfilling this obligation, something it should have done months earlier, the GCHA bumbled its way through additional unproductive months. Its members repeatedly claimed remarkable progress only to have frustrated government investigators discover they had exaggerated their successes. So the WPA waited for the DLC, and the DLC waited for the GCHA. And the river, waiting for no one, flowed past a town entrenched right where Michael Sprinkle had opened his trading post a century and half earlier.

The first substantial construction loan from the DLC arrived in mid-

1938. It took the GCHA almost that long to acquire land for the new site. Within days of the flood crest, Mayor Brinkley had selected an ideal plot across the highway from the high school. Inexplicably, the GCHA waited a year to approach the owner of one of the desired parcels. Discussions with the other proprietors went nowhere. Knowing they had considerable leverage, the landlords held out for as much as they could get. At one point Galt offered $300 an acre for land with an appraised value of $75 an acre.[31]

Galt's bid meant little. The GCHA had no money, and the DLC would never finance such an egregious overpayment. Tempers flared as the stand-off dragged on. Arthur Lord dismissed the proceedings as "a farce." Francis Harrington warned Galt it was "imperative that this matter be taken care of without further delay." The banker insisted the property was a good deal at any price because land values were sure to skyrocket after the move. Galt appealed to Washington's idealism, arguing that with a little patience and a small financial outlay New Dealers could lead his "blighted and der-elict" community toward its prosperous destiny. Galt's entreaties bought the breathing space he needed. In mid-1938 the DLC paid $48,000, or $150 an acre, for the new site.[32]

Silence emanating from the *Democrat* convinced most residents that Whitmore's model would never take shape. Apathy gripped the town as momentum for relocation dissipated. Seventy-seven-year-old Albert Venters epitomized the community's fading interest in social engineering schemes. "It don't make much difference to me if they do move," he declared, "I will be here even though left alone." Venters spent his days in a rickety old chair under a tree on the empty lot where his house once stood, selling chickens and eggs from a stall next to Rudy's Barbecue and moving his seat to stay in the shade as the day progressed.[33]

GCHA members finally asked residents to reserve lots in the new town soon after the Disaster Loan Corporation purchased the site. Although the *Democrat* reported a "mad rush" to sign up, the town's elite stood at the head of the line. Brinkleys, Galts, Harmons, Howells, and Riches grabbed the choicest locations. Property owners sold their land to the state in ex-change for credits to purchase a spot at the new site. Low-interest loans from the DLC would cover residual expenses. Relocation was not free, as many assumed—and the GCHA had done nothing to discourage those whisperings—but it came at a nominal price.[34]

Lincoln Rogers announced that crews would transport the first house in July. Anticipating rapid progress, Arthur Lord moved to town to supervise

WPA personnel. Lord's promise to run a transparent operation with high standards of quality was a tacit admission of the GCHA's sloppiness and feeble public relations skills. In return he asked locals to "fall into line," trust the outsiders, and subordinate individual interests to the general good. Lord showed a canny awareness of the community's self-image. "The very act of relocation," he said, "is new evidence that the proud pioneer spirit of Shawneetown is still dominant in the hearts of the people."[35]

A vocal minority apparently rejected the pioneer spirit he invoked, for a cohesive anti-relocation movement emerged when it became clear that a decisive break from the past lay on the horizon. A village that once concealed its social prejudices behind a facade of shared history split into quarreling factions that never fully resolved their differences.

Opponents criticized the move out of a desire to respect ancestral roots or because they believed they could force a better deal from the government if they obstructed progress. Skeptics in Springfield blamed delays on the "natural lethargy of the people." Divisions also reflected the upper class's alienation from the masses. Poor residents stuck in fetid bottomlands wanted to vacate the old site but disliked the idea of going into debt to purchase a new house. The revelation that the government would not cover the entire cost of moving convinced some have-nots that local elites had tricked them into supporting the scheme. Apprehensive of any white-led endeavor, African Americans suspected that the GCHA's lengthy moving contracts contained traps garbed in legalistic rhetoric.[36]

Doubts grew as urbane, urbanized WPA technicians arrived. Unskilled local workers resented the high wages newcomers earned. Gossip spread that government bureaucrats had hatched the relocation plot to further communistic ideas of social engineering. Hostility kept incoming WPA managers on edge. Well-educated professionals who saw the ruined village as a stopover rather than a destination chafed at the intense scrutiny they faced. One complained that he could not have a beer in a tavern without hearing stories that he had started a barroom brawl. Galt exhibited this parochialism when he grumbled that the project would be better off if "high salaried outsiders" stopped stirring up trouble with their big-city arrogance and curious ways.[37]

Galt himself aroused the suspicion of anti-movers. For all his bonhomie, he was a controversial figure subject to rumors of corruption. Everything he touched in his business career turned to coal, yet he kept smelling like a rose. His loan company failed, his insurance company failed, and the bank wobbled during the early 1930s financial crisis. No one knew how Galt maintained his prosperous image. Conventional wisdom in some circles held that he skimmed off the top. There is little evidence to support these stories. The most anyone can be sure of is that he engaged in nepotism, a common sin in small-town life, since both he and Mayor Howell put relatives on the WPA payroll.[38]

Galt and Howell's GCHA ensured that Shawneetown's haves benefited from relocation. Members rejected a proposed community building fund that would enable poor homeowners to borrow extra money for construction because it would reduce the pool available to the wealthy. They fought to spend federal dollars on cheap, low-maintenance rental housing instead of seeking ways to broaden homeownership. Howell floated a plan to transfer every house regardless of its current condition and let owners make repairs at their own expense, thus guaranteeing a wide disparity between rich and poor. As Lord noted, "Slums now will still be slums." These hard-nosed proposals drove the WPA official to distraction. "The plain fact is that this group does not want to see the poor families of Shawneetown taken care of with decent housing," he fumed.[39]

Anti-movers despised project manager Lincoln Rogers, whose wide experience in housing developments did not translate into good people skills. His brusqueness alienated many, as did his long absences from the job site and his unwillingness to explain complex details to bewildered clients. Rogers expected people to shut up, accept his word as gospel, and fill out the forty-seven forms required to complete a moving contract. He is "a source of constant irritation and friction," Lord observed. Rogers's downfall came when inquisitive Shawneetowners unearthed his extramarital romp with Mary Long Whitmore, the architect who designed the model of the community. Matters reached a head when Whitmore's mother stormed into town with a gun, promising to execute the man who had defiled her daughter. Galt fired the manager soon after, ostensibly because the relocation no longer required his services. Rogers took a post with the U.S. Housing Authority, divorced his wife, and left for Chicago with Whitmore to work on a new housing project.[40]

Businessmen occupying the sturdy brick stores on Main Street opposed the move for economic reasons. High waters destroyed their stocks but inflicted little damage on the buildings themselves, so the cost of reopening was small. Merchants would have to fund construction of new outlets from their own shallow pockets because the WPA's charter prevented it from building businesses. Beyond this financial consideration, no one dared move without first being sure their patrons were coming with them. Everyone had to move together for the transfer to succeed, and unity was a scarce commodity.[41]

A gloomy spirit pervaded the village through 1938. Charges of incompetence, graft, and profiteering haunted the GCHA. Political discord widened as local Republicans cursed the "damned New Dealers" among them. Another minor spring flood incited further hostilities. Paranoid anti-movers accused pro-movers of plugging storm sewers to keep water from draining out of town in order to emphasize the risk of flooding.[42]

Galt's childhood friend Al Lowe was the chief rabble-rouser. Lowe was a balding, middle-aged businessman whose main objection to moving, like June Rowan's, was that he wanted to remain in the marvelous home his grandfather had built a century earlier. He called an October 1938 meeting of three hundred moving opponents hoping to forge them into a cohesive bloc with himself as its leader. The gathering came after the GCHA announced an election to consider annexing property for the new town, a necessary precursor to construction and the only way to keep the WPA interested in the faltering project. Lowe's followers plastered walls with handbills reading "Save Shawneetown, Vote 'No'" and implored citizens not to "dig up good solid roots and try to get them to thrive in quicksand." Voters nevertheless approved the measure 715 to 240. Their approval allowed the town to incorporate territory across from the high school and a strip of land a few yards wide along the highway connecting the two sites.[43]

Subsequent elections confirmed the pro-move majority. In April 1939 voters agreed to sell bonds to pay for conveying the city's waterworks to the new development, a transfer that deprived the old town of running water. Three months later Gallatin County approved bonds to build a new courthouse at the WPA site. As Lowe's allies feared, these decisions drained population and amenities from the riverside area.[44]

The annexation election suggested a great leap forward, and in fall 1938 the hilltop site did indeed hum. Four large grading machines prepared the ground for roads. A ditcher trenched the earth to receive sewer pipes. WPA workers tossed up temporary barracks and a plumbing shop, concrete-mixing shop, and woodworking shop. They devoted more care to a demonstration home erected behind the nearly completed host house. Arthur Lord, elevated to executive chairman of the GCHA after Lincoln Rogers's ignominious departure, praised the modest four-room structure as an example of the "best and cheapest type of house construction." Most exciting for those who had lived in squalor for the past two years, a house-moving crew arrived from Indianapolis.[45]

Once again the appearance of progress exceeded actual progress. House movers lolled around the construction site drinking coffee and playing cards, because the GCHA had not yet acquired a single completed relocation contract. The $3,000 they charged every month for their inactivity epitomized a project hemorrhaging money. WPA administrators spent $200,000 building field offices, roads, public buildings, sidewalks, and sewers for a town with no houses. The understaffed GCHA needed more draftsmen, contract writers, and stenographers, but additional help was hard to find. Shawneetown natives lacked the education needed, and outsiders refused to come without assurances of long-term employment. The one lawyer in the area able to handle complex titles and abstract jobs was an elderly man on the verge of a work-induced nervous breakdown.[46]

Francis Harrington's threat to kill the project inspired a brief spurt of action. The GCHA finally started handing over signed agreements, then had to spend months redrawing them when an oil rush necessitated a clause reserving mineral rights. Mother Nature added to the problems when yet another minor flood, this one in March 1939, filled Shawneetown with seep water. WPA outsiders dubbed the soggy village "Lake Shawnee." A fire at the WPA office building the next month destroyed technical books, equipment, and architectural plans. An exhausted Arthur Lord tried to find a bright spot in the jet black picture. "If everything at Shawneetown is as thoroughly accomplished as the burning of the field office building, there can be no cause of complaint," he wrote to a friend.[47]

Just when the night seemed darkest, dawn broke. The April 13, 1939, edition of the *Gallatin Democrat* blared amazing news. Construction crews had started on the first house and scheduled a score more to commence within a week. "It seems almost unbelievable," the paper remarked. WPA workers laid off during inhospitable winter months returned to the payroll to dig foundations, grade landscaping, seed lawns, and construct a sewage treatment plant. Other teams rebuilt the burned-out high school gym. An optimistic editorial predicted that the hammering of studs would silence dissidents. "Why not forget differences that may exist and pull together for mutual benefit to build one of the best towns in the country?" it asked in a rare acknowledgment of community tensions.[48]

Tidy homes popped up on the flat, treeless plain opposite the refurbished school. They contained from three to seven rooms, including a bathroom—a feature only five houses in the preflood town possessed. Older buildings started arriving five months later when movers jacked Ewing Hobbs's small frame house onto beams for a one-hour procession up Route 13. James Coleman's seven-room, two-story home and Marsh Wiseheart's two-and-a-half-story mansion followed it west.[49]

Ordinary citizens believed relocation was proceeding without a hitch. Even Ralph Harmon and Earl Rich signed contracts for new homes, ending an embarrassingly long period of indecision for the two GCHA members. Visitors to the construction site watched heavy equipment rumble down wide dirt lanes and thrilled to see familiar homes in unfamiliar places. An enormous red, white, and blue WPA sign facing the highway promised glory for this city reborn upon a hill. Spectacularly floodlit at night, the banner depicted an ultramodern yet somehow quaint community center, courthouse, and museum surrounding a green mall. "Oldest and Newest City of Illinois," the sign proclaimed. Within that image lay an entire philosophy of government and American life. Its promise of continuity coexisting with innovation suggested that the New Deal could improve life without meddling in it. New Shawneetown represented the mutually beneficial melding of Washington with the grass roots. It epitomized the dreams of Franklin Roosevelt and other New Dealers who extolled greenbelt communities, masterpieces of human planning that gave defeated farmers and discontented urbanites a chance to thrive in an environment that combined orderly streets with untrammeled green spaces.[50]

Lingering difficulties lurked beneath this gleaming exterior. Building the newest city in Illinois cost far more than the WPA anticipated. Interminable delays meant high overhead and idle employees. Families who demanded customized homes created extra work and more overruns. The GCHA's inability to deliver contracts on time scotched the WPA's plan to use assembly line methods to hold down expenses. Crews worked haphazardly on whatever lot was ready for construction rather than moving efficiently from one project to the next. WPA officials had already spent most of their appropriation when Galt requested an additional $250,000 to complete the town. Lord dismissed the suggestion out of hand. "I have come reluctantly to the conclusion that the Housing Authority of Gallatin County is itself the chief obstacle to the prosecution of the project," he

After years of delays a new Shawneetown rises from the earth. Courtesy of Shawneetown Public Library.

told a colleague. He sympathized with Galt and Howell, two small-town businessmen juggling the thirteen state and federal agencies involved in the relocation as best they could. But much as it pained him, he was ready to walk away.[51]

After touring the desolate work site, Walter Wesselius of the Red Cross joked that he "hoped to live to see the day that Shawneetown was moved, which was tantamount with wishing for long life." He believed the transfer would "go on indefinitely and probably end up in a divided city." Lord had neither the patience nor the resources to find out whether Wesselius was right. WPA workers had relocated Leavenworth, Indiana, a town of about four hundred, months earlier. Shawneetown, in contrast, seemed in no hurry to go anywhere. Frustrated with the plodding pace, Lord announced a pullout date of September 30. When Galt pleaded for more time, he granted three additional months. Crews focused on homes they could complete by the end of the year. Technical workers packed up their blueprints and architectural equipment and headed off to other jobs.[52]

Shawneetown no longer existed as a separate federal project as of January 1940, the first time the *Democrat* acknowledged rumors of the WPA's changing relationship with the GCHA. The State of Illinois folded the move into its larger WPA roster, relegating it to being just another item on a

chock-full agenda. Illinois's WPA assumed responsibility for constructing public buildings and infrastructure. Responsibility for transporting
existing homes and building new ones fell to the destitute, shorthanded
GCHA.

Bitter temperatures brought halting progress to a standstill. That winter was so cold that people walked across the frozen Ohio. The barren, icy
work zone echoed the horrible scene three years earlier. Twenty-seven
houses, twelve new and fifteen moved, stood on the site, their isolated
peaks thrusting upward against a lifeless landscape. Though the surface
was frozen earth, not water, the topographies of 1937 and 1940 were equally
lonely. Deep gashes crisscrossed unpaved streets waiting to receive sewer
and water pipes. Unconnected stretches of sidewalk suggested a town long
gone rather than one waiting to be born. The unfinished host house could
not shelter visitors even if any came.

As of late 1940, new Shawneetown boasted about 120 homes. About
1,000 people, half the village's population, lived in the development. Many
of the community's landmarks sat in updated surroundings. People gaped
as the old town's 132-foot, fifty-ton water tower rolled up the highway.
Moving the century-old courthouse bell required an especially deft touch;
laborers ripped out the floors below the old building's belfry, guided the
bell through the holes, and wrestled it onto a truck bound for the new
courthouse.[53]

An endeavor that embodied the New Deal's best impulses limped toward an inconclusive finish. A March 1940 tornado that tore the roof off
the rebuilt high school symbolized the project as a whole. One step forward, one step back. WPA enrollees dismantled their workshop, once tabbed
as the centerpiece of a regional construction program, to reuse as part of
a munitions plant sixty miles to the east. Desperate for cash, the GCHA
sold lots in the northeast corner of town that had no access to city services.
Mayor Howell reasoned that "persons who do not want water and sewer
facilities can thus move or build in the new town at a greatly reduced expense."[54]

Dreams of a model community evaporated in the face of cold financial
reality. What began as a test of the New Deal's ability to engineer a better
society ended up as another example of an activist government's providing
security for a select group of people. This was no small achievement. Neither was it what ambitious New Dealers had set out to accomplish. Washington never harmonized its agenda with the goals of the various local

interests. New Dealers perhaps expected too much of small-town businessmen unaccustomed to dealing with miles of red tape, and too much of
parochial people wary of outsiders' meddling in their affairs. At the same
time, Shawneetowners showed an inability to overcome ingrained social
divisions and prejudices that limited decision making to a handful of powerful men and left the bulk of the population in the dark. Centralized planning encountered local realities at Shawneetown. The result was something neither side imagined back in those heady, tragic days of early 1937.

GCHA OFFICIALS USED THEIR last DLC dollars to erect a row of commercial buildings on the central mall's west side. They finally accepted
that Main Street businessmen were not going to pay to relocate and that
the expected rush of outside employers would never materialize. Merchants who balked at the expense of building their own stores agreed to
lease space at the new site. Ralph Harmon's grocery and Harry Howell's
department store occupied two-story structures. A bank, a variety store,
a clothing store, a jewelry store, a barbershop, an electrical shop, and a
movie theater improved the quality of life at the new site while pinching
customers from the old town.[55]

Business leaders spent 1941 trumpeting the area's abundant timber and
coal reserves, easy river transport, and cheap labor in a futile bid to attract
defense industries. A potential source of traffic and tourist revenue vanished when plans to construct a bridge over the Ohio collapsed amid war-
time steel shortages. Pearl Harbor killed any remaining federal support for
relocation. The WPA diverted its laborers to war needs in summer 1942.
With no money to spend and no revenue streams to tap, the GCHA had
taken the move as far as it could.[56]

"We'll have a nice little town here in about ten years," one inhabitant
of the new site commented. Many missed the old town's neighborly spirit.
People no longer stopped to exchange stories, no longer dropped by the
post office at ten in the morning to pick up their mail and meet friends.
They blamed the town's unblemished originality for the lack of sociabil-
ity. We just need to break in New Shawneetown enough to be able to relax
in it, the argument went. We will loosen up once the shade trees grow large
enough to provide comfortable places to chat.[57]

Old Shawneetown, stagnant and poverty-stricken, retained its lure.
Some residents of the new town made six to eight trips back there every
day. People without cars hung around the host house to hitchhike to the

river and loitered outside the former courthouse to catch a ride uphill. Shawneetown's bipolar geography necessitated this commute. The post office remained in the old town, but the courthouse was at the new site. Merchants who once cooperated to attract shoppers to a single commercial district now competed to draw them to one section or the other. Their rivalry embittered both sides and contributed to a growing sense of separation between the village's two parts.[58]

New Shawneetown was a river community without a river. People felt an inherent need to visit La Belle Rivière, acting like salmon in reverse as they journeyed downhill to recapture their past. "You don't know how I miss the river since we moved out here," one new towner told an interviewer. "It's funny, when we lived in the old town, I don't suppose I went up to look at the river once in six months. Now every time I go to town, I have to see that river." Villagers gained security in exchange for a piece of their souls. "Out there it won't be old Shawneetown as we have known it," one man said as he stood before the levee. *The history is all here.*"[59]

LEGACIES

~~~~~~

IN 1938, AFTER YEARS of debates, arguments, and false starts, the flood control issue entered a new phase. Man's large-scale encroachment on floodplains, in the form of great industrial cities, made its resolution a life-and-death matter crucial to America's economic security. Congressman Will Whittington, who knew as much as anyone in Washington about the currents and countercurrents swirling through flood control circles, saw untamed waterways as an existential threat to the American way of life. "Every civilization stands or falls according to its ability to utilize and conserve the forces of nature," he observed in January 1938. "All water falling as rain must find its way to the sea to be evaporated, condensed into clouds and complete the cycle that has been going on for ages. If that cycle fails men die; if that cycle continues, men live."

Whittington rejected the notion popular among scientists and government bureaucrats that man either caused floods or made them worse through deforestation and poor land management. He did accept that humans had ignored the omnipresent dangers of river life. "It is not improper to charge the Ohio flood of 1937 to the lack of political leadership," he said. "We had the money, and we had the men—ten million of them begging for work, and we did not do the job." He promised to bring the interminable legislative process to a conclusion. "We have had enough of planning, we have had enough of investigation," he said. "It is time for cooperation and action."[1]

Waterways management advocates had spent decades calling for cooperation and action without changing man's basic relationship with the

Ohio. But forces were coming together that might break the long stalemate. A large segment of the American public craved flood control and seemed willing to pay for it, within reason. Congress and the administration believed the time was ripe for an ambitious new program. Except for the physical labor involved in constructing flood works, the greatest remaining challenge was uniting the various factions behind an affordable plan that met everyone's definition of "comprehensive."

The 1938 Flood Control Act was far from perfect. Like any legislative compromise, it left everyone a little disappointed. To a great extent it vindicated Charles Ellet Jr., the first to advocate a system of flood control reservoirs in the Ohio basin. Its passage also destroyed Franklin Roosevelt's dream of centralizing flood control, land and water use, public power, wildlife, recreation, and pollution abatement within a board of experts under executive control. New Deal dreams of a rational, comprehensive approach to environmental matters lost out to a broad series of fixes to individual problems. The law also robbed *Little Waters* acolytes of their last, best chance to implement their bold initiatives. Neither did it satisfy Will Whittington and others who focused on the Mississippi River and its lower tributaries.

National legislators stifled the arguments of those who favored ceding territory to the rivers. Except for a few thousand Shawneetowners and several hundred people in Leavenworth, Indiana, Americans resolved to stay put. They banked on the uncertain promise that the government would appropriate money to implement the program the law authorized and that the resulting structures would work as intended. For the most part their faith in Washington proved justified. The system created under the law validated the New Deal's mission to provide basic security for every American. Ohio valley residents have not experienced widespread, devastating flooding since the act took effect. Today valley residents' greatest flood control challenge is not so much defending themselves from high water as ensuring that dams, levees, and walls stay in working order. But nature has not quite repeated the conditions seen in early 1937.

The legacy of the 1938 Flood Control Act encompasses the entire United States. It exists in scores of man-made lakes that provide refuge for animals and recreation for humans. It touched off back-to-the-river movements in Paducah, Louisville, and other communities eager to rediscover their brawny waterside pasts. These campaigns could not have occurred unless the public perceived the river as a pleasant view from their windows rather than a disaster waiting to happen. The act also redefined the role of the federal government. After decades of waffling and debate, Washington established itself as the nerve center for planning, financing, and operating flood control structures. It therefore furthered the New Deal's overall expansion of federal power and added to the central government's responsibility to protect its citizens.

WHITTINGTON, AS ALWAYS WITH one eye toward winning improvements for the Yazoo basin, pressured colleagues to pass sweeping waterways reform during the 1938 legislative session. He branded the makeshift 1937 law that he steered through Congress "utterly inadequate" and criticized its adherence to the 1936 Flood Control Act's stipulation that locals pay for land, flowage rights, and operational expenses. The Mississippian kept up his fight against Roosevelt's National Resources Committee, an agency that undermined his and the Corps of Engineers' authority over water policy and submerged traditional flood control in a New Deal soup of questionable environmental priorities. Lawmakers should rely on "established agencies," meaning the Corps of Engineers, not on untested bureaucracies.[2]

President Roosevelt had to move fast enough to prevent Whittington's supporters from controlling the debate while at the same time delaying the proceedings enough to give his planning group time to draft an alternative to whatever Whittington and the Corps produced. National Resources Committee researchers were busy compiling material from the Agriculture and Interior Departments, the Federal Power Commission, the Public Health Service, and other interested agencies into a new comprehensive report. Working largely on its own, the Corps of Engineers crafted its own recommendations. Eager to avoid duplication, fearful of confusing lawmakers and the public with two definitive plans, and convinced that the Corps had a narrow definition of "comprehensive," Roosevelt cut the army out of the picture when he ordered the War Department to hand over its data to the planning board and directed agriculture secretary Henry Wallace, who had been cooperating with the War Department, to assist the competing investigation.[3]

Despite having the field to itself as a result of Roosevelt's machinations, 1938's *Water Planning and Policy for Drainage Basins of the U.S.* disappointed most readers. Far from the comprehensive plan FDR promised, it was a progress report for a project nowhere near completion. It repeated often-stated goals without explaining how to reach them. It said that water policy must treat drainage basins as interconnected entities and consider the combined impact of flood control, antipollution, wildlife, and public power programs. But this was nothing new, nor did the report offer specific steps toward these ends. Committeemen just rewrote the question.[4]

Board members confessed they faced so many gaps in basic data that they considered it unwise to articulate clear conclusions. Their caution reflected the prudence appropriate to a massive undertaking. Congressmen anxious to appease nervous constituents wanted more immediate gratification. Confusion mounted when, having described the impossibility of issuing a comprehensive plan, the board enumerated a six-year slate of power, erosion, conservation, and flood control studies and projects it considered both economically feasible and compatible with its nonexistent overall agenda. Congress had authorized many of the suggested works in the 1936 Flood Control Act and elsewhere without voting appropriations. Other recommendations reflected a consensus of strategists from the National Resources Committee and Corps of Engineers that they were necessary to any national plan. Readers nevertheless identified the conflict between *Water Planning and Policy*'s two parts and blanched at the $2 billion price tag attached to the first stage of a multistep waterways program.[5]

Roosevelt found himself hewing to a difficult political line at a troublesome moment in his presidency. At his insistence, the report included a list of projects ready for immediate action. He believed high-profile groundbreaking ceremonies would keep his favored agency in the spotlight and satisfy critics pushing for action. Roosevelt also understood that Americans had one shot at crafting a long-term fix for their water problems. He wanted to let the planning board move at its own pace to ensure getting it right. Complicating this tightrope walk between haste and deliberation was the looming threat of a congressional bill placing the Corps of Engineers in charge of a scaled-down water program.[6]

FDR's calls for patience could not slow the momentum for an immediate overhaul. Detractors joined Whittington in denouncing the requirement that states and localities foot part of the bill. Legislators asked the oracle in the White House for guidance on the thorny question. After opposing federal funding the previous year, the elusive Roosevelt now called it "a plausible and reasonable thing to do" without endorsing it outright. Preoccupied with the deteriorating situation in Europe and an economic recession that resulted in part from the same belt tightening that had overridden last year's demands for a broader flood bill, FDR ignored advisers' requests for a more definitive statement. He deferred a final opinion on federal financing until after his vacation to Warm Springs.[7]

Whittington opened hearings on a new rivers and harbors bill while the president was away. As he had the year before, the Mississippian established the tone from the outset. While his first witness, new chief engineer Major General Julian Schley, scanned his prepared remarks, Whittington announced that he intended to send a $300 million bill to the House floor and that the Corps of Engineers' April 1937 report, not the National Resources Committee's *Water Planning and Policy*, provided the basis for the proceedings.[8]

Schley, like Markham before him, offered authoritative testimony. Using crisp, precise language, he explained how the Corps determined the economic viability of proposed projects, detailed its plans for major drainage basins, and discussed the surveys conducted over the last twelve months. He lamented funding shortages and problems with local governments that prevented the army from constructing local protection works authorized under the previous flood control act. In a cross-examination that sounded rehearsed, Chairman Whittington allowed the general to walk him through the particulars of various projects, most of them on the lower Mississippi, and endorsed the Corps's recommendations for protecting the Ohio valley.[9]

Whittington next explored the local financing requirement. Good soldier that he was, Schley refused to choose a side in this political debate, though he hinted that he agreed with the congressman. Neither did he discourage the chairman from describing numerous failed attempts to coordinate multiple states behind a single project. John McClellan of Arkansas, another state desperate for waterways improvements but unable to scrape together money to fund them, seconded Whittington's sentiments. Schley left unchallenged the congressman's contention that a local contributions clause made progress impossible.[10]

Whittington spent the next few days interviewing Schley's subordinates. While declining to offer definitive policy statements, all agreed that difficulties in financing and coordination hampered the implementation of plans Congress had approved. "Has the inability of local interests to furnish rights-of-way held up your work?" Representative Phil Ferguson of Oklahoma asked Colonel R. G. Powell, lead engineer of the Corps's Ohio River division. "Oh, yes; very much," Powell replied. Congressman Robert

Secrest of Ohio, a longtime advocate of abolishing local funding requirements who had sponsored the previous year's bill to create valley authorities, stated in mock amazement, "It appears to me . . . that if the existing
provisions of law are allowed to stand with respect to local contribution,
that we can have little to expect in the way of construction of reservoirs in
the Ohio Valley." Whittington turned to his colleague and declared himself "in absolute accord with your very wise, pertinent, and proper statement."[11]

As in 1937, the Agriculture Department waited for the military men to
finish their performance before taking the stage. Undersecretary of agriculture M. L. Wilson merited about ten minutes of the committee's time.
He spent most of it complaining that his bureau received only token sums
for flood control tasks. Committee members gave Wilson a verbal pat on
the back, then ushered in a few of his coworkers for similarly brief appearances.[12]

The committee spent the next few weeks taking statements from politicians and civic leaders who touted the importance of protecting their
town, city, or valley. Mayors, levee board commissioners, and congressman all begged Washington to assume financial and organizational control over waterways. Victor O'Shaughnessy, chair of the Lawrenceburg,
Indiana, levee committee, recounted his town's proud tradition of self-
sufficiency before stressing that it now faced problems too big to combat alone. Lawrenceburg could not prevent upstream communities from
dumping sewage into the river and could not defend itself when floods
rushed down on it. Mayor George Seamonds of Huntington, West Virginia,
similarly explained that his constituents might help finance a local protection floodwall but would not surrender local autonomy to join a mul-
tistate compact aimed at tackling upstream issues. "Are you prepared to
make any contributions to the building of reservoirs on the tributaries of
the Ohio above Huntington?" Whittington asked. "We are not," Seamonds
replied.[13]

After the three-week hearings closed, Whittington's committee reported
out a new flood control bill. At $375 million it exceeded the chairman's
initial budget limits but otherwise embraced his priorities. It provided
money for Yazoo River basin reservoirs and made Washington liable for
70 percent of the cost of land, rights-of-way, and easements necessary to
construct reservoirs. Federal crews would also operate and maintain them.
Whittington's bill reaffirmed the Corps of Engineers' control over select-

ing and constructing flood works. In a jab at the administration, committee members chided recent planning efforts as "too theoretical, lacking in
practical results," and too eager to incorporate "related activities" into the
nuts and bolts of flood control.[14]

Whittington viewed his proposal as "truly comprehensive." He defined
"comprehensive" in geographical rather than functional terms, jettison-
ing Roosevelt's desire for a system that linked land- and water-based issues
within a single agency dedicated to long-term thinking in favor of a program that provided a reasonable level of flood protection throughout the
national watershed. House colleagues deferred to his opinion, passing the
legislation after a single day of debate. Prospects for passage in the Senate
looked good until Roosevelt jammed on the brakes. "It is not a step in the
right direction in the set-up provided for general government planning,"
he said. Objecting to the authority it granted the Corps of Engineers, he
asked legislators to recognize his board as the entity best able to coordinate all the relevant agencies and interest groups. Although he did not say
so, Roosevelt was also fighting for the extension of executive power and
the entire planning ideology of the New Deal.[15]

The National Resources Committee, except for its representative from
the War Department, recommended a veto on the grounds that waiving
local contributions would encourage states to sponsor unnecessary projects in order to win federal dollars without anteing up their own money.
Left unstated was its fear that Whittington's act marginalized the board.
Federal Power Commission members resented a bill that strengthened the
Corps at their expense, and they criticized Whittington's nebulous language regarding control over hydropower generated at federally built dams.
FDR's budget director warned of the fiscal difficulties inherent in transferring millions of dollars worth of obligations incurred under the 1928 and
1936 Flood Control Acts from the states to the federal government.[16]

Senate Majority Leader Alben Barkley, facing a veto threat on legislation
he needed to pass in order to satisfy restless Kentuckians, rammed through
amendments enabling the Federal Power Commission to assess the viability of outfitting dams with hydroelectric generators. In exchange for this
victory the administration allowed the Paducahan to insert a clause requiring Washington to pay the entire cost of acquiring land and rights-of-way
on reservoirs, rather than the 70 percent the House version demanded, and
giving the federal government title to those sites. Barkley's addition placed
most decisions regarding flood control and dam construction in federal

hands. States could criticize Washington's decisions but could do little to stop them. Senators approved the amended bill after less than two hours of debate. Their vote put Roosevelt in the difficult position of achieving one priority at the expense of another. Signing the bill meant surrendering locals' power to influence national environmental planning in order to gain literal power, in the form of electricity coursing through lines running from new dams.[17]

FDR harbored grave doubts about the legislation but in the end accepted it as a positive step forward that Congress could improve on in subsequent sessions. Elections were coming in the fall, and political allies from river districts wanted something to show constituents. Signs that conservatives would do well in the upcoming congressional contests indicated that the odds of passing a better bill next session were slim. With FDR's halfhearted blessing, and with the added incentive of an impending adjournment, the conference committee adopted the Senate's changes.[18]

Whittington and Majority Leader Sam Rayburn eased the revised bill through the House. Clearing the Senate proved more difficult. As majority leader, Barkley had to invoke a series of parliamentary maneuvers to break a filibuster from states' rights proponents who opposed his amendment. The bill passed 51–32.[19]

It remained unclear whether Roosevelt, who had retired to Hyde Park, would sign the bill. He had just vetoed an act creating a Division of Water Pollution within the U.S. Public Health Service—an idea he favored in theory—because, like the proposed flood control law, it did not funnel the agency's responsibilities through the National Resources Committee. Administration members offered conflicting advice. Clyde Seavey of the Federal Power Commission recommended approval on the grounds that Barkley's amendments cleared the way for huge public power benefits. Interior secretary Harold Ickes urged a veto because the bill cut both his department and Agriculture out of the waterways loop.[20]

A nervous Will Whittington monitored FDR's last-second indecision from his home in Greenwood, Mississippi. His secretary in the capital passed along messages from anxious associates seeking insight into the president's mood. Whittington implored colleagues to lean on Roosevelt. Barkley fired off a telegram to Hyde Park to remind FDR that a veto "would be a severe blow to the whole Ohio Valley." House Majority Leader Rayburn sent a "vital importance" message from Bonham, Texas. "No greater disappointment could come to the country at this time than would the disapproval of a flood authorization bill," he wrote.[21]

Roosevelt ended the suspense when he signed the Flood Control Act into law with little ceremony and "some reluctance." He told reporters he questioned the merits of some projects it authorized. More important, he objected to Congress's determination to vest supreme policymaking power in the Corps of Engineers. "Coordination of all such public works involves a wider survey and the examination of more national problems than any one bureau or department is qualified for," he explained. FDR promised to raise the issue of a permanent National Resources Committee in future sessions. He may not have realized, or may not have wanted to admit, that his signature killed planners' quest for a rational, comprehensive, national environmental program.[22]

Roosevelt's doubts about the law did not stop him from claiming credit for it. "We, in Washington, have worked out a definite national policy," he told a cheering crowd at an event in Louisville for Senate candidate Happy Chandler. "The Ohio Basin and other great river basins subject to floods can and are going to be made safe for our American civilization." Publicly he embraced the dominant narrative of inevitable progress and vanquishing nature. Privately the president knew the act undermined his planning agenda. Congress deleted the National Resources Committee from the watered-down version of the executive branch reorganization bill it passed in 1939. The Corps of Engineers' lobby bore primary responsibility for an excision that sealed the War Department's authority over flood control. The NRC's umbrella agency, the National Resources Planning Board, passed out of existence in 1943. Its members insisted to the end that proper land use and "control of little waters," tools the army all but ignored, offered "the principal method of reducing flood damage." Until the end of his life Roosevelt pleaded for more comprehensive waterways plans and for greater interagency cooperation.[23]

"I WANT TO LIVE IN a constructive age," Will Whittington exclaimed in one of his rhapsodic moments. "I want the age in which I live to build." His excitement was well founded, for the act he guided through Congress envisioned a lot of building. Its five-year, $375 million agenda authorized scores of new or strengthened levees, flood control reservoirs, and local protective works. These joined the hundreds of projects authorized in the flood control acts of 1928, 1936, and 1937 that were either in progress or awaiting funding.[24]

It proved easier for Congress to declare its intention to spend money than to find the dollars needed to turn words into reality. Roosevelt's desire to cut the budget, his hope that future laws might again change the rules of flood control, and the need to allocate resources to the burgeoning defense effort conspired to push waterways spending far below necessary levels. In 1939 army engineers requested $195 million for flood control, exclusive of funds for the lower Mississippi and for upkeep. FDR countered with $110 million, enough to continue current projects but too little to initiate significant new construction. He sympathized with the desire to protect everyone as soon as possible but found the costs of doing so prohibitive under current financial conditions.[25]

Budgetary limitations ensured that the 1938 Flood Control Act initiated evolutionary, not revolutionary, change. Its gradual implementation nevertheless impressed a New Deal legacy on America's industrial heartland. Memories of New Deal building programs often revolve around imposing western dams or utilitarian public buildings. In this case the New Deal's imprint is more subtle but no less enduring. It lives on in scores of recreational and wildlife areas created by multipurpose dams. It lives on in the expanded supply of hydropower that helped fuel a post–World War II economic boom. It lives on in a new sense of security along the Ohio valley, a new confidence that one can settle near a river without having to run away every few years. And finally, it lives on in a changed psychological relationship with the environment, a feeling that the river is a friend, an ally, a boon, rather than an enemy.

Determining the flood's legacy is really a question of finding trends in the collective history of the communities that endured its wrath. Such a task proves frustrating if not impossible. A thousand towns spread along a thousand miles of riverfront experienced and recovered from the disaster in a thousand ways. Decisions from each city's past, choices individual citizens and local leaders made during and after the deluge, and debates occurring in Washington created an array of futures that follow no single prototype. What any examination of the postflood Ohio valley makes clear is that the catastrophe resonates today, even though most inhabitants have no idea how much those far-off events dictated their contemporary world. Sometimes the flood's lasting impact is obvious, sometimes it is subtle yet profound.

Louisvillians remember the thousand-year flood with words similar to Mayor Neville Miller's boastful characterizations. "During that harrowing period, the most serious crisis in our city's history, our community rose to new heights of generosity, ingenuity, stamina, and courage," a local organization noted in its fifty-year retrospective on the event. Old-timers proudly, and mistakenly, claim that no one died in the deluge. These rosy assessments suggest that the flood heightened tendencies already present within the community, enabling it to extend a history of success that inevitably pointed toward a better future. The flood actually marked a decisive break from the city's past that freed Louisville to assume its modern form. It was "a blessing in disguise," Father Clyde F. Crews wrote in the *Courier-Journal* in 1987.[26]

Mayor Miller capitalized on the momentum for change that rose as the waters sank. He championed a plan to buy out residents of the low-lying Point and Shippingport areas and turn the land into parks, replicating on a small scale what William Brinkley and Max Galt wanted for Shawneetown. Houses in these slum neighborhoods sat on land belonging more to the river than to the city. Floodwaters damaged them beyond repair. Politicians had tendered similar proposals for years without success. Miller, however, was determined to gain victory. He won over the Municipal Housing Commission and the Zoning Commission but faced a divided Board of Aldermen. Board meetings devolved into free-for-alls as angry riverfront residents screamed at representatives to defend their homes. Opponents sought the moral, not the geophysical, high ground. "The city of Louisville is not so poor that it has to take away from even the poorest citizens their rights," one detractor argued. Red Cross officials walked a fine line between the warring sides, delaying payments to victims who might be forced to move while staying mum on the relocation scheme itself.[27]

Miller prevailed in the end. The city converted the land into a string of gorgeous recreational areas straddling River Road. Crews dismantled Shippingport, leaving a few rugged fishermen behind to reminisce about the good old days. These stragglers departed in 1958 when the federal government razed the neighborhood's last decaying buildings in order to widen the Portland Canal and construct a new dam across the Ohio.

The flood's impact on local settlement patterns went beyond the riverfront. As happened elsewhere, the disaster touched off a migration that robbed Louisville of some of its original character. A town founded because of the river became less of a river town. St. Matthew's, east of downtown, grew from an expanse of potato farms into a major suburb. Many West Enders headed a few miles south to Shively, which picked up the nickname New Portland. These burgeoning districts grew exponentially after World War II, in part because of a federal decision to deny FHA and VA housing loans to applicants seeking to settle in flood-prone areas.[28]

People who stayed in downtown Louisville demanded better city services. Miller and his successors improved sanitation and sewers, banned outdoor privies, and beefed up the public health system. As was the case elsewhere, floodtime typhoid immunizations benefited long-term health. Louisville Gas and Electric and other utility companies moved their plants well above the 1937 high-water mark, ensuring that the long power outage that imperiled thousands would not be repeated.[29]

Louisville's impressive recovery invited enthusiastic pronouncements of an amazing transformation. Nowhere was this more true than on the issue of race. It is nice to imagine that a disaster shared by blacks and whites might usher in a new era of tolerance. In fact, the city's race relations remained essentially unchanged for decades. Louisville, one of the South's northernmost cities, never exhibited the vicious racism seen elsewhere. Black Louisvillians won the right to vote in 1870, and few local politicians resorted to overt race baiting. At the same time, the white community indulged in what one historian called "polite racism." African Americans attended segregated schools, worked menial jobs, and congregated in a few substandard neighborhoods in the West End and East End.[30]

Here and elsewhere, floodwaters disproportionately affected African Americans, who often lived in poor riverside districts. Black refugees sheltered in segregated schools, churches, and tent camps. Moments of apparent racial harmony carried great tension. An all-white church's congregation initially refused to admit black flooders seeking shelter. They relented when a group of miserable black refugees appeared outside their windows. These new arrivals automatically adopted the groveling, fawning demeanor white Louisvillians expected from their racial inferiors. "The Negro tenants of the church were most grateful to their white benefactors," one contemporary noted, "and thanked them publicly in their nightly prayer service." His report later implies that blacks worshipped apart from whites even when they shared a sacred roof.[31]

Segregation survived the flood. Louisville newspapers printed separate lists of black and white refugees found in camps. Residents racialized flood control, as African Americans had to form a Negro Citizens Flood

Committee to gain a voice in postflood political discussions. Officially color-blind, the Red Cross's rehabilitation program drew cries of discrimination from both sides. Angry whites complained that "the colored people are getting furniture and bedding while the deserving white people are not being taken care of at all." An American Civil Liberties Union investigator, on the other hand, argued that caseworkers favored white applicants.[32]

Louisville's Red Cross chapter decided after much debate to allow African Americans to join the local advisory committees it created as a way to improve its response to future emergencies. Organization heads believed the community would accept biracial commissions "provided the right type of negro citizen was selected for committee membership," meaning well-heeled individuals who posed no threat to the racial status quo. Most districts, however, wanted no part of this egalitarian venture. Only four of fifteen committees, all of them in areas with large black populations, accepted black members.[33]

Postwar agitation for civil rights, not the flood, wrenched Louisville from its tradition of racial discrimination. Public libraries and city colleges opened their doors to African Americans in the late 1940s and early 1950s. Public schools desegregated in 1956. Racial resentments persisted, and many neighborhoods stayed off-limits to blacks until the 1970s. A bloody race riot in 1968 shattered the veneer of racial harmony, as did violent resistance to a 1975 court order to bus black students to white schools.[34]

Just because the flood did not change everything should not obscure its immense impact on the city. Louisville finally acknowledged the need to defend itself from the Ohio. "It is not a riverfront, it is a floodway," mused urban analyst Grady Clay, "and we . . . all of us, ventured there at our peril." Mayor Miller and Senator Barkley successfully lobbied for inclusion in the 1938 Flood Control Act. Army engineers drew up a wall high enough to restrain a crest three feet higher than the one in 1937. When presented with this golden opportunity, the city struggled to uphold its end of the bargain. Local officials stalled as they tried to establish the wall's exact location and price tag. Another delay occurred when the federal government withdrew construction funds because of defense needs and a shortage of steel and other materials.[35]

Louisville remained unprotected when spring 1945 rains pushed the Ohio to its second-highest level ever, ten feet below 1937's mark. Many who remembered the earlier disaster concluded that stagnant surface water on the streets and backed-up sewers in their basements heralded the arrival of another big one. Mayor Wilson Wyatt, a political protégé of Neville Miller, used a series of soothing radio appearances to stamp out talk of major flooding. "This is a send a truck flood, not a send a boat one," became his mantra.[36]

The thousand-year flood laid the foundation for a smoother response this time around. Wyatt staged a get-acquainted meeting with representatives from relief agencies days before the situation grew critical. His preparations kept lines of authority tangle-free when the water arrived. Improved topographical maps the Corps of Engineers assembled after 1937 enabled the administration to inform people in safe areas to stay put while dispatching trucks to endangered neighborhoods before they got wet. On the mayor's initiative, local radio stations followed a protocol for broadcasting assistance calls so as to avoid the confusion surrounding the previous emergency. Wyatt did not need to worry about utility companies because they had moved uphill years before. Oil companies now bolted their big tanks to the ground to prevent them from leaking or drifting as had happened in 1937.[37]

The WPA and CCC were no more, but World War II provided the beleaguered city with alternative sources of manpower. Air-raid wardens moved furniture, and naval trainees from the University of Louisville ferried stranded pedestrians. Fort Knox and the Jeffersonville Quartermaster Depot sent five hundred German prisoners of war to carry sandbags and help clean up. Along with laborers from the Office of Civilian Defense and other groups, their involuntary service held damage to a minimum.[38]

"The question of whether Louisville needs a flood wall is just about as completely settled . . . as the question of whether Noah needed an ark," one editorialist declared. Indeed, the 1945 flood and the end of the war several months later kick-started the long-delayed project authorized in 1938. City officials started acquiring land for a wall that autumn. Washington released the first installment of its financial contribution a year later. Groundbreaking ceremonies occurred in spring 1947.[39]

Engineers figured the nineteen-mile project would take four years to complete. Lower-than-expected appropriations from Congress extended the schedule considerably. Local politicians joined their congressional allies in a ceaseless battle to boost federal aid or, at the very least, ensure that the trickle of dollars kept flowing. Periodic bursts of austerity in Washington nearly killed the project more than once. The workers building the wall tried not to worry about their employment status. Day after day they poured concrete, packed dirt (some of it cannibalized from Shippingport Island), and bound the soil with Kentucky bluegrass.

Construction wrapped up in early 1956. Louisville conquered the Ohio for a total cost of $28.5 million, six times more than expected. The barrier began in the eastern highlands, hugged the riverfront through downtown and the West End, and ended at the high ground to the southwest. Pumping stations heaved groundwater into the river. Dozens of openings permitted passage through the wall except during emergencies. A few dozen men followed a precise script to seal the gaps whenever the Ohio rose. Step 1: inspect a seven-by-seven-foot sluice gate in the sewer at Fourth and Main when the water reaches seventeen point eight feet. Step 292: close the opening just south of Western Parkway pumping plant when the water reaches fifty-eight feet—eleven inches higher than 1937's crest.[40]

Louisville's flood wall was an engineering masterpiece that has rebuffed the Ohio for over fifty years, except for a snafu in 1964 when workers could not locate parts needed to close holes, allowing significant water into parts of downtown. Although groundwater sometimes accumulates in basements, the odds of another 1937 are basically nil unless the city and county neglect the structure's maintenance. "It can happen," Corps of Engineers spokesman Chuck Schumann said of a devastating flood, "but the likelihood of it happening is up in the stratosphere."[41]

With this legacy of 1937 in place, the city opened a new chapter in its history. Public officials had long argued that flood protection would lead to a better Louisville. Local industry boomed now that businessmen no longer worried about overflows. A new cultural vibrancy swept the community. Author William Manchester captured these changes in a 1955 *Harper's* article written to bookend George R. Leighton's harsh feature from 1937. Manchester marveled at the city's sudden shift "from stagnation to prosperity." Population was rising, businesses were thriving, and civic enthusiasm pervaded every street corner. He credited the big flood for jolting the town from its torpor. "Modern Louisville started with it," he wrote.[42]

After a generation of running from the Ohio, Louisvillians in the 1960s embraced the waterway responsible for their city's existence. Office towers sprang up in the once moribund downtown. Developers lured young professionals to pedestrian-friendly neighborhoods in the former red-light district near Fourth and Liberty. Shuttered in the 1970s, the downtown Seelbach and Brown hotels reopened as the riverfront stirred to life. Retail outlets set up shop, with mixed success, along the Fourth Street corridor.

Louisville's reincarnation is very much a product of 1937. By changing attitudes toward flood control and putting the city in a position to build its barrier, in a roundabout way the disaster actually made the community more comfortable with its river identity. "Had that floodwall not been built," former mayor Wyatt said in 1987, "the downtown renaissance of the city today would not have been possible. . . . No one in his right mind would ever have considered such construction without this protection."[43]

Federally funded local protective works authorized under the 1937 and 1938 Flood Control Acts proved key to reversing other cities' declines as well. Newport, Kentucky, and Jeffersonville, Indiana, are among the many secure Ohio River towns. Paducah's postflood story also parallels Louisville's. Residents from both cities scurried to suburban high grounds after the catastrophe. Avondale Heights and other safe areas swelled as Paducah's historic center emptied. This demographic shift sent a community already suffering from the Depression into an economic funk that took years to overcome.[44]

Political and business elites recognized that a floodwall represented the best way to lure investors and bring the town together. Captain Miles Reber, the newly appointed head of the Army Engineers' Louisville District, which encompassed Paducah, agreed. He broached the subject in a meeting with a few dozen leading citizens held in a garage near the government-business-relief shantytown on the city's western edge. A small minority argued that a wall would advertise Paducah's dangerous location. Everyone else backed Reber. Commercial leaders organized a Paducah Flood Control Committee committed to forging connections with engineers and congressional representatives. The Paducah Lions Club, Rotary Club, and Junior Chamber of Commerce contributed time, resources, and influence. Senator Barkley proved a natural ally, as did General Markham, who discussed the proposal during a visit to town.[45]

Captain Reber testified at the 1937 Flood Control Act hearings that Paducah's importance as a manufacturing and population center merited a federal investment in an earth-and-concrete floodwall. Alben Barkley's influence in the Senate ensured that Congress incorporated Reber's suggestion into the 1937 Flood Control Act. Work on the structure began in 1939. Crews packed down earthen levees through World War II. Steel shortages prevented them from finishing the wall until 1949. Paducah's redemption arrived in 1952 when the federal government opened a uranium enrichment plant a few miles west of the city, a move it would never have made had there been a risk of flooding. Barkley (now the vice president), who had proved so important to passing the 1938 act, probably applied pressure to locate the installation there. Washington's willingness to place a pivotal cold war factory in Paducah acted as an unmistakable announcement of its flood-free status. New industries, stores, and entertainment outlets opened as a boomtown spirit lifted two decades of malaise at the Ohio's confluence with the Tennessee. Construction companies worked at full tilt to keep pace with a soaring population.[46]

Modern Paducah owes its character, prosperity, and revival to the most devastating disaster in its history. Artists' communities flourish in low-lying downtown areas once subject to inundation. Funky cafes and eclectic galleries lure in visitors who view the Ohio as a nice place to picnic rather than an existential threat. Paducahans began a full-fledged "back to the river" movement in the early 1990s. Long dismissed as a relic of the past, the waterfront district's cobblestone streets and brick facades gained new life as the city reconnected with its roots. The rebirth began when the American Quilter's Society opened a quilt museum within sight of the Ohio. This unexpectedly popular attraction anchored downtown redevelopment. Soon after, a nonprofit organization opened a River Heritage Museum in the old Petter Supply building, site of the carbide fire that almost incinerated Charlie Jackson's foundry and machine shop.

The Center for Maritime Education building occupies the corner that once hosted Jackson's business. A mural celebrating Paducah's glorious steamboat era adorns a panel on the floodwall across the street, part of a series of magnificent paintings of local history that have turned the hulking structure into a tourist site. Close by is a panel depicting scenes from the 1884, 1913, and 1937 floods. An oval insert showing boat crews paddling past city hall dominates the scene. Bossie the cow looks down from the upper right-hand corner. Although appropriately gray and downcast, the images of flooded buildings, a man standing on his roof with his dog, and a group posing around a Model T plowing through a foot of water somehow give the impression that these disasters offered as much fun as fright. It is hard to feel a sense of menace, particularly because the Ohio itself is invisible except for the representations painted on the wall.

Narrow gaps in the barrier let one substitute the real river for the ersatz versions along Water Street. From the top of the levee the Ohio is a placid stream rolling so far below the protective works that one cannot imagine the quantity of water needed to raise it to dangerous heights. Paducahans

One stretch of Paducah's floodwall, a monument to the city's flood-ridden past and its dry present. Grooves in the exposed edge receive steel doors in times of high water. Photo from the author's collection.

have great faith in their wall; asking if they feel safe behind it produces guffaws, as if the question is too absurd to merit consideration. Like Louisville, the community's biggest river problem today is not so much protection as maintenance. The wall's sixty-year-old pumps, pipes, and motors need upgrading. Unlike the days when locals bore responsibility for their own defense, however, the Corps of Engineers is already procuring federal dollars to carry out the repairs.

Not every community gained long-term benefits from the flood. In Cairo, for example, historical tensions combined with stresses born from the flood to condemn the town to permanent irrelevance. Today it is a curiosity instead of the national marketplace its many founders imagined. Cairo's jury-rigged mudboxes and the engineers' decision to wash out the Bird's Point floodway spared it from a fatal blow. Town fathers hoped to turn the narrow escape into a civic renaissance akin to what happened in Louisville and elsewhere. Features in the *Evening Citizen and Bulletin* enticed potential migrants with news of Cairo's ample available housing— the result of population loss over the previous few decades—and quality schools. Community leaders worked to mollify their furious neighbors across the Mississippi. "Cairo did not make the Jadwin plan and had nothing to do with the ridiculously low compensation paid for flowage rights," one writer pleaded. More than public favor was at stake; the city's battered economy depended on warehousing and transport business from farmers on the other side of the river.[47]

Rather than uniting in the aftermath of a narrow escape, Cairoites launched another round of bickering that tainted the fractious community for decades to come. Uncertainty over who was responsible for paying men who had enrolled, volunteered, or been drafted to toil on the levees drove the discord. Mayor August Bode interpreted Harry Hopkins's order to save the city at all costs as an announcement that the WPA would compensate everyone he put to work. Bode believed Hopkins confirmed this policy when the relief head visited Cairo during his flood tour. The truth is more complicated. Hopkins apparently agreed to reimburse anyone the city hired for flood control duties between the morning of Black Sunday and the afternoon of February 3, when he arrived. To qualify for payment, employees had to be registered with the WPA and show proof of their floodtime service. The WPA would not compensate volunteers.[48]

In the confusion, the Bode administration failed to keep accurate records of temporary employees. Later, local officials who expected WPA dollars to wash over Cairo compiled a haphazard list of names and hours worked. Washington derided the application as either incompetent or fraudulent, and perhaps both. Bode returned an amended request that eliminated five hundred of the original eighteen hundred claimants on the grounds that the city could not prove they existed. Bureaucrats further trimmed the list by crossing off people the WPA had already paid. Federal officials suggested that "persons who gave their address as the city jail" had been compelled to work or that someone was padding the roster to grab extra cash for themselves.[49]

Hopkins's refusal to write a check sent Bode running to four-term congressman Kent Keller, a former schoolteacher, lawyer, and mining entrepreneur with close links to Governor Horner and the Roosevelt administration. Keller, who was among the loudest advocates for federal flood aid, considered himself a progressive champion of the downtrodden. He dedicated himself to winning a favorable settlement for the storm-tossed unfortunates who saved Cairo. The congressman blanketed Hopkins with memos demanding that emergency workers get what they deserved. Hopkins responded with equal vigor that the city, not the WPA, had ordered the construction of mudboxes and was therefore liable for the costs. Hopkins also noted that few of the men clamoring for restitution could produce work cards or find their names on time sheets. Keller dismissed these serious objections without answering them. "It would be a mistake on the part of the government for you to fail to accept this obligation and provide some means of paying these men for their work," he retorted.[50]

The imbroglio spawned a string of backroom recriminations that fractured even the limited solidarity Cairo possessed during the crisis. Suspicious local Democrats accused the Republican Bode of driving the city into bankruptcy, then bilking the Roosevelt administration to balance the books. Bode was "desirous of discrediting our Democratic administration, among the colored population especially, by giving the men a hard way to go," one local politician thundered. According to this line of thinking, Bode's flailing disguised a cunning attempt to turn working-class African Americans, recent converts to the Democratic Party who made up a sizable portion of those seeking restitution, against the New Deal.[51]

Most of these workers had no inkling of the charges and countercharges flying between Cairo, Springfield, and Washington. They just wanted to get paid, and, so far as they could tell, no one was making progress toward that objective. As had so often been the case in Cairo, honest men suffered at the hands of corrupt or incompetent neighbors. Five hundred frustrated former levee workers hired a sharp, well-connected attorney from Mound City named J. Kelly Smith to get what was owed them—in exchange for a 25 percent commission. Smith was a tenacious shyster who smeared opponents and milked every contact to maximize financial returns. He privately believed the city should pay the men but, knowing that the local money pot was empty, focused on persuading the WPA to make good on its hazy promises.[52]

Cairoites grumbled as weeks passed with no perceptible movement in the logjam. A group of unpaid levee workers invited Ed Parker, an organizer for the Illinois Workers Alliance (IWA), to whip them into a unit capable of publicizing their plight. The IWA was affiliated with the Workers Alliance of America, an agglomeration of liberal, socialist, and communist groups formed in 1935 to represent the interests of the unemployed. It acted as a trade union for WPA enrollees, devoted to raising wages on public works projects and promoting the rights, dignity, and essential decency of those surviving on work relief.[53]

Parker tapped the frustration seething within Cairo's dispossessed. Hundreds showed up at IWA rallies to cheer as speakers ripped the WPA and area relief officials who stiffed deserving levee workers. Parker tried to force a resolution when in early April he led a racially mixed group of one thousand WPA enrollees and unpaid mudboxers to present their demands at the courthouse. Bode brushed them off. The next morning Parker marched two thousand men, women, and children to the county relief offices. They found the building empty and locked. Angry protesters milled about, smoking, discussing tactics, letting their anger fester. Someone set up a cry to seize the building. Demonstrators held it unopposed through the morning before shifting their attention to lunch. Some abandoned their posts to visit groceries and restaurants. Others procured supplies from a state-run food bank. In the meantime, Parker led a delegation to persuade the county judge to arbitrate a settlement, but the judge refused to serve on the grounds that the mob was guilty of breaking and entering.

Tensions rose as the day wore on. "Several large negroes" beat another black man, Essie "Doughbelly" Taylor, for being a suspected informant. Although Taylor escaped with bruises and a small knife wound in his back, the incident further soured the mood. One faction trooped across the street to acquire guns from a jewelry store. A skirmish broke out when the mayor dispatched a team of negotiators. Police wounded two black men, including a minister, and abducted Parker. They hustled the union man to a prison in Jonesboro, thirty miles to the north, then moved him another twenty miles up the road to Murphysboro, where they held him incommunicado. Parker's kidnapping enraged the mob. Facing a deteriorating situation, Mayor Bode closed the town's saloons and assembled a force of policemen, American Legionnaires, Kiwanis, Chamber of Commerce members, and other solid citizens to evict the strikers.

Hoping to catch the sleepy rabble unawares, the deputy brigade stormed the relief office at two in the morning. Their approach scared off many protestors. Those who remained disregarded orders to disband. Someone lobbed a fruit jar at an officer's head as the forces of law and order waded into the throng. Cairoites lashed out with sticks, stones, and fists. Shots rang out, although no one ever established who fired them. It took Bode's army a few hours to win control of the battlefield. Police arrested four African Americans for carrying weapons and sent the other strikers home. Authorities later released the men without charges. Highway patrolmen guarded the relief office and beefed up their street presence to discourage further disorder.[54]

Local power brokers ignored the root causes of discontent. They blamed the disturbance on "professional and amateur agitators," many of them strangers in town, and moved to silence dissent. With the conservative *Evening Citizen and Bulletin* as their ally, city councilmen campaigned to expel "undesirable and trouble-making residents." In their opinion, the problems started because the flood brought in "outside forces . . . people who contribute nothing but trouble to the community." Cairo needed to banish these parasites. IWA supporters offered easy targets. Policemen seized the union's property and arrested many members, particularly African Americans, on trumped-up charges, then released them after they promised to leave town. Longtime black residents who got caught in the dragnet had to flee their homes or face prosecution.[55]

Officials justified their actions as an assault against a lawless element that hampered a postflood revival. Others saw a brutal suppression of decent, hardworking citizens. A "reign of terror exists against colored members of IWA," the union's state chairman complained to Governor Horner. Sympathy for the organization came from around the nation. The New Kensington, Pennsylvania, branch of the United Electrical and Radio Workers of America sent Horner a resolution decrying the bogus charges against Parker, a man who led workers desiring "a decent standard of living in the richest country in the world." Its petition lauded the brave men who rescued a city only to find injustice on the other side of the crest. Facing rejection at every turn, they had no choice but to defend their rights through collective action.[56]

A grand jury charged Ed Parker with rioting, inciting a riot, and three counts of assault with deadly intent—one for each of the officers beaten during his arrest. It also indicted him for arson after he started a fire in his cell. He stewed in jail for weeks before making his $6,500 bond. Procedural issues delayed his trial several times. It eventually disappeared from the city's docket without explanation.[57]

The insurrection did nothing to help those who started it. State WPA officials eager to avoid further trouble considered allowing Mayor Bode to pay whomever he wanted whatever sum he thought fair, then compensating Cairo by cooking the books on future projects. This shady proposal died not so much because of its questionable legality as because the city could not raise enough money to satisfy workers' demands. Bode instead reduced the city's obligation by eliminating more names from its IOU list, reversing the approach taken when he thought WPA would pay everyone.[58]

Congressman Keller recognized that the Bode team maintained shoddy records and padded the reimbursement request to enrich itself, but he kept his disgust to himself. His goal was to win restitution for the workers while keeping whatever money Washington coughed up away from Bode's corrupt administration. In 1940 he persuaded Congress to appropriate $21,000 for the Cairo levee workers who survived the purges to the list. It took three years for the men whose backbreaking labors had saved Cairo to get their thirty cents an hour—minus 10 percent to pay attorney J. Kelly Smith for the small part he played on their behalf. Even though Smith reduced his original fee, this commission annoyed Keller, who regretted that "these poor devils . . . have to share the little pay they will get with someone else." Keller's success brought a misplaced feeling of resolution to Cairoites, who believed they had closed the book on the 1937 flood saga. They did not realize that the high water's impact would echo for decades to come.[59]

The riot and its aftermath further polluted Cairo's fetid racial waters and hastened the town's decline. Segregated African Americans withdrew deeper into their own isolated community. Persistent threats of renewed violence fostered a reluctance to speak out. Area politicians reinforced racial hierarchy by keeping public offices in white hands. Cairo's system of electing city councilmen at large prevented African Americans, who made up about 40 percent of the population, from winning seats on the board. White businessmen froze out black job applicants, who eventually sought employment elsewhere. Racial prejudices ran so deep that the city closed its public pool in 1962 rather than integrate it. Three days of race riots in 1967 after the suspicious death of a black soldier arrested for driving a car with a defective taillight sealed Cairo's reputation for intolerance. Social clubs such as the Kiwanis, Knights of Columbus, and Veterans of Foreign Wars remained lily-white into the 1970s.[60]

Racial tensions were not the only reasons for Cairo's inability to remake itself. Its problems dated back to the town's multiple inceptions. Speculators chose the location based on geography rather than actual conditions. Their faulty relationship with the rivers condemned Cairo to mediocrity. Greed compounded their original sin as generations of leaders more interested in moneymaking than community building neglected to foster civic pride. Kiwanis, Rotarians, the Ministerial Association, and women's groups who trumpeted a postflood revival could not rouse a populace raised on apathy. Indifferent citizens tossed empty whiskey bottles into roads already covered with broken glass. A crackdown on gambling collapsed when juries failed to convict businessmen who owned illegal slot machines. "The city administration has bowed submissively to the will of the slot machine racketeers, admitting its own tragic weakness and lack of interest in making Cairo a decent town," lamented an *Evening Citizen and Bulletin* editorial. "The vast majority of the public is voiceless, apparently devoid of courage, [and] lacking in vision."[61]

Ed Parker's rabble-rousing and the desultory revival campaign inverted Cairo's floodtime narrative. Rather than a triumphant story of neighbors pulling together, Cairo's flood legacy centered on the social pressures unleashed in the deluge. Those divisions shoved it toward irrelevance and perhaps extinction. Racial hostilities and lingering doubts about its floodworthiness discouraged new industries from moving in. Job shortages prompted an exodus unlikely to be reversed. Cairo's population today is a quarter of its 1937 figure. Except for a few posh neighborhoods on the west side, it feels like a ghost town. Crumbling shells of buildings line the waterfront. Ohio Street, once raucous and vibrant, is deserted.

"IT IS A SAD commentary on civilization that people in one part of the world are struggling to enrich the land, while those in another part seek only to spread destruction," soil guru H. H. Bennett wrote soon after the Nazis invaded France. He believed the administration remained committed to its environmental agenda regardless of the widening war. Unlike Bennett, Roosevelt saw little room for waterways in a crowded fiscal picture. His 1941 budget message included a demand that Congress appropriate no money for flood control or navigation improvements unless those projects contributed to national defense. FDR permitted legislators to authorize new reservoirs and local works only because the Corps of Engineers needed a backlog of worthy ventures ready for groundbreaking the moment the emergency ended.[62]

Little changed in the Ohio basin between 1938 and Pearl Harbor. Authorizations piled up, engineers conducted surveys and crafted blueprints, and residents waited for the protection elected officials had promised. With money, manpower, and construction materials in short supply during the war, the wait extended through the early 1940s. Advocates who hoped peace would spark activity cried foul when President Harry Truman slashed waterways appropriations as a means of curbing postwar inflation and debt. One national rivers conference blasted the move as "ill-advised, untimely, detrimental to the control and utilization of the nation's great inland waterways and harbors, and fraught with potential danger to human life and property."[63]

Construction in Louisville, Paducah, and elsewhere crawled along, hampered by small appropriations and sporadic resistance from landowners determined to defend their property from federal intrusion. A 1951 report from the Water Resources Policy Commission, a temporary board Truman created to develop "a consistent and comprehensive program" of waterways improvements, bemoaned the slow pace of change. Engineers had completed 24 of the 80 Ohio valley reservoirs authorized under the 1938 Flood Control Act and about one-tenth of the 240 authorized local protection schemes. These shortfalls, in combination with the large number of people living in lowland areas, made high water an ongoing threat to life and property.[64]

Truman's panel detailed a string of problems that FDR had tried to fold into a comprehensive environmental agenda. Such parallels could be expected, since many commission members were holdovers from the earlier administration. Pollution in the valley was getting worse. Erosion and deforestation leached soil-based nutrients and hastened precipitation's path to the river. Potential hydroelectric reserves went untapped owing to resistance from coal interests, utilities companies, and the politicians beholden to them. The board also cited the inadequacy of "basic data essential for planning a program for development."[65]

These findings in no way marked a return to the heady days of national planning. Congress's neutering of Roosevelt's executive reorganization bill ended any realistic possibility of a permanent national resources committee. After years of frustration and false starts, liberals had lost faith in comprehensive environmental planning. Washington's frustrating experience with economic planning during the war further diminished enthusiasm for similar experiments in other fields. President Truman proved unreceptive to talk of centralized planning. Cold war America, with its abhorrence of anything bearing the faintest resemblance to communism, offered a hostile climate for planning advocates.[66]

Subsequent decades saw a series of incremental measures that addressed some of the commission's concerns. Although inundations will always occur, it is unlikely that Ohio valley residents will experience another superflood—even the monstrous 2011 overflow passed with minimal damage. By the mid-1970s engineers had completed almost all of the flood control reservoirs authorized in 1938, creating a network of man-made lakes that can hold ten trillion gallons of water out of the main river. Army engineers funnel information into computers that tell them whether to raise or lower the steel gates regulating the flow of water from reservoirs. Technicians maintain a stable pool in the summer to maximize a reservoir's recreation value, then draw it down in the fall to prepare for spring rains and snowmelt. Complementing this system is a series of floodwalls and levees protecting major towns fronting the river.[67]

Technological advancements such as satellites improved the Weather Bureau's ability to predict rainfall and crest heights, adding another layer of protection for riverside residents. Increased appropriations in the wake of 1937 enabled the bureau to expand and modernize its river and flood service. Its personnel cooperated with the Corps of Engineers to set up additional rain gauges and open new stations. Today's meteorologists have a far better understanding than their predecessors of how precipitation affects river basins and are therefore able to provide accurate forecasts of flood heights well ahead of the crest.

Congress has passed several flood control acts that broadened the Corps of Engineers' mission to include tasks Roosevelt counted among his goals. Once limited to evaluating proposals based on their flood control and navigation merits, the Corps now considers recreational opportunities and wildlife preservation when deciding whether to green light an application. In certain cases it can build additional storage space in flood control reservoirs to enhance the supply of drinking water. This expanded portfolio encompasses elements of the New Dealers' environmental agenda without achieving what Roosevelt most desired: a permanent planning agency responsible to the president, not to Congress, that coordinates all government bureaus, whether federal, state, or local, interested in land and river questions in order to provide long-term solutions to resource issues.[68]

Pollution remains a major problem in the valley despite a long campaign to restore water quality. Industrial chemicals and contaminated agricultural wastewater still pour into streams. Although cleaner than it was in 1937, the river carries enough pollutants and bacteria to make swimming in it risky and eating fish from it ill-advised. "I wouldn't eat anything out of the Ohio River," one Cincinnati chef laughed in 2004. "Would you?"[69]

La Belle Rivière will never again resemble the stream that inspired awe among seventeenth-century French pioneers. There are too many people, too many gasoline-powered boats, too many commercial farms, and too many factories for mankind to undo the damage it has inflicted upon the river over the previous century. It remains to be seen whether the era of intensive human intervention in the Ohio's affairs that began in 1937 will ultimately benefit the river itself. Man's interference has to this point left a mixed record of success. The Ohio is in some ways a better neighbor than in 1937, while in others it is more dangerous.

EPILOGUE

~~~~~~

MEMORIES OF THE GREAT experiment that was Shawneetown faded as the war dominated headlines and the New Deal's work-relief programs fell beneath the budgetary ax. In 1943 a baffled Illinois Department of Public Works employee sent a memo to the bureau's director. "I didn't know we owned the First National Bank Building in Old Shawneetown," he wrote. "What do you think we had better do about it?" His query sent bureaucrats scrambling to discover that the state indeed owned large chunks of the village, including most of its historic buildings. But what to do about it? Illinois did not hold enough contiguous plots to convert the site into a park. Persistent flooding and a dearth of automobile traffic made the idea even less feasible. "I think the best thing to do with this place is to give it back to the Indians," one staffer laughed.[1]

About four hundred die-hards still huddled along the river. Among them were Louis and Fannie Goetzman, uncle and aunt to Max Galt's brother-in-law Carroll Goetzman. The elderly couple occupied the second floor of a ninety-year-old brick house overlooking the levee and spent their days watching the Ohio glide past from their living room, which had been underwater in 1937. From their front yard they could see the old bank, with a waterline etched high on its sandstone columns. "There's never a lonesome moment," Louis said in 1947. "We can hear the boat whistles, and we can look out at the water, and the gulls and the ferry." Most Old Shawneetowners lived in tar paper shacks or decrepit, state-owned buildings. Their career options consisted of fish markets, an antifreeze storage depot, and gravel companies. A handful of nondescript stores survived, as did a pool hall, a filling station, four lightly patronized bars, and unlikeliest of all, a popcorn stand, a nod to the region's large fields of popcorn plants. With their water system removed to the new site, old-town residents drank from wells and relieved themselves in outhouses.[2]

Confidence in a riverside renaissance persisted. They believed rebirth would come if they could free themselves from the more populous new development. An independence movement blossomed in the 1940s, led by Paul Stefko, a World War I veteran and former owner of the raucous Moon Mullins floating roadhouse. Stefko, his wife, and their two young sons rented quarters in the state-owned Posey Building, a decaying three-story brick structure that once housed the offices of noted nineteenth-century freethinker Robert Ingersoll and a young attorney named Abraham Lincoln.[3]

Besides running a restaurant, a planing mill, and a small bootlegging operation, the balding, bespectacled Stefko served as one of Old Shawneetown's two aldermen. He spent years agitating to separate old from new Shawneetown, a move opposed by Max Galt, who served nine years as mayor in the 1940s and 1950s. Stefko resented the riverside community's second-class status. Living behind the levee was like "living behind the Iron Curtain," he thundered. "You can't get a permit to build a building, we don't have any water, sewers, or fire protection, and they"—meaning new Shawneetowners—"won't let a carnival or any other entertainment come in."[4]

New Shawneetown and the State of Illinois saw Stefko as a pest. On various occasions authorities arrested him for possessing slot machines, selling liquor without a license, and discharging a firearm within the city limits. Parks Department officials tried to evict him on the grounds that the Posey Building was unfit for human occupation. Part of its roof was missing, its walls were crumbling, and pigeons had broken most of the windows. Stefko got himself arrested again when he tore down official notices to leave. At one point administrators urged the state to forcibly remove the family. Stefko rumbled about buying the building and persisted in his crusade to divorce the Shawneetowns.[5]

It took years for Stefko's supporters to wear down the opposition. The city council agreed in 1956 to separate Old Shawneetown from the new site. Illinois's oldest surviving settlement became its newest municipality. Stefko, elected as the town's first mayor 144–141, insisted the break meant a bright future for his fellow river rats. With a bridge to Kentucky opened a few months earlier, he reasoned that a revitalized riverside location chock full of historic buildings could draw waves of vacationers. Pessimists recognized that independence marked the final chapter for a dying community. "I honestly believed the town would make a come back," store owner Louis Brooks wrote twenty years after the flood. "Now I am beginning to have my doubts."[6]

Max Galt, the man most responsible for moving the village he loved to safe ground, lived just long enough to see the literal and symbolic end to his dream of a unified, vibrant Shawneetown. A stroke claimed his life just six weeks after his longtime nemesis Stefko became Old Shawneetown's mayor. During his time as mayor, Galt presided over a community convinced that prosperity and population growth were just around the corner. Such optimism had waned by the time he resigned without explanation in 1952. Galt chaired the county housing authority until he died, still an important figure in a village so modest that it had neither street signs nor house numbers. His Nebraska birth deprived him of the most coveted line in local obituaries, one that marked an indelible boundary between insiders and outsiders in a parochial, tradition-bound village: "Shawneetown pioneer."[7]

Contrary to Stefko's expectations, Old Shawneetown's deterioration accelerated after the breakup. A 1964 study classified 95 of its 106 dwellings as either "deteriorating" or "dilapidated." Wrecking crews dismantled the Posey Building. The magnificent Riverside Hotel was long gone. Even the bank, the town's most prized landmark, fell on hard times. Workers from the Parks Department refurbished the building every so often only to let it fall into disrepair again. A trickle of visitors squinted and cocked their heads, trying to perceive the beauty behind its boarded-over windows and weed-choked grounds. Illinois officials rejected Old Shawneetown's request for a new sewer system. They had spent too much money persuading residents to leave to turn around and encourage them to stay. The levee itself was overgrown with vegetation and shot through with rodent holes. In its shadow stood a row of dodgy bars, a sad echo of the town's rowdy past.[8]

Today Shawneetown is a powerful if forgotten reminder of the flood's enduring legacy. It resembles any number of small towns along America's rural highways. Law-abiding motorists approaching on Illinois Route 13 slow down to forty miles an hour for about a thousand yards, grumble at the inconvenience, then mash the accelerator without a second glance at the place they just passed. Those heading east, toward the bridge to Kentucky, might notice a smallish brick building a hundred yards down the road—probably an old school. Any thought of Shawneetown is gone by the time they cross the Ohio or, if they are traveling west from Kentucky, before they reach Harrisburg twenty minutes later.

A modest business district offers few inducements to exit the highway. Those who do pull onto Lincoln Boulevard get a firsthand look at the optimism of the New Deal era. Shawneetown's central mall remains intact, although few residents take advantage of its unbroken green space. Aged stores dominate the west side while unpretentious public buildings line the east side. As its designers intended, the mall serves as a social divide, a physical reminder of the tensions pervading the village long before the flood. West side lots are generously proportioned with well-tended lawns and comfortable homes. A handful of houses from the relocation era survive. It is a pleasant place whose tidy neighborhoods promise the best of village life. New Shawneetown's east side, the section the GCHA sold without sewer or water lines, tells a different story. Trailer homes and other humble structures in need of major repairs dominate this district. Pickup trucks and random farm equipment clutter empty lots. Drainage is so poor that any significant rain or snowmelt turns the ground near Galt Avenue into a swampy mess.

Contrary to the expectations of the GCHA and the WPA, jobs never came to Shawneetown in any notable numbers. Einar Dyhrkopp and his two partners opened a cabinetmaking company, long since gone, that employed seventy-five people back in the days when Rudy Phillips would barbecue your goat for just two dollars. The major industries the Kiwanis always seemed on the verge of landing never materialized. Shawneetown's status as the county seat provides some work. Even so, poverty rates are high and opportunities for advancement rare.

Despite these problems, people are friendly and welcoming. Few of them know much about the relocation beyond the simple fact that it occurred. Though part of the town's cosmology, the great flood is trivia more than an essential touchstone. Shawneetowners do not speak of it as their ancestors spoke of General Lafayette's visit and Ulysses S. Grant's honeymoon stay. They have little sense of the forces it unleashed, the debates it spawned, or its continuing impact. It is enough to say, "the town moved."

Shawneetown joined other school districts in the early 1990s to build a modern K–12 building three miles west of the new town. Private investors converted the old high school into a bare-bones apartment complex for migrant farmworkers. Shapeless heaps of rusted metal cover the back

Shawneetown's old high school building, a refuge of last resort that now serves a different community of dispossessed people. Photo from the author's collection.

lot. Depressing as the scene is, it is somehow apropos. The twisted rubbish and helter-skelter surroundings evoke memories of a tornado ripping off a room, a gymnasium demolished by fire, a mound of personal belongings gone up in flames, and terrified flooders wondering whether rescue would come.

If few motorists visit Shawneetown, even fewer realize that Old Shawneetown exists. Once a monument to American commerce and persistence, the town is now invisible and forgotten. A thick row of trees screens it from the highway, and the earthen levee hides it from the river. A small brown sign marks its main entrance, a grim-looking road heading straight into a dark forest. Sitting just yards from the Ohio, the marker is easy to miss. Eastbound travelers are looking at the bridge ahead, while those headed west are readjusting to dry land after crossing the river. Motorists blow past the sign without seeing it.

Old Shawneetown claims a population of about three hundred. A pervasive, eerie silence engulfing its dozen or so streets suggests that may be an exaggeration. Trailer homes, many housing squatters rather than permanent residents, dot otherwise vacant lots. There is no order or symmetry. Its haphazard layout stands as a sad travesty of the well-ordered utopia New Dealers envisioned for the new town. Its only thriving business is Hogdaddy's, a biker bar occupying a two-story brick building hard up against the levee.

A quick scramble to a small concrete wall atop the levee reveals a stunning panorama. Thirty feet below flows the Ohio. The river is narrow here, perhaps one-third of a mile across, but the water owns this piece of earth. If one blocks out the drone of cars whizzing over the bridge a few hundred yards downstream, it becomes easy to understand why this place exerted such a hold for so long. Silent and noble, the river provides a majestic foreground for the Kentucky hills gracing the opposite shore. To be here is to understand power cloaked in the guise of serenity. The river is an unpredictable force that inspires calm. It is both terrible and beautiful. "Why don't we leave?" one resident asked herself when the Ohio again menaced the village six decades after the thousand-year flood. "I don't know, really," she concluded. "I guess it's just home. I'll always live by the river."[9]

Turning around obliges a visitor to ponder the sad shell of this once-thriving community. Old Shawneetown cowers beneath the levee, its ragged desolation a heartbreaking contrast to the natural splendor on the other side. Hogdaddy's stands to the right, a rusty water tower to the left. Between them are empty roads, tumbledown homes, and unkempt lots. Impressions of Shawneetown's former greatness dissipate, the glow of river life dims.

But the bank is still here, an incongruous neoclassical masterpiece rising from the weeds. If you look at it hard enough while shutting out its surroundings, you can recapture some glimmer of Shawneetown's glory years. Stately columns conjure memories of a frontier village laughing at a request for credit from someplace called Chicago, of a boisterous trading center known to boatmen up and down the Ohio. One can almost see Max Galt fishing from the third-story window and hear dogs in the attic wailing for Harry Howell to feed them. Shawneetown comes to life, and you can understand why, decades after the flood subsided, a handful of survivors still loved what it once was. "It was a beautiful little town," one former resident recalled seventy years later, "but the flood damn near destroyed it."[10]

Others interpreted the past differently. Reflecting on the actions of town founders who settled flood-prone ground; of politicians and a public reluctant to address environmental issues until an emergency demanded action; of the New Deal's inability to fuse Washington's idealism with realities on the ground; and of local leaders who decided in 1937 that enough was enough, longtime resident Joe Chamberlain offered his own assessment of Shawneetown's fate. "See, this town," he told an interviewer in 1978, "the *flood* didn't destroy it. . . . *Man* destroyed it."[11]

Chamberlain's assessment rings true for the valley as a whole. Man put himself in nature's path. Man failed to accommodate the Ohio despite frequent reminders of its deadly strength. Some cities used a combination of good leadership, political clout, community spirit, and sheer luck to emerge from the disaster as better places to live. Other towns proved unable to rebound. From that mixed record of success came a new and to some extent wiser valley. Flood survivors and their descendants did not realize all the optimistic dreams that horrible moment in 1937 unleashed. Because of their actions, and the actions of their countrymen, they did at least put themselves in a position to prevent catastrophe should the next thousand-year flood thunder down the basin centuries ahead of schedule.

ACKNOWLEDGMENTS

OF ALL THE PEOPLE I encountered while working on this book, none described surviving the flood as purely an individual feat. Similarly, I am not sure I would have survived researching and writing about the 1937 flood without help from a great number of selfless archivists and librarians and encouragement from a multitude of old and new friends.

Like so many historians, I am deeply grateful to the outstanding team at the National Archives II in College Park, Maryland. They patiently answered my obscure questions, pointed me down paths I would never have found on my own, and even let me peek into one of the archive's vast storage halls, an experience I can only compare to the final scene of *Raiders of the Lost Ark*. Thanks also to Virginia Lewick, Mark Renovitch, Alycia Vivona, and the rest of the magnificent crew at the Franklin D. Roosevelt Presidential Library in Hyde Park, New York. Ed Frank guided me through the University of Memphis's local history collections. G. Wayne Dowdy provided expert assistance in the Memphis Public Library's Memphis and Shelby County Room. Jennifer Ford welcomed me to the University of Mississippi's Archives and Special Collections division. E. J. Abell gave me the run of Paducah's River Heritage Museum, and Vonnie Shelton essentially handed me the keys to the McCracken County Public Library. I am also indebted to Sherry Hinant at the Harrisburg, Illinois, District Library and Cynthia Vickery at the Shawneetown Public Library. Seth Cohen at the Louisville Free Public Library devoted more hours responding to my queries than I am comfortable thinking about. I am also grateful to the staffs of the Abraham Lincoln Presidential Library, the Arkansas History Commission, the Cairo Public Library, the Illinois State Library, the National Archives Great Lakes Region branch in Chicago, the University of Illinois's Rare Books and Manuscripts Library, the University of Kentucky's Special Collections library, and the University of Louisville Archives and Records Center.

I benefited tremendously from my interactions with other scholars who I am quite certain know more about the 1937 flood than I do. Thanks go to the Three Wise

305

ACKNOWLEDGMENTS

Men (although they don't know I think of them that way): Rick Bell, John E. L. Robertson, and Chuck Parrish, who gladly spent their precious time reading a manuscript from a perfect stranger. Special thanks to John for giving that same stranger a guided tour of Paducah. I also appreciate my conversations with Robert Reid, who is hard at work on his own book about the disaster. Lorien Foote and Mike Schaefer offered incisive comments on portions of the manuscript. Aram Goudsouzian not only read the entire manuscript with his usual sharp eye, but also housed me during my visits to Memphis. Jack Pointer offered lodging in Chicago and his usual good humor. Dave Hardy put me up, and put up with me, on my trip to Champaign. Brad Mehrtens and Brian Moline enlivened that same trip. Michelle Wick-Patterson brightened my sojourn in College Park and got a parking ticket for her trouble.

The University of Central Arkansas has been a consistent supporter of my work. I could not have finished this book without the painstaking labors of UCA's Interlibrary Loan department. A grant from the University Research Council funded most of my travels. The Department of History provided reassign time to allow me to continue my research. I also benefited from a sabbatical semester that enabled me to write much of the book with minimal interruptions.

The University of Chicago Press has far exceeded my expectations for any publisher. Robert Devens has been all that I could ever hope for in an editor, a source of wit and wisdom who has been a magnificent cheerleader for this project since our first contact. Our conversations—some of them, anyway—have had an immeasurable impact on this book. Anne Summers Goldberg did an extraordinary job of preparing the manuscript and of handling the innumerable minor issues that crop up during publication. The legendary Alice Bennett did a wonderful job of copyediting the manuscript. Joan Davies, Andrea Guinn, Carol Saller, and Levi Stahl contributed their time and expertise as well. Two anonymous reviewers offered thorough reads bristling with insights and helpful suggestions. Thanks also to Karen Lucas for her mapmaking skills.

I am fortunate to have a wonderful family that, for reasons I have never figured out, has stuck with me through many years and many projects. My wife Ali has exhibited Joblike patience ever since we met all those years ago. She does so many things that make the lonely task of writing not just enjoyable but worthwhile. I cannot honestly say I could not have written this book without her, but it would not have been nearly as much fun. While working on "the flood book" I have seen our son Jude grow from a toddler into a wonderful little boy whose amazement at the big world around him reminds me that there is more to life than Depression-era natural disasters. Our daughter Kate, once our brand-new flood baby, is now a precocious toddler whose infatuation with water suggests that she resembles me more than I hoped she would. To them, and to my extended family, I offer the biggest thank you of all.

306

ABBREVIATIONS

ALPL	Abraham Lincoln Presidential Library, Springfield, Illinois
Chandler	Albert B. Chandler Papers, University of Kentucky Special Collections, Lexington, Kentucky
Conservation	Department of Conservation Collection, Illinois State Archives, Springfield, Illinois
Crump	E. H. Crump Collection, Series IV, Memphis–Shelby County Room, Memphis Public Library, Memphis, Tennessee
FDRL	Franklin D. Roosevelt Presidential Library, Hyde Park, New York
Hopkins	Papers of Harry Hopkins, Franklin D. Roosevelt Presidential Library, Hyde Park, New York
Horner	Henry Horner Papers, Abraham Lincoln Presidential Library, Springfield, Illinois
ISA	Illinois State Archives, Springfield, Illinois
Keller	Kent Keller Papers, Abraham Lincoln Presidential Library, Springfield, Illinois
NARA	National Archives and Records Administration, College Park, Maryland
OF	Official File
Overton	Watkins Overton Papers, University of Memphis Special Collections, Memphis, Tennessee
Overton Office	Watkins Overton Office Papers, Memphis–Shelby County Room, Memphis Public Library, Memphis, Tennessee

PPF	President's Personal File
PSF	President's Secretary's File
RC	Records of the American Red Cross, National Archives and Records Administration, College Park, Maryland, Record Group 200
RG 27	Record Group 27, Records of the Weather Bureau, General Correspondence of the Weather Bureau, 1912–42, National Archives and Records Administration, College Park, Maryland
RG 69 Central	Record Group 69, Work Projects Administration, Central Files: General 1935–44, National Archives and Records Administration, College Park, Maryland
RG 69 State	Record Group 69, Work Projects Administration, Central Files: State, 1935–44, National Archives and Records Administration, College Park, Maryland
RG 77	Record Group 77, Office of the Chief of Engineers, National Archives Great Lakes Branch, Chicago, Illinois
RG 92	Record Group 92, Office of the Quartermaster General, Jeffersonville Quartermaster Unit, Jeffersonville, Indiana, General Correspondence, 1920–39, National Archives Great Lakes Branch, Chicago, Illinois
STFU	Papers of the Southern Tenant Farmers' Union (microfilm edition)
UARC	University Archives and Records Center, University of Louisville, Louisville, Kentucky
Whittington	William M. Whittington Collection, University of Mississippi Archives and Special Collections, Oxford, Mississippi
Wyatt	Wilson Wyatt Papers, University of Kentucky Special Collections, Lexington, Kentucky

NOTES

Preface

1. I credit John Barry's masterful *Rising Tide: The Great Mississippi Flood of 1927 and How It Changed America* (New York: Simon and Schuster, 1997) for the attention given to that inundation. Interested parties should also read Pete Daniel, *Deep'n as It Come: The 1927 Mississippi River Flood* (New York: Oxford University Press, 1977).

2. For a sampling of the quickie volumes, see *Souvenir of the 1937 Louisville, Jeffersonville, New Albany Flood* (Louisville: K. S. Caulfield, 1937); Willard Rouse Jillson, *The Great Flood of 1937 in Louisville, Kentucky* (Louisville: Standard Printing Company, 1937); C. P. Malory, *Hickman's 1937 Flood: A Tragedy Averted* (n.p., 1937); Fred G. Neuman, *Paducah's Super-flood, January–February 1937: The Story of Paducah's Greatest Disaster in Words and Pictures* (Paducah: Young Publishing, 1937); *Flood: The Great 1937 Disaster* (Wilkes-Barre, PA: Picture Press, 1937); *Flood Stories by Shawnee High School Girls, Louisville Kentucky, 1937* (Louisville: Standard Printing, 1937); Lowell Thomas, *Hungry Waters: The Story of the Great Flood, Together with an Account of Famous Floods of History, and Plans for Flood Control and Prevention* (Philadelphia: John C. Winston, 1937); *The Union Central and the 1937 Flood* (Cincinnati: Union Central Life Insurance Company, 1937). Nathan C. Grover, *Floods of Ohio and Mississippi Rivers, January–February 1937* (Washington, DC: Government Printing Office, 1938), contains a wealth of statistical information and a brief narrative of the flood. Elisabeth Peck's *Tibb's Flooders: A Tale of the Ohio River Flood of 1937* (New York: House of Field, 1941) is a work of fiction that reflects its author's familiarity with the experience of small towns during the event. Frederick Simpich, "Men Against the Rivers," *National Geographic* 71 (June 1937): 767–94 is the best of the many magazine surveys of the flood. There is also much to recommend in Gustave A. Breaux, "1937 Flood at Louisville," *Filson Club History Quarterly* 11 (April 1937): 109–19. For a more technical contemporary view of the disaster see Paschal N. Strong, "The Great Flood of the Ohio," *Military Engineer* 29 (May–June 1937): 157–62. Since I began work on this book Rick Bell has brought out his

lavishly illustrated *The Great Flood of 1937: Rising Waters, Soaring Spirits, Louisville, Kentucky* (Louisville: Butler Books, 2007). Finally, consult Patrick O'Daniel, *Memphis and the Superflood of 1937: High Water Blues* (Charleston, SC: History Press, 2010).

Introduction

1. *New York Times*, 21 January 1937.

2. Harold Ickes Diary, 24 January 1937, FDRL, Ickes Diary, reel 2.

3. *New York Times*, 21 January 1937.

4. *New York Times*, 21 January 1937; Harold Ickes Diary, 24 January 1937, FDRL, Ickes Diary, reel 2.

5. *New York Times*, 21 January 1937.

6. *New York Times*, 21 January 1937; Harold Ickes Diary, 24 January 1937, FDRL, Ickes Diary, reel 2.

7. *New York Times*, 21 January 1937.

8. Stephen Early Diary, 20 January 1937, FDRL, Papers of Stephen T. Early.

9. Federal Writers' Program, *Arkansas: A Guide to the State* (New York: Hastings House, 1941), 101; Jerold S. Auerbach, "Southern Tenant Farmers: Socialist Critics of the New Deal," *Arkansas Historical Quarterly* 27 (Summer 1968): 114.

10. *Memphis Commercial Appeal*, 8 January 1937; *Dunklin (MO) Democrat*, 12 January 1937.

11. *Blytheville (AR) Courier News*, 20 January 1937.

12. *Memphis Commercial Appeal*, 20 January 1937.

13. W. L. McFarland to Carl Bailey, 20 January 1937, Carl Bailey Papers, Arkansas History Commission, Little Rock, Arkansas, reel 4.

14. K. Goodwin to Howard Hunter and F. C. Harrington, 16 January 1937, RG 69 Central, box 292.

15. *Louisville Courier-Journal*, 14 February 1937; *Memphis Commercial Appeal*, 26 January 1937.

16. For more on human responsibility for Depression era environmental disasters, see Timothy Egan, *The Worst Hard Time: The Untold Story of Those Who Survived the Great American Dust Bowl* (New York: Houghton Mifflin, 2005); Ted Steinberg, *Down to Earth: Nature's Role in American History* (New York: Oxford University Press, 2002); and Donald Worster, *Dust Bowl: The Southern Plains in the 1930s* (New York: Oxford University Press, 1980).

17. For more on the New Deal and African Americans see Cheryl Greenberg, *To Ask for an Equal Chance: African Americans in the Great Depression* (Lanham, MD: Rowman and Littlefield, 2009); Lauren Rebecca Sklaroff, *Black Culture and the New Deal: The Quest for Civil Rights in the Roosevelt Era* (Chapel Hill: University of North Carolina Press, 2009); and Patricia Sullivan, *Days of Hope: Race and Democracy in the New Deal Era* (Chapel Hill: University of North Carolina Press, 1996).

18. For discussions of the concept of environmental "agency," see Linda Nash, "The Agency of Nature or the Nature of Agency?" *Environmental History* 10 (January 2005): 67–69; Jared Farmer, *On Zion's Mount: Mormons, Indians, and the American Land-*

scape (Cambridge, MA: Harvard University Press, 2008); Ari Kelman, *A River and Its City: The Nature of Landscape in New Orleans* (Berkeley: University of California Press, 2003); Robert Kelley Schneiders, *Unruly River: Two Centuries of Change along the Mississippi* (Lawrence: University Press of Kansas, 1999); Coll Thrush, *Native Seattle: Histories from the Crossing-Over Place* (Seattle: University of Washington Press, 2007); and Richard White, *The Organic Machine* (New York: Hill and Wang, 1995).

Chapter One

1. R. David Edmunds, "Heron Who Waits at the Speleawee-thepee: The Ohio River and the Shawnee World," *Register of the Kentucky Historical Society* 91 (Summer 1993): 249; Henri Joutel, *Joutel's Journal of La Salle's Last Voyage, 1684-7* (1714; reprint, Albany, NY: Joseph McDonough, 1906), 185; Thomas Jefferson, *Notes on the State of Virginia* (1784; reprint, Boston: David Carlisle, 1801), 14.

2. Richard Elwell Banta, *The Ohio* (New York: Rinehart, 1949), 61–65.

3. Ibid., 62–63.

4. Ibid., 266.

5. Ibid., 510.

6. Leland R. Johnson, *The Falls City Engineers: A History of the Louisville District, Corps of Engineers, United States Army* (Washington, DC: U.S. Army Corps of Engineers, 1975), 44–50.

7. Ibid., 88–101.

8. Gene D. Lewis, *Charles Ellet, Jr.: The Engineer as Individualist* (Urbana: University of Illinois Press, 1968), 3–5.

9. Ibid., 5–8.

10. Ibid., 10–12.

11. Ibid., 19.

12. Ibid., 53.

13. Ibid., 61.

14. Ellet quoted in David McCullough, *The Great Bridge: The Epic Story of the Building of the Brooklyn Bridge* (New York: Simon and Schuster, 1983), 77.

15. McCullough, *Great Bridge*, 77.

16. Lewis, *Charles Ellet, Jr.*, 119–26.

17. Ellet quoted in ibid., 127.

18. Lewis, *Charles Ellet, Jr.*, 135.

19. Joseph L. Arnold, *The Evolution of the 1936 Flood Control Act* (Fort Belvoir, VA: U.S. Army Corps of Engineers, 1988), 6; Ellet quoted in Lewis, *Charles Ellet, Jr.*, 139.

20. John M. Barry, *Rising Tide: The Great Mississippi Flood of 1927 and How It Changed America* (New York: Simon and Schuster, 1997), 42–45.

21. Humphreys quoted in Barry, *Rising Tide*, 42; Ellet quoted in Lewis, *Charles Ellet, Jr.*, 139.

22. Charles Ellet Jr., "Report on the Overflows of the Delta of the Mississippi," in House Committee on Flood Control, *Reports on the Ohio and Mississippi Rivers*, 70th Cong., 1st sess., 1928, 49, 62, 57–59, 63–64.

23. Ibid., 112–18.

24. Charles Ellet Jr., *The Mississippi and Ohio Rivers* (1853; reprint, New York: Arno, 1970), 280, 306, 315–16, 311, 303–4.

25. Donald Worster, *Nature's Economy: A History of Ecological Ideas*, 2nd ed. (Cambridge: Cambridge University Press, 1994), 30–51.

26. S. H. Long, "Report on the Nature and Progress of the Delta Surveys of the Lower Mississippi," in House Committee on Flood Control, *Reports on the Ohio and Mississippi Rivers*, 70th Cong., 1st sess., 1928, 19; Barry, *Rising Tide*, 46.

27. W. Milnor Roberts, *Practical Views on the Proposed Improvement of the Ohio River* (Philadelphia: Franklin Institute, 1857), 31, 18–19, 23–29, 40.

28. Lewis, *Charles Ellet, Jr.*, 147, 177–81, 186–92, 196–207.

29. A. A. Humphreys and Henry L. Abbot, *The Physics and Hydraulics of the Mississippi River* (Philadelphia: J. B. Lippincott, 1861), 30.

30. Ibid., 353, 410, 381, 120.

31. Ibid., 379, 30, 418; Barry, *Rising Tide*, 53.

32. Barry, *Rising Tide*, 47–55.

33. Johnson, *Falls City Engineers*, 155–56, 162–72, 185–88, 191.

34. Arthur E. Morgan, *Dams and Other Disasters: A Century of the Army Corps of Engineers in Civil Works* (Boston: Porter Sargent, 1971), 263; George Perkins Marsh, *Man and Nature, or Physical Geography as Modified by Human Action* (1864; reprint, Cambridge, MA: Harvard University Press, 1965), 194–201, 326–43.

35. The eminent environmental historian Donald Worster has contributed a quartet of books useful to anyone seeking more information on late nineteenth-century conservation and environmental policy. *Nature's Economy* provides an excellent introductory survey. *Rivers of Empire: Water, Aridity, and the Growth of the American West* (New York: Pantheon, 1985) examines the powerful forces working to control the most precious resource in America's dry country. It is best read in conjunction with Richard White's brief but powerful *The Organic Machine* (New York: Hill and Wang, 1995). Worster's *A River Running West: The Life of John Wesley Powell* (New York: Oxford University Press, 2001) and *A Passion for Nature: The Life of John Muir* (New York: Oxford University Press, 2008) are excellent biographies of two of the most important figures in American environmental history.

36. Samuel P. Hays, *Conservation and the Gospel of Efficiency* (Cambridge, MA: Harvard University Press, 1959), 105–14, 199–209. Also see Douglas Brinkley, *The Wilderness Warrior: Theodore Roosevelt and the Crusade for America* (New York: Harper, 2009).

37. Francis Shunk to William Rossell, 17 April 1913, RG 77; Francis Shunk to Dan Kingman, 11 August 1914, RG 77.

38. Francis Shunk to Dan Kingman, 11 August 1914, RG 77; "Preliminary Report of the Army Engineers on the Central States Floods," *Engineering News* 70 (9 October 1913): 726; Lindley Garrison to Champ Clark, 15 April 1914, RG 77.

39. Lowell Thomas, *Hungry Waters: The Story of the Great Flood, Together with an Account of Famous Floods of History, and Plans for Flood Control and Prevention* (Philadelphia: John C. Winston, 1937), 300–304.

40. Arthur Maass, *Muddy Waters: The Army Engineers and the Nation's Rivers* (Cambridge, MA: Harvard University Press, 1951), 66.

41. Floyd Clay, *A Century on the Mississippi: A History of the Memphis District, U.S. Army Corps of Engineers, 1876-1976* (Washington, DC: U.S. Army Corps of Engineers, 1976), 100.

42. *Charleston (MO) Enterprise-Courier*, 14, 21 April 1927.

43. *New Madrid (MO) Weekly Record*, 30 December 1927; *Dunklin (MO) Democrat*, 24 January 1928; Senate Committee on Commerce, *Hearings before the Committee on Commerce, United States Senate relative to Flood Control on the Mississippi River*, 70th Cong., 1st sess., 49.

44. Waterways Experiment Station, *Model Study of Effects of Operating Bird's Point-New Madrid Floodway: Paper C of the U.S. Waterways Experiment Station, Vicksburg, Mississippi* (Vicksburg: Waterways Experiment Station, 1933), 7; "Narrative Report—Rehabilitation Period—Region H," RC, box 1271.

45. Sarah T. Phillips, *This Land, This Nation: Conservation, Rural America, and the New Deal* (Cambridge: Cambridge University Press, 2007), 47-48; David P. Billington and Donald C. Jackson, *Big Dams of the New Deal Era: A Confluence of Engineering and Politics* (Norman: University of Oklahoma Press, 2006), 87-91.

46. Morgan, *Dams and Other Disasters*, 228-30.

47. Lucille Lawler, *Gallatin County: Gateway to Illinois* (Ridgway, IL, 1968), 11; Mary Catherine Kershaw, "Early History of Shawneetown, Illinois, from 1812 to 1832" (MA thesis, University of Illinois, 1941), 85.

48. Jon Musgrave, ed., *Handbook of Old Gallatin County* (Marion, IL: IllinoisHistory .com, 2002), 7; Lawler, *Gallatin County*, 1.

49. Lawler, *Gallatin County*, 7, 25.

50. Stanley Griswold to Josiah Meigs, 14 August 1813, Reports and Instructions re: Surveying Shawneetown, 1810-14, ISA; Curtis Small, "River, Stay Away from My Door," *Saturday Evening Post* 213 (7 December 1940): 101.

51. Lawler, *Gallatin County*, 38, 17.

52. Ibid., 61; William H. Nicholas, "Shawneetown Forsakes the Ohio," *National Geographic* 93 (February 1948): 283.

53. *Gallatin Democrat*, 22 February 1940; Musgrave, *Handbook of Old Gallatin County*, 53.

54. WPA Illinois, *Work Progress Aids: A Pictorial Journal of Cooperative Effort*, April 1939, 5.

55. Lawler, *Gallatin County*, 31, 50, 58, 69; Lisabeth Lowe Parsons, "Shawneetown," 6 December 1932, unpublished paper in Shawneetown Public Library, Shawneetown, Illinois.

56. *Shawneetown News* quoted in Small, "River, Stay Away from My Door," 101.

57. John Crebs to John Tanner, 4 April 1898, John Riley Tanner Papers, ISA.

58. Executive Relief Committee of Shawneetown, Illinois, *The Shawneetown Flood, April 3rd, 1898: Final Report of the Executive Relief Committee* (Shawneetown, IL, 1900), 6-10; Ephraim Banning to John Tanner, 7 April 1898, John Riley Tanner Papers, ISA.

59. Robert William Janes, "The Collective Action Involved in the Removal and Relocation of Shawneetown, Illinois" (PhD diss., University of Illinois, 1942), 179.

Chapter Two

1. Mary Helen Dohan, *Mr. Roosevelt's Steamboat: The First Steamboat to Travel the Mississippi* (New York: Pelican, 2004), 1-3.

2. F. Kevin Simon, ed., *The WPA Guide to Kentucky* (1939; reprint, Lexington: University of Kentucky Press, 1996), 176-84.

3. Jay Feldman, *When the Mississippi Ran Backwards: Empire, Intrigue, Murder, and the New Madrid Earthquakes* (New York: Free Press, 2005), 12, 18-19, 24, 106-18.

4. Ibid., 149-50, 159.

5. Nicholas Roosevelt was great-uncle to FDR's fifth cousin, President Theodore Roosevelt.

6. Neil M. Maher, *Nature's New Deal: The Civilian Conservation Corps and the Roots of the American Environmental Movement* (New York: Oxford University Press, 2008), 28.

7. Ibid., 28-32, 188; Sarah T. Phillips, *This Land, This Nation: Conservation, Rural America, and the New Deal* (Cambridge: Cambridge University Press, 2007), 13.

8. Maher, *Nature's New Deal*, 190, 39.

9. Franklin Roosevelt, "Speech Accepting the Democratic Vice-Presidential Nomination," 9 August 1920, in *Franklin D. Roosevelt and Conservation, 1911-1945*, ed. Edgar B. Nixon (New York: Arno, 1972), 38.

10. Franklin Roosevelt Form Letter [1927], FDRL, FDR Family, Business, and Personal Papers, box 42, folder Letters re: Flood Relief in the Mississippi Valley.

11. Ibid.; *New York Times*, 22 August 1928.

12. Otis L. Graham Jr., "The Planning Ideal and American Reality: The 1930s," in *The Hofstadter Aegis: A Memorial*, ed. Stanley Elkins and Eric McKitrick (New York: Alfred A. Knopf, 1974), 275, 257-60, 263-73.

13. Lewis Mumford, *The Culture of Cities* (New York: Harcourt, Brace, 1938), 374, 329-36; George Henry Soule, *A Planned Society* (New York: Macmillan, 1933), 265, 29-54, 230-58. Also see Otis L. Graham Jr., *Toward a Planned Society: From Roosevelt to Nixon* (New York: Oxford University Press, 1976).

14. Mumford, *Culture of Cities*, 367, 376-81.

15. Phillips, *This Land, This Nation*, 63-71; Franklin Roosevelt, "Address at the Thomas Jefferson Dinner," in *Public Papers and Addresses of Franklin D. Roosevelt*, ed. Samuel I. Rosenman (New York: Random House, 1938), 5:181.

16. Griffith quoted in Graham, "Planning Ideal and American Reality," 284; Bennett quoted in Maher, *Nature's New Deal*, 204.

17. Graham, "Planning Ideal and American Reality," 267; Donald Worster, *Nature's Economy: A History of Ecological Ideas*, 2nd ed. (Cambridge: Cambridge University Press, 1994), 237-41.

18. Franklin Roosevelt to Lewis Douglas, 20 April 1933, FDRL, OF 25, War Department, box 25, folder Mississippi River Commission.

19. *Congressional Record*, 13 April 1934, 52845-10188.

20. United States House of Representatives, *Development of the Rivers of the United States*, 73rd Cong., 2nd sess., H.R. Doc. 395, 3–4.

21. Ibid., 219–21.

22. Franklin Roosevelt to George Dern, 6 June 1934, FDRL, OF 25, War Department, box 27, folder Mississippi River Commission.

23. Press release, 26 December 1934, FDRL, Leland Olds Papers, box 86, folder Mississippi Valley Committee. See also *Report of the Mississippi Valley Committee of the Public Works Administration* (Washington, DC: Government Printing Office, 1934).

24. http://www.presidency.ucsb.edu/ws/index.php?pid=14715. Accessed 10 September 2008.

25. National Resources Board, "A Report on National Planning and Public Works in relation to Natural Resources and Including Land Use and Water Resources with Findings and Recommendations," 1 December 1934, FDRL, Leon Henderson Papers, box 7, folder National Resources Board.

26. Joseph L. Arnold, *The Evolution of the 1936 Flood Control Act* (Fort Belvoir, VA: U.S. Army Corps of Engineers, 1988), 27–28, 37–38, 42–43.

27. Ibid., 47–54.

28. Ibid., 56–57.

29. Daniel Bell to Franklin Roosevelt, 20 July 1935, FDRL, OF 132, Floods, box 1, folder 1935; Franklin Roosevelt to Daniel Bell, 22 July 1935, FDRL, OF 132, Floods, box 1, folder 1935.

30. H. S. Person, *Little Waters: A Study of Headwater Streams and Other Little Waters, Their Use and Relation to the Land* (Washington, DC: Government Printing Office, 1936), 3, 1.

31. For more on the idea of a limited economy, see Alan Brinkley, *The End of Reform: New Deal Liberalism in Recession and War* (New York: Knopf, 1995).

32. American National Red Cross, *Spring Floods and Tornadoes, 1936: Official Report of Relief Operations* (Washington, DC: ANRC, 1938), 5–15.

33. Crest heights are inconsistent at various points along a stream and to some degree are arbitrary. Engineers establish a zero-foot mark at the riverbed or at an assumed lowest level for the stream at a specific location and work upward from there. The width of the river and the topography of the banks affect the height at which a river achieves flood stage. For example, although a thirty-four-foot crest produces a considerable flood at Pittsburgh, a thirty-four-foot crest would be far below flood stage at Cincinnati, which has its own set of markers and a different topography.

34. Victor Weybright, "Runaway Rivers," *Survey Graphic* 35 (May 1936): 296–98.

35. Roger Pickenpaugh, *River on a Rampage: The 1936 Flood from Chester to Marietta* (Baltimore: Gateway Press, 2002), 1, 27, 109; Weybright, "Runaway Rivers," 295; ANRC, *Spring Floods and Tornadoes*, 27.

36. Arnold, *Evolution of the 1936 Flood Control Act*, 69–70; *Flood News*, April 1936, 1.

37. Markham quoted in Arnold, *Evolution of the 1936 Flood Control Act*, 77.

38. Arnold, *Evolution of the 1936 Flood Control Act*, 77, 70–72, 79.

39. "Environmentalism" can refer to a movement that grew up after World War II and was dedicated to the idea that mankind needs to reduce or eliminate its influence

over nature. When used this way "environmentalism" carries moral and preservationist overtones. Here and throughout this book I use a broader definition that simply refers to discussions about the environment.

40. Henry Wallace to Franklin Roosevelt, 25 March 1936, FDRL, OF 132, Floods, box 1, folder 1936; Franklin Roosevelt to Henry Wallace, 26 March 1936, FDRL, OF 132, Floods, box 1, folder 1936; George Dern et al. to Franklin Roosevelt, 31 March 1936, FDRL, OF 132, Floods, box 1, folder 1936.

41. Franklin Roosevelt Press Conference, 28 April 1936, in Nixon, *Franklin D. Roosevelt and Conservation*, 508; Franklin Roosevelt to Joseph Robinson, 1 May 1936, FDRL, OF 132, Floods, box 1, folder 1936; Harold Ickes to Franklin Roosevelt, 13 April 1936, in Nixon, *Franklin D. Roosevelt and Conservation*, 506.

42. Arnold, *Evolution of the 1936 Flood Control Act*, 89–90.

43. National Resources Committee, *Drainage Basin Problems and Programs* (Washington, DC: Government Printing Office, 1937), 1, 3, 4–5.

44. Ibid., 37–38, 212–14.

45. Maher, *Nature's New Deal*, 165, 77–103, 116, 146, 163–64; Jason Scott Smith, *Building New Deal Liberalism: The Political Economy of Public Works, 1933–1956* (Cambridge: Cambridge University Press, 2006), 19.

46. *Gallatin Democrat*, 10 May 1962; Lucille Lawler, *Gallatin County: Gateway to Illinois* (Ridgway, IL, 1968), 144.

47. Robert William Janes, "The Collective Action Involved in the Removal and Relocation of Shawneetown" (PhD diss., University of Illinois, 1942), 96–108, 79–85.

48. Ibid., 65–70; *Gallatin Democrat*, 29 February 1940, 13 September 1956; *History and Families of Gallatin County* (Paducah, KY: Turner, 1988), 125.

49. G. Cullom Davis and Horace Waggoner, *Memories of a Bank: Final Report, an Oral History and Documentary Inventory at Old Shawneetown* (Springfield, IL: Sangamon State University Oral History Office, 1979), 4:453, 3:290, 3:276; Rudy Phillips, *Rudy's Life in Shawneetown, 1928–1980* (n.p.: Rudy Phillips, 1980), 41.

50. Janes, "Collective Action Involved in the Removal and Relocation of Shawneetown," 59–62.

51. Ibid., 163, 159, 65, 42.

52. Ibid., 129.

53. Phillips, *Rudy's Life in Shawneetown*, 1; Birbeck, quoted in Lawler, *Gallatin County*, 22.

Chapter Three

1. Weather and river-gauge information comes from Nathan C. Grover, *Floods of Ohio and Mississippi Rivers, January–February 1937* (Washington, DC: Government Printing Office, 1938).

2. *Cairo Evening Citizen and Bulletin*, 1 January 1937; *Golconda (IL) Herald-Enterprise*, 14 January 1937.

3. Grover, *Floods of Ohio and Mississippi Rivers*, 61–63.

4. Lowell Thomas, *Hungry Waters: The Story of the Great Flood, Together with an Ac-*

count of *Famous Floods of History, and Plans for Flood Control and Prevention* (Philadelphia: John C. Winston, 1937), 2–18.

5. William Hillinger to Marvin McIntyre, 14 October 1936, FDRL, OF 132, Floods, box 1, folder 1936.

6. House Committee on Flood Control, *Hearings on Amendments to Flood Control Acts of 1936, 1937 and 1938, Including H.R. 4291*, 67th Cong., 1st sess., 1939, 40.

7. Patrick Hughes, *A Century of Weather Service: A History of the Birth and Growth of the National Weather Service* (New York: Gordon and Breach, 1970), 14; Donald R. Whitnah, *A History of the United States Weather Bureau* (Urbana: University of Illinois Press, 1961), 4, 9.

8. Hughes, *Century of Weather Service*, 7.

9. Whitnah, *History of the United States Weather Bureau*, 23–28.

10. Hughes, *Century of Weather Service*, 23, 41; Whitnah, *History of the United States Weather Bureau*, 31.

11. Hughes, *Century of Weather Service*, 37, 61–63; Whitnah, *History of the United States Weather Bureau*, 103–13.

12. Whitnah, *History of the United States Weather Bureau*, 144, 155, 158–61, 166; *Hearings on Amendments to Flood Control Acts of 1936, 1937 and 1938*, 33–34.

13. *Cincinnati Enquirer*, 18, 19, 20, 22 January 1937.

14. *Cincinnati Enquirer*, 23 January 1937.

15. *Cincinnati Enquirer*, 24, 25, 26 January 1937.

16. E. E. Brownell to John Boehne Jr., 20 April 1937, RG 27, box 215; Phillip Hertzberger to Willis Gregg, 17 April 1937, RG 27, box 215.

17. *Memphis Commercial Appeal*, 21, 22 January 1937; *Cape Girardeau Southeast Missourian*, 22, 23 January 1937.

18. *Blytheville (AR) Courier News*, 22, 23 January 1937.

19. "Narrative Report—Region H" [1937], RC, box 1271.

20. Thomas Hart Benton, *An Artist in America* (1937; rev. ed., New York: Twayne, 1951), 146.

21. David Eugene Conrad, *The Forgotten Farmers: The Story of Sharecroppers in the New Deal* (Urbana: University of Illinois Press, 1965), 15; William Cobb and Donald H. Grubb, "Arkansas' Commonwealth College and the Southern Tenant Farmers' Union," *Arkansas Historical Quarterly* 25 (Winter 1966): 294–95.

22. Jonathan Daniels, *A Southerner Discovers the South* (New York: Macmillan, 1938), 135.

23. M. E. Venkatarami, "Norman Thomas, Arkansas Sharecroppers, and the Roosevelt Agricultural Policies, 1933–1937," *Arkansas Historical Quarterly* 24 (Spring 1965): 8, 14, 13.

24. Donald H. Grubbs, *Cry from the Cotton: The Southern Tenant Farmers' Union and the New Deal* (Chapel Hill: University of North Carolina Press, 1971), 27–29.

25. "Report to the Third Annual Convention" [January 1937], STFU, reel 4; "Statement of the Southern Tenant Farmers' Union," 4 January 1937, STFU, reel 4.

26. "Auditor's Preliminary Report to the Convention" [January 1937], STFU, reel 4; Daniels, *Southerner Discovers the South*, 121–22.

27. *New York Post*, 11 February 1937; *Nashville Tennessean*, 23 February 1935; *Muskogee (OK) Daily Phoenix*, 15 January 1937.

28. "Report to the Third Annual Convention" [January 1937], STFU, reel 4; Aaron Levenstein to unnamed recipient, 17 January 1937, STFU, reel 4; "Ceremony of the Land" [January 1937], STFU, reel 4.

29. C. J. Spradling to H. L. Mitchell, 24 January 1937, STFU, reel 4; H. L. Mitchell to C. J. Spradling, [January 1937], STFU, reel 4.

30. *United Progressive News* (Los Angeles), 2 February 1937.

31. *Cape Girardeau Southeast Missourian*, 22, 23, 27 January 1937; "Narrative Report—Region H" [1937], RC, box 1271.

32. "Ohio River Flood of 1913—a Pioneering Relief Task," *Red Cross Courier* 16 (March 1937): 15; John M. Barry, *Rising Tide: The Great Mississippi Flood of 1927 and How It Changed America* (New York: Simon and Schuster, 1997), 311–13.

33. "Day by Day Developments in the Flood Crisis," *Red Cross Courier* 16 (March 1937): 11; American National Red Cross, *The Ohio-Mississippi Valley Flood Disaster of 1937* (Washington, DC: ANRC, 1938), 28.

34. Alwyn W. Knight, "Nursing Waterlogged America," *Hygeia* 15 (June 1937): 494, 568; Paul Gascoigne, "The Part Played by Telephones in the Crisis," *Red Cross Courier* 16 (April 1937): 11.

35. Knight, "Nursing Waterlogged America," 494–95, 568; I. Malinde Havey, "Disaster Report" [1937], RC, box 1256.

36. "Suggestion and Friendly Advice to a Nurse Assigned to Red Cross Disaster Service" [1937], RC, box 1255.

37. Maurice Reddy, "Ohio and Mississippi Valley Floods—1937. Region B—Ohio. Final Report," July 1937, RC, box 1268; W. C. Conover, "Final Report of the Regional Supply Officer, Region B, American Red Cross," 15 May 1937, RC, box 1267; "Summary Report of Disaster Relief Committee," 15 February 1937, RC, box 1266; Gus Meyer to Richard Allen, 11 July 1937, RC, box 1266.

38. "Narrative Report—Rehabilitation Period—Region H" [1937], RC, box 1271; "Narrative Report—Region I" [1937], RC, box 1270.

39. American National Red Cross, *Ohio-Mississippi Valley Flood Disaster of 1937*, 44–47, 28.

40. Ibid., 46–48; Finis Dunaway, *Natural Visions: The Power of Images in American Environmental Reform* (Chicago: University of Chicago Press, 2005), 70.

41. "Coast Guard Operations in Flood Area," 22 January 1937, FDRL, OF 83, Disasters, box 1, folder 1937 Floods; "Report of Operations, Coast Guard Flood Relief Forces, Ohio and Mississippi Valleys, from 19 January, 1937 to 11 March, 1937," 19 April 1937, RC, box 1251.

42. *Cincinnati Enquirer*, 23 January 1937; Harry Hopkins to Franklin Roosevelt, 22 January 1937, FDRL, OF 83, Disasters, box 1, folder 1937 Floods.

43. Harry Hopkins to Wayne Coy, 22 January 1937, Hopkins, box 74; Harry Hopkins to Franklin Roosevelt, 22 January 1937, RG 69 Central, box 292; Francis Harrington to Floyd Sharp, 23 January 1937, Hopkins, box 54, folder Flood—January 1937.

44. "Special Report on Civilian Conservation Corps Activities during Ohio, Mississippi Floods of January and February, 1937" [August 1937], RC, box 1251.

45. Stephen Early Diary, 22, 23 January 1937, FDRL, Papers of Stephen T. Early.

46. *Paducah Sun-Democrat*, 21 January 1937; Francis Harrington to Lt. Col. Crawford, 23 January 1937, Hopkins, box 54, folder Flood—January 1937; Harry Hopkins to Howard Hunter, 23 January 1937, Hopkins, box 73, folder Transcripts of Telephone Conversations.

47. Francis Harrington to Wayne Coy, 23 January 1937, Hopkins, box 54, folder Flood—January 1937.

48. Garry J. Nokes, *Jeffersonville, Indiana* (Chicago: Arcadia, 2002), 85–86, 9.

49. Ibid., 10, 91, 96–98.

50. Ibid., 103.

51. "Clark County" [1937] RC, box 1258; Nokes, *Jeffersonville*, 23.

52. *Jeffersonville (IN) Evening News*, 16, 20, 21 January 1937, 11 March 1937; "Clark County" [1937], RC, box 1258.

53. "Memorandum of Phone Conversation from Colonel Alfonte," 20 January 1937, RG 92; M. G. Holliday to Alvin K. Baskette, 22 January 1937, RG 92.

54. "Proceedings, Board of Officers Convened February 1, 1937 to Report on Flood Damage and Loss to Buildings, Machinery, Stocks and Utilities at the Jeffersonville Quartermaster Depot," 1 February 1937, RG 92.

55. Henry Gibbons to General Warfield, 22 January 1937, RG 92.

56. *Jeffersonville (IN) Evening News*, 24, 9 March 1937; Nokes, *Jeffersonville*, 108.

57. "Report on Flood Damage and Loss to Buildings, Machinery, Stocks and Utilities at the Jeffersonville Quartermaster Depot"; Henry Gibbins to General Warfield, 22 January 1937, RG 92.

58. "Report on Flood Damage and Loss to Buildings, Machinery, Stocks and Utilities at the Jeffersonville Quartermaster Depot."

59. Ibid.

60. Ibid.; *Jeffersonville (IN) Evening News*, 18 June 1937; *Louisville Courier-Journal*, 27 January 1937.

61. "Report on Health Conditions," 15 February 1937, Overton Office, box 6, folder Flood Disaster (Army); Curtis R. Hay, "Flood Report," Horner, box 322; *Louisville Courier-Journal*, 22 January 1937; Keen Johnson to Alben Barkley, 22 January 1937, Chandler, box 100, folder Flood, 1937; *Kentucky Medical Journal, Part II—Women's Auxiliary Section* 6 (April 1937): 68.

62. Alexander Maxwell, "Floods Give Fair Warning," *Scientific American* 159 (October 1938): 193.

63. Maurice Reddy, "Ohio and Mississippi Valley Floods—1937. Region B—Ohio, Final Report," July 1937, RC, box 1268.

64. *Louisville Courier-Journal*, 22, 23 January 1937; Joseph Scholtz to Neville Miller, 23 January 1937, Neville Miller Scrapbook, 1937 Ohio River Flood Collection, University of Louisville Special Collections; *Cairo Evening Citizen and Bulletin*, 20 January 1937.

Chapter Four

1. *Louisville Courier-Journal*, 24 January 1937.

2. W. O. Ulrey, "The Volunteers in Kentucky" [1937], pamphlet, Louisville Free Public Library.

3. R. E. Tarbett, "Federal Facilities to Expedite Emergency Sanitation Measures," *American Journal of Public Health* 28 (September 1938): 1091–92; *Paducah Sun-Democrat*, 25 January 1987.

4. Eliot Curtis to Franklin Roosevelt, 26 January 1937, FDRL, OF 83, Disasters, box 1, folder 1937 Floods; phone message from Tobey Miller, 25 January 1937, FDRL, OF 83, Disasters, box 1, folder 1937 Floods; Chicago Board of Women's International League for Peace and Freedom to Franklin Roosevelt, 2 February 1937, FDRL, OF 83, Disasters, box 1, folder 1937 Floods.

5. Richard F. Allen, "Minutes of Meeting," 25 January 1937, RC, box 1251.

6. Harold Ickes Diary, 30 January 1937, FDRL, Ickes Diary, reel 2.

7. Jonathan Daniels, ed., *Complete Presidential Press Conferences of Franklin D. Roosevelt* (New York: DaCapo, 1972), 9:105.

8. *Memphis Commercial Appeal*, 26 January, 11 February 1937; *Vicksburg Evening Post*, 29, 31 January 1937.

9. "Confidential Memo," 28 January 1937, RC, box 1253; "Plan of Action in Case of Major Break in the Mississippi River" [January 1937], FDRL, Papers of Stephen T. Early, box 29, folder Flood—Mississippi River.

10. Malin Craig to Commanding General, Sixth Area Corps, 27 January 1937, FDRL, OF 83, Disasters, box 1, folder 1937 Floods.

11. Ibid.; "News Flashes," 27 January 1937, FDRL, OF 83, Disasters, box 2, folder 1937–1945 Floods.

12. *Harrisburg (IL) Daily Register*, 31 January 1937; *New Orleans Times-Picayune*, 27, 28, 29 January 1937; *Golconda (IL) Herald-Enterprise*, 4 February 1937; *London News Chronicle*, 28 January 1937.

13. M. A. Bell, "Data on Red Cross Rescue Division, Mississippi River, during the Ohio-Mississippi Flood, January-February 1937" [1937], RC, box 1256.

14. Maurice Reddy, "Ohio and Mississippi Valley Floods-1937. Region B–Ohio, Final Report," July 1937, RC, box 1268.

15. *Cincinnati Enquirer*, 19, 20, 21, 22, 23, 24 January 1937.

16. Geneva A. Seybold, "Dykstra in Cincinnati: Portrait of a Scholar in Action," *Survey Graphic* 26 (April 1937): 205; Walter Davenport, "Cincinnati's Dyke," *Collier's* 99 (10 April 1937): 83–84.

17. "Flood-Master," *Scholastic* 30 (20 February 1937): 23; Davenport, "Cincinnati's Dyke," 13; Seybold, "Dykstra in Cincinnati," 204–5.

18. Seybold, "Dykstra in Cincinnati," 206; Davenport, "Cincinnati's Dyke," 84.

19. *The Union Central and the 1937 Flood* (Cincinnati: Union Central Life Insurance Company, 1937), 8; *Cincinnati Enquirer*, 25 January 1937.

20. *Cincinnati Enquirer*, 25, 24 January 1937.

21. *Cincinnati Enquirer*, 26, 29, 25 January 1937; *Louisville Courier-Journal*, 27 January 1937.

22. *Cincinnati Enquirer*, 25 January 1937; *Louisville Courier-Journal*, 30 January 1937; "Flooded Industry," *Literary Digest* 123 (6 February 1937): 37; Lewis Crossley interview, 3 July 1957, University of Illinois-Springfield Oral History Collection, Archives/Special Collections, www.idaillinois.org/cgi-bin/Showfile_exe?CISROOT=/uis&CISOPTR =163&filename=164.pdf. Accessed 25 May 2007.

23. *Cincinnati Enquirer*, 25 January 1937.

24. *Louisville Courier-Journal*, 7, 21 February 1937. Kentucky's State Office Building sits on the site today, built in part with stones salvaged from the old prison.

25. Beverly Vincent to A. B. Chandler, 10 February 1936, Chandler, box 79, folder Reformatory; A. T. McCormack to A. B. Chandler, 24 January 1937, Chandler, box 101, folder Flood, 1937.

26. *Cape Girardeau Southeast Missourian*, 22 January 1937; *Louisville Courier-Journal*, 5 March 1937.

27. *Louisville Courier-Journal*, 5 March 1937; *Cincinnati Enquirer*, 26 January 1937; Mrs. James Brown to A. B. Chandler, 11 February 1937, Chandler, box 78, folder Reformatory, 1937.

28. *Memphis Commercial Appeal*, 26 January 1937; *Cincinnati Enquirer*, 25 January 1937.

29. Handwritten note [January 1937], Chandler, box 100, folder Flood, 1937; *Memphis Commercial Appeal*, 24 January 1937.

30. *Cincinnati Enquirer*, 25 January 1937; *Louisville Courier-Journal*, 24 January 1937; *New Orleans Times-Picayune*, 26 January 1937.

31. Mary Bowman to A. B. Chandler, 26 January 1937, Chandler, box 101, folder Flood, 1937; Norman Thomas to A. B. Chandler, 26 January 1937, Chandler, box 101, folder Flood, 1937.

32. *Frankfort (KY) State Journal*, 26 January 1937; *Cincinnati Enquirer*, 29 January 1937.

33. Frances Dyhrkopp interview by Horace Waggoner, 15 November 1978, http:// www.idaillinois.org/cgi-bin/showfile.exe?CISROOT=/uis&CISOPTR=216&filename =217. Accessed 11 August 2008.

34. Curtis R. Hay, "Flood Report," Horner, box 322.

35. *Harrisburg (IL) Daily Register*, 21, 22 January 1937; *Gallatin Democrat*, 10 May 1962.

36. Robert William Janes, "The Collective Action Involved in the Removal and Relocation of Shawneetown, Illinois" (PhD diss., University of Illinois, 1942), 237, 269.

37. William H. Nicholas, "Shawneetown Forsakes the Ohio," *National Geographic* 93 (February 1948): 286; Frances Dyhrkopp interview, 10–12.

38. *Gallatin Democrat*, 30 June 1960.

39. Rudy Phillips, *Rudy's Life in Shawneetown, 1928–1980* (n.p.: Rudy Phillips, 1980), 24–26; *Harrisburg (IL) Daily Register*, 29 January 1937.

40. *Harrisburg (IL) Daily Register*, 26 January 1937.

41. G. Cullon Davis and Horace Waggoner, *Memories of a Bank: Final Report, an Oral History and Documentary Inventory at Old Shawneetown* (Springfield, IL: Sangamon

State University Oral History Office, 1979), 2:117, 4:448; Janes, "Collective Action Involved in the Removal and Relocation of Shawneetown," 181.

42. *Paducah Sun-Democrat*, 25 January 1987.

43. *Paducah Sun-Democrat*, 20, 21 January 1937.

44. *Paducah Sun-Democrat*, 21 January 1937, 26 July 1956; Nathaniel B. Kell, "Boots on Broadway," unpublished typescript [1986], McCracken County Library, Flood of 1937 file, 7.

45. *Paducah Sun-Democrat*, 4 February, 7 March 1937.

46. *Mayfield (KY) Messenger*, 25 January 1937.

47. Fred G. Neuman, *Paducah's Super-flood, January-February 1937: The Story of Paducah's Greatest Disaster in Words and Pictures* (Paducah: Young, 1937); *Paducah Sun-Democrat*, 25 January, 3 February 1937.

48. *Paducah Sun-Democrat*, 31 January, 7 March 1937; *Cincinnati Enquirer*, 1 February 1937.

49. Federal Writers' Project, *Cairo Guide* (Cairo, IL: Cairo Public Library, 1938), 11–19; John McMurray Lansden, *A History of the City of Cairo, Illinois* (1910; reprint, Carbondale: Southern Illinois University Press, 1976), 22.

50. *Cairo Guide*, 16; "City of Cairo," 1818, in *Documents Printed relating to the City of Cairo* (New York: H. Cogswell, 1847).

51. *Cairo Guide*, 16–17.

52. Larry Heid, *River City: A Home-Town Remembrance of Cairo, Illinois* (New York: Exposition Press, 1966), 20–22; Lansden, *History of the City of Cairo*, 53–55.

53. Heid, *River City*, 20–22.

54. Charles Dickens, *American Notes for General Circulation* (1842; reprint, London: Chapman and Hall, 1850), 118.

55. Lansden, *History of the City of Cairo*, 198–203; *Cairo Guide*, 24–28.

56. *Cairo Guide*, 24–26; Heid, *River City*, 39, 72.

57. Lansden, *History of the City of Cairo*, 71–74; *Cairo Guide*, 29; Heid, *River City*, 44–45.

58. Herman R. Lantz, *A Community in Search of Itself: A Case History of Cairo, Illinois* (Carbondale: Southern Illinois University Press, 1972), 132, 135.

59. Quoted in Christopher K. Hays, "Way Down in Egypt Land: Conflict and Community in Cairo, Illinois, 1850–1930" (PhD diss., University of Missouri, 1996), 88.

60. Ibid., 85–89, 93–105.

61. Ibid., 410–16; Dora Artis interview by Gregory Taylor, 23 July 1975, http://www.shawneecc.edu/library/History/artisd-1.asp. Accessed 19 February 2009.

62. Lansden, *History of the City of Cairo*, 146; Hattie Kendrick interview by Mattie Woods, 18 August 1975, http://www.shawneecc.edu/library/History/kendrickh-1.asp. Accessed 19 February 2009.

63. *Cairo Evening Citizen*, 19 February 1916.

64. Lantz, *Community in Search of Itself*, 68, 82, 53, 105; *Cairo Evening Citizen and Bulletin*, 16 January 1937.

65. *Cairo Evening Citizen and Bulletin*, 22 January 1937; "Narrative Report Covering

Emergency Period of the Ohio-Mississippi Flood of 1937. Pulaski and Alexander Counties, Illinois" [1937], RC, box 1270.

66. Floyd Clay, *A Century on the Mississippi: A History of the Memphis District, U.S. Army Corps of Engineers, 1876–1976* (Washington, DC: U.S. Army Corps of Engineers, 1976), 149.

67. *Cairo Evening Citizen and Bulletin*, 25 January 1937; *Memphis Commercial Appeal*, 25 January 1937.

68. Clay, *Century on the Mississippi*, 149–50.

69. *Cairo Evening Citizen and Bulletin*, 25, 27 January 1937.

70. *Cairo Evening Citizen and Bulletin*, 26 January 1937; "Narrative Report—Region H," RC, box 1271.

71. *Cairo Evening Citizen and Bulletin*, 25, 28 January 1937; "Telephone Report from Charles Carr," 25 January 1937, RC, box 1270.

72. *Cairo Evening Citizen and Bulletin*, 25, 27 January 1937; *Memphis Commercial Appeal*, 27 January 1937.

73. Hattie Kendrick interview.

74. *Cairo Evening Citizen and Bulletin*, 26 January 1937; Henretta Moore interview by Edward Whitaker, 6 November 1975, http://www.shawneecc.edu/library/History/mooreh-1.asp. Accessed 19 February 2009.

75. *Cairo Evening Citizen and Bulletin*, 28, 30, 31 January, 10 February 1937.

76. Kent Keller to Richard Elliott, 7, 28 April 1938, Keller, box 146; John J. Kingman to Kent Keller, 21 February 1938, Keller, box 146; W. H. Sullivan to Kent Keller, 15 April 1937, Keller, box 82.

77. *Cairo Evening Citizen and Bulletin*, 25, 27, 29 January 1937.

78. W. C. Ropiequet, "Ol' Man River, He Jes Kept Rollin'," *Illinois Alumni News* 15 (March 1937): 9; "Narrative Report Covering Emergency Period of the Ohio-Mississippi Flood of 1937. Pulaski and Alexander Counties."

79. Ropiequet, "Ol' Man River," 9.

80. August Bode to Henry Horner, 28 January 1937, Horner, box 398; *Cairo Evening Citizen and Bulletin*, 28 January 1937.

81. Harry L. Bolen, "Plan 'A'" [1937], Horner, box 398.

82. *Cairo Evening Citizen and Bulletin*, 31 January 1937.

Chapter Five

1. Stephen Early Diary, 30 January 1937, FDRL, Papers of Stephen T. Early.

2. Ibid., 29 January 1937; Harry Hopkins, handwritten memo [January 1937], Hopkins, box 10, folder Speeches, 1937.

3. Scripts of the performances appear in FDRL, PSF, box 159, folder FDR Birthdays: 1933–37.

4. Harry Hopkins to Happy Chandler, 22 January 1937, Hopkins, box 74, folder Transcripts of Telephone Conversations; "Memorandum re: Happy Chandler," 1 March 1938, FDRL, PPF 4754, Chandler, A. B.

5. Press Release, 30 January 1937, FDRL, Stephen Early Papers, box 46; audio recording of FDR, 30 January 1937 speech, FDRL.

6. American Red Cross, *The Ohio-Mississippi Valley Flood Disaster of 1937* (Washington, DC: American Red Cross, 1938), 43, 45, 48.

7. The *New York Times* claimed in its coverage of Roosevelt's party that "the stunts were omitted tonight" out of respect for the recent passing of FDR's political guru, Louis Howe. *New York Times*, 31 January 1937.

8. John M. Barry, *Rising Tide: The Great Mississippi Flood of 1927 and How It Changed America* (New York: Simon and Schuster, 1997), 280, 287.

9. "Radio Battles Old Man River," *Popular Mechanics* 67 (April 1937): 481; Chris Chandler, "The Whole World Is Listening," *American History* 42 (August 2007): 59; Lizabeth Cohen, *Making a New Deal: Industrial Workers in Chicago, 1919–1939* (Cambridge: Cambridge University Press, 1990), 325–29.

10. Nettie G. Horn, "How Did Highland Baptist Church Help Louisville Meet the Flood," 18 February 1937, University of Louisville Special Collections, 1937 Ohio River Flood Collection; J. Kenneth Jones, "They Also Served . . . WHAS," unpublished manuscript in Louisville Free Public Library, 1937 Flood Reports.

11. William E. Ellis, "The Bingham Family: From the Old South to the New South and Beyond," *Filson Club History Quarterly* 61 (January 1987): 6–32; *Louisville Courier-Journal*, 11 June 1986.

12. Credo Fitch Harris, *Microphone Memoirs of the Horse and Buggy Days of Radio* (Indianapolis: Bobbs-Merrill, 1937), 13, 79.

13. *Louisville Courier-Journal*, 11 June 1986; WHAS Twentieth Anniversary Show (1942), www.lkyradio.com/WHASairchecks.htm. Accessed 13 January 2009.

14. *Louisville Courier-Journal*, 11 June 1986.

15. Neville Miller Scrapbook, 1937 Ohio River Flood Collection, University of Louisville Special Collections.

16. Frank Caldwell to Harold Bingham [March 1937], Louisville Free Public Library Flood Reports.

17. Rick Bell, *The Great Flood of 1937: Rising Waters, Soaring Spirits, Louisville, Kentucky* (Louisville: Butler Books, 2007), 16–19. Trollope quoted in Bell, *Great Flood of 1937*, 22.

18. *Louisville Courier-Journal*, 21, 22 January 1937; Willard Rouse Jillson, *The Great Flood of 1937 in Louisville, Kentucky* (Louisville: Standard Printing, 1937), 33.

19. Jillson, *Great Flood of 1937*, 33; Jones, "They Also Served."

20. *Louisville Courier-Journal*, 18, 22, 23 January 1937.

21. David Potts to Linda Raymond [January 1987], UARC, Flood Memories: Letters Submitted by Readers, 1987, box 1; *Flood Stories by Shawnee High School Girls, Louisville Kentucky, 1937* (Louisville: Standard Printing, 1937), 43, 75; WHAS 1937 Flood Coverage Documentary, www.lkyradio.com/WHASairchecks.htm. Accessed 13 January 2009.

22. Gustave A. Breaux, "1937 Flood at Louisville," *Filson Club History Quarterly* 11 (April 1937): 112; *Flood Stories by Shawnee High School Girls*, 16.

23. Jones, "They Also Served."

24. Ibid.; "Rose Hudson Community Center," Louisville Free Public Library 1937 Flood Reports; *Louisville Courier-Journal*, 28 January 2007; Paul B. Williams, "Health in the Flood Area," *Hygeia* 15 (March 1937): 203.

25. Jonathan Van Dyke Norman Jr., "The 1937 Flood at Louisville," Jonathan Van Dyke Norman Jr. and Morey L. Boothie File, UARC.

26. "Rose Hudson Community Center"; A. L. Crabb, "The 1937 Flood in Louisville via Radio Broadcasts," *Kentucky Explorer* (December 2003–January 2004): 60; Jones, "They Also Served."

27. *Louisville Courier-Journal*, 7 March 1937.

28. Jones, "They Also Served."

29. *Cincinnati Enquirer*, 25 January 1937.

30. Jones, "They Also Served"; Jillson, *Great Flood of 1937*, 19.

31. WHAS 1937 Flood Coverage Documentary.

32. Jones, "They Also Served"; Crabb, "1937 Flood in Louisville," 58, 59; WFBR Transmission of WSM Flood Coverage. www.lkyradio.com/WHASairchecks.htm. Accessed 13 January 2009.

33. *Memories of Louisville's 1937 Flood* (Louisville: PCR, 1991), 1.

34. Jillson, *Great Flood of 1937*, 33; Jones, "They Also Served."

35. Norman, "1937 Flood at Louisville."

36. City Program Presented by Neville Miller, 7 October 1933, Wyatt, box 1, folder Election—Mayoral, 1933; "Speech Made by Neville Miller at the Opening of Democratic Campaign," 7 October 1933, Wyatt, box 1, folder Election—Mayoral; Bell, *Great Flood of 1937*, 28.

37. "Suggestions regarding Administration of the Mayor's Office" [November 1941], Wyatt, box 36, folder Mayoral—Neville Miller; "'Confiscation' Claims in Louisville, Kentucky" [1937], RC, box 1266.

38. Crabb, "1937 Flood in Louisville," 59–60; Jones, "They Also Served."

39. Jones, "They Also Served"; *Louisville Courier-Journal*, 28 January 2007.

40. WHAS Flood Coverage Documentary; *Memories of Louisville's 1937 Flood*, 7; *Kentucky Medical Journal, Part II—Women's Auxiliary Section* 6 (April 1937): 71–72, 74.

41. WHAS Flood Coverage Documentary.

42. *Louisville Courier-Journal*, 27 January 1937; Norman, "1937 Flood at Louisville."

43. Albert Chandler to Franklin Roosevelt, 24 January 1937, Chandler, box 101, folder Flood, 1937; handwritten note, 25 January 1937, Chandler, box 100, folder Flood, 1937; Neville Miller to Albert Chandler, 25 January 1937, Chandler, box 100, folder Flood, 1937; G. L. McClain to Malin Craig, 25 January 1937, Chandler, box 100, folder Flood, 1937.

44. Albert Chandler, "Executive Order and Proclamation," 25 January 1937, Chandler, box 100, folder Flood, 1937; Alben Barkley to Albert Chandler, 26 January 1937, Chandler, box 100, folder Flood, 1937; *Louisville Courier-Journal*, 28, 29 January 1937.

45. Bingham quoted in Bell, *Great Flood of 1937*, 136.

46. *Louisville Courier-Journal*, 6 May 1937, 18 January 1987; Elmer Vogel to Linda Raymond, 8 January 1987, UARC, 1937 Flood Memories: Letters Submitted by Readers, 1987, box 1.

47. *Louisville Courier-Journal*, 6 May 1937, 18 January 1987; Bell, *Great Flood of 1937*, 90.

48. *Flood Stories by Shawnee High School Girls*, 22; *Louisville Courier-Journal*, 30 January 1937.

49. *Louisville Courier-Journal*, 29 January 1937.

50. Crabb, "1937 Flood in Louisville," 61.

51. Norman, "1937 Flood at Louisville"; *Louisville Courier-Journal*, 28 January 1937.

52. Jones, "They Also Served."

53. Ibid.

54. *Cairo Evening Citizen and Bulletin*, 1 February 1937.

55. *Cincinnati Enquirer*, 31 January 1937; *Louisville Courier-Journal*, 2 February 1937.

56. *Louisville Courier-Journal*, 1, 2 February 1937.

57. Robert T. Kutak, "The Sociology of Crises: The Louisville Flood of 1937," *Social Forces* 17 (October 1938): 66; "Final Narrative Report, Region C—Kentucky, Ohio and Mississippi Valley Flood, 1937" [1937], RC, box 1261; E. W. Bedinger, "Some Afterthoughts," Louisville Free Public Library 1937 Flood Reports; Chandler, "Whole World Is Listening," 59.

58. "Radio Battles Old Man River," 481, 484, 485; *Memphis Commercial Appeal*, 7 February 1937; *Cincinnati Enquirer*, 28 January 1937.

59. *Paducah Sun-Democrat*, 18 February 1937; *Memphis Commercial Appeal*, 28 January 1937.

Chapter Six

1. *Louisville Courier-Journal*, 29 January 1937.

2. Gustave A. Breaux, "1937 Flood at Louisville," *Filson Club History Quarterly* 11 (April 1937): 113; Paul B. Williams, "Health in the Flood Area," *Hygeia* 15 (March 1937): 204; Dot to Mary [February 1937], UARC, 1937 Flood—Vertical File; *Louisville Courier-Journal*, 18 January 1947; *New Orleans Times-Picayune*, 1 February 1937.

3. Unless otherwise noted, this and subsequent paragraphs come from "Report from: Life Savers Hotel," UARC, Hammer Family Collection, box 1, folder Flood Memorabilia, and from information gleaned from the *Louisville City Directory*, obituary notices in the *Louisville Courier-Journal*, and census data.

4. Agnes Crume to Linda Raymond [January 1987], UARC, 1937 Flood Memories: Letters Submitted by Readers, 1987, box 1.

5. Bill Hammer to George Hammer, 6 February 1937, UARC, Hammer Family Collection, box 1, folder Flood Memorabilia.

6. *Mayfield (KY) Messenger*, 10 February 1937; *Louisville Courier-Journal Magazine*, 18 January 1987.

7. Rick Bell, *The Great Flood of 1937: Rising Waters, Soaring Spirits, Louisville, Kentucky* (Louisville: Butler, 2007), 101; interview with Rick Bell, 2 June 2009.

8. *Louisville Courier-Journal*, 24, 26 January 1937; J. Kenneth Jones, "They Also Served . . . WHAS," unpublished manuscript in Louisville Free Public Library, 1937 Flood Reports.

9. Neville Miller to Wilson Wyatt, 27 January 1937, Neville Miller Scrapbook, 1937 Ohio River Flood Collection, University of Louisville Special Collections; Jonathan Van Dyke Norman Jr., "The 1937 Flood at Louisville," UARC, Jonathan Van Dyke Norman Jr. and Morey L. Boothie file.

10. *Paducah Sun-Democrat*, 2, 3, 4, 9, 17 February 1937.

11. Material for this and the following paragraphs comes from John E. L. Robertson, "'High Water and Hell So Far': A Paducahan Remembers the 1937 Ohio Valley Flood," *Register of the Kentucky Historical Society* 102 (Spring 2004): 183–206.

12. Gus Meyer to Richard Allen, 11 July 1937, RC, box 1266.

13. *Paducah Sun-Democrat*, 2 January 1934, 2, 3 February 1937.

14. *Paducah Sun-Democrat*, 2 February 1937.

15. Jimmie Huston's story can be found in Barron White, *My Paducah: From the Early Years to the Present* (Paducah: Barrons, 2002), 80–86; *Paducah Sun-Democrat*, 25 January 1987.

16. A photograph of Bossie appears in Frederick Simpich, "Man Against the Rivers," *National Geographic* 71 (June 1937): 786.

17. *Paducah Sun-Democrat*, 4 February 1937.

18. *Paducah Sun-Democrat*, 7, 12 February 1937.

19. *Paducah Sun-Democrat*, 1, 12 February 1937.

20. *Louisville Courier-Journal*, 7 February 1937; Simpich, "Man Against the Rivers," 777.

21. G. Cullom Davis and Horace Waggoner, *Memories of a Bank: Final Report, an Oral History and Documentary Inventory at Old Shawneetown* (Springfield, IL: Sangamon State University Oral History Office, 1979), 4:418, 3:259.

22. Ibid., 4:364; *Gallatin Democrat*, 8 April 1937; William H. Nicholas, "Shawneetown Forsakes the Ohio," *National Geographic* 93 (February 1948): 287.

23. *Gallatin Democrat*, 22 April 1937.

24. Davis and Waggoner, *Memories of a Bank*, 3:282.

25. Ibid., 3:261–62; 2:110–11; 4:376, 415, 433; Pauline Harmon interview by Horace Q. Waggoner, 1978, at http://www.uis.edu/archives/memoirs/HARMON.pdf. Accessed 24 May 2007.

26. Davis and Waggoner, *Memories of a Bank*, 2:108; 4:405–7.

27. Ibid., 2:105–7.

28. Robert William Janes, "The Collective Action Involved in the Removal and Relocation of Shawneetown, Illinois" (PhD diss., University of Illinois, 1942), 182–83.

29. *History and Families of Gallatin County* (Paducah: Turner, 1988), 52; Janes, "Collective Action Involved in the Removal and Relocation of Shawneetown," 182–83; *Gallatin Democrat*, 10 May 1962.

30. Janes, "Collective Action Involved in the Removal and Relocation of Shawneetown," 180; *Harrisburg (IL) Daily Register*, 20 May 1937; Sophie Foote to Walter Wesselius, 25 March 1937, RC, box 1270.

31. *Harrisburg (IL) Daily Register*, 30 March 1937.

32. *Harrisburg (IL) Daily Register*, 30 March 1937.

33. Lona Trott to Mrs. Vaughn, 31 January 1937, RC, box 1270.

34. *Harrisburg (IL) Daily Register*, 25 January, 2 February 1937.

35. *Harrisburg (IL) Daily Register*, 23 January 1937.

36. Unless otherwise noted, my account of conditions inside Shawneetown High School comes from Lona Trott to Mrs. Vaughn, 31 January 1937, RC, box 1270, and Lona Trott, "Diary of a Nurse in the Great Flood" [1937], RC, box 1251.

37. "Report of Evacuation and Establishment of Refugee Camps" [1937], RC, box 1270; Trott, "Diary of a Nurse in the Great Flood."

38. *Harrisburg (IL) Daily Register*, 25 January 1937.

39. *Gallatin Democrat*, 18 January 1940; *Harrisburg (IL) Daily Register*, 25 26 January 1937.

40. Trott, "Diary of a Nurse in the Great Flood."

41. Sophie Foote to Walter Wesselius, 25 March 1937, RC, box 1270; *Harrisburg (IL) Daily Register*, 27 January 1937.

42. "Report of Emergency Operations, Region G" [1937], RC, box 1270; Rebecca W. Ford, "Resume of the Nursing Service Activities, Region G—Marion, Illinois" [1937], RC, box 1270; *Gallatin Democrat*, 30 June 1960.

43. Sophie Foote to Walter Wesselius, 25 March 1937, RC, box 1270.

44. Ibid.; Trott, "Diary of a Nurse in the Great Flood."

45. *Harrisburg (IL) Daily Register*, 10 February, 30 March 1937.

46. *Cape Girardeau Southeast Missourian*, 30 January 1937.

47. *Cape Girardeau Southeast Missourian*, 27, 29 January, 18 February 1937.

48. *Cape Girardeau Southeast Missourian*, 29, 30 January 1937.

49. *Charleston (MO) Democrat*, 28 January 1937.

50. *Cape Girardeau Southeast Missourian*, 4 February 1937; *Dunklin (MO) Democrat*, 5 February 1937.

51. *Dunklin (MO) Democrat*, 5 February 1937; *New Madrid (MO) Weekly Record*, 5, 12 February 1937.

52. "Narrative Report-Region H," RC, box 1271.

53. C. M. Roos, "Cairo and the Superflood of 1937," *Journal of the American Water Works Association* 29 (September 1937): 1281, 1284; *Cairo Evening Citizen and Bulletin*, 27 January 1937.

54. Roos, "Cairo and the Superflood of 1937," 1285; Cecil Baltzar Jacobson, "Ground-Water Phenomena behind the Levees at Cairo, Illinois," (MA thesis, University of Illinois, 1941), 37–38.

55. *Cairo Evening Citizen and Bulletin*, 8, 9 February 1937. One company proposed using dry ice to freeze sand boils. The Corps of Engineers elected to stick to traditional means of battling these outbreaks.

56. *Cairo Evening Citizen and Bulletin*, 1, 2 February 1937.

57. *Cairo Evening Citizen and Bulletin*, 2, 3, 4 February 1937.

58. *Paducah Sun-Democrat*, 2 February 1937; transcript of telephone conversation: Harry Hopkins to Martin Davey, 29 January 1937, Hopkins, box 73, folder Transcripts of Telephone Conversations.

59. Transcript of telephone conversation: Lawrence Westbrook to Eugene Reybold and Francis Harrington, 30 January 1937, Hopkins, box 54, folder Flood-January

1937; Franklin Roosevelt to Harry Hopkins, 3 February 1937, Hopkins, box 96, folder Roosevelt, Franklin D. (signed correspondence, 1933–1940).

60. *Cairo Evening Citizen and Bulletin*, 4, 6 February 1937.

61. *Cairo Evening Citizen and Bulletin*, 8, 11, 12 February 1937; *New Madrid (MO) Weekly Record*, 12 February 1937.

Chapter Seven

1. *Louisville Courier-Journal*, 24 January 1937.

2. *Paducah Sun-Democrat*, 25 January 1937.

3. American Red Cross, *The Ohio-Mississippi Valley Flood Disaster of 1937* (Washington, DC: American Red Cross, 1938).

4. Richard Allen to DeWitt Smith, 9 March 1937, RC, box 1251; "Narrative Report Covering Emergency Period of the Ohio-Mississippi Flood of 1937, Pulaski and Alexander Counties, Illinois" [1937], RC, box 1270.

5. Henry Baker to Richard Allen, 27 February 1937, RC, box 1261; "Narrative Regional Report of the Emergency Period of the 1937 Flood in Kentucky" [1937], RC, box 1261; memorandum of telephone conversation between George Myer and James Fieser, 1 February 1937, RC, box 1251.

6. "Final Narrative Report, Region C—Kentucky, Ohio and Mississippi Valley Flood, 1937" [1937], RC, box 1261.

7. "Narrative Regional Report of the Emergency Period of the 1937 Flood in Kentucky."

8. Miriam Dailey to Malinde Havey, 4 February 1937, RC, box 1268; *The Union Central and the 1937 Flood* (Cincinnati: Union Central Life Insurance Company, 1937), 9–11, 32–36. At the time the second-tallest skyscraper in Cincinnati, the Union Central building is now known as the PNC Tower.

9. *Cincinnati Enquirer*, 24, 27 January 1937; *Union Central and the 1937 Flood*, 38–40.

10. "Summary by Regions of Emergency Relief" [1937], RC, box 1253; "Summary by Region of Camps and Concentration Centers" [1937], RC, box 1253.

11. Mildred Lanphere Martin, "I'm Tired" [1937], RC, box 1271; R. M. Muirhead, "Medical Service Report" [1937], RC, box 1270; "Report of Emergency Operations, Region G" [1937], RC, box 1270.

12. *Harrisburg (IL) Daily Register*, 2 February 1937.

13. Bruce Uthus to F. C. Harrington, 11 March 1937, RG 69 Central, box 293.

14. *Paducah Sun-Democrat*, 1 February 1937; *Cape Girardeau Southeast Missourian*, 27 January 1937; "Report on Rockport, Indiana," 14 February 1937, RC, box 1256.

15. William DeKleine and William Scarlett, "Cerebrospinal Meningitis in a Flood Refugee Center," *Southern Medical Journal* 31 (January 1938): 76; "Narrative Report of Meningitis Epidemic," 9 March 1937, RC, box 1270.

16. Luella Landwehr, "A Resume of the Spinal Meningitis Epidemic in North Eastern Arkansas" [1937], RC, box 1256.

17. Ibid.

18. DeWitt Smith to Regional Directors, 7 February 1937, RC, box 1255.

19. Ramone S. Eaton to DeWitt Smith, 10 March 1937, RC, box 1256.

20. "Juniors Make Little Refugees Happy," *Red Cross Courier* 16 (April 1937): 9.

21. Ramone S. Eaton to DeWitt Smith, 10 March 1937, RC, box 1256; Dan Sharp to Ramone S. Eaton, 7 March 1937, RC, box 1256.

22. William Jacobs to Ramone S. Eaton, 6 March 1937, RC, box 1256.

23. "Final Rehabilitation Period Summary, Region I—Arkansas" [1937], RC, box 1270.

24. Robert W. Chowning, *History of St. Francis County, Arkansas* (Forrest City, AR: Times-Herald, 1954), 5–6; Vivian Hansbrough, "The Crowleys of Crowley's Ridge," *Arkansas Historical Quarterly* 13 (Spring 1954): 52–62.

25. Chowning, *History of St. Francis County*, 16–36.

26. *Marianna (AR) Courier-Index*, 10 December 1936.

27. *Memphis Commercial Appeal*, 30 January 1937.

28. Thomas Hart Benton, *An Artist in America* (1937; rev. ed., New York: Twayne, 1951), 147; John Handcox to H. L. Mitchell, 5 February 1937, STFU, reel 4; Elgan Robertson to Hattie Caraway, 22 January 1938, RC, box 1270.

29. *Paducah Sun-Democrat*, 4 February 1937; W. A. Elliott to John E. Miller, 3 February 1938, RC, box 1270; Elgan Robertson to Hattie Caraway, 22 January 1938, RC, box 1270; *Memphis Commercial Appeal*, 15 February 1937.

30. H. L. Mitchell to Gardner Jackson, 27 January 1937, STFU, reel 4.

31. Douglass Cobb to J. R. Butler, 7 February 1937, STFU, reel 4; Aaron Levenstein to Roger Baldwin, 27 January 1937, STFU, reel 4.

32. J. R. Butler to Otis Peoples, 27 January 1937, STFU, reel 4; C. J. Spradling to H. L. Mitchell, 31 January 1937, STFU, reel 4.

33. J. R. Butler to Godfrey Cabot, 17 February 1937, STFU, reel 4.

34. *Memphis Commercial Appeal*, 13 February 1937; J. R. Butler to the *Commercial Appeal*, 14 February 1937, STFU, reel 4.

35. Scottie Spears to H. L. Mitchell, 16 February 1937, STFU, reel 4; J. R. Butler to F. C. Cotton, 3 February 1937, STFU, reel 4.

36. Jarod Heath Roll, "Road to the Promised Land: Rural Rebellion in the New Cotton South, 1890–1945" (PhD diss., Northwestern University, 2006), 240–46, 257.

37. C. C. Brooks to H. L. Mitchell, 28 January 1937, STFU, reel 4.

38. *Memphis Commercial Appeal*, 4 February, 24 January 1937.

39. *Memphis Commercial Appeal*, 23, 29 January 1937.

40. Watkins Overton to Walter Chandler, 28 January 1937, Overton, box 4, folder 35; Carl Bailey to Watkins Overton, 29 January 1937, Overton, box 4, folder 35.

41. *Memphis Commercial Appeal*, 1 February 1937; Floyd Clay, *A Century on the Mississippi: A History of the Memphis District, U.S. Army Corps of Engineers, 1876–1976* (Washington, DC: U.S. Army Corps of Engineers, 1976), 152.

42. *Memphis Commercial Appeal*, 1 February 1937.

43. *Memphis Commercial Appeal*, 14 February 1937.

44. "Narrative Report Red Cross Disaster Relief Operations Shelby County Tennessee, January 27–March 15, 1937" [1937], RC, box 1268.

45. Ibid.; Karl N. Pollard, "Flood Conditions of 1937," presentation to the Annual Re-union of the "Fighting Sixty," 27 February 1937, Overton, box 4, folder 35.

46. *Memphis Commercial Appeal*, 23, 24, 25 January 1937.

47. I. Malinde Havey, "Disaster Report" [1937], RC, box 1256.

48. Pollard, "Flood Conditions of 1937"; *Memphis Commercial Appeal*, 29 January 1937.

49. *Memphis Commercial Appeal*, 28 January 1937.

50. *Memphis Commercial Appeal*, 28 January 1937.

51. E. H. Crump to Walter Chandler, 27 January 1937, Crump, box 148; G. Wayne Dowdy, *Mayor Crump Don't Like It: Machine Politics in Memphis* (Jackson: University Press of Mississippi, 2006), 90.

52. E. H. Crump to Watkins Overton, 30 January 1937, Crump, box 142.

53. *Memphis Commercial Appeal*, 1 February 1937.

54. *Memphis Commercial Appeal*, 2 February 1937; Kathleen West Caradine, "Tennessee Works Progress Administration, Tennessee Division, Fifth District Activities in Mississippi 1937 Flood, Memphis Area," Memphis Public Library Mid-South Flood Collection, box C, 19–20.

55. E. B. Maynard, "Report on Health Conditions," 15 February 1937, Overton Office, box 6, folder Flood Disaster (Army).

56. Ibid.

57. *Chicago Defender*, 27 February 1937; Kate Born, "Memphis Negro Workingmen and the NAACP," *West Tennessee Historical Society Papers* 28 (1974): 91.

58. Bobby Joe Williams, "Mid-South Views the Floods of 1912 and 1913," *West Tennessee Historical Society Papers* 39 (October 1975): 77.

59. *Chicago Defender*, 20 February 1937.

60. G. Wayne Dowdy, "Expansion of the Crump Machine: Politics in Bedford County, 1928–1936," *West Tennessee Historical Society Papers* 56 (2002): 29; Born, "Memphis Negro Workingmen and the NAACP," 90–104; Roger Biles, "The Persistence of the Past: Memphis in the Great Depression," *Journal of Southern History* 52 (May 1986): 208.

61. John Barry, *Rising Tide: The Great Mississippi Flood of 1927 and How It Changed America* (New York: Simon and Schuster, 1997), 307–17.

62. American National Red Cross, "Case Statistics: Summary by Regions" [1937], RC, box 1253. Absolute data on black and white refugees are impossible to determine, since the Red Cross recorded cases by family rather than by individuals. One can reach a rough estimate of the number of people involved by multiplying the number of families receiving aid by the size of the average American family in 1937—about 3.8, according to information from the 1930 and 1940 census—and comparing those figures with contemporary approximations of black and white populations in various places.

63. Roy Wilkins to Harry Hopkins, 25 January 1937, RG 69 Central, box 292; *Pittsburgh Courier*, 30 January, 6 February 1937; *Chicago Defender*, 30 January 1937.

64. Untitled memorandum, 26 April 1937, RC, box 1255.

65. NAACP Report of the Secretary, 8 March 1937, Papers of the NAACP, part 1, reel

6; Roy Wilkins to Cary Grayson, 17 March 1937, RC, box 1251; Aminda Wilkins to Walter White [February 1937], Papers of the NAACP, part 2, reel 18.

66. Gladyce Badger to Malinde Havey, 3 April 1937, RC, box 1255; *Chicago Defender*, 13 March 1937.

67. William DeKleine to Cristine Limbert, 9 April 1937, RC, box 1255; "Report of Nursing Service—Region F" [1937], RC, box 1268.

68. *Memphis Commercial Appeal*, 29 January 1937; *Blytheville (AR) Courier News*, 27 January 1937; Dr. L. M. Thompson to Henry Baker, 17 February 1937, RC, box 1266.

69. *Chicago Defender*, 20, 13 February 1937.

70. *Chicago Defender*, 30 January, 6, 20 February 1937.

71. *Pittsburgh Courier*, 6 February 1937.

72. Claude Barnett, "Report on Visit to Flood Area," 26 April 1937, RC, box 1257; *Pittsburgh Courier*, 13 February 1937; *Chicago Defender*, 20 February 1937.

73. *Chicago Defender*, 6 March 1937.

74. Watkins Overton to E. H. Crump, 2 February 1937, Crump, box 142.

75. *Marianna (AR) Courier-Index*, 4 February 1937; *Paducah Sun-Democrat*, 11 February 1937; *Memphis Commercial Appeal*, 29 January 1937; Lenah Brock Anderson to A. B. Chandler, 2 February 1937, Chandler, box 101, folder Flood, 1937.

Chapter Eight

1. John E. L. Robertson, "'High Water and Hell So Far': A Paducahan Remembers the 1937 Ohio Valley Flood," *Register of the Kentucky Historical Society* 102 (Spring 2004): 205–6.

2. *Vicksburg Evening Post*, 7 February 1937.

3. *Vicksburg Evening Post*, 8 February 1937; *New Orleans Times-Picayune*, 1 February 1937.

4. *Vicksburg Evening Post*, 21 February 1937; *New Orleans Times-Picayune*, 19 February 1937.

5. *Memphis Commercial Appeal*, 19 February 1937.

6. *Cincinnati Enquirer*, 1 February 1937; *Paducah Sun-Democrat*, 26 July 1956; *Louisville Courier-Journal*, 23 February, 3 March 1937.

7. *Memphis Commercial Appeal*, 3 March, 14 February 1937.

8. Minutes of Meeting, 28 February 1937, RC, box 1252; Albert Evans to Regional Headquarters Staff, 18 February 1937, RC, box 1270; *Memphis Commercial Appeal*, 18 March 1937.

9. J. R. Butler to C. J. Spradling, 6 February 1937, STFU, reel 4; Fred Coleman to STFU, 15 February 1937, STFU, reel 4.

10. "Final Rehabilitation Period Summary, Region I—Arkansas" [1937], RC, box 1270.

11. J. R. Butler to John Heath, 16 February 1937, STFU, reel 4; Mary Pratt to H. L. Mitchell, 17 May 1937, STFU, reel 4.

12. J. R. Butler to Robert La Follette, 25 May 1937, STFU, reel 4; J. R. Butler to Carl Bailey, 24, 28 May 1937, STFU, reel 4; John Doe's Statement, 31 May 1937, STFU, reel 4.

13. Jarod Heath Roll, "Road to the Promised Land: Rural Rebellion in the New Cotton South, 1890–1945" (PhD diss., Northwestern University, 2006), 290–357; *Chicago Defender*, 14 February 1942.

14. *Cincinnati Enquirer*, 5 February 1937.

15. Clarence W. Klassen interview by Ida Klassen, October–December 1981, www .idaillinois.org_cgi-bin_showfile.exe_CISOROOT=_uis&CISOPTR=413&Filename= 414.pdf. Accessed 15 May 2008.

16. Willie Mae Leglet to Louie Lewis, 23 March 1937, ALPL, Louie Lewis Papers, box 2.

17. *Louisville Courier-Journal*, 5, 8 February 1937; *Cincinnati Enquirer*, 6, 10 February 1937.

18. *Cincinnati Enquirer*, 10 February 1937; Frederick Simpich, "Men Against the Rivers," *National Geographic* 71 (June 1937): 768.

19. "The Louisville Free Public Library in the Flood of 1937," May 1937, UARC, 1937 Flood—Vertical File.

20. Nathan C. Grover, *Floods of Ohio and Mississippi Rivers, January–February 1937* (Washington, DC: Government Printing Office, 1938), 800.

21. "Flood Forces Destruction of Vast Quantities of Food," *Science News Letter* 31 (20 February 1937): 124.

22. *Paducah Sun-Democrat*, 13 February 1937.

23. *Louisville Courier-Journal*, 20 April 1937; *Memphis Commercial Appeal*, 5 February 1937.

24. Harry Hopkins to Howard Hunter et al., 29 January 1937, RG 69 Central, box 292; *Memphis Commercial Appeal*, 13 February 1937.

25. William Pryor to Woodrow Wilson, 28 January, 2 February 1937, RG 69 Central, box 292.

26. *Paducah Sun-Democrat*, 18, 23 March, 11, 19 April 1937.

27. J. Blaine Gwin, "Recruiting a Staff for Flood Relief" [1937], RC, box 1256.

28. American Red Cross Award Slip, 7 July 1937, RC, box 1255.

29. Financial and Statistical Report, 31 December 1937, RC, box 1253.

30. Ella McFalls to Albert Chandler, 11 May 1937, Chandler, box 101, folder Flood, 1937.

31. Richard Allen to DeWitt Smith, 7 July 1937, RC, box 1266.

32. Richard Allen to William Fortune, 20 July 1937, RC, box 1266; Report of telephone conversation, 15 July 1937, RC, box 1266; Minutes of Meeting, 16 July 1937, RC, box 1265; DeWitt Smith to Raymond O'Neal, 22 July 1937, FDRL, OF 124, American Red Cross, box 2, folder American Red Cross 1937.

33. *Louisville Times*, 2 August 1937; Richard Allen to William Fortune, 20 July 1937, RC, box 1266.

34. Henry Baker to DeWitt Smith, 5 August 1937, RC, box 1266.

35. *New Orleans Times-Picayune*, 2 February 1937.

36. *New Orleans Times-Picayune*, 23 February 1937.

37. *Memphis Commercial Appeal*, 5 February 1937; Roger Biles, "The Persistence of the Past: Memphis in the Great Depression," *Journal of Southern History* 52 (May 1986): 186–88.

38. Biles, "Persistence of the Past," 190–94; Watkins Overton, Statement, 31 December 1936, Overton, box 10, folder 9; *Memphis Commercial Appeal*, 8 January 1937.

39. *Memphis Commercial Appeal*, 3 February 1937; Marvin Pope to Louise Gambill, 13 February 1937, Memphis Public Library Mid-South Flood Collection, box A, folder 13; W. H. Jasspon to Members of Memphis Chamber of Commerce, 9 April 1937, Overton Office, box 3, folder Chamber of Commerce.

40. *Memphis Commercial Appeal*, 10 March 1937.

41. *Memphis Commercial Appeal*, 9 May 1937.

42. G. Wayne Dowdy, "Expansion of the Crump Machine: Politics in Bedford County, 1928–1936," *West Tennessee Historical Society Papers* 56 (2002): 17, 21–23.

43. *Memphis Press-Scimitar*, 16 December 1939; *Memphis Commercial Appeal*, 19 December 1939.

44. G. Wayne Dowdy, *Mayor Crump Don't Like It: Machine Politics in Memphis* (Jackson: University Press of Mississippi, 2006), 90–91; William D. Miller, *Mr. Crump of Memphis* (Baton Rouge: Louisiana State University Press, 1964), 320.

45. Dot to Mary [February 1937], UARC, 1937 Flood—Vertical File; *Louisville Courier-Journal Magazine*, 18 January 1987; *Louisville Courier-Journal*, 26 January, 2 February 1937.

46. *Louisville Courier-Journal*, 11 May 1937; *Memphis Commercial Appeal*, 5 February 1937.

47. Minutes of Meeting of Board of Directors, 24 February 1937, UARC, Louisville Area Chamber of Commerce Records, 1862–1988, box 27; *Louisville Courier-Journal*, 3, 5 February 1937.

48. *Louisville Courier-Journal*, 28 January 2007. A pledge card can be found in UARC, 1937 Flood—Vertical File.

49. *Louisville Courier-Journal*, 26 January 1958; Minutes of Meeting of Board of Directors, 24 February 1937, UARC, Louisville Area Chamber of Commerce Records, 1862–1988, box 27; *Louisville Courier-Journal*, 13 February 1937.

50. Minutes of Meeting of Board of Directors, 24 February 1937, UARC, Louisville Area Chamber of Commerce Records, 1862–1988, box 27; *Louisville Courier-Journal*, 4, 16, 17 February 1937; William Stoll, "Louisville Marches On," *Louisville Board of Trade Journal* 21 (March 1937): 4.

51. *Louisville Courier-Journal*, 17, 18 February 1937.

52. *Louisville Courier-Journal*, 10, 11 February, 4 March 1937; "Press and Church Help Fight High Water in Louisville," *Life* (15 February 1937): 11.

53. *Louisville Courier-Journal*, 3, 13 February, 5 March 1937; Sidney Appel to Mark Ethridge, 27 February 1937, Chandler, box 98, folder Derby, 1937.

54. *Louisville Courier-Journal*, 4, 18 March, 4 April, 5 May 1937.

55. *Louisville Courier-Journal*, 5 May 1937.

56. *Louisville Courier-Journal*, 5 May 1937.

57. *Louisville Courier-Journal*, 5 May 1937.

58. "Progress Report Number One," 26 July 1937, RC, box 1266; *Louisville Courier-Journal*, 2, 6, 8 May 1937.

59. *Louisville Courier-Journal*, 6, 8, 9 May 1937, 18 January 1957.

60. *Louisville Courier-Journal*, 25, 29 April, 1, 8, 19 May 1937; "Civic Matters," *Louisville Board of Trade Journal* 21 (May 1937): 24.

61. *Louisville Courier-Journal*, 11 May 1937; Program for Testimonial Dinner in Honor of Neville Miller, 10 May 1937, Neville Miller Scrapbook, 1937 Ohio River Flood Collection, University of Louisville Special Collections.

62. George R. Leighton, "Louisville, Kentucky: An American Museum Piece," *Harper's Monthly* 175 (September 1937): 400, 402, 408, 416.

Chapter Nine

1. *Louisville Courier-Journal*, 8 March 1937.

2. Rajah Waw to Wilson Wyatt, 5 November 1937, Wyatt, box 1, folder City of Louisville; untitled poem [1937], McCracken County Library, folder Flood of 1937.

3. *Memphis Commercial Appeal*, 10 February 1937; *Jeffersonville (IN) Evening News*, 8 March 1937; Nathaniel Wheat to Franklin Roosevelt, 28 April 1937, Chandler, box 102, folder flood control.

4. *Cincinnati Enquirer*, 1 February 1937; *Memphis Commercial Appeal*, 7 February 1937.

5. Gilbert F. White, *Human Adjustment to Floods: A Geographical Approach to the Flood Problem in the United States* (Chicago: University of Chicago Press, 1945), 2.

6. *Cincinnati Enquirer*, 28 January 1937; "Report Accompanying H.R. 7646," 28 June 1937, National Archives Great Lakes Branch, Chicago, RG 187, Records of the National Resources Planning Board, Region IV, Correspondence and Related Records, 1934–43, folder 240. Converting historical dollars to today's values is almost impossible, but one billion 1937 dollars is the equivalent of about fifteen billion 2008 dollars when adjusted for inflation. When taken as a percentage of annual gross national product, one billion 1937 dollars equals about $155 billion today. http://www.measuringworth.com/calculators/uscompare/resultwithad.php#. Accessed 20 December 2010.

7. *Louisville Courier-Journal*, 7 February 1937; Hugh Horn to Stephen Early, 17 February 1937, FDRL, OF 132, Floods, box 1, folder 1937 January–June.

8. *Mayfield (KY) Messenger*, 8 February 1937; Charles Berkey, "Population Centers Should Be Moved from Flood Zones," *Science News Letter* 31 (6 February 1937): 83.

9. *Cairo Evening Citizen and Bulletin*, 8 February 1937; "Flood Curbs," *Scientific American* 156 (April 1937): 216.

10. "Bennett and Silcox Map Flood Step," *Forestry News Digest*, March 1937.

11. Finis Dunaway, *Natural Visions: The Power of Images in American Environmental Reform* (Chicago: University of Chicago Press, 2005), 60–73.

12. Paschal N. Strong, "The Great Flood of the Ohio," *Military Engineer* 29 (May-June 1937): 162; Paul Sears, "Half-Hearted Measures Won't Succeed for Flood Control," *Science News Letter* 31 (6 February 1937): 84; *Vicksburg Evening Post*, 12 February 1937.

13. *Cincinnati Enquirer*, 4 February 1937; Press Release, 5 February 1937, FDRL, Papers of Stephen T. Early, box 46.

14. *Cincinnati Enquirer*, 2 February 1937.

15. *Cincinnati Enquirer*, 5 February 1937; *Memphis Commercial Appeal*, 5 February 1937.

16. Jonathan Daniels, ed., *Complete Presidential Press Conferences of Franklin D. Roosevelt* (New York: DaCapo, 1972), 9:149.

17. Harry Hopkins Appointment Book, 9 February 1937, Hopkins, box 104, folder Mr. Hopkins's Engagements, 1937; *Cincinnati Enquirer*, 11 February 1937.

18. Richard White, *The Organic Machine* (New York: Hill and Wang, 1995), 50–56. For more on the role of publicly generated electricity in the New Deal agenda, see Jordan Schwartz, *The New Dealers: Power Politics in the Age of Roosevelt* (New York: Vintage, 1993).

19. Matthew Todd Pearcy, "Will Whittington and the Legislative History of Flood Control for the Yazoo Basin" (MA thesis, University of Mississippi, 1991), 1; Will Whittington, "The Next Step in Flood Control in the Lower Mississippi Valley," 19 January 1938, Whittington, box 17, folder Flood Control Speeches—1938.

20. Will Whittington, "Extension of Remarks," 26 April 1937, Whittington, box 17, folder Flood Control Speeches—1937; Will Whittington, "The Next Step in Flood Control," 28 September 1937, Whittington, box 17, folder Flood Control Speeches—1937; Will Whittington, "National Flood Control," 20 January 1938, Whittington, box 17, folder Flood Control Speeches—1938.

21. *Cairo Evening Citizen and Bulletin*, 11 February 1937.

22. Stephen Early Diary, 18 February 1937, FDRL, Papers of Stephen T. Early.

23. Mississippi Valley Association, *Proceedings of a Conference on Flood Control and Its Related Problems* (St. Louis: Mississippi Valley Association, 1937), 8.

24. Ibid., 10.

25. Ibid., 12, 16, 21.

26. Ibid., 33, 34.

27. Ibid., 35–38.

28. Ibid., 61.

29. *Mayfield (KY) Messenger*, 12 February 1937.

30. *Dunklin (MO) Democrat*, 9 February 1937; *Harrisburg (IL) Daily Register*, 6 February 1937.

31. *Memphis Commercial Appeal*, 12 February 1937.

32. *Cairo Evening Citizen and Bulletin*, 15 February, 22 May 1937.

33. *Paducah Sun-Democrat*, 7, 25 February, 6 April 1937.

34. *Cairo Evening Citizen and Bulletin*, 7 April 1937.

35. Franklin Roosevelt to Henry Woodring, 3 April 1937, FDRL, OF 25, War Department, box 28, folder War Department, Chief of Engineers, 1933–37; Henry Woodring to Franklin Roosevelt, 8 April 1937, FDRL, OF 25, War Department, box 28, folder War Department, Chief of Engineers, 1933–37.

36. *Paducah Sun-Democrat*, 15, 12 April 1937.

37. Press Release, 20 April 1937, Kenneth McKellar Papers, Memphis-Shelby County, Series-Speech and Press Releases, box 7; *Paducah Sun-Democrat*, 21 April 1937.

38. Water Resources Committee Memorandum, 17 April 1937, FDRL, OF 25, War Department, box 28, folder War Department, Chief of Engineers, 1933–37.

39. House Committee on Flood Control, "Comprehensive Flood-Control Plan for Ohio and Lower Mississippi River, Letter from the President of the United States and

Report of the Chief of Engineers," 10 February 1937, 75th Cong., 1st sess. (Washington, DC: Government Printing Office, 1937).

40. Franklin Roosevelt to Henry Woodring, 28 April 1937, FDRL, OF 25, War Department, box 28, folder War Department, Chief of Engineers, 1933–37; Franklin Roosevelt to Henry Wallace, 28 April 1937, FDRL, OF 25, War Department, box 28, folder War Department, Chief of Engineers, 1933–37.

41. Will Whittington to Franklin Roosevelt, 5 May 1937, FDRL, OF 25, War Department, box 28, folder War Department, Chief of Engineers, 1933–37.

42. Charles Reynolds to Brent Spence, 17 May 1937, Brent Spence Papers, University of Kentucky Special Collections, Lexington, Kentucky, box 3, folder Flood Control 1938; *Paducah Sun-Democrat*, 27 April 1937.

43. *Jeffersonville (IN) Evening News*, 6, 17, 20 March, 12 May, 23 June 1937.

44. *New Madrid (MO) Weekly Record*, 5 February 1937.

45. *Dunklin (MO) Democrat*, 23 February 1937; *Charleston (MO) Democrat*, 11 March 1937.

46. Charles Dillon to Mr. Grissemer, 3 April 1937, RC, box 1253; Floyd Clay, *A Century on the Mississippi: A History of the Memphis District, U.S. Army Corps of Engineers, 1876–1976* (Washington, DC: U.S. Corps of Engineers, 1976), 154.

47. Franklin Roosevelt, "Message of the President of June 3, 1937, relating to Regional Planning Agencies," FDRL, FDR Speech Files, box 33, folder 1057.

48. Arthur Maass, *Muddy Waters: The Army Engineers and the Nation's Rivers* (Cambridge, MA: Harvard University Press, 1951), 87–90.

49. John McClellan to Franklin Roosevelt, 10 June 1937, FDRL, OF 132, Floods, box 2, folder 1937 January–June; Will Whittington, "H.J. Resolution 175," 29 July 1937, Whittington, box 17, folder Flood Control Speeches—1937; Englebright quoted in Maass, *Muddy Waters*, 90.

50. Franklin Roosevelt to Frederic Delano, 12 August 1937, FDRL, OF 132, Floods, box 2, folder 1937 July-December.

51. Franklin Roosevelt, "Message of the President of August 13, 1937 relating to Vetoing S.J. Res. 57," FDRL, FDR Speech Files, box 33, folder 1065; George Henry Soule, *A Planned Society* (New York: Macmillan, 1933), 230.

52. House Committee on Flood Control, *Comprehensive Flood Control Plan for Ohio and Mississippi Rivers: Hearings on H.R. 7393 and H.R. 7646*, 75th Cong., 1st sess., 1937, 29, 35, 51; Pearcy, "Will Whittington and the Legislative History of Flood Control for the Yazoo Basin," 73, 174.

53. *Comprehensive Flood Control Plan for Ohio and Mississippi Rivers*, 60.

54. Ibid., 91, 179, 246, 265.

55. Ralph Cessna, "River, Stay Away from My Door . . . ," *Christian Science Monitor* 20 (5 January 1938): 8.

56. Pearcy, "Will Whittington and the Legislative History of Flood Control for the Yazoo Basin," 74–75.

57. Will Whittington, "Diversions Must Be Definitely Provided for in Next Flood Control Bill," 6 November 1937, Whittington, box 17, folder Flood Control Speeches—1937.

Chapter Ten

1. *Gallatin Democrat*, 1 April 1937; A. R. Lord to O. K. Yeager, 12 July 1937, RG 69 Central, box 1225.

2. *Gallatin Democrat*, 22 March, 25 February 1937.

3. Rudy Phillips, *Rudy's Life in Shawneetown, 1928–1980* (n.p.: Rudy Phillips, 1980), 6, 29–31.

4. *Gallatin Democrat*, 2 April, 31 March 1937; "Report of Emergency Operations, Region G" [1937], RC, box 1270.

5. *Gallatin Democrat*, 1 April 1937.

6. *Harrisburg (IL) Daily Register*, 30 January 1937.

7. Handbill [February 1937], RC, box 1271.

8. Robert William Janes, "The Collective Action Involved in the Removal and Relocation of Shawneetown, Illinois" (PhD diss., University of Illinois, 1942), 184; "Memorandum of Meeting of Citizens of Shawneetown," 21 February 1937, RC, box 1271.

9. "Memorandum of Meeting of Citizens of Shawneetown," 21 February 1937, RC, box 1271; Curtis Small, "River, Stay Away from My Door," *Saturday Evening Post* 213 (7 December 1940): 101–2; *Gallatin Democrat*, 10 May 1962.

10. *Harrisburg (IL) Daily Register*, 26 February 1937; Walter Wesselius to DeWitt Smith, 26 February 1937, RC, box 1271.

11. *Harrisburg (IL) Daily Register*, 26 February, 5 March 1937; Janes, "Collective Action Involved in the Removal and Relocation of Shawneetown," 184.

12. Memorandum regarding Proposed Removal, 9 March 1937, Horner, box 398; Charles J. Masters, *Governor Henry Horner, Chicago Politics, and the Great Depression* (Carbondale: Southern Illinois University Press, 2007), 124–32, 140.

13. DeWitt Smith to Colin Herrle, 18 March 1937, RC, box 1271; Memorandum of Telephone Conversation with Congressman Claude E. Parsons, 12 March 1937, RC, box 1271; *Harrisburg (IL) Daily Register*, 24 April 1937.

14. *Gallatin Democrat*, 1, 15 April 1937; L. H. Jacobson to F. C. Harrington, 26 March 1937, RG 69 Central, box 1225; Jason Scott Smith, *Building New Deal Liberalism: The Political Economy of Public Works, 1933–1956* (Cambridge: Cambridge University Press, 2006), 112–14. For more on the WPA see Nick Taylor, *American Made: The Enduring Legacy of the WPA: When FDR Put the Nation to Work* (New York: Bantam, 2008).

15. *Gallatin Democrat*, 8 April 1937.

16. Janes, "Collective Action Involved in the Removal and Relocation of Shawneetown," 199.

17. Lela Horlick to Henry Horner, 26 March 1937, Horner, box 126; *St. Louis Post-Dispatch*, 26 March 1937. It is indicative of the Red Cross's attitude that someone in the organization forwarded a clipping of the "Shawneetown is heaven" article to DeWitt Smith with "DeWitt—You evidently don't know a good town when you see one" written across the top.

18. *Harrisburg (IL) Daily Register*, 21 April 1937; *Gallatin Democrat*, 29 April 1937; Small, "River, Stay Away from My Door," 104.

19. *Gallatin Democrat*, 22, 15 April, 6 May 1937; Small, "River, Stay Away from My Door," 104.

20. *Gallatin Democrat*, 20 May 1937; *Harrisburg (IL) Daily Register*, 20 May 1937.

21. A. D. Hovey to Leo Lyons, 21 April 1937, Horner, box 398.

22. *Gallatin Democrat*, 30 September, 17 June, 5 August 1937.

23. *Gallatin Democrat*, 27 May 1937; A. R. Lord to O. K. Yeager, 12 July 1937, RG 69 Central box 1225; Notes on telephone conversation, 15 July 1937, RG 69 Central, box 1225.

24. F. C. Harrington to Charles Miner, 15 June 1937, RG 69 Central, box 293; *Gallatin Democrat*, 24 June 1937.

25. George Field to Francis Harrington, 14 June 1937, RG 69 Central, box 1225; Frances Harrington to Charles Miner, 21 July 1937, RG 69 Central, box 1225; *Gallatin Democrat*, 12 August 1937.

26. *Gallatin Democrat*, 22 July 1937; Charles Miner to Claude Parsons, 1 July 1937, RG 69 Central, box 1225; Arthur Lord to O. K. Yeager, 16 October 1937, RG 69 Central, box 1225.

27. *Gallatin Democrat*, 8 July 1937. With minor modifications, present-day Shawneetown reflects Whitmore's design.

28. Arthur Lord to Bruce Uthus, 26 July 1937, RG 69 Central, box 1225.

29. WPA Project Application, 1 December 1937, RG 69 Central, box 1225. The proposal called for the WPA to demolish unsafe structures, erect public buildings, pave streets, install sidewalks and sewer lines, and transfer the water system from the old site to the new one. The GCHA was liable for constructing private homes and for 70 percent of the nonlabor cost of moving buildings.

30. WPA Project Proposal, 7 December 1937, RG 69 Central, box 1225.

31. *Gallatin Democrat*, 24 February 1938; Arthur Lord to Francis Harrington et al., 16 August 1937, RG 69 Central, box 1225; Francis Harrington to Max Galt, 3 March 1938, RG 69 Central, box 1225.

32. Arthur Lord to Francis Harrington et al., 16 August 1937, RG 69 Central, box 1225; Francis Harrington to Max Galt, 9 April 1938, RG 69 State, box 1222; Max Galt to O. K. Yeager, 25 February 1937, RG 69 Central, box 1225.

33. *Gallatin Democrat*, 8 July 1937.

34. *Gallatin Democrat*, 19 May 1938; GCHA, "Approved Plan for Moving Shawneetown" [June 1938], RG 69 Central, box 1225.

35. *Gallatin Democrat*, 14 July, 30 June 1938.

36. Carter Jenkins to Lynden Smith, 13 April 1939, Conservation.

37. Janes, "Collective Action Involved in the Removal and Relocation of Shawneetown," 116, 240, 302–4; Arthur Lord to O. K. Yeager, 25 January 1939, RG 69 State, box 1221.

38. Lela Stricklin to Henry Horner, 28 September 1933, Horner, box 126; Carter Jenkins to Lynden Smith, 13 April 1939, Conservation.

39. Arthur Lord to Lincoln Rogers, 13 October 1938, RG 69 Central, box 1225; Arthur Lord to Howard Hunter, 28 October 1938, RG 69 Central, box 1225.

40. Arthur Lord to O. K. Yeager, 5 December 1938, RG 69 Central, box 1225; Carter Jenkins to Lynden Smith, 13 April 1939, Conservation.

41. Janes, "Collective Action Involved in the Removal and Relocation of Shawnee-town," 176–77, 262.

42. Ibid., 242–43, 275.

43. *Gallatin Democrat*, 6 October 1938; handbill [1938], Conservation; Arthur Lord to Howard Hunter, 28 October 1938, RG 69 Central, box 1225.

44. *Gallatin Democrat*, 13 April, 27 July 1939.

45. *Gallatin Democrat*, 18 August, 10 November, 8 September 1938.

46. O. K. Yeager to Francis Harrington, 14 December 1938, RG 69 Central, box 1225; A. D. Morrell to B. M. Harloe, 27 February 1939, RG 69 State, box 1221; Arthur Lord to O. K. Yeager, 25 January 1939, RG 69 State, box 1221.

47. Arthur Lord to Charles Miner, 15 April 1939, RG 69 State, box 1222.

48. *Gallatin Democrat*, 13, 20 April, 4, 25 May 1939.

49. *Gallatin Democrat*, 4 May, 7, 28 September, 19 October 1939.

50. *Gallatin Democrat*, 17 August 1939.

51. "Proposed Plan of Operation Subsequent to December 31, 1939 and an Accounting of the Affairs of the Housing Authority of Gallatin County," 6 November 1939, RG 69 State, box 1221; Arthur Lord to Charles Miner, 15 June 1939, RG 69 State, box 1221.

52. Walter Wesselius to Charles Burkett, 24 November 1939, RC, box 1271; Walter Wesselius to DeWitt Smith, 13 November 1939, RC, box 1271; Arthur Lord to O. K. Yeager, 26 October 1939, RG 69 State, box 1221.

53. *Gallatin Democrat*, 4 April, 5 September 1940.

54. Janes, "Collective Action Involved in the Removal and Relocation of Shawnee-town," 212–13; *Gallatin Democrat*, 7 March, 4 April 1940.

55. Arthur Lord to Charles Miner, 29 November 1940, RG 69 State, box 1221; *Gallatin Democrat*, 25 July 1940, 29 May 1941.

56. *Gallatin Democrat*, 26 September 1940, 13 February 1941. A bridge connecting Illinois Route 13, which passes in front of Shawneetown, to Kentucky opened in 1955.

57. Janes, "Collective Action Involved in the Removal and Relocation of Shawnee-town," 310–12, 323–24.

58. Ibid., 314–18.

59. Ibid., 323, 236; italics in original.

Chapter Eleven

1. Will Whittington, "National Flood Control," 20 January 1938, Whittington, box 17, folder Flood Control Speeches—1938.

2. Ibid.; Will Whittington, Press Release, 19 January 1938, Whittington, box 17, folder Flood Control Speeches—1938; Will Whittington, "Flood Control Bill in 1938 Imperative" [1938], Whittington, box 17, folder Flood Control Speeches—1938.

3. Harry Woodring to Franklin Roosevelt, 29 October 1937, FDRL, OF 25, War De-

partment, box 28, folder Chief of Engineers, 1933–37; Franklin Roosevelt to Henry Wallace, 20 October 1937, FDRL, OF 25, War Department, box 28, folder Chief of Engineers, 1933–37.

4. National Resources Committee, *Water Planning and Policy for Drainage Basins of the U.S.* (Washington, DC: Government Printing Office, 1938), 11–15.

5. Ibid., 11, 16, 30.

6. Franklin Roosevelt to Daniel Bell, 23 April 1938, FDRL, OF 25, War Department, box 28, folder War Department, Chief of Engineers, 1933–37.

7. Jonathan Daniels, ed., *Complete Presidential Press Conferences of Franklin D. Roosevelt* (New York: DaCapo, 1972), 11:91, 246; Daniel Bell to Franklin Roosevelt, 15 February 1938, FDRL, OF 132, Floods, box 2, folder 1938.

8. House Committee on Flood Control, *Comprehensive Flood-Control Plans: Hearings on Amendments to the Flood Control Acts of June 15, 1936, June 22, 1936, and August 28, 1937,* 75th Cong., 3rd sess., 1938, 1.

9. Ibid., 3, 7, 8–9.

10. Ibid., 11–13, 22–23.

11. Ibid., 130, 178.

12. Ibid., 213.

13. Ibid., 423, 451.

14. Daniel Bell to Franklin Roosevelt, 23 May 1938, FDRL, OF 132d, Floods, box 5, folder Flood Control Act of 1938.

15. FDR quoted in Arthur Maass, *Muddy Waters: The Army Engineers and the Nation's Rivers* (Cambridge, MA: Harvard University Press, 1951), 86.

16. Maass, *Muddy Waters,* 155–56; Clyde Seavey to James Roosevelt, 23 May 1938, FDRL, OF 132d, Floods, box 5, folder Flood Control Act of 1938; Daniel Bell to Franklin Roosevelt, 28 May 1938, FDRL, OF 132d, Floods, box 5, folder Flood Control Act of 1938.

17. Franklin Roosevelt to Alben Barkley, 28 May 1938, FDRL, OF 132d, Floods, box 5, folder Flood Control Act of 1938.

18. Memorandum, 10 June 1938, FDRL, OF 132, Floods, box 2, folder 1938.

19. *New York Times,* 15, 16 June 1938.

20. Franklin Roosevelt, "Memorandum of Disapproval," 25 June 1938, Brent Spence Papers, University of Kentucky Special Collections, Lexington, Kentucky, box 3, folder Flood Control 1938; Clyde Seavey to Franklin Roosevelt, 28 June 1937, FDRL, OF 132d, Floods, box 5, folder Flood Control Act of 1938; Harold Ickes to Franklin Roosevelt, 27 June 1938, FDRL, OF 132d, Floods, box 5, folder Flood Control Act of 1938.

21. Will Whittington to Gerald Montgomery [June 1938], Whittington, box 28, folder Letters, Legislation, and Publications—Flood Control 1938; Alben Barkley to Franklin Roosevelt, 28 June 1938, FDRL, OF 132d, Floods, box 5, folder Flood Control Act of 1938; Sam Rayburn to Marvin McIntyre, 28 June 1938, FDRL, OF 132d, Floods, box 5, folder Flood Control Act of 1938; Sam Rayburn to Franklin Roosevelt, 28 June 1938, FDRL, OF 132d, Floods, box 5, folder Flood Control Act of 1938.

22. *New York Times,* 30 June 1938.

23. "Informal Remarks of the President," 8 July 1938, FDRL, FDR Speech Files, box

40, folder 1145; Maass, *Muddy Waters*, 94, 122–23; "First Revision, Regional Development Plan, Lake States and Ohio Valley," 1941, NARA, RG 187, Records of the National Resources Planning Board, Central Office Records, Working Reports of the National Resources Planning Board and Regional Offices, 1934–1942, box 49.

24. Will Whittington, "Flood Control and States' Rights," 23 March 1939, Whittington, box 17, folder Flood Control Speeches—1939.

25. Daniel Bell to Franklin Roosevelt, 20 March 1939, FDRL, OF 132, Floods, box 2, folder 1939.

26. Water Tower Arts Association, "The 1937 Flood: A Chronology of Louisville's Greatest Challenge," Louisville Free Public Library, 1, 9; *Louisville Courier-Journal*, 18 January 1987.

27. *Louisville Courier-Journal*, 9 February, 10 March, 22 April 1937; "General Report for the Building Department," 24 July 1937, RC, box 1266.

28. *Louisville Courier-Journal*, 18 January 1987; "1937 Flood: A Chronology of Louisville's Greatest Challenge," 11.

29. *Louisville Courier-Journal*, 28 January 2007; Rick Bell, *The Great Flood of 1937: Rising Waters, Soaring Spirits, Louisville, Kentucky* (Louisville: Butler Books, 2007), 133–34.

30. *Louisville Courier-Journal*, 28 January 2007; George C. Wright, *Life behind a Veil: Blacks in Louisville, Kentucky, 1865–1930* (Baton Rouge: Louisiana State University Press, 1985), 5–6, 12.

31. Robert I. Kutak, "The Sociology of Crises: The Louisville Flood of 1938," *Social Forces* 17 (October 1938): 69.

32. *Louisville Courier-Journal*, 29 January, 22 March 1937; Fannie Chandler to Red Cross Headquarters, 19 March 1937, RC, box 1266; Lucille Milner to DeWitt Smith, 11 February 1937, RC, box 1266.

33. Henry Baker to DeWitt Smith, 14 April 1937, RC, box 1266.

34. George H. Yater, *Two Hundred Years at the Falls of the Ohio: A History of Louisville and Jefferson County* (Louisville: Heritage Corporation, 1979), 219, 244; Wright, *Life behind a Veil*, 1. Also see Tracy E. K'Meyer, *Civil Rights in the Gateway to the South: Louisville, Kentucky, 1945–1980* (Lexington: University Press of Kentucky, 2009).

35. Grady Clay interview by Louise Chawla and Caroline Taylor Chadwell, 26 July 1989, University of Kentucky Oral History Collection; *Louisville Courier-Journal*, 4, 11 March 1945.

36. *Louisville Courier-Journal*, 7 March 1945; Edward Kirwan to Wilson Wyatt, 13 March 1945, Wyatt, box 24, folder Mayoral—Flood.

37. *Louisville Courier-Journal*, 28 February, 4, 7 March 1945; *Louisville Times*, 7 March 1945; Wilson Wyatt to Lee Coulson, 17 April 1945, Wyatt, box 24, folder Mayoral—Flood.

38. *Louisville Times*, 8 March 1945; *Louisville Courier-Journal*, 12 March 1945; Wilson Wyatt to C. L. Hall, 12 April 1945, Wyatt, box 24, folder Mayoral—Flood.

39. *Louisville Courier-Journal*, 7 March, 24 August 1945, 5 November 1946, 26 January 1947. After subsequent expansions the floodwall now runs for twenty-nine miles.

40. *Louisville Courier-Journal*, 18 July 1948, 19 October 1947, 15 January 1956; *Louisville Times*, 19 April 1948, 9 May 1958, 12 March 1964.

41. *Louisville Times*, 11 March 1964; *Louisville Courier-Journal*, 18 July 1993.

42. William Manchester, "Louisville Cashes in on Culture," *Harper's* 211 (August 1955): 77–78.

43. Yater, *Two Hundred Years at the Falls of the Ohio*, 231–41; *Louisville Courier-Journal*, 18 January 1987.

44. John E. L. Robertson, *Paducah, 1830–1980: A Sesquicentennial History* (Paducah: Image Graphics, 1980), 103.

45. *Mayfield (KY) Messenger*, 13 February 1937; *Paducah Sun-Democrat*, 21, 19 February, 2, 3, 12 March 1937.

46. House Committee on Flood Control, *Comprehensive Flood Control Plan for Ohio and Mississippi Rivers: Hearings on H.R. 7393 and H.R. 7646*, 75th Cong., 1st sess., 1937, 301; Robertson, *Paducah, 1830–1980*, 103–5.

47. *Cairo Evening Citizen and Bulletin*, 6 February 1937; *Charleston (MO) Democrat*, 25 February 1937.

48. *Cairo Evening Citizen and Bulletin*, 12 April 1937; A. G. Foote to August Bode, 6 February 1937, Keller, box 146.

49. Aubrey Williams to Kent Keller, 17 March 1937, Keller, box 82.

50. Harry Hopkins to Kent Keller, 3 April 1937, Keller, box 82; Kent Keller to Harry Hopkins, 14 April 1937, Keller, box 82.

51. J. Kelly Smith to Louie Lewis, 15 March 1937, ALPL, Louie Lewis Papers, box 2.

52. J. Kelly Smith to Kent Keller, 29 May 1940, Keller, box 146.

53. Chad Alan Goldberg, "Contesting the Status of Relief Workers during the New Deal: The Workers Alliance of America and the Works Progress Administration, 1935–1941," *Social Science History* 29 (Fall 2005): 348–51.

54. *Cairo Evening Citizen and Bulletin*, 9, 10 April 1937; *Paducah Sun-Democrat*, 24 May 1937; Lloyd Oller to Henry Horner, 14 April 1937, Horner, box 115.

55. *Cairo Evening Citizen and Bulletin*, 10, 12 April 1937; *Paducah Sun-Democrat*, 24 May 1937.

56. Charles Rossio to Henry Horner, 24 April 1937, Henry Horner Collection, Illinois State Archives; Andrew Panezich to Henry Horner, 10 July 1937, www.sos.state.il.us/departments/archives/hard_times/doc42.html. Accessed 9 January 2009.

57. *Cairo Evening Citizen and Bulletin*, 11, 25 May, 9 June 1937.

58. Charles Miner to August Bode, 19 May 1937, Keller, box 146; W. H. Sullivan to Kent Keller, 15 April 1937, Keller, box 82.

59. Kent Keller to Ray Williams, 10 July 1940, Keller, box 146.

60. Paul Good, *Cairo, Illinois: Racism at Floodtide* (Washington, DC: U.S. Commission on Civil Rights, 1973), 11–15.

61. *Cairo Evening Citizen and Bulletin*, 6, 13 April, 5 June 1937.

62. H. H. Bennett to Morris L. Cooke, 25 May 1940, FDRL, Morris L. Cooke Papers, box 138, folder Bennett, Hugh H.

63. "Resolution Unanimously Adopted at a National Conference Held in New Orleans," 20 September 1946, Brent Spence Papers, University of Kentucky Special Collections, Lexington, Kentucky, box 2, folder Floodwall, Newport 1946.

64. Harry Truman to Morris L. Cooke, 3 January 1950, www.presidency.ucsb.edu/

ws/index.php?pid=13456, accessed 30 April 2009; President's Water Resources Policy Commission, *The Rivers in America's Future*, no. 9, *The Ohio* (Washington, DC: Government Printing Office, 1951), 6, 11–12, 21.

65. *Rivers in America's Future*, 15, 58, 46, 33.

66. Otis L. Graham, *Toward a Planned Society: From Roosevelt to Nixon* (New York: Oxford University Press, 1976), 67–93; Neil M. Maher, *Nature's New Deal: The Civilian Conservation Corps and the Roots of the American Environmental Movement* (New York: Oxford University Press, 2008), 208–9.

67. Leland R. Johnson, *The Falls City Engineers: A History of the Louisville District, Corps of Engineers, United States Army, 1970–1983* (Louisville: U.S. Army Engineer District, 1984), 161.

68. Ibid., 4.

69. *Cincinnati Enquirer*, 23 January 2004.

Epilogue

1. Walter Rosenfield to T. B. Casey, 20 October 1943, Conservation; W. C. Rebhan to George Williams, 12 April 1945, Conservation.

2. William H. Nicholas, "Shawneetown Forsakes the Ohio," *National Geographic* 93 (February 1948): 284, 277; *Gallatin Democrat*, 29 May 1947.

3. *Southern Illinoisan* (Carbondale, IL), 1 December 1949; Mary Ann Stefko to Walter Rosenfield, 19 August 1948, Conservation.

4. *Southern Illinoisan* (Carbondale, IL), 1 December 1949; *Harrisburg (IL) Daily Register*, 12 May 1953.

5. Ray Hubbs to Scerial Thompson, 21 December 1949, Conservation; Charles Casey to Ivan Elliott, 14 May 1951, Conservation.

6. *Gallatin Democrat*, 2 August 1956; Louis Brooks to Division of Parks, 17 January 1957, Conservation.

7. *Gallatin Democrat*, 13 September 1956.

8. General Planning and Resource Consultants, *A Comprehensive Community Plan: Old Shawneetown, Illinois* (St. Louis: GPRC, 1964), 9; William Allen to Louis Aaron, 9 July 1956, Conservation; William Smith to Henry Mitchell, 31 January 1963, Conservation; "Shawneetown: A Tale of Two Cities," *Hi-Lines*, February 1968, 5–7.

9. *Cincinnati Enquirer*, 13 March 1997.

10. *Evansville (IN) Courier and Press*, 21 January 2007.

11. http://www.uis.edu/archives/memoirs/CHAMBERLAINJOE.pdf. Accessed 1 June 2009.

Index

Page numbers in italics refer to figures.